ACKNOWLEDGMENTS

This publication was a project of the department of development policy of the research division, Urban Land Institute. Terry Jill Lassar, research counsel at ULI, directed the study of the 65 downtowns initially surveyed, conducted the on-site visits, and wrote the text.

Carrots & Sticks: New Zoning Downtown examines relationships between downtown zoning regulations, urban design issues, and the development process and is a companion piece to other ULI publications that focus on downtown development—*Cities Reborn, Designing the Successful Downtown, Downtown Development Handbook, Downtown Retail Development,* and *Urban Waterfront Development.*

Although no list of acknowledgments can be complete, I wish nonetheless to single out a few people for special note. First to be thanked are the members of ULI's advisory committee for the project, listed herein, who made valuable comments on the approach and the draft chapters. Especially helpful were Alan Billingsley, Richard Clotfelter, and Ralph Guthrie. In addition, Rosalyn Doggett's analysis of the District of Columbia's housing/residential (HR) overlay district formed the basis for the discussion of that zoning technique in Chapter 11.

Special thanks also go to all those public officials, planners, developers, architects, lawyers, and consultants across the country who gave generously of their time for interviews and, many times, reinterviews. They supplied guidance through the intricacies of their zoning regulations and recounted the impacts of these rulings on local downtown development. The large number of individuals who helped in this way makes it infeasible to name them here, but many are referred to in the pages of the book. Their continuing assistance in offering and verifying information was not only gratifying but essential. Special credit, however, must go to Peter Spitzner, Hartford's chief staff planner; Mark Hinshaw, city architect and lead urban designer for Bellevue, Washington; Patrick Ping-Tze Too, principal urban designer for New York City's planning department; Jeffrey Heller, San Francisco architect; Peter Bosselmann, director of the Environmental Simulation Laboratory, University of California, Berkeley; Walter Fields III, zoning coordinator for the planning commission in Charlotte-Mecklenburg, North Carolina; Michael McGill, executive director of SPUR in San Francisco; Bill Duchek, senior planner with the Seattle Office for Long-Range Planning; and Michael Harrison and John Southgate of Portland, Oregon's bureau of planning.

Finally to be thanked is Douglas Porter, ULI's director of development policy research, who steadily offered valuable insights, direction, and encouragement throughout the course of the project.

In a manuscript of this length and complexity, some errors will doubtless survive the publication process. For these, the author accepts all responsibility, as for the general approach and analysis.

ULI ADVISORY COMMITTEE

Alan C. Billingsley
Principal
Economics Research Associates
San Francisco, California

Richard Bradley
President
International Downtown Association
Washington, D.C.

Richard C. Clotfelter
President
Prescott
Seattle, Washington

4

CONTENTS

PREFACE 6

INTRODUCTION Why Write New Regulations? 8

CHAPTER 1 Incentive Zoning 12

CHAPTER 2 Four Bonuses in Closeup: Public Art, Employment and
Job Training, Human Services, and Downtown Daycare 39

CHAPTER 3 Development and Design Reviews 53

CHAPTER 4 Design Review Overdose, San Francisco–Style 70

CHAPTER 5 Zoning As Shaper of Building Design 77

CHAPTER 6 Environmental Impacts of Tall Buildings: Light Access
and Shadows, Street-Level Winds, and View Protection 87

CHAPTER 7 Retail Uses 106

CHAPTER 8 Open Space and Streetscapes 129

CHAPTER 9 Skywalks 153

CHAPTER 10 Parking and Transportation 160

CHAPTER 11 Housing 174

APPENDICES 195

INDEX 201

PREFACE

Zoning is one of New York's most important boring subjects.

–Jack Newfield [1]

Zoning laws have been for real estate what the Marquis of Queensberry Rules were to boxing. They set up rules of conduct and define what constitutes a "low blow" against the public interest. . . .

–Jonathan Barnett [2]

Innovative zoning techniques. Although the mere thought is enough to send chills up and down the spines of developers, it was largely private property owners who spearheaded the nation's first major downtown zoning controls in 1916. In that year, fearful of the invading garment industry's impact on their district's carriage trade, Fifth Avenue merchants welcomed public regulations as protection from the vexing uncertainty of private land use anarchy. Ten years later, the U.S. Supreme Court upheld the basic constitutionality of local zoning controls in its decision on *Village of Euclid* v. *Ambler Realty Company*.

To many, the term "innovative zoning" is an oxymoron. After all, the essence of traditional Euclidean zoning—segregating incompatible land uses within a hierarchical scheme—means maintaining the status quo. Nowhere was the stabilizing influence of zoning more welcome than in the newly risen suburbia, which was the main arena of zoning action for decades to come. Even here, however, zoning was already being viewed by critics as "a negative tool to retard the forces of inevitable change." [3]

Downtown zoning, meanwhile, historically took a back seat to economic revitalization. But some 20 years ago, taking a decidedly more activist approach to zoning, cities began discarding their traditional laissez-faire attitudes. Instead of as impediments to change, new interventionist land use regulations were seen as strategies to encourage particular kinds of growth in the CBD. This transformation in the purpose of zoning was the subject of a 1969 conference, whose proceedings were published in Groves and Marcus's *The New Zoning: Legal, Administrative, and Economic Concepts and Techniques*. In the introduction, Donald H. Elliott defined "the new zoning" as "a complex symbiotic relationship in which growth is conditioned upon development 'in the public interest'. . . ." [4]

Carrots & Sticks: New Zoning Downtown attempts to build on Groves and Marcus's work, as well as on the 1979 book, *City Zoning*, in which Richard Babcock and Clifford Weaver predicted: "Zoning in cities shows some hope of becoming a vital tool of positive change. The stale ideas and negative controls that characterize most of suburban zoning practice are clearly insufficient to deal with the land use problems of our cities. As city zoners thrash about for new ways to skin a cat, it seems a good bet that they will move quickly to the forefront of land use theory." [5]

In 1987, ULI research staff asked planning officials in more than 65 cities to describe their newest land use controls, including those created especially for use in the downtown. The study was confined to those techniques that had been implemented through zoning regulations. The Institute found an impressive array of zoning innovations. Downtowns throughout the country, mostly in major and second-tier cities, have developed a formidable arsenal of zoning tools to shape downtown development and stimulate specific activities. Cities as diverse as Seattle and Bellevue, Washington; Hartford, Connecticut; San Francisco; Boston; Cincinnati; New York City; Charlotte, North Carolina; and Portland, Oregon, are experimenting with activist zoning controls to pursue such goals as bolstering ailing retail cores, strengthening pedestrian networks, preventing shadows on parks and plazas, and upgrading building design.

The new downtown zoning weaves rather conventional techniques such as overlay districts, special use districts, and height and density limits with newer mechanisms such as linkage requirements, commercial development caps, and tiered bonus programs. Many cities also use incentive zoning systems to award developers additional height or density allowances in exchange for building or financing given amenities. At a time when public funds are scarce, cities increasingly are looking to incentive zoning to obtain for them some much-needed public benefits. The menu of bonus choices has been expanded greatly to include not only design features physically related to the bonused building (outdoor plazas and internal atriums) but also social amenities and services (daycare centers, low-cost housing, human services facilities, and employment and job training programs).

Aimed at effecting changes in the downtown, the new interventionist regulations look forward to what is possible, rather than merely what is. They may not always correspond directly to existing market realities. Office developers routinely protest that mandates to provide a percentage of street-level retail uses, for example, are too ambitious, forcing retail beyond the level the market can now support and thus requiring burdensome subsidies. Such tactics must achieve a delicate balance, reflecting present market conditions yet pointing to a city's vision of its future self.

In keeping with ULI's tradition of examination of land use practices, *Carrots & Sticks* neither endorses nor promotes particular regulatory techniques, although it assesses their impacts on development. And because guidance of downtown development by the private sector is clearly on the rise, scrupulous efforts were made to elicit viewpoints representing both the public and private sectors. Many developers, architects, economic and real estate consultants, city officials, planners, lawyers, urban designers, and businesspeople contributed their thoughts and observations on the effectiveness of particular zoning controls.

The book is intended to be a practical guide for planning professionals, architects, developers, academics, and public officials. Discussion of each zoning technique includes several examples, specific code selections, and an analysis of that technique's application in several downtowns. Successes and failures are examined equally. Some cities' notorious practice of xeroxing zoning regulations and mechanically adopting them without any fine tuning or tailoring to local needs is legendary. This book is not intended to provide such ready-made blueprints, but rather to kindle thinking on inventive approaches to common problems.

With a few exceptions, this volume pays scant attention to the political skirmishes that invariably accompany the adoption of new zoning regulations. But anyone who has vied in the land use arena knows zoning is usually a political issue, subject to the push and pull of many competing interest groups—environmentalists, housing advocates, developers, and historic preservationists. And such battles do not end with passage of a new code. Administration and interpretation of the new regulations, often entailing public hearings, planning board actions, and city council votes, are equally fraught with political perils.

Because the focus of this book is zoning, discussion is limited almost entirely to privately developed projects. With the exception of New York City, most of the discussion involves medium-sized cities. Zoning, however, represents but one of the mechanisms that can be used to direct downtown development activity. It would be a mistake for any city to rely solely on zoning to revive a moribund retail core or enhance downtown housing opportunities. Cities should explore other incentive tools, including tax abatement, land assemblage programs, tax increment financing, land writedowns, special service areas financing, and other subsidies while they are experimenting with innovative zoning systems.

Finally, it must be emphasized that many of the zoning programs discussed here were put in place when real estate markets were robust. The downtown market's seemingly insatiable appetite for office space enabled cities more or less to call the shots by demanding that new office projects provide more public benefits. At the same time, traditional municipal funding sources were shrinking rapidly, and many cities looked to zoning to leverage the provision of public amenities and facilities. Not surprisingly, in the Midwest and other parts of the country where development pressures have been less intense, cities have hesitated to impose new regulatory hurdles and instead have looked to economic inducements to lure development downtown. The question remains whether the newer carrot-and-stick zoning will survive a less bullish downtown development market.

Notes

1. Jack Newfield in the *Village Voice*.
2. Jonathan Barnett, *Introduction to Urban Design* (New York: Harper & Row, 1982), p. 66.
3. Clifford L. Weaver and Richard F. Babcock, *City Zoning: The Once and Future Frontier* (Chicago: American Planning Association, 1979), p. 10.
4. Donald H. Elliott, "Introduction," in *The New Zoning*, eds. Norman Marcus and Marilyn W. Groves (New York: Praeger, 1970), p. xvi.
5. Weaver and Babcock, op. cit.

INTRODUCTION:
WHY WRITE NEW REGULATIONS?

The decision to implement new downtown regulations is influenced by several factors. In some instances, the existing dowdy code, which may be more than 20 years old, does not respond to current development pressures and so calls for constant massaging and manipulation via negotiated variances and special permits. Boston's 1987 Interim Planning Overlay District (IPOD), for example, is part of an incremental overhaul of a 1964-vintage code, compliance with which meant that almost all major downtown projects had to apply for some type of zoning relief.

Similarly, more than 2,500 exceptions were added to New York's first 1916 zoning ordinance before the comprehensive code revision was adopted in 1961. The revision in turn has been substantially amended. In Cincinnati, the 1987 downtown code marked the city's first comprehensive rezoning since 1962. For some years before the new regulations, almost all new development in the city had exceeded the FAR and height limits of the old code, and the city council passed some 22 ordinances accommodating projects that did not comply. These ordinances permitted projects "notwithstanding" the zoning requirements. The 1987 incentive regulations for the downtown established height and bulk limits that more accurately reflect the scale of projects currently coming on line.

Whereas Cincinnati wanted its zoning code to mirror the scale of current development projects, many other cities are more interested in using their codes as tools to actively shape the character and scale of downtown buildings. For example, many of the design requirements of San Francisco's 1985 ordinance were aimed explicitly at paring down the density of office high rises and preventing the "Manhattanization" of the downtown.

Sometimes, it is a major new project and the possibility that its gargantuan scale will be cloned that galvanize a city to rethink its zoning. Indeed, the country's first major zoning effort, in New York, was in part a reaction to the huge mass of the Equitable

T. J. Lassar

135 East 57th Street, New York City.

Building. This was also the situation in Seattle. In response to a dark-glassed behemoth of an office tower that, at 954 feet, loomed 350 feet above its nearest rival, then-Mayor Charles Royer vowed there would be no more 76-story buildings in Seattle. That city's rezoning, however, was mainly undertaken because the city's 1960s-vintage code was markedly out of sync with the galloping rate of new building in the area.

Hartford, too, in the early 1980s, underwent unprecedented commercial activity, and its 1983 incentive zoning system was an attempt to shape its own destiny and exert more control over the size and quality of downtown development. For much the same reason, Bellevue, Washington, rewrote its land use code in 1981 and used density bonuses to steer development activity to an intensified downtown core and discourage pell-mell development on the periphery.

TO BONUS OR NOT?

When a city tackles the job of writing new zoning regulations, the first decision, generally a highly political one, is whether to go the mandatory or incentive route. In many downtowns (particularly those sustaining soft markets or high vacancy rates for the foreseeable future), it would not be politically expedient to mandate that office towers come equipped with daycare centers or sassy sculptured rooftops, or be subject to affordable housing obligations as they are in San Francisco. The more palatable approach is to integrate these features into an incentive zoning system whereby developers gain something in return (usually greater density) for the extra expenses they incur.

Incentive zoning is also attractive because it enables cities to secure public benefits without spending public funds and without imposing development fees or exactions. Cities also welcome the additional real estate tax revenues garnered from the increased density.

One of the first considerations in any incentive zoning scheme is the base FAR. This is the underlying floor/area ratio that allows cities to control the density of future development. The concept of floor/area ratio, invented to facilitate the then-new technique of incentive zoning in New York's 1961 Zoning Resolution, represents the relationship between a building's total floor area and the size of its site. Rather than the direct relationship of building bulk to street width, the FAR becomes the primary bulk control mechanism. The FAR is the multiplier developers apply to the number of square feet in their projects. In Hartford's downtown commercial core, for example, the as-of-right FAR (that achieved without the use of incentives) is 10, which means that developers can build 10 times the amount of square feet in their lots. Developers may prefer to mass the space in a squat building or to build higher, covering less of the lot area.[1]

Unfortunately, if the as-of-right FAR limits are set too high, developers will have no incentive to exceed the basic regulations and take advantage of the density bonuses. On the other hand, if the base FAR is too stringent, development generally will be discouraged altogether. (This delicate balance is discussed more fully in Chapter 1, "Incentive Zoning.") Moreover, according to a 1988 American Planning Association survey, several cities with incentive systems in place have no takers for the available bonuses: Either their real estate market conditions (as in Denver) do not warrant it, or existing FAR limits "satisfy demands without additional enticements."[2]

Therefore, for the density bonuses to function as real inducements, incentive zoning systems usually call for big reductions in existing FAR limits. As Babcock and Weaver note, "It must be trumpeted that

the scheme [incentive zoning] will not work in most cities unless the political climate permits a substantial reduction in what is now allowed as a matter of right."[3] The basic message to the developer must be: "We will give you something more than you are permitted as-of-right if you'll give us something in return."[4]

A case in point: Seattle's 1985 incentive ordinance was accompanied by a major downzoning, particularly in the retail core, where the base FAR went from 10 to 5 and the maximum height from 400 feet to 240 feet, with some exemptions for providing certain public benefit features. Although no height limits were imposed in the office sector, the base FAR was set at 10, and a maximum density of 20 FAR may be achieved through the provision of various bonuses.[5]

Downzonings may also be accomplished through less direct means, such as parking requirements. In Hartford, for example, the city set no parking requirements until the Downtown Development District zoning was passed in 1984. The imposition of minimum parking standards (one space per 1,000 square feet of net office space) in the new zoning effectively downzoned the downtown by more than 20 percent.

Many developers therefore view incentive zoning as a glorified name for a downzoning followed by an "upzoning with strings."[6] In this regard, Cincinnati's bonus system, enacted in 1987, is something of an anomaly. Whereas the old code set the maximum FAR at 9, the as-of-right limit in the downtown under the new code is 13. If all of the bonus options were exercised, a project's FAR could theoretically exceed 30. Parking requirements, however, were instituted for the first time. Although a major goal of the new code was to reflect more accurately the present scale of new development in the downtown, the FAR constraints are nevertheless generous. For this reason, some skepticism has been voiced about the potential effectiveness of the city's incentive approach.

In contrast, incentive zoning regulations in Hartford and Seattle, two downtowns where current development pressures are much greater than in Cincinnati, limit as-of-right projects to FARs of 10, so that developers have a strong incentive to avail themselves of the various bonus options. In an even more extreme example, Los Angeles's 1974 Central City regulations downzoned as-of-right FARs from 13 to 6. Because the base may be pushed up to 13 through the purchase of development rights transfers, most downtown projects exceed the base. It should be noted, however, that Cincinnati's base floor/area ratios deliberately were made generous to preserve the essential as-of-right development ethos of the downtown code.

9

CARROTS OR STICKS?

The trend in many recent zoning systems is to combine requirements with incentives. Moreover, some zoning features are deemed so important that they are mandated, even within incentive zoning regimes—the theory being that no incentive works like a mandatory one. For instance, some incentive zoning systems also require certain parking ratios, massing alternatives, build-to lines (whereby projects must be flush with the street wall and push out to the lot line), view corridors, and percentages of transparency and retail uses at the ground level. Another approach is to grant additional density for a mandated amenity. In Seattle, Bellevue, and Hartford, developers may earn increased commercial space for providing active street-level uses on designated streets in excess of the retail requirement.

Because continuity of retail uses and uninterrupted active pedestrian streetscapes are deemed crucial to a robust downtown retail core, it makes sense in some downtowns to mandate such features, rather than to depend on the vagaries and differing timetables of private development. Similarly, build-to lines and view corridors are far less effective if implemented randomly.

Because mandated activities or features generally apply only to new development, achieving retail or streetscape continuity in mature downtowns is no easy task. Likewise, critics claim that because view planes have already been disrupted, regulations preserving view corridors are merely academic exercises. Orlando, Florida, is one of the few cities where the requirement to incorporate a percentage of active street-level uses applies not only to new construction but also to existing structures. The requirement is triggered by a change in occupancy.

Historic preservation is another goal that is probably best achieved through mandatory rather than incentive techniques. Preserving older structures and incorporating them into new commercial development can be extremely expensive, so that additional density alone (unless the increase is truly large) is not generally sufficient inducement. On the other hand, using density bonuses to reinforce an existing delay or anti-demolition ordinance may be an effective and politically acceptable method for saving older buildings.

In Hartford, where the bonus ratio for preserving historic buildings is 1 to 3 (each square foot of historic space preserved earns three additional commercial square feet) with an internal cap of 2.5, only one project has yet been approved to use the bonus. The bonus criteria state that the entire structure must be conserved in compliance with the U.S. Secretary of the Interior's rehabilitation standards, thus discouraging the phenomenon of "façadomies." At one time, the city considered charging what it called a negative bonus penalty, whereby the destruction of a historic building would result in a loss of FAR at the same rate as set by the bonus ratio. The proposal, however, was politically inflammatory and never passed.

Although historic preservation is not one of Seattle's 28 bonus options, the city's incentive code provides that none of the bonus features will be available to a development involving the destruction of a historic structure or a designated feature, or of a portion thereof, unless authorized by the Seattle Landmarks Board.

Portland, Oregon, recently adopted an extensive bonus system in its 1988 Central City Plan, although it had earlier rejected the use of incentive zoning. In Portland's 1975 downtown ordinance, the city reasoned that it wanted all projects, not just those electing to use the bonuses, to incorporate a percentage of retail uses at the ground floor, to avoid the use of blank walls, and to preserve views of the hills and the Willamette River.

San Francisco, on the other hand, expunged almost all bonuses from its 1985 Downtown Plan, replacing them mainly with TDRs (development rights transfer programs). Now, increased density may only be acquired through the purchase of TDRs for historic buildings or open space, or through the inclusion of housing in downtown commercial projects. The 1985 code cut back greatly on allowable densities throughout most of the downtown, but by availing themselves of TDRs, developers may often build to density levels comparable to those under the earlier code.

Other cities have been known to offer a particular feature as an elective bonus selection, only later to remove it. For example, when Bellevue, Washington's incentive system was first instituted, developers earned significant density credits for building below-grade parking. On further consideration, the planning department recognized that steep land costs alone gave sufficient inducement to drive parking underground, so Bellevue no longer awards major density credits for constructing these facilities.

Hartford found it necessary to supplement one of its bonus options with a related requirement. Although it awarded additional density at the rate of 8 to 1 for including housing in downtown commercial projects (eight additional commercial square feet for each square foot of housing), the incentive was inadequate and only one developer applied to use the bonus. More recently, Hartford created a housing overlay district, operative in designated areas of the CBD, requiring that at least 25 percent of the gross floor area proposed for commercial projects be devoted to residential uses. Within the overlay district, the housing bonus may still be elected but only after meeting the initial 25 percent requirement.

A hybrid package of regulatory carrots and sticks also is often integrated within "special district" regulations. These provide tailor-made zoning unique to a particular area, most frequently a historic or a neighborhood district.

In summary, downtown zonings, which evolved from piecemeal amendments during the period of strong growth from the 1950s through the 1970s, erupted into a wave of comprehensive rewrites in the 1980s. This trend will likely continue. Many recent rezonings, which generally combine incentives and requirements, also have entailed significant reductions in base FARs, followed by "upzonings with strings" to ensure the viability of bonus systems.

Notes

1. The FAR is calculated by dividing the amount of floor area allowed in a new building by the lot area of the property; therefore, the greater the floor area in relation to the lot size, the higher the building intensity. For example, a one-story structure covering all of the lot would have an FAR of 1. A two-story structure covering half the lot also would have an FAR of 1, and a 200,000-square-foot structure on a 20,000-square-foot lot would have an FAR of 10, as explained by Robert S. Cook, Jr., in *Zoning for Downtown Urban Design* (Lexington, Massachusetts: D.C. Heath and Company, 1980), p.10.
2. Judith Getzels and Martin Jaffe, with Brian W. Blaesser and Robert F. Brown, *Zoning Bonuses in Central Cities*, Planning Advisory Service Report no. 410 (Chicago: American Planning Association, 1988), p. 2.
3. Clifford L. Weaver and Richard F. Babcock, *City Zoning* (Chicago: American Planning Association, 1979), pp. 58–59.
4. Ibid., p. 58.
5. With the passage of the citizens' initiative called the Citizens Alternative Plan (CAP) in May 1989, height limits were imposed for the first time in Seattle's office core at 450 feet, and height limits in the retail core were reduced significantly. (See Chapter 1, "Incentive Zoning," for more information on CAP.)
6. William H. Whyte, *City: Rediscovering the Center* (New York: Doubleday, 1989), p. 229.

INCENTIVE ZONING

Incentive zoning is catching on with city officials and urban planners. It has been incorporated to varying degrees within the revised land use codes of many downtowns, including Bellevue, Hartford, Austin, Burlington, Cincinnati, New York, Orlando, Portland, Oregon, Sacramento, and Seattle. In some downtowns, the bonus options may be limited to one or two features, such as providing mixed-use projects or devoting a percentage of the floor area to public open space; other incentive systems offer an extensive menu of amenity selections. In most instances, the bonus award is additional density; less frequently, it is additional height.

NEGOTIATED OR AS-OF-RIGHT?

Incentive zoning systems are either discretionary, as-of-right, or a hybrid of the two. The first type, a largely negotiated method whereby the city retains considerable discretion, characterizes many first-generation incentive systems, including New York City's 1961 Zoning Resolution, as well as its special district zoning. New York's special district approach developed simultaneously with the city's use of incentive zoning. Density bonuses were awarded for building plazas, "through-block arcades" (continuous, covered pedestrian walkways connecting parallel streets), housing, and theaters.

In an effort to stiffen the 1960s code, which contained inadequate bonus standards so that density awards had to be negotiated on a project-by-project basis, New York later developed explicit bonus criteria in its 1982 Midtown Zoning. Under the earlier, "wait-and-see" system, developers had had little indication of just how much density would be credited for the provision of individual public amenities until they met at the bargaining table to outline their proposals and negotiate with the city. Los Angeles's first-generation incentive system, which is still in place, is another excellent example of the discretionary approach.

By contrast, as-of-right, or automatic, incentive zoning systems spell out the precise elements of each bonus feature and its corresponding potential density gain. In theory, this self-administrative system gives developers advance notice of the criteria on which the bonus award will be made and offers a high level of predictability.

An argument can be made for either approach. Although negotiating bonuses on a site-specific basis affords maximum flexibility and a better chance to fine-tune the regulations, the disadvantages of the discretionary approach are well known. Such protracted negotiations are expensive and time-consuming for both the public and private sectors. Moreover, site-specific negotiations for bonuses may raise undue doubts of a city's intentions and finally erode the integrity of the underlying zoning. When ad hoc negotiation is the rule, it is also more difficult to ensure that all landowners are treated fairly; such systems are therefore more vulnerable to legal challenge. (See discussion of New York's Columbus Center decision later in this chapter.)

For these reasons, many cities have scuttled their discretionary negotiated incentives in favor of as-of-right bonuses. Planning officials point out, however, that even within as-of-right systems, the additional density is not entirely automatic. It is only granted if the bonus amenity *in fact* benefits the public. This decision, which is usually made by the planning department, review board, or, in some instances, city council, does involve some degree of discretion.

One potential drawback of the across-the-board approach is that there is less flexibility to encourage those aspects of a design proposal that promote the spirit, though not necessarily the letter, of the code. In other words, unless a feature is explicitly included as one of the bonus selections, a city, lest it be accused of giving something away, is not free to reward the developer for installing the amenity.

In a Bellevue project, for instance, sculptured water features were deftly designed to disguise the exhaust vents from an underground parking garage. Because the water features were on the downtown's Major Pedestrian Corridor, where pedestrian improvements and design embellishments are automatically required, the city refused to grant any more floor space. This same project also features a grand piano in the interior lobby, available for public use. City planning policy, however, generally proscribes awarding credit for amenities provided indoors, with the reasoning that interior space is not readily seen as available for public use.

THE HYBRID APPROACH

In practice, many cities combine the two kinds of programs, using one or the other according to the scale and environmental impact of a particular bonus selection. A project offering a major public benefit, such as a department store or theater, might reasonably be subjected to a heightened, more discretionary review process.[1] Seattle's multitiered system distinguishes between public benefit features (sculptured building tops, shopping corridors, and sidewalk widenings) and *special* public benefit features (transit station access plus development of a department store, performing arts theater, or museum), which require more discretionary input. Special public benefit features, which generally cost more to provide, are therefore assigned higher density credits and are subject to public notice and comment as well as review by the city council. (See Insert 1.)

Insert 1.
Seattle's Public Benefit Features
(code excerpt)

III. General Public Benefit Features:
A. Human services, B. Daycare, C. Cinema, D. Shopping atrium, E. Shopping corridor, F. Retail shopping, G. Parcel park, H. Residential parcel park, I. Street park, J. Rooftop garden: street-accessible, K. Rooftop garden: interior-accessible, L. Hillclimb assist, M. Hillside terrace, N. Sidewalk widening, O. Overhead weather protection, P. Voluntary building setback, Q. Sculptured building tops, R. Short-term parking, S. Small-lot development, and T. Harborfront open space.

IV. Special Public Benefit Features:
U. Performing arts theater, V. Museum, W. Urban plaza, X. Transit station access: mechanical, Y. Transit station access: grade-level, Z. Transit station access easement, and A A. Public atrium.

V. Housing Bonus Program Guidelines:
Housing bonus for DMR zones, Inclusion of affordable . . . units, Transfer of development rights from low-income housing, and Combined-lot development.

Although some by-right bonuses in New York City may be approved directly by the building department, others require certification and authorization by the planning department and planning commission. Still other discretionary bonuses, those that are part of a special permit process, must undergo the full-blown Uniform Land Use Review Process (ULURP). In Midtown Manhattan, for instance, bonus applications for subway improvements, urban parks, and renovations of designated theaters are subject to a ULURP. The highly negotiated review entails three phases: public hearings before a community board, hearings before the planning commission, and finally approval by the board of estimate.

It should be noted that New York City—the hotbed of incentive zoning—has tried to eliminate the abuse and overuse of negotiated variances and the need for discretionary actions, in favor of a more predictable, as-of-right development process. This effort has been attributed in part to pecuniary concerns. Burdened by lengthy discretionary review protocols during the fiscal crisis of the late 1970s, the city began to encourage as-of-right bonuses just to speed up development in Midtown.

In 1982, a sweeping revision of Midtown's zoning shrank the number of bonus options to four. Although the plaza bonus was retained, the FAR density credit was cut by one-third. Allowable FARs in Midtown were also reduced from a range of 10 to 21.6 to a range of 15 to 18. Higher ratios were maintained on the West Side, where development was encouraged. The bonuses currently permitted in Midtown are: urban parks, plazas, special subway station improvements, and through-block galleries. Besides the 1982 bonus for renovation of legitimate Broadway theaters (as named in the code) that might otherwise have been demolished, a separate theater retention bonus aimed at maintaining and continuing a structure's present use as a live theater was added in 1988.

According to a 1987 report on the results of the new zoning in Midtown, the city planning department has found that the number of as-of-right projects has swelled since 1982. The report recounts that whereas only 28 percent of Midtown buildings were developed as-of-right between 1977 and 1982, since then the percentage of as-of-right projects has risen to about 80 percent. [2]

Despite these report findings, some critics maintain that ad hoc decision making and discretionary review for most significant projects is still the rule in New York and many other cities. Paul Goldberger says that New York has perfected "the art of the deal," wherein "zoning laws are less rules that a city enforces for the public good than they are the starting point[s] in a negotiation." [3] (For a look at a court case that revolved around this point, see "Zoning for Sale," the last section of this chapter.)

The remainder of Chapter 1 falls roughly into two parts. The first part outlines the steps involved in devising an incentive system. Mainly, these steps determine which public amenities to encourage, then assign values to each bonus feature. The second portion of the chapter highlights various administrative issues, including enforcement and maintenance, coordination with other regulations, transitional matters, and legal considerations.

WHAT TO BONUS AND HOW MUCH?

Once the decision is made to adopt an incentive zoning system, whether as-of-right or discretionary, a city should take several critical initial steps: 1) determine which public goals to promote; 2) adopt public policies, preferably in the general plan, that reflect those goals, thus providing a tangible and legal basis for the zoning; and 3) analyze the market and potential financial impediments to achieving those goals.

The determination of what to bonus is highly political and inevitably reflects the priorities of a community. Bellevue, Washington, for instance, which is working to create a viable neighborhood in its new-born downtown, offers increased density for including grocery stores, hardware stores, public meeting rooms, and public restrooms in downtown development. In like fashion, Seattle's bonus provision for building daycare centers complements the city's overall effort to make the downtown living environment more hospitable to families and children.

First, the intent of the incentive should be clearly enunciated in a statement of purpose, which, as Judith Getzels and Martin Jaffe note, may be articulated in several different places:

> It can be contained in the overall purpose or intent statement covering the zoning district in which the bonuses are offered [see Insert 2 for Hartford's code], or it can appear in a separate section of the ordinance covering bonus provisions, or it can be spelled out in a set of published administrative guidelines. Wherever it appears, the community should be as explicit as possible about what the bonuses are intended to accomplish. A general

statement, such as "to improve the urban environment," ought to be translated into specifics. [4]

Insert 2.
Hartford's Statement of Purpose for New Downtown Zoning (code excerpt)

Sec. 35-5.40. B-1 Downtown Development District.
35-5.41. *Purpose.* The purpose of the B-1 Downtown Development District is to promote the health, safety, social, and economic welfare of the residents of the city by increasing the city's tax base and promoting the long-term economic growth of the downtown area. By implementing an expeditious administrative process, the city desires to encourage development that will be compatible with the character of the downtown area and conform to the downtown development plan. These regulations further the following additional goals:

(a) To foster and promote the orderly expansion of commercial office development so that the city will enchance its position as a center for economic and business affairs;

(b) To provide for an expanding source of employment opportunities for the city's inhabitants, and encourage the development of a desirable working environment;

(c) To implement a plan for improved pedestrian and vehicular circulation and parking management;

(d) To retain and promote the establishment of a variety of retail consumer and service businesses so that the needs of the area's residential and working populations will be satisfied;

(e) To encourage excellence in urban design;

(f) To preserve the unique character and historic fabric of the downtown;

(g) To reinforce the role of the downtown as a community center and a meeting place for people from all walks of life and all economic groups;

(h) To provide an incentive for development in a manner consistent with the foregoing objectives; and

(i) To provide for an increased presence and integration of the arts and related cultural activities in the Downtown Development District. . . .

In Seattle's downtown code, a brief statement of intent precedes each bonusable amenity. Shopping corridors, for example, are

> intended to provide weather-protected through-block pedestrian connections and retail frontage where retail activity and pedestrian traffic are most concentrated downtown. Shopping corridors create additional "streets" in the most intensive area of shopping activity, and are intended to complement streetfront retail activity.

Similarly, cinemas "are intended to enliven an area with activity during the evening hours, as well as maintain public entertainment uses downtown. Cinema design should promote activity on the street."

Bonus alternatives run the gamut and can be clustered around several general categories:

- building amenities—urban spaces, ground-floor retail, retail arcades, artwork, sculptured rooftops, atriums, and daycare;

- pedestrian amenities—sidewalk canopies and other overhead weather protection devices, landscaping, multiple building entrances;
- pedestrian movement—sidewalk widening and through-block connections;
- housing and human services—employment and job training; low-income health clinics; low-income, affordable, and market-rate housing;
- transportation improvements—transient parking, below-grade parking, and transit station access and upgrading;
- cultural amenities—cinemas, performing arts centers, art galleries, and live theaters; and
- preservation—historic structures, theaters, and low-rent housing stock. (Although a few incentive codes bonus historic structures, preservation is generally encouraged instead through the availability of transferable development rights [TDRs].)

THE PUBLIC INTEREST: WHICH PUBLIC?

As an exercise of the police powers, incentive zoning must promote the public interest, and individual bonus options must in fact benefit the public. One of the primary fears of municipalities that adopt incentive zoning systems is that they will be perceived as giving away the store. Should bonuses be granted, for instance, for the construction of underground parking garages to serve the general public? Or would steep downtown land costs drive parking below grade, regardless of the density credits? What about awarding bonuses for downtown daycare, which initially needed to be encouraged but which is now regarded as a hot ticket in many cities? Should bonuses be reserved exclusively for those features that *but for* the incentive would not likely get built?

Also, to what extent do building amenities such as retail arcades, lavishly appointed atriums, or urban plazas, which always benefit building tenants and enhance rent potential, also benefit the general public? Do such amenities as rooftop gardens or interior courtyards not readily available to the general public truly qualify as public benefits? Is it necessary to separate those benefits that accrue to the building tenants from those that accrue to the larger public, and are these necessarily in conflict?

The "public interest" usually refers to the greater good. Incentives for transient parking, for instance, with rating structures favoring downtown shoppers, visitors, clients, and so forth, are clearly intended to benefit the larger public rather than office workers. However, because some bonus selections favor one community sector over another, it may also be necessary to make distinctions among several different "publics." Are the intended beneficiaries the building tenants, office workers, downtown residents, tourists, or shoppers? In the case of downtown housing incentives, Seattle and some other cities award different density amounts depending on whether the housing is low-income, affordable, or market-rate. Many other cities make no such distinction and are satisfied just to get some housing built in the downtown.

With regard to child care incentives, cities need to determine which economic market will be targeted. If a facility is to be made available to all income categories, it will need subsidies. Will tenants have priority, or will the spaces be open equally to the general downtown workforce? Whose interests are paramount? Some jurisdictions may also opt to give precedence to city residents.

One way to ensure that a bonus amenity in fact benefits the public, or one of the intended publics, is to develop explicit, easy-to-follow bonus criteria and design guidelines. "In the matter of zoning bonuses and incentives," writes William H. Whyte, "what you do not specify you do not get." [5] (See Chapter 3, "Development and Design Reviews," for examples of bonus criteria.)

Another important decision is whether to confine bonuses to on-site amenities or to permit some bonus obligations to be met off site. Seattle's code awards increased densities for off-site child care centers, as well as for human services facilities, although in both instances, the bonus ratio for the off-site amenity is roughly half that awarded for on-site construction.

Density bonuses for housing also frequently permit the housing obligation to be met off site. In these cases, those areas targeted for the housing construction may be designated by the city, as are the receiving areas in TDR systems.

It is also important to target the appropriate geographic locations for on-site bonuses. The most direct method is to map out those streets or parts of the downtown where various bonuses are permitted. For example, credits for pedestrian amenities are usually confined to streets in the retail sector or in other areas with heavy pedestrian use. Furthermore, some cities refuse to award bonus credits for plazas and other urban open spaces that get little sunlight.

Another decision is whether to permit an in-lieu fee option whereby, instead of building a particular bonus feature, developers may opt to pay into a city fund whose monies will be used to develop affordable housing, public artwork, child care centers, or human services facilities.

Finally, it is essential that the selection of bonus features be carefully tailored to the particular locale. An incentive in one city may be a disincentive in another. Each bonus alternative should be economically driven, and the particular application must be thoroughly tested to determine the appropriate value. To illustrate: Allowing a height increase beyond a specific threshold would not be an incentive if subsoil conditions would unduly escalate costs for digging the foundation.

HOW MUCH VALUE?

Next, cities must determine the value to assign to each amenity option, a decision that not only must reflect community priorities but also must be grounded in economic reality. This determination is first affected by market demand, both demand for the extra commercial space and demand for the given amenity. Also, in an overly strict bonus system, when the as-of-right FAR is set too low and when many bonus selections must be assembled to reach desired densities, costs are driven up and developer interest is discouraged. This benefits neither the city nor the general public. On the other hand, in an overly generous incentive system, developers get a windfall and incur public distrust.

Achieving this delicate balance involves exhaustive analysis of the potential public benefit gained from the amenity, as well as of the economic benefit accruing to the developer via the bonus. Some bonus features—urban open spaces and plazas, shopping corridors, or artwork—generally boost a building's value, thereby benefiting both the public and the developer. Because many developers would install some service amenities and design-enhancing features regardless of the potential for greater density, these options generally trigger fewer bonus credits than those that do not directly enhance a project's marketability.

Although a comprehensive cost/benefit analysis is basic to the formulation of an effective incentive system, it is not always undertaken. According to a 1988 report, the office of the state comptroller in New York found that the amenities associated with 15 special permit projects approved in Manhattan during the 1980s cost about $5 million. This amount may be compared with the market value of the bonused floor area given the developers under these permits—an estimated $108 million.[6] When informed of the discrepancy, the city planning department responded that instead of focusing on developer costs and gains, it had been more interested in the potential public benefit from the amenity.

Although such trades need not be precisely equal, the extent of the imbalance in the above example is symptomatic of a problem. Because regulatory permissions (for instance, for additional density) are not direct cash outlays, city staff may tend to undervalue them. As planning professor Bernard Frieden observes, "Noncash elements in a deal should be evaluated with the same care as dollar outlays, and cities need to develop defensible procedures for analyzing all the costs and returns of their development agreements."[7]

In theory, a comprehensive cost/benefit analysis entails at least four distinct variables: construction cost for providing the bonus amenity, developer benefit derived from the amenity, public benefit derived from it, and any harm incurred by the public as a result of the bonus gain (traffic congestion, loss of light and air, and the like). The last two variables defy precise measurement. The rationale that density is increased in return for a feature that ameliorates the adverse effects of the increased density is paradoxical. To make sense, the amenity space must more than offset the adverse effects of added density and greatly improve the quality of the public environment.[8]

The bonus value must also be generous enough to offset costs for providing the amenity, with an increment to cover any time delays incurred through participation in the bonus review process or other additional risks. If the bonus value is set too high, however, it benefits the developer rather more than the public and opens the door to a claim that the public interest is not being adequately served.

For some critics, there is no such thing as a fair cost/benefit offset. As William H. Whyte writes, "No matter how pleasant an atrium might be for those who use it, it does not itself temper the downdrafts induced by the tower. . . . And suppose it wasn't even a good atrium? The offset concept is a sloppy one—rather like robbing Peter to pay Paul, but without conceding the robbery."[9]

Another cost consideration is whether the added density will raise or lower the average construction cost per square foot. In calculating the right bonus value, one needs to consider the complete menu of bonus alternatives and how they function as a system. If too many options are available, the chances of any one being used may be reduced, especially with those selections that are seen as risky or that tend to cost the most, such as historic preservation or housing. In Hartford, for example, commercial space may be earned either by paying into a housing trust fund or by building the residential units. Developers have opted to beg the question of housing entirely by using other bonus alternatives available under the city's incentive zoning program (such as retail or daycare).

Finally, in the case of such public initiatives as downtown housing, the amount of subsidy needed to close the gap between commercial and residential development may be so great that, to reach its goal, a city may have to supplement the incentive with more direct subsidies, like tax breaks.

A BONUS FORMULA

One of the hallmarks of an as-of-right incentive system is that developers know in advance both the precise value assigned to each bonus selection and the method used for calculating the bonus credits. The methods differ from city to city. One approach is to describe bonus gain (normally, added density) in terms of a given number of square feet for each square foot of amenity provided. In Seattle, for instance, the bonus ratio for providing a parcel park is 1 to 5: for each square foot of park provided, five more square feet of commercial space is granted. Cincinnati expresses the bonus gain as a percentage of the project size.

A further variable is the frequency with which a bonus may be used in any one project. Most second-generation bonus systems establish bonus caps. In Hartford, four square feet of commercial space is allowed for every square foot of art gallery space, but no credit is awarded beyond an FAR increment of 1, meaning that the bonus caps at 1 FAR. The housing bonus, on the other hand, caps at 4, so that eight square feet of office space is awarded for each square foot of housing. This bonus may be used up to four times. (See Inserts 3 and 4 for Hartford and Seattle's bonus systems.)

Bonus gains are also influenced by the various methods for calculating FAR. Although below-grade construction is generally exempt from the FAR count, some codes include basements, underground parking, and mechanical floors. Codes also should clearly state whether the bonused amenity space is to be counted into the new total floor area calculation. Cincinnati and Seattle explicitly exempt bonused space from the total count.

A formula for calculating bonus awards is perhaps even more critical in the situation of in-lieu fee contributions. In those cities that permit density gain in exchange for cash contributions to a trust fund (such as Hartford, where developers may earn density by paying into a housing/employment and job training trust fund), it is imperative that the incentive regulations provide a precise formula, lest a city be accused of "selling" bonuses and subjected to an onslaught of

Insert 3.
Hartford's Bonus Ratios
(code excerpt)

Use, Improvement, or Facility	Bonus Ratio	FAR Cap
Residential uses	1:8	4
Pedestrian-oriented retail uses	1:3	2
Transient parking	1:4	2
Cultural/entertainment facilities:		
Visual arts space	1:4	–
Performing arts space	1:4	1
Motion picture theaters	1:4	–
Visitor- and convention-related housing	1:1	1
Pedestrian circulation improvements:		
Sidewalk widening	1:4	–
Arcades	1:4	–
Through-block arcades	1:4	1
Plazas	1:4	–
Urban parks	1:4	–
Daycare centers/nurseries	1:6	1
Preservation of historic buildings	1:3	2.5
Employment	1:625	6
Streetscape improvements:		
Street	1:2	1
Sidewalk	1:1.5	1

(a) *Payment in lieu of providing residential uses or employment and job training.* Applicants for residential and/or employment bonuses may choose to receive additional floor area in lieu of residential construction and/or the provision of employment by contributing to the linkage trust fund an amount equal to fifteen dollars ($15.00) per square foot for each foot of bonus floor area. . . .

legal challenges. Moreover, once a formula is devised, it must be strictly followed, with no opportunity for additional voluntary payments. (For a further examination of this issue, see the discussion of New York's Columbus Center project later in this chapter.)

The formula also must undergo routine evaluation and necessary adjustment, accounting for fluctuations in assessed land values and so forth. One of the conclusions drawn by the New York Office of the State Comptroller in its evaluation of special permit bonuses is that "at a minimum, any section of the zoning resolution that requires an amenity with a specific value should contain a formula, so that the value can be adjusted over time, thereby making the process fairer to the affected community and the city as a whole." Market conditions fluctuate as well: Once a critical mass of housing is built downtown, the market is more favorable, so that a smaller bonus award becomes appropriate.

Opportunities for formula readjustments gain in importance in the case of involuntary exactions. San

**Insert 4.
Seattle's Bonus Ratios
(code excerpt)**

B. Public Benefit Features

If the director approves the design of public benefit features according to Subsection A, floor area bonuses shall be granted as follows:

Public Benefit Feature	Bonus Ratio[1]	Maximum Area of Public Benefit Feature Eligible for Bonus
Human Service Use in New Structure	7[6]	10,000 square feet
Human Service Use in Existing Structure	3.5[6]	10,000 square feet
Daycare in New Structure	12.5[6]	10,000 square feet[5]
Daycare in Existing Structure	6.5[6]	10,000 square feet[5]
Cinema	7	15,000 square feet
Shopping Atrium, in areas shown on Map IIB	6 or 8[2]	15,000 square feet
Shopping Corridor, in areas shown on Map IIB	6 or 7.5[3]	7,200 square feet
Retail Shopping, in areas shown on Map IIB	3	0.5 times the area of the lot, not to exceed 15,000 square feet
Parcel Park	5	7,000 square feet
Rooftop Garden, Street-Accessible	2.5	20 percent of lot area
Rooftop Garden, Interior-Accessible	1.5	30 percent of lot area
Hillclimb Assist, in areas shown on Map IIB	1.0 FAR[4]	Not applicable
Hillside Terrace, in areas shown on Map IIB	5	6,000 square feet
Sidewalk Widening, if required by Section 23.49.22	3	Area necessary to meet the required sidewalk width
Overhead Weather Protection, on Pedestrian I streets designated on Map IID	3 or 4.5[3]	10 times the street frontage of the lot
Sculptured Building Top	1.5 square feet per square foot of reduction	30,000 square feet
Small-Lot Development	2.0 FAR[4]	Not applicable
Short-Term Parking, above grade, in areas shown on Map IIB	1	200 parking spaces
Short-Term Parking, below grade, in areas shown on Map IIB	2	200 parking spaces
Performing Arts Theater	12	Subject to the Public Benefit Features Rule
Museums	5	30,000 square feet
Urban Plaza	5	15,000 square feet
Public Atrium	6	5,500 square feet
Transit Station Access Easement	25,000 square feet	2 per lot
Grade-Level Transit Station Access	25,000 square feet	2 per lot
Mechanical Transit Station Access	30,000 square feet	2 per lot
Housing	Subject to the Public Benefit Features Rule	Subject to the Public Benefit Features Rule; maximum amount of bonus is 7 times the area of the lot.

[1] Ratio of additional square feet of floor area granted per square foot of public benefit feature provided.
[2] Amount depends on height of the shopping atrium.
[3] Higher bonus is granted when skylights are provided.
[4] This is the amount of bonus granted when the public benefit feature is provided, regardless of its size.
[5] Daycare space from 3,001 to 10,000 square feet is bonused at same ratio as human service uses.
[6] Human services and daycare may be provided in another downtown zone; in that case, bonus ratio subject to Public Benefit Features Rule.

Francisco's 1985 code requires that the city's Downtown Park Fund, which is mandated as part of its comprehensive fee program, be reviewed every three years. The city's daycare requirement also calls for annual evaluation. The code clearly states that if the evaluation shows the fee requirement is too high, the planning commission must "refund that portion of any fee paid or permit a reduction of the space in the office development project dedicated for child care."

BONUS CALIBRATION MODELS

A technique used to relate the value of additional commercial space to developer costs for supplying a public amenity is the bonus calibration model. In 1988, Chicago's planning staff and consultants examined incentive zoning systems throughout the country and found that few cities relied on economic models for assigning FAR value to bonus amenities. Many cities indicated, however, "that they were moving in the direction of quantifying this relationship, because of the perception of unfair trade-offs in their existing system." [10]

The Chicago study examines the following five approaches that have been used or are still being tested: 1) the equivalent land-cost model, 2) the equivalent development rights approach, 3) the return on investment approach, 4) the marginal cost-to-profit approach, and 5) the cost-plus formula.

The equivalent land-cost model compares the cost of providing an amenity to the cost of buying additional land to reach the desired density. According to this model, a particular incentive option would be provided only if its cost per square foot of FAR were less than or equal to the cost of purchasing more land to construct the same-sized project under the site's base zoning. A 1988 report by the American Planning Association confirms the Chicago study's finding that—although the equivalent land-cost model has worked well in Bellevue and Seattle by giving developers specific options based on actual numbers and on assumptions they understand—a major question is how to determine boundaries for the land districts so as to generalize land costs. Therefore, the Chicago report concluded, this technique works best in those cities with relatively stable land costs throughout the downtown. It would be cumbersome to apply in a larger city like Chicago, where big differences in land costs exist from district to district and sometimes from block to block; these discrepancies mean devising too many different prototypes.

The return on investment (ROI) approach, relied on by Denver and Hartford, assumes that developers will choose the public amenity option that maximizes the return on their investment in a downtown office project. Unlike the other models, which measure implicit costs of acquiring more land or air rights to build to desired densities, this approach measures the potential benefits to the developer of the amenities and bonus gain. One difficulty with this model is getting a developers' consensus on land and construction costs. Although figures can easily be pulled from developers' pro formas, "there is an incentive for the developer to understate net operating income to obtain artificially higher bonus ratios. Variables such as net operating income and land costs would move with the market, but the cost inputs in the model would have to be updated to reflect such changes." [11] Developers might be more comfortable sharing this particular information with an independent consultant.

The marginal cost-to-profit model, used extensively in San Francisco before the 1985 Downtown Plan was passed, compares the marginal profits derived from bonus office space to the cost of the amenity chosen by a developer. Based on traditional appraisal techniques, the model assumes that developers will build to a point where they get the greatest profit per square foot at the margin. The Chicago study concluded that in a situation like Chicago's, with land values often differing from block to block, this model, which does not rely largely on land costs, is particularly useful.

One crucial decision that cannot be derived through any amount of economic modeling is the initial selection of public amenities and their comparative worth. The bonus value attached to each, generally first decided as a matter of policy, must be accomplished through hardheaded choices and political compromises.

SECOND-GENERATION INCENTIVE ZONING SYSTEMS

BELLEVUE, WASHINGTON

Bellevue's 1981 hybrid code, a mixture of requirements and incentives, offers more than 20 distinct bonus selections and corresponding density ratios, which differ with their locations within the downtown. They are: pedestrian-oriented frontage, landscape feature, arcade, marquee, awning, sculpture, water feature, plaza, active recreation area, residential use, public meeting room, Major Pedestrian Corridor, child care services, retail food, public restrooms, performing arts space, space for nonprofit social services, and donation of park property. Regardless of project size, developers must devote space in a new project or major expansion to any combination of the first seven amenity features (according to a formula), after which they are free to amass more density through any bonus combination.

HARTFORD

The heart of Hartford's 1984 Downtown Development District regulations is the schedule of density bonuses. (See Insert 3 for an inventory of the full bonus platter and for density ratios.) Events leading up to the rezoning are discussed in Chapter 7, "Retail Uses."

PORTLAND, OREGON

When Portland rewrote its downtown land use regulations in the late 1970s, it considered and then rejected the idea of incentive zoning because it wanted *all* projects to incorporate those public amenities that would have been elective within a bonus system. The 1972 Downtown Plan referred vaguely to an incentive system, while the zoning regulations of 1979 included only one incentive provision, a residential bonus that was used in only one project.

As part of the downtown development process set up by the 1979 code, the Portland City Council followed a policy of granting exceptions to bulk limits if developers could show that their projects would better meet the intent of the code. A dozen projects received such exemptions within nine years. These ad hoc density awards were criticized for the inconsistent manner in which they were granted, and developers claimed the practice was too unpredictable. An across-the-board incentive program, it was thought, might be preferable to this highly discretionary system.

Thus, density bonuses were reconsidered during discussion on Portland's Central City Plan and were ultimately adopted in the zoning regulations that became effective in July 1988. Encompassing roughly 2,750 acres, including the downtown, the Central City Plan reflects the community's recognition of the need to guide future patterns of business investment, office and retail growth, and redevelopment in the expanding city core. For example, Lloyd Center, Portland's first regional shopping center, located less than two miles away from the downtown core and now on the light-rail line, is part of the Central City Plan and regarded as an extension of the downtown retail sector.

The area affected by the Central City Plan is really an expanded version of the downtown development zone, and many of the same code requirements apply. For example, those requirements in the downtown code—the ground-floor retail use requirement, the prohibition against blank walls, and the explicit development review design guidelines—also apply in the Central City area. Similarly, the bonuses in the Central City Plan also apply within the downtown development zone.

The Central City Plan includes density bonuses for providing daycare, retail, public art, rooftop gardens, theaters, water features, public fountains, or residential units within mixed-use projects. The zoning also calls for bonus height awards in the case of each of these amenities, if the "increased height . . . [does] not interfere with the protection of established view corridors, preservation of the character of historical districts, protection of public open spaces from shadow, and preservation of the city's visual focus on important buildings. . . . "

Separate height and density limits are set for different parts of the Central City, with bonuses available in each sector. The FAR range in some areas is 1 to 2, while in others it is 1 to 15. Heights also vary from 45 feet to 460 feet. Within limited areas of the financial core, the maximum height is 460 feet and the highest base FAR is 15. Because Portland's downtown blocks are small (200 feet), the buildings are relatively small, and the addition of, say, 120,000 square feet to a building in the 15 FAR range (about 600,000 square feet) is substantial. Much of the development downtown is within the 9-to-1 range, with FAR limits set at 4 for projects near the river or abutting residential neighborhoods. Although these limits are retained within the downtown zone, permitted heights and densities in other Central City districts are reduced greatly. In some instances, FARs have been reduced from 12 to 2. Strict height limits are also imposed on development along the Willamette River, and development is stepped back to preserve river view corridors.

A CASE IN POINT: SEATTLE'S ZONING SAGA

Home of the most elaborate incentive zoning system in the United States, Seattle first experimented with incentives in the mid-1960s and got a 1.5 million-square-foot office tower that shot up to an unprecedented 76 stories across the street from the city's planning office. The city's first-generation incentive zoning code contained neither maximum height nor FAR limits, and developers were permitted (some say encouraged) to stack one bonus upon another, with few constraints except those imposed by the market. Furthermore, some of the bonus-winning amenities, particularly retail, were built in inappropriate locations: This same 76-story high rise, located in the government sector and separated from the traditional retail core, is loaded with some 60,000 square feet of retail space on a triple-level arcade and has had difficulty in leasing some of this space. Yet the developer's aggressive use of bonuses to reap more leasable space complied completely with the rules of the city's zoning game. It is the fault of the city, not the developer, that some of the retail space affords negligible public benefit.

THE 1985 ZONING OVERHAUL

The chance that this Darth Vader of a building, clad in black glass, could be cloned helped prod the city to rethink its zoning. The zoning overhaul, however, took place largely because the 1960s-vintage code was out of step with the galloping gait of new building in the area. As part of an eight-year city-wide rezoning effort, work on the *Land Use and Transportation Plan for the Downtown*—the basis for the new ordinance—started in 1980. It first addressed many issues regarding single-family and multifamily neighborhoods: overbuilding in residential sections, the loss of low-income housing stock, the need for moderate-income downtown housing, public concern over rapid development's impacts on the infrastructure as well as on neighborhood character, and consternation over the density and overall design quality of new development. In 1984, interim controls were put into effect until the downtown plan and zoning were simultaneously adopted a year later.

Seattle's new code expanded the palette of bonuses from five to 28, established base FARs for all downtown sectors, and capped the maximum FAR at 20 in the densest commercial area. Although no height limits were imposed in the primary office core, they were applied elsewhere: Heights in the retail sector were set at 240 feet but could be pushed up to 400 feet by incorporating a department store or performing arts center.

It is no longer possible to stack bonus upon bonus indefinitely. The maximum value that will be assigned to the retail space bonus, for example, is 0.5 FAR or 15,000 square feet, whichever is less. Any greater retail space will receive no density credit.

Furthermore, with densities for each of the 11 downtown zoning districts tied to their distinct functions and transit capacities, the city simultaneously retains certain absolute requirements for view corridors, setbacks, street wall standards, street classifications, and ground-floor retail uses.

The multitiered bonus system establishes a hierarchy for each of the 28 bonus features. (See Insert 4

for a table of Seattle's bonus options and ratios.) Within the densest portion of the office core, as-of-right development is permitted up to 10 FAR; to build beyond that point (from 10 to 15 FAR), developers must provide certain "general" public benefit features, such as street parks, retail atriums, daycare services, small-lot development, or cinemas. The FAR may also be increased to 15 by using a mix of general bonuses, affordable housing bonuses, and development rights transfers for low-income housing or historic landmarks. The only way to exceed an FAR of 15, however, is to use the downtown housing bonus. Development in the office core sector typically goes in at FARs of 17 and 18, so the requirement that projects of such size provide housing virtually ensures that some housing will be built. (See Insert 5 for a diagram clarifying bonus tiering within the office core.)

(In current practice, although the tiered system still stands, the success of a recent voter initiative called the Citizens Alternative Plan [CAP] has debarred structures with a higher FAR than 14 from the office core. For details, consult the later subsection of this chapter entitled "The Citizens' Response to the New Zoning.")

Seattle's 1985 incentive zoning scheme also dictates that none of the bonus features will be avail-

Insert 5.
Seattle's FAR System

DOWNTOWN OFFICE CORE-1:
FLOOR/AREA RATIO SYSTEM

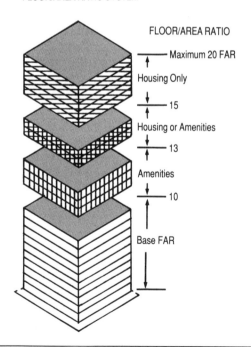

FLOOR/AREA RATIO

— Maximum 20 FAR

Housing Only

— 15

Housing or Amenities

— 13

Amenities

— 10

Base FAR

Source: City of Seattle Department of Construction and Land Use.

able to a project entailing destruction of a designated structure or portion thereof, unless authorized by the city's landmarks board.

ZONING WITH SOUL

Former Deputy Mayor Carol Lewis characterizes Seattle's code as "zoning with soul." Indeed, over and above the bonus options, transferable development rights are also available for building low-income housing. And under the daycare bonus, 20 percent of the spaces in the child care center must be allocated to the children of low-income workers. The human services bonus, designed to obtain new nonprofit health, social services, and drug treatment facilities, can be met by building these facilities on the same or a different downtown lot or by giving to a fund. Bonuses for performing arts theaters and museums will expand the city's cultural offerings; the overhead weather protection bonus will improve pedestrian comfort along major pedestrian routes during the rainy season; and the hillclimb assist bonus will "aid pedestrian movement in areas of concentrated employment and pedestrian activity on lots located along steeply sloping streets."

Whereas the amenity options of Seattle's first-generation incentive zoning system contained almost no review standards, the current bonus menu is replete with criteria and design guidelines, better ensuring that bonuses will benefit the public.

For example, retail-related and weather protection features are permitted only in locations with high pedestrian use and are evaluated within the context of their surroundings. Rooftop gardens must be "directly accessible and visible from an adjacent street or public open space," and their locations must "be clearly identified so that access from the street is apparent to pedestrians." Except in the downtown's three special districts (the International District, Pioneer Square, and Pike Place Market), private construction is not often subject to design review; however, the city's comprehensive bonus evaluation procedure entails a form of design review, at least for those public benefit features incorporated into a project.

BONUSES BEGET TEST TUBE BUILDING

Washington Mutual Tower, a postmodern office high rise built in the financial core, was conceived while the downtown code was being revised. Anchor tenant Washington Mutual Savings Bank occupies 120,000 square feet of the 55-story project, located at 1201 Third Avenue. Although the project was permitted under the 1984 interim zoning provisions, developer Jon Runstad opted to follow the new code provisions. As the first offspring of the new zoning, the 1 million-square-foot Wright Runstad & Company development amassed sufficient bonus credits to more than double its as-of-right density. An extra 28 stories were gained by providing a bus transit tunnel entrance, downtown housing, retail space, daycare, and other public amenities (see Insert 6).

Insert 6.
How Seattle's Washington Mutual Tower Stacked Up

This tower originally qualified for 27 stories. The building grew to 55 stories by acquiring bonus points.

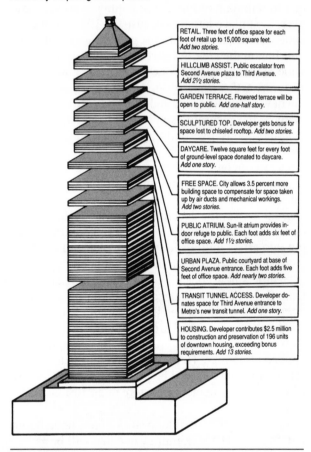

RETAIL. Three feet of office space for each foot of retail up to 15,000 square feet. *Add two stories.*

HILLCLIMB ASSIST. Public escalator from Second Avenue plaza to Third Avenue. *Add 2½ stories.*

GARDEN TERRACE. Flowered terrace will be open to public. *Add one-half story.*

SCULPTURED TOP. Developer gets bonus for space lost to chiseled rooftop. *Add two stories.*

DAYCARE. Twelve square feet for every foot of ground-level space donated to daycare. *Add one story.*

FREE SPACE. City allows 3.5 percent more building space to compensate for space taken up by air ducts and mechanical workings. *Add two stories.*

PUBLIC ATRIUM. Sun-lit atrium provides indoor refuge to public. Each foot adds six feet of office space. *Add 1½ stories.*

URBAN PLAZA. Public courtyard at base of Second Avenue entrance. Each foot adds five feet of office space. *Add nearly two stories.*

TRANSIT TUNNEL ACCESS. Developer donates space for Third Avenue entrance to Metro's new transit tunnel. *Add one story.*

HOUSING. Developer contributes $2.5 million to construction and preservation of 196 units of downtown housing, exceeding bonus requirements. *Add 13 stories.*

Source: *Seattle Post-Intelligencer* (April 18, 1988).
Based on original art by Duane Hoffman.

Because the building and the code were shaped simultaneously, the Washington Mutual Tower served as a "test tube for the plan," notes Wright Runstad's senior executive vice president, Steve Trainer.[12] The whimsical wedding-cake cupola had to be redesigned more than a dozen times to qualify for the sculptured rooftop bonus. Finally, the code formula itself was adjusted to make the bonus workable.

Other glitches in the code have called for readjustments. At first, the city insisted that the project's urban plaza border on Third Avenue, which carries heavy pedestrian traffic but incidentally receives no sunlight. So the city took stock of its position and allowed the developer to place the plaza on a sunnier street, Second Avenue. Washington Mutual Tower's hillclimb assist feature, an outdoor public escalator giving the Second Avenue plaza access to Third Avenue and alleviating a steep east/west climb, was patterned after an escalator that had worked well in an earlier Wright Runstad project.

The largest amount of bonus density (13 stories) was gained for a contribution of more than $2.5 million in housing improvements. The contribution aided construction of 101 new affordable housing units in three buildings and the rehabilitation of 155 low-rent units. Runstad paid a cash fee for the new construction and bought transferable development rights from three residential buildings to provide rehabilitation funding. The housing contribution per commercial square foot came to roughly $9.60.

Some critics question whether the city's incentive zoning system is rewarding developers for features they would include anyway or whether some amenities—say, roof gardens or handsomely appointed atriums—provide much public benefit. Another issue is whether the enhancement features should primarily benefit the downtown public or the building tenants. Although 20 percent of the places in Washington Mutual Tower's daycare program are set aside for the children of low-income employees, the 22 places have all gone to workers in the building rather than to the general downtown population.

Jon Runstad says that without the bonus he would never have considered the subsidies for downtown housing or such amenities as the rent-free daycare and the public atrium. He concedes, however, that the sculptured top was chosen mainly for aesthetic reasons and that he would have built the urban plaza and retail shops regardless of the bonus value.

The money spent on the building's public features—approximately $6 million—is substantial, but relatively modest compared with the project's $175 million price tag. And, of course, higher profits will be generated by the extra 28 stories.

The office tower, designed by Kohn Pederson Fox in association with McKinley Architects of Seattle, has been praised for its fastidious attention to elegant details. It has a sumptuous mahogany- and marble-trimmed, hotellike lobby, is enhanced externally by a pinkish-beige Brazilian granite skin, and presents a snappy silhouette. One point of controversy, though,

is that the bonus system yielded 0.5 million additional square feet, placing new strains on city services. It is estimated, for example, that the 13 floors gained from the housing bonus payments will bring some 1,040 more office workers downtown, who will need more parking spaces and expanded transit service.

One former developer compares the incentive zoning system to the medieval church practice of selling indulgences. The test is "whether the indulgences are remotely proportional to the transgressions. . . . " [13] To many critics of the downtown plan, the balance between public benefits and public costs is not remotely proportional. For example, as Seattle architect Peter Steinbrueck observes, recent surveys suggest that 40 percent of downtown workers want child care services downtown. Applying this ratio to the Washington Mutual Tower, which can house about 80 office workers per floor, the daycare needs for the building could amount to 32 child care spaces for every floor, which in the case of this 55-story structure would be 1,760 daycare spaces.[14] This is a far cry from the daycare center that ultimately was built to serve 22 children. Perhaps the center, which gleaned an extra floor for the developer, should at least have met the child care needs of workers on that one floor.

THE CITIZENS' RESPONSE TO THE NEW ZONING

Concern about Seattle's capacity to absorb more buildings of this size, and about the concomitant burdens laid on the infrastructure and transportation system, prodded the city's slow-growth gang to call for more stringent height caps and numerical curbs on commercial development. The growth controversy has been aggravated by the surge of recent construction, most of which involves projects granted use permits before the 1985 ordinance and forced to get building permits within two years or risk losing their permit rights. During 1986 alone, five new office projects were completed. Five million square feet of construction broke ground in 1987 and is slated for completion in 1989 and 1990, raising concerns about overwhelming the existing inventory.

At the same time, the construction of several major public projects—Westlake Center, the convention center, and the transit tunnel—has temporarily transformed the downtown into "Little Beirut."

Granted, it is unlikely that the 5 to 10 million square feet of commercial space vested under the old code will all get built. The difficulty of assembling available land parcels makes it likelier that smaller projects will be erected in the future.

Seattle's downtown skyrush.

Annual downtown construction in the 1980s has run close to 1 million square feet on the average, with absorption running from 800,000 to 1 million square feet. In 1988, close to 1.5 million square feet was absorbed in the downtown, and two recent projects are 75 percent and 65 percent preleased; clearly, the recent rate of construction is not out of line with the demand.

Increased fears about the crush of new development and a downtown skyrush, however, helped foment the revolution leading to the Citizens Alternative Plan (CAP). The CAP initiative puts an annual lid on office development, slashes height and FAR limits throughout the downtown, and mandates a comprehensive growth management plan.

By early November 1988, CAP had secured enough signatures to be placed on the May 1989 ballot in a special election. The Seattle City Council responded by passing an emergency five-month moratorium on all new downtown construction. Effective in late November 1988, the moratorium was a stopgap measure to prevent a rush of projects into the approval pipeline before the initiative election.

In this David-and-Goliath struggle, opponents of CAP spent 10 times the amount available to the low-budget grass-roots campaign, decrying the "blunt instrument" of the CAP and warning that the measure would worsen traffic congestion, escalate rents, contribute to suburban sprawl, and eventually shut down development. CAP supporters, fed up with what they saw as runaway growth and the "Manhattanized" silhouette of the downtown, trounced their opponents in the May 16 election, capturing 62 percent of the votes.

Although CAP leaves intact the basic bonus system, it metes out development by limiting total office space to 500,000 square feet a year for the next five years (85,000 square feet for low-rise buildings). The limit doubles to 1 million square feet annually between 1995 and 1999. CAP also sets stricter FAR and height limits throughout the downtown. For instance, the base FAR in the densest office sector is reduced from 10 to 5, and a new height limit of 450 feet (comparable to a 38-story building) is imposed. The plan also shrinks height limits in the retail core from 400 feet (with inclusion of a major retail store or performing arts theater) to 150 feet.

CAP leaves open the question of how the limitations will be administered. Rejecting a first-come, first-served approach, former Mayor Charles Royer advocated a competition based on building design and its "enhancement of the cityscape of downtown." Other voices have suggested that projects be judged in light of the public amenities they offer. The city's planning office has proposed preliminary criteria for evaluating competing projects, some of which are the project's contribution to a high-quality pedestrian-oriented street environment, architectural design and provision of public art, as well as minimization of traffic and transportation impacts. The competition rules will likely be adopted in late summer 1989, in time for the first round in the fall.

The ceiling on new office development under CAP resembles San Francisco's much-ballyhoo'ed "office rationing program" (Proposition M), the only other commercial space allocation program enacted in any American city. Unlike CAP, however, which may be changed through legislative action after two years,

San Francisco's Proposition M is permanent. (See Chapter 4, "Design Review Overdose, San Francisco–Style," for a history and analysis of Proposition M.)

One ramification of Seattle's five-year annual limit of one-half million square feet of new downtown office space will be to reduce markedly the number of office projects applying for housing credits, or indeed for any of the array of public benefit features. Inevitably, indexing the provision of public amenities to the amount of office space means the incentives to build low-cost housing, daycare, theaters, and pedestrian improvements become more dependent on the market for office development. This dependency is made all too explicit in the case of commercial caps.

The CAP initiative corrects for this dependency to some extent. For example, the housing obligation is triggered sooner. To build beyond an FAR of 7, office developers must participate in the city's housing or historic preservation program, and beyond an FAR of 10, they must buy TDRs for low-income housing. (For further discussion, see Chapter 11, "Housing.") Meanwhile, the planning office is considering a major overhaul of the bonus system and possible removal of some bonus selections altogether. Some open space options, such as those for parcel parks, street parks, and rooftop gardens, as well as the bonuses for daycare and human services, may be mandated instead.

One of the unfortunate consequences of Seattle's new development lid is that it threatens to torpedo, almost from the start, a bold, comprehensive incentive zoning system (some eight years in the making) that has not yet had a chance to strut its stuff.

EVALUATING AN INCENTIVE SYSTEM

One method for judging the effectiveness of an incentive system is to examine the frequency with which individual amenity features are used by developers. Sparse use of a bonus selection might be attributed, say, to overly complicated, obscure bonus criteria. The level of administrative ease also influences bonus use; burdensome enforcement mechanisms, for instance, may impede use of particular bonus features. In Hartford, lack of developer interest in the bonus for employment and job training has been laid mainly to administrative difficulties. In this connection, developers complain that because many new downtown projects are speculative, the unknown tenant mix precludes their (developers') exercising the necessary control to set up or monitor hiring and employment agreements.

Cost is always paramount in the choice of bonus options. Those features that are most expensive for developers, such as preserving historic structures or allotting several floors of a commercial project to residential use, might get short shrift, depending on the bonus value assigned to each. As already discussed, costs for building a bonus, including any perceived risks, must be scrupulously balanced against the expected reasonable return on investment.

On the other hand, extensive use of an amenity might show that the assigned bonus value is too high or that the feature should not be bonused at all. In Bellevue's first experiment with incentive zoning, some projects amassed hundreds of thousands of unused square footage that developers banked for subsequent project phases, indicating that the system was too generous. Most of this excess largesse was blamed on the bonus award for underground parking, and the policy was later discontinued. From the time the first code went into effect in Bellevue in 1981, land values skyrocketed overnight, and it was the economics as much as the bonus that drove parking underground and gave rise to a demand for larger-scale development. Nonetheless, the city saw no reason to continue bonusing an item that would be built with or without the incentive.

Similar criticism has been levelled against Hartford's transient parking incentive, which has been offered as a bonus for some projects under the city's 1984 incentive code. Hartford has been accused of virtually giving away the additional commercial space. After all, in Bellevue, Portland, and Seattle, downtown developers must automatically set aside a percentage of spaces for short-term parking with no bonus award.

The flip side of the issue is the efficacy of using bonuses to force a market. For example, in some downtowns with ailing retail cores, the added ground-floor retail uses generated by bonus systems may, at least in the beginning, require large subsidies or may even lie vacant for a time. Although one would assume that developers would refrain from incorporating bonuses for which no market yet exists, the chance to acquire greater density might more than compensate for other possible losses. Indeed, for some cities, the very raison d'être of incentive zoning is to encourage the visionary and to ensure that cities will get those amenities they would like to have, rather than those they are already getting.

The issue of which bonuses are used the most and why may also be influenced by politics. In Hartford's downtown regulations, contributions to a trust fund may be earmarked either for low-income housing or for employment and job training. Given the choice of paying for low-income housing, in a city wracked by severe housing shortages, or supporting employment opportunities, it may be politically more expedient for developers to be associated with the former.

As with any other zoning system, putting a bonus program into practice invariably requires a certain amount of trial-and-error tinkering and sometimes calls for revision. Capricious design tastes and tenant preferences, as well as the fluctuating economics of the commercial building market, need continuous monitoring and may render a bonus selection ineffective or irrelevant. Cities must be prepared to adjust their zoning schemes accordingly. Some bonus systems, therefore, call for periodic evaluation. Under Seattle's code, the city council must demand a yearly status report on the downtown incentive regulations. The code also entails a "review and adjust" approach to the housing and human services policies. If after 1 million square feet of downtown office space has been bonused, less than 40 percent of the space has been achieved through housing bonuses or development rights transfers for affordable housing, the overall incentive system must be adjusted accordingly.

Continuous monitoring is also needed to balance, on the one hand, the costs of incorporating a given bonus feature against, on the other hand, the value of the extra commercial space and the public benefit of the bonus amenity.

ADMINISTRATIVE ISSUES: ENFORCEABILITY AND MAINTENANCE

Maintenance and enforceability issues must be considered within any land use regulatory system, although they are probably more complex within the context of incentive zoning. As part of their mandates to protect the general welfare, cities are responsible for ensuring that bonused spaces, which are the quid pro quo for the grant of additional density, do in fact benefit the public. Bonus features most likely to raise maintenance and enforcement concerns are those in which a project sponsor has a continuing obligation to keep up an amenity. For instance, those developers who earn extra commercial density for providing short-term parking must monitor the lot or garage to ensure that the spaces are indeed reserved for shoppers, clients, or visitors. Similarly, bonus provisions for urban open spaces and public plazas often contain detailed guidelines for the compulsory maintenance of lighting, seating, and landscaping.

ENFORCEMENT

Public Access. One of the most direct enforcement mechanisms is the demand that a plaque or other permanent sign be conspicuously displayed on any open space for which a bonus is granted. It should announce that the area is open to the public and state the hours of operation. This requirement, which bolsters public vigilance of bonused spaces and the agreed-upon improvements, was suggested by William Holly Whyte as a result of his research on New York's urban open spaces. The plaque requirement was eventually written into the city's zoning criteria for the plaza bonus and has since been enshrined in the downtown regulations of many other cities. (See Chapter 8, "Open Space and Streetscapes," for further information.) As a result, all bonused open spaces in New York, including the sumptuous retail-lined atrium of Trump Tower, all bear the same familiar plaque with the tree image, identifying them as public spaces (see Insert 7).

Insert 7.
Plaque Requirement for Urban Plazas, 1982 Midtown Zoning, New York
(code excerpt)[1]

(l) Plaque

A plaque or other permanent *sign* with a *surface area* not less than two nor more than four square feet shall be displayed in a prominent location on any urban plaza for which a bonus is granted. Such *sign* shall indicate the following:

Plaque designates bonused public space in New York City.

1. The number of trees required on the urban plaza and *street* trees required on the *street* sidewalk area.
2. The number of movable chairs required on or adjacent to the urban plaza.
3. The name of the owner and the person he has designated to maintain the urban plaza and that person's address and a telephone number where he can be reached between the hours of 8:00 a.m. and 7:00 p.m.
4. The symbol for a city planning commission–certified urban plaza.
5. The International Symbol of Access and the statement: "This urban plaza is accessible to the physically handicapped."
6. The statement: "To ensure compliance with requirements regarding this urban plaza, a bond has been posted with the Comptroller of the City of New York."

---

[1] In New York inserts, all italics are original.

In addition, many states have barrier-free access regulations for the handicapped, which also affect the public availability of bonused areas. Seattle's code states that any "public benefit feature that has a publicly accessible exterior or interior space shall provide access in accordance with the Washington State Rules and Regulations for Barrier-Free Design [with some exceptions]." (See Insert 8 for New York's code language.)

Insert 8.
Access for the Disabled to Urban Plazas, 1982 Midtown Zoning, New York
(code excerpt)[1]

(o) Standards of accessibility for the handicapped:
   1. There shall be at least one path of travel conforming to the standards set forth in Subparagraph (2) and providing access to each of the following:
      (a) The major portion of the urban plaza;
      (b) Any *building* lobby accessible to the urban plaza; and
      (c) Any *use* that may be present on or adjacent to the urban plaza.
   2. The following standards shall apply to assure access for handicapped persons:
      (a) Such paths shall have a minimum width of five feet, except where specific provisions require a greater width, free and clear of all obstructions.
      (b) Ramps are to be provided alongside any stairs or steps for such paths. Ramps shall have a minimum width of 36 inches, a slope of not greater than 1 in 12, a nonskid surface, and, for open-edged ramps, a two-inch-high safety curb. At each end of a ramp, there shall be a level area, which may be a public sidewalk, at least five feet long.
      (c) All stairs or ramps within such paths shall provide handrails. Handrails shall be 32 inches high, have a midrail 22 inches high, and extend at least 18 inches beyond the stair or ramp ends.
      (d) Where stairs are used to effect changes of grade for such paths, they shall have closed risers, no projecting nosings, a maximum riser height of 7.5 inches, and a minimum tread width of 11 inches.

---

[1] Italics are original.

Timeliness. How promptly an amenity is built is another enforcement issue. As recounted earlier, in 1988, the office of the state comptroller of New York reviewed the public amenities of a sample of 15 special permit projects throughout Manhattan whose permits had been issued in the 1980s. The review disclosed that several developers had been permitted to complete construction, get temporary certificates of occupancy, and begin to rent offices or sell apartments in a building before completing work on the related amenity. Although a principal aim of many bonus amenities is to reduce or mitigate the undesirable impacts of larger structures on the downtown or surrounding neighborhoods, in these instances the impacts were experienced long before any benefit had been derived from the amenity. In several cases of density awards for subway station improvements, projects had been fully leased for several years before the promised amenities had been provided. In other cases, they were never provided. The comptroller's office strongly recommended that certificates of occupancy be withheld until developers had thoroughly satisfied all amenity obligations.

This situation was explicitly addressed in the 1982 Midtown Zoning. Bonus criteria clearly state that before obtaining any certificate of occupancy, building owners must first post a performance bond with New York City's comptroller to ensure fulfillment of the bonus obligations and any maintenance responsibilities for the lifetime of the project (see Insert 9).

Insert 9.
Failure to Provide Amenities in Urban Plazas, 1982 Midtown Zoning, New York
(code excerpt)[1]

4. Performance Bond
   Prior to obtaining any certificate of occupancy from the department of buildings, the building owner shall post with the comptroller of the city of New York, a performance bond, city securities, or fixed-income securities, at the comptroller's discretion, to ensure the mandatory tree planting, movable seating exclusive of any seating for open air cafes, and the litter-free maintenance of the urban plaza, including the replacement of such trees and movable furniture, during the life of the *development*.
   In the event of a failure in the required performance, the chairman of the city planning commission shall notify the building owner in writing of such failure and shall stipulate the period of time in which the building owner has to correct the failure. If the failure is not corrected in the stipulated time, the chairman may declare the building owner in default in the required performance, and the city may enforce the obligation by whatever means may be appropriate to the situation, including letting contracts for doing any required planting, installation, or maintenance and paying all labor, material, and other costs connected with such work from the bond or city securities the building owner is required to provide.
   In the event that the city enforces the aforesaid obligation as provided for in this paragraph, the *building* owner shall, within 90

days of such enforcement, provide the city with an additional bond or city securities in an amount not less than that which was expended to cure the default.

The value of the bond or city securities, if tendered prior to January 1, 1983, shall be at a rate of $300 per required tree, $100 per movable chair, and $100 per 1,000 square feet of urban plaza for litter removal, as set forth in this section.

...

(t) Penalties for Violations
Failure to comply with the conditions or restrictions of the bonused urban plaza shall constitute a violation of this resolution and shall constitute the basis for denial or revocation of a building permit or certificate of occupancy and for all other applicable remedies.

---

[1] Italics are original.

Lease Commitments. One popular enforcement mechanism, in the case of bonuses for retail uses, cinemas, performing arts centers, and daycare facilities, is to require evidence of lease commitments before a city will issue a certificate of occupancy. Some codes also stipulate specific time durations for the leases. Seattle developers using the cinema bonus, for instance, "shall secure at least a 15-year lease from a motion picture theater operator before a certificate of occupancy for the project using the bonus is issued," whereas in the case of the daycare bonus, the "developer shall secure at least a five-year lease with the operator of the daycare center." In Cincinnati, the "owner shall covenant to make the center available for a period of 40 years for the exclusive use and operation as a children's daycare center. . . ."

In some situations, particularly in those downtowns where retail uses may need to be forced and subsidized in the early stages, retailers may be reluctant to commit until the office tenants have moved in and supplied a ready-made market. Cities, therefore, may need to be reasonably flexible about enforcement of these requirements. (See summary in Chapter 7, "Retail Uses.")

Covenants, deeds, and easements are also used to "grant the public and the city the right of use and access to all public bonus areas for the life of the building." (See Insert 10a, "Covenants and Easements," for the remainder of the Cincinnati code's discussion of this point; also, refer to 10b for Portland's wording.) Most cities call for maintenance of a bonused space over the life of the project, although Hartford limits the time to 20 years. If a bonused space is not well maintained, Hartford may "place a lien on the property, do the maintenance or repair work, and seek reimbursement from the owner."

Although Cincinnati's enforcement provision has not yet been exercised, the code subjects the errant owner of the bonused space to criminal and civil ac-

tions. Noncompliance with the covenant or easement may also be cause for a nuisance claim (see Insert 10a, "Enforcement"). Elsewhere, Cincinnati's code addresses the matter of enforcing bonused space in the situation of phased development (see same insert, relevant section):

The site may be further subdivided, and title to the various parcels held by different owners, provided that appropriate deed restrictions, covenants, and easements be provided as determined to be necessary by the director of city planning to ensure that the arrangement of building density and public amenities used to calculate allowable floor area is maintained for as long as any building erected on the site pursuant to this provision remains.

Insert 10.
Requirements before Issuance of a Certificate of Occupancy or Building Permit: Two Cities

10a. Cincinnati (code excerpts)
Sec. 2406.4. Covenants and Easements. Prior to the issuance of any certificate of occupancy for any work that includes floor area allowed as a bonus for providing public amenities or work for which a downtown development variance has been granted, the director of buildings and inspections shall obtain from the owner appropriate covenants and easements. The covenant shall bind the owner, his successors, and assigns for the life of the building to comply with all provisions of this zoning code regarding maintenance and all other terms and conditions as may have been imposed upon the work. The owner shall further covenant to maintain all landscaping that was indicated on the approved plans and specifications in good order and to replace with like kind any trees or plantings that fail to survive. The easement shall grant the public and the city the right of use and access to all public bonus areas for the life of the building. The covenants and easements shall be in form approved by the city solicitor, may incorporate as exhibits any decision of the director of city planning, and shall be entered upon the records of the Hamilton County Recorder at the expense of the owner.
Sec. 2406.5. Enforcement. The provisions of this chapter and any covenants and easements that may have been obtained from the owner pursuant to any provision shall be subject to criminal and civil enforcement in the manner provided by Section 401.3. Further, failure to comply with any such provision of this chapter, covenants, or easement is declared to be a nuisance and may be abated in the manner provided by Revised Code Section 715.261, and the costs thereof collected as provided therein.
Sec. 2406.7. Phased Developments. Where the owner of a lot or lots in the DD District intends to phase the development by first erecting one building and then enlarging that building, or erecting one or more additional buildings, or both, the owner shall, prior to commencing development of the site, file a master plan with the director of city planning. The master plan shall be a schematic of the intended development of the entire site, showing the locations, uses, heights, and floor areas of every building and identifying any public amenities which may qualify for bonus area. . . . Compliance with the DD District regulations imposed by Division 2402 and, as applicable, Section 2401.4, Required Residential Uses, shall be determined each time a permit for construction of a new building or enlargement of an existing building is made. Compliance with the maximum floor area and the residential floor

area shall be determined by calculating the base building floor area, the residential floor area, and the bonus floor area of any public amenities qualifying for bonus floor area within the entire site, including all previously constructed buildings and the proposed new work within the application. . . . The site may be further subdivided and title to the various parcels held by different owners, provided that appropriate deed restrictions, covenants, and easements be provided as determined to be necessary by the director of city planning to ensure that the arrangement of building density and public amenities used to calculate allowable floor area [is] maintained for as long as any building erected on the site pursuant to this provision remains.

10b. Portland, Oregon (code excerpt)
33.702.090 Covenants with the City

A. **Purpose**. To assure continuation of amenities and housing built to qualify the project for bonus and/or transfer of floor area, the property owner must execute a covenant with the city. The covenant is required in consideration of the city's issuing a building permit allowing additional floor area beyond the amount permitted, based on Supplemental Zoning Map C.

B. **Requirements**. The covenant must run with the land and be attached to the land. It must provide that in the event of the property owner's failure to abide by the covenant, the city is empowered to terminate occupancy of the structure and to obtain, in the name of the city, injunctive relief in a court of competent jurisdiction enjoining future occupancy of the structure while a violation of the covenant exists. All covenants must be approved in form by the city attorney and be recorded in the appropriate records of the county in which the project site is located. Covenants must be recorded prior to issuance of any building permit and must specify that the owner will comply with all approval conditions, conditions listed for approval of the applicable bonus provision, and the provisions of this section.

When bonused space is built off site, it is preferable to burden the project that receives the additional density rather than the existing building where the bonus is installed. One of the options under Seattle's bonus for child care facilities, for example, is to provide a center off site in another existing downtown building. The use of this option, however, has been impeded by the code requirement "that if the daycare center leaves and is not replaced within six months," the lien or deed of trust must be placed, not on the new project that received the extra FAR, but on the existing building in which the center was placed. Lenders chafed at this stipulation and refused to finance these projects. Hence, the city is looking into other mechanisms by which the burden would be borne by the recipient of the bonus credit.

Protective covenants and easements are also typically used to enforce agreements for transferring development rights (TDRs). One of the options under Seattle's housing bonus program is to purchase TDRs for retaining and rehabilitating low-income housing in the downtown. The owners of sending and receiving sites must file a TDR agreement with the city certify-

ing that the owner of the receiving lot will complete the rehabilitation and that the residential owner will maintain the units as low-income housing for 20 years. Moreover, Seattle imposes a rehabilitation requirement in the case of TDR use for preservation of landmarks. The TDR agreement, which obliges the owner of the receiving lot to rehabilitate the landmark structure and the owner of the landmark to preserve the structure for the life of the new development on the receiving site, is enforced through a protective covenant or conservation easement.

San Francisco's deputy planning director, George Williams, suggests that financial institutions may act as an auxiliary enforcement check. Concerned that they may be financing leases for projects that might violate particular zoning provisions, local banks and other financial institutions, says Williams, are likely to police an area where they have a financial interest.

Another technique is to require a performance instrument. To get a certificate of occupancy, project sponsors in Bellevue must show a letter of credit or an assigned savings account to ensure that required landscaping will be maintained. After one year, if it has been demonstrated that the plants have survived, the instrument is returned. However, in other cities, where development pressures are not as great, planning officials might be reluctant to tie up developer funds for long periods to guarantee completion of bonus features. (Return to Insert 9 for details of the performance bond requirement in the New York Midtown Zoning.)

Finally, one of the most effective and least onerous enforcement mechanisms is administrative simplicity. Incentive zoning regulations should be written with sufficient clarity and detail to be self-enforcing. One approach is to consolidate all bonus provisions within a single section of the land use code for easy access. Planning departments are also encouraged to give building inspectors checklists of the criteria they must look for if they are responsible for approving the bonuses.[15]

MAINTENANCE

The matter of maintenance overlaps with that of enforcement. Such amenities as plazas, arcades, and rooftop gardens often must meet specific code standards relating to street furniture, landscaping, lighting, and sometimes artwork. Seattle's ordinance explicitly states that landscaping requirements for bonused public open spaces may "include a wide variety of living trees, shrubs, groundcovers, and seasonal plantings, as well as fountains and planters . . . [and that] all required landscaping shall be located in permanently installed beds or planters or in large containers, which, while movable, cannot be readily removed." And "[u]nless otherwise stated in the specific conditions for a public benefit feature, the property owner shall maintain all elements of bonused features, including but not limited to landscaping, parking, seating, and lighting, in a safe and attractive condition." (See Inserts 11a and b for New York and Charlotte's related provisions.)

Insert 11.
Responsibility for Maintenance of Open Spaces: Two Cities

11a. Charlotte, North Carolina (code excerpt)
   8. *Maintenance.* The building owners, lessee, management entity, or authorized agent are jointly and severally responsible for the maintenance of the urban open space area, including litter control and care and replacement of trees and shrubs.

11b. New York's Urban Plazas, 1982 Midtown Zoning (code excerpt)[1]
   (s) Maintenance
   1. The building owner shall be responsible for the maintenance of the urban plaza, including, but not limited to, the confinement of permitted obstruction, litter control, and the care and replacement of vegetation within the *zoning lot* and in the *street* sidewalk area adjacent to the *zoning lot.*
   2. Litter receptacles shall be provided with a minimum capacity of one cubic foot for each 2,000 square feet of urban plaza area, excluding the area of any sidewalk widening. An additional capacity of one cubic foot of litter receptacle shall be provided for each 2,000 square feet of urban plaza in connection with outdoor eating services or other *uses* permitted on urban plazas which generate litter.
   3. Location of urban plaza *uses* and furniture shall be confined within area designated on *building* plans as available for occupancy by such *uses.* Encroachment of an urban plaza *use* outside an area so designated shall be valid ground for complaint and removal.

   ---
   [1] Italics in Insert 11b are original.

Safety and Security. Maintenance matters may raise safety considerations. Seattle's code states that trees and shrubs "shall be planted and maintained so that they do not promote a public safety problem, interfere with normal lines of sight, or negate the effects of nighttime security lighting."

Security concerns are also triggered by code requirements for continuous use. Although the more typical requirement is that a space be open during ordinary business hours, in some downtowns the bonused areas must be accessible to the public 24 hours a day. Pittsburgh's open space provision, which is mandated rather than bonused, was amended so that the space, which previously had to be open continuously, now could be gated in the evening, and movable chairs and tables could be stored away at closing time. As a result, the quality of the fixtures used in the spaces—

fountains, benches, lights, artwork, and so on—can be markedly higher.

Some Costs of Maintenance. Indeed, because bonused spaces must be accessible to the public so much of the time, all street hardware, including light standards, benches, planters, and artwork, are subject to the wear and tear of everyday use. It is advisable to address maintenance issues directly in the zoning ordinance and spell out such obligations (and their potential costliness) in advance. Under Seattle's daycare bonus program, when a nonprofit center is subsidized, the operator is "not charged rent but may be required to pay a portion of the utility, insurance, and maintenance expenses for the space." According to San Francisco's code, the space must be provided to a "nonprofit child care provider without charge for rent, utilities, property taxes, building services, or any other charges of any nature." (See Chapter 2 and its section on downtown daycare.)

Code provisions for artwork bonuses often impose maintenance criteria and even specify that insurance be carried. Cincinnati's code calls for developers who receive density bonuses for installing artworks to "keep the work sufficiently insured to restore or replace it in the event that the work is damaged or destroyed. The city shall be named an additional insured." Portland, Oregon's code states that "[i]nstallation, future preservation, maintenance, and replacement, if necessary, of the public art provided to qualify for this bonus is assured by the property owner executing a covenant with the city. . . . "

Reduction, Elimination, or Replacement. Although many incentive regulations state that bonused spaces may neither be eliminated nor reduced in size without a corresponding reduction in floor area, other codes permit changes under certain limited circumstances. (See Insert 12a for language from New York's Midtown Zoning.)

Insert 12.
Decrease, Discontinuance, or Replacement of Amenities: Two Cities

12a. New York's Urban Plazas, 1982 Midtown Zoning (code excerpt)[1]
   81-232 Existing plazas or other public amenities
   No existing *plaza, urban open space,* or other public amenity open or enclosed for which a *floor area* bonus has been received pursuant to regulations antedating the effective date of this amendment shall be eliminated or reduced in size anywhere within the *Special Midtown District* without a corresponding reduction in the *floor area* of the *building* or the substitution of equivalent complying area for such amenity elsewhere on the *zoning lot.* Any elimination or reduction in size of such an existing public amenity shall be permitted in the *Special Midtown District* only by special permit of the city planning commission, subject to board of estimate action and to a finding by the commission that the proposed change will provide a greater public

benefit in the light of the public amenity's purpose and the purposes of the *Special Midtown District*.

12b. Seattle (code excerpt)

Section 23.49.35 Replacement of Public Benefit Features

A. All public benefit features, except housing, shall remain for the life of the structure, which includes the additional gross floor area. A public benefit feature may only be diminished or discontinued if the additional gross floor area permitted in return for the specific feature is permanently removed; or if the public benefit feature is replaced by another approved public benefit feature of at least equivalent floor area value; or by buying out the equivalent floor area value of the benefit feature according to the requirements of the Public Benefit Features Rule.

B. In addition to the provisions of Subsection A, this subsection shall apply in downtown zones when additional gross floor area is granted for any of the following public benefit features: human service uses, daycare centers, retail shopping, cinemas, performing arts theaters, major retail stores, and museums.

 1. In the event that the occupant or operator of one of the public benefit features listed in this subsection moves out of a structure, the owner or owner's agent is responsible for notifying the director within five days of the date that notice of intent to move is given or that the occupant or operator moves out, whichever is earlier.

 2. Starting from the fifth day after notice is given or that the occupant or operator moves out, whichever is first, the owner or owner's agent shall have a maximum of six months to replace the use with another one which meets the provisions of this code and the Public Benefit Features Rule.

 3. When the public benefit feature is replaced, any portion of the gross floor area formerly occupied by that feature and not reoccupied by a replacement feature may be either:

   a. Changed to other uses which are exempt from FAR calculations in the zone in which the structure is located; or

   b. Changed to uses which are not exempt from FAR calculations, provided that this would not cause the structure to exceed the maximum FAR limit for the zone in which it is located, and that gross floor area in an amount equivalent to the gross floor area proposed to be changed shall be achieved through provision of public benefit features, or transfer of development rights, according to the provisions of the zone in which the structure is located.

 4. During the time that the space is vacant, it shall be made available to nonprofit community and charitable organizations for events at no charge.

---

[1] Italics in Insert 12a are original.

Seattle's code goes the furthest toward anticipating the measures that must be taken if a developer wants to alter or replace a bonused space. The code contains an explicit provision, entitled "Modifications," governing replacement of public benefit features:

[A] public benefit feature may only be diminished or discontinued if the additional gross floor area permitted in return for the specific feature is permanently removed, or if the public benefit feature is replaced by another approved public benefit feature of at least equivalent floor area value, or by buying out the equivalent floor area value of the benefit feature according to the requirements of the Public Benefit Features Rule.

(See Insert 12b. For specific examples of bonus modifications, refer to this chapter's later section on "Transitional Issues"; also, turn to the section on open space retrofits in Chapter 8, "Open Space and Streetscapes.")

Seattle's code anticipates similar possible dilemmas when a bonused space is vacated (again, see Insert 12b). A retail tenant might pull out and the developer fail to re-lease the space, or the operator of a child care center or cinema might renege on a lease commitment. Under the code, the owner has no more than six months to replace the use with another that complies with the Seattle Public Benefit Features Rule. While the space lies vacant, however, the bonused area no longer functions as a public benefit; therefore, the ordinance specifies that while the space is vacant, it shall be made available free of charge to nonprofit community and charitable organizations.

In his analysis of effective urban design controls, New York zoning attorney Robert Cook writes that

enforcement mechanisms [should not] . . . be so weak that it is economically attractive to violate the ordinance by paying a small fine. Enforceability is also a function of clarity, meaning that obligations must be easily understood. . . . Violations of requirements that a property owner act in a certain way—such as leaving doors open to provide public access, or providing a service—are particularly difficult to enforce. Inspection staff must be adequate in size and properly trained to deal with such complexity.[16]

Misuse or, more probably, underuse of bonus areas in a large downtown may sometimes be difficult to detect, and as Cook observes, cities might not be adequately staffed to monitor such infringements. For this reason, Seattle's ordinance requires that the "leases for human services, daycare centers, cinemas, retail shopping uses, performing arts theaters, and museums shall contain a clause that provides that the director shall be notified if the use no longer occupies the leased space." The code states, further, that the "owner or owner's agent is responsible for notifying the director within five days of the date that notice of intent to move is given or that the occupant or operator moves out, whichever is earlier."

Parking and Retail. Similarly, various zoning incentives and requirements for parking may be hard to monitor. For instance, some downtown codes mandate that a percentage of the permitted parking spaces be allotted to short-term parking. It is no easy matter ensuring that the space set aside for transient parking is not encroached on by commuters, or that spaces for carpools or vanpools are adequately marked so they do not remain empty. (See Chapter 10, "Parking and Transportation.")

Marginal retail uses, which may meet the technical requirements of the code but not its intent, raise an additional enforcement issue. In downtowns where the retail activity may be fragile, for example, a lower caliber of retailers may be leasing than had been foreseen for prime downtown locations. Such marginal uses may be going in where former retail tenants might have failed or where otherwise the space would stand empty. Although incentive regulations may hand down criteria and design guidelines for bonused retail spaces, controlling the quality and character of the uses is more difficult. (For a closer look at the retail quality issue, see Chapter 7, "Retail Uses.")

COORDINATION WITH OTHER REGULATIONS

Potential overlaps and contradictions caused by related regulatory regimes often bring clashes. As is the case with any zoning system, incentive zoning provisions must be coordinated with other regulatory programs, such as health and building codes, in addition to other municipal, state, and federal laws. In the regulation of child care centers, for example, state daycare licensing laws, which typically oblige a center to be located on the ground level and to give access to adjacent open space, pose formidable obstacles for downtown daycare. Thus, some cities may need to amend their building codes, as did Seattle and San Francisco, to allow centers on upper levels. (See the section on daycare in Chapter 2, "Four Bonuses in Closeup.")

Cities must also consider the injunctions imposed by other municipal codes—fire, building, safety, transportation, and the like—so as to avoid potential conflicts. For example, many innovative zoning codes discourage the use of mirrored glass and limit the percentage of reflectivity, which may directly contravene the strict energy-saving rules that some cities adopted during the gas shortage years of the early 1970s. Although many cities try to combine the separate reviews of various governmental departments and agencies into one streamlined process of development application review, anticipation of potential conflicts is the better approach.

TRANSITIONAL ISSUES

Setting aside a transitional period from an old code to a new one helps accommodate differences between the two systems. During this period, particularly in downtowns with second-generation incentive zoning programs, like New York and Seattle, it may be useful to spell out the procedures for modifying a public benefit feature bonused under the earlier code. Now, this feature might have to comply with a different, more explicit set of bonus criteria.

SEATTLE'S BONUS MODIFICATIONS

Seattle's code states that

[the] modification of plazas, shopping plazas, arcades, shopping arcades, and voluntary building setbacks which resulted in any increase in gross floor area under Title 24 of the Seattle Municipal Code [the old zoning] shall be encouraged in any downtown zone, if the change makes the plaza, arcade, or setback more closely conform to the requirements of this chapter. The director shall review proposed modifications to determine whether they provide greater public benefits and are consistent with the intent of the Public Benefit Features Rule. . . .

(Refer back to Insert 12b for other code criteria.)

The first such modification under Seattle's revised incentive zoning scheme involved the plaza of a 50-story office tower (originally, the Seafirst National Bank Building) designed in the "tower-in-the-park" style of the 1960s. After the code modification, the building's new owner chose to redesign the plaza, making it more remunerative, attractive, and usable. The formerly austere, empty space was retrofitted with perimeter retail uses, landscaping, canopies, a coffee bar and other food facilities, and a glassed-in public winter garden. Although the bonus modifications and additional expenses were completely voluntary, the redesign was subject to discretionary review under the Public Benefit Features Rule. (This project is discussed more fully in Chapter 8, "Open Space and Streetscapes," under the heading of "Open Space Retrofits.")

Some modifications entail doing away with portions of a bonused area. For instance, when Seafirst National Bank sold the building described above in the mid-1980s, it moved its branch bank to the 75-story Columbia Center. To make room for the ground-floor branch bank, the Columbia Center developer needed to eliminate some of the retail arcade bonused under the former code, as well as tack on some 10,000 square feet. In addition to these changes, the developer wanted to fill in a portion of the retail/restaurant arcade on the third floor. In exchange, the developer contributed to the low-income housing bonus program, gave to a fund subsidizing downtown daycare, and agreed to build a public observation deck on the top floor.

Other bonus modifications may involve alterations to paper projects that have been permitted under Seattle's old zoning but have not yet been built. In these situations, the bonused areas are treated as if they were already in place, and any changes to the benefit features must meet the code requirements. Two such modifications were applied to two entire projects within the retail core. Those projects with permits granted under the old code are particularly valuable, for they are exempt from the more stringent height and FAR limits of the 1985 ordinance.

In the case of one mixed-use office tower, a series of financial problems delayed the project, and the new owner decided to make strategic program and design alterations to raise the project's efficiency and profit margin. In return for some of these changes, which affected bonused areas, the developer agreed to incorporate some of the newly available public benefit features, namely, shopping corridors, movie theaters, and a daycare center with a rooftop garden. (Although the developer expected approval of the modifications within 90 days, the actual review time exceeded one year.)

FORCING DEVELOPMENT

Another transitional issue in any major rezoning effort, particularly when the new regulations are more restrictive than the old, is the artificial forcing of new development to preserve permits for those projects-in-progress that have been vested under the old code. In San Francisco and Seattle, representatives from the private and public sectors generally agree that the new zoning regulations have transmuted the old permits into gold and, in many instances, assured that these projects would be built regardless of market demand. Both cities anticipated this problem and set time limits. Although permits in Seattle must be acted on within two years, developers have been allowed to renew permits for up to six years, so that construction may be delayed for a more favorable market. The city is considering cutting the renewal period to three years.

Ironically, the zoning revisions in both cities are encouraging the development of buildings with the very characteristics that the newer regulations have sought to eliminate. In 1987, Seattle land use attorney Judy Runstad conceded that but for the new code, many of the commercial projects then underway in downtown

Seattle probably would have been delayed for several more years, until the market could guarantee more favorable absorption rates. Runstad observed, however, that the problem of forced development was a short-term one, and the actual effects of the new zoning would not be clear for several years. Furthermore, although temporary overbuilding in both San Francisco and Seattle can be laid in part to the adoption of new zoning regulations, other contributing factors might include fluctuating interest rates and the recent infusion of foreign real estate investment throughout the country.

In contrast to Seattle and San Francisco, Portland, Oregon, deliberately wrote a vesting period into its 1988 Central City Plan, so that the new requirements were not effective until four months after the enactment date. Because the new ordinance includes bonuses for the first time and in some ways is seen as more generous than the old code, most developers apparently chose to wait and come in under the new zoning regime. But then development pressures in Portland are not nearly as great as they are in Seattle or San Francisco.

The approach taken by many cities—that of adopting an interim ordinance that "looks forward to" the new zoning—still raises the same issue of forced development. But differences exist. Depending on the clout of the planning department, a city may be more, or less, successful in negotiating for those features it wants.

One sure method to avoid forcing development prematurely is to enact major zoning revisions when the real estate market is down. Most cities, however, would probably hesitate to saddle themselves with additional land use regulations at a time when development interest is already marginal.

Another, more drastic method for avoiding the forced vesting issue is to impose a moratorium restricting all, or a major part of, new development for a stated time period. Temporary moratoriums usually are used as emergency measures to allow time for completing plans or devising solutions to specific growth crises like inadequate infrastructure or sewer facilities.

Recognizing the potential for accelerated building under new zoning rules, New York City used a sunset clause as a growth management tool deliberately to steer development toward strategic parts of the downtown. At the same time as the 1982 Midtown Zoning reduced development potential on much of the congested East Side, it gave rise to a West Side growth area. In this area, extending from the Avenue of the Americas to Eighth Avenue between 40th and 60th Streets, the FAR limit was increased from 15 to 18 on selected avenues. The rush of activity here sprang directly from the sunset provision, whereby any projects without full foundation work completed within six years had to forfeit the 20 percent bonus. The sunset provision has been compared to the city's now-expired 421a tax-abatement program to encourage residential building south of 96th Street. Steven Spinola, president of the New York Real Estate Board, predicted that the six-year limit might be too short: "There's concern that the deadline may force people to start construction before the market is ripe for the space."[17] Indeed, this has been the case. The construction of some 9 million square feet of rentable space on the West Side is attributed largely to the incentive deadline. At the same time, however, the area is suffering from record-high vacancy rates.

In 1988, at the end of the six-year period, FARs on the West Side reverted to pre-1982 limits. In an effort to make densities on the East and West Sides more consistent, the board of estimate further reduced densities for some West Side midblocks.

STEROID ZONING?

The injection of bonus incentives into development systems—in what might be called "steroid zoning"—has been blamed by some critics for the oversized projects that have contributed to rampant speculation and artificially raised land values. The problem is too much density. Despite the use of fine-tuned bonus criteria, assiduous economic calibrations, and sophisticated design guidelines to ensure that bonus amenities are well designed, actively used, and beneficial to the public, there is a limit, these critics maintain. At some point, the purported benefits will never compensate for the concomitant losses of light and air, not to mention the alteration in scale and character of a neighborhood, brought on by the added square footage.

Land use scholar John Costonis believes that this point has been reached. He even characterizes the bonus programs in some cities as "Frankenstein zoning." New York City, writes Costonis,

has sanctioned buildings that outstrip even the bulky, light- and air-blocking slabs that frightened the city into adopting zoning in 1916. . . . [T]he public is demoralized by a "system" that has spun out of control, and puzzled by "amenities" that are unused, unwanted, or if attractive, would have been built without zoning bonuses. Whether the buildings constructed under that system are "better architecture" than those that would have been built without it is conjectural at best. That many of them fail to respect their urban design context is clear.[18]

Slow-growth advocates in Seattle agree. Vociferous critics of the city's incentive regulations, they as-

sert, among other claims, that base FARs in the downtown are excessive and that the overly generous platter of amenity options encourages office towers of overwhelming densities. Indeed, as described earlier, the Washington Mutual Tower, the first building designed under Seattle's incentive regulations, swelled to 1 million square feet. More than half of this space was acquired through bonuses. And within certain commercial sectors of Chicago, it is possible to expand the base FAR from 16 to 30 by using only the city's by-right open space and setback bonuses. The bonus density calculation is apparently based on the setback for each floor above ground, as well as on the setback at street level.

One difficulty is that if base FARs and bonus ratios are set too low, so that developers must provide many different amenities to get desired densities, their construction costs are driven up and they tend to assemble large sites to make their projects feasible. Paradoxically, incentive systems may also prod developers into assembling larger land parcels to *avoid* amenity construction costs.[19] To alleviate some of the potential problems of increased density, some commentators simply suggest offering different types of incentives, such as setbacks, reduced parking requirements, or raised height allowances, instead of increases in FAR.[20]

Finally, yet another density problem is the failure of many incentive regulations to address the development of superblocks. For example, as discussed below, the initial proposal for the development of New York City's old Coliseum site—an enormous superblock covering two full city blocks and the street area between them—would have profited from an FAR that permits a much larger building than could go up on a normal parcel. Opponents claim, therefore, that bonus density awards should be reduced for superblock projects.

The public objections to increased density, however, should be viewed in light of the effective downzoning that accompanies most incentive-based ordinances. San Francisco economic consultant Alan Billingsley traces some of the density criticism to the prevailing slow-growth sentiment that has recently taken hold in many cities. In some parts of the country, says Billingsley, any amount of density is criticized as excessive.

ZONING FOR SALE: THE COLUMBUS CENTER CASE

One would think that community groups would champion any device of incentive zoning that encourages private sector funding of daycare, affordable

Drawing by Stevenson; copyright 1987, The New Yorker Magazine, Inc.

housing, pedestrian amenities, or other much-needed public improvements. Public reaction, however, is mixed. As John Costonis notes, community groups fear that official discretion "will be exercised contrary to, rather than in favor of, their interests, as indeed it can be. Consequently, even concessions that appear to favor community group interests often fail to escape unscathed."[21]

This certainly was the situation in the 1987 court decision *Municipal Art Society of New York* v. *City of New York*.[22] A New York trial court ruled illegal a deal that allowed a developer to build a project in New York City 20 percent denser than the base FAR in exchange for hefty contributions to the city's transit system. In the decision, Judge Edward H. Lehner wrote that "government may not place itself in the position of reaping a cash premium because one of its agencies bestows a zoning benefit upon a developer. Zoning benefits are not cash items."

Unshaken by the decision, Mortimer Zuckerman, co-head of Boston Properties, said "the controversy has more to do with the city's volatile political scene than with legal or urban design matters."[23] Nonetheless, Judge Lehner's indictment of a cash sale for a zoning bonus raises important questions.

In 1985, Boston Properties beat out more than a dozen firms in a city-sponsored competition to develop the 4.5-acre site of the old Coliseum on the southwest rim of Central Park. The stadium had been rendered obsolete by the Jacob Javits Convention Center. Moshe Safdie's winning design would have produced one of the biggest private buildings in the world, a pinkish-grey granite, 925-foot-high structure with street-level shops, cinemas, several hundred lux-

ury condominiums, and a 300-room hotel. Sandwiched between would be 2 million square feet of office space, most of which was committed to new headquarters for Salomon Brothers, Inc., joint investors in the project.

In exchange for the city-owned site and for permission to exceed the zoning by 20 percent, Boston Properties agreed to pay the city $455.1 million, in addition to its commitment of up to $40 million for improvements to the nearby Columbus Center subway station at 59th and Broadway. With the bonus, which stretched the allowable density from 15 to 18 FAR, the project shot up to 2.7 million square feet. The city would have realized about $100 million in taxes each year from the proposed project.

The Municipal Art Society (MAS), watchdog over the city's physical environment, filed suit along with the Metropolitan Chapter of the American Planning Association and the New York Parks Council. The suit asserted, among other matters, that the city's financial stake in the sale tainted the "fundamentally and fatally flawed approval process" and that the environmental impact reviews were "manipulated" and "glaringly incomplete."

In October 1987, the "parasol set," organized by the MAS, staged its Stand against the Shadow demonstration in Central Park. When the signal was given, more than 800 protesters unfurled black umbrellas, simulating the mile-long shadow the project would purportedly cast in the park.

In his decision, Judge Lehner focused exclusively on the matter of exchanging density bonuses for money. He based his reasoning largely on a straightforward statutory interpretation of the bonus provision in the 1982 Midtown Zoning. The $40 million pledged to upgrade the Columbus Center station met the regulation's primary requirement for a subway improvement bonus—that the developer build a substantial subway entrance improvement next to the site that enabled direct access.

The pivotal issue in the case was the contractual clause allowing Boston Properties to cut its payment by $57 million should the city withhold the 448,500-square-foot bonus. To Judge Lehner, this clause indicated that "the city [was] obtaining not only $35 to $40 million of local subway improvements, but an additional $57 million in cash to be employed for other purposes."

The case might have been decided differently if the price reduction had been more closely related to the subway improvements. Even so, the Midtown Zoning explicitly precludes the practice of awarding density for off-site subway station improvements. The regula-

STAND AGAINST THE SHADOW
SUNDAY, OCTOBER 18, 1987 AT NOON. CENTRAL PARK BANDSHELL
Bring a black umbrella, rain or shine!

Join the Municipal Art Society and other New Yorkers to protest the proposed Coliseum site building by opening black umbrellas in the path of its shadow. Meet in Central Park at the bandshell at 72nd Street.

The shadow superimposed onto this photo demonstrates what will happen to the walks and playgrounds of Central Park on afternoons in spring if New Yorkers allow the 925-ft. tower proposed for Columbus Circle to be built.

Municipal Art Society
457 Madison Avenue
New York, NY 10022
(212) 935-3960

Poster for the Stand against the Shadow demonstration in Central Park.

tions state that an "off-site subway station improvement [in this case, the additional $57 million to be used for other purposes] does not provide any compensating reduction in density. The proposed bonus [in this resolution] is justified because it improves di-

rect access to the larger development. For off-site subway improvements, direct financial incentives appear to be more appropriate than zoning measures."

Moreover, Judge Lehner intimated that his decision might have been different had the full $92 to $97 million been earmarked for public improvements in the immediate vicinity of the project. "A proper quid pro quo," wrote Lehner, "for the grant of the right to increase the bulk of a building may not be the payment of additional cash into the city's coffers for citywide use." In trying to use zoning to reap the highest dollar return, the city was acting beyond its delegated powers, and the contract was declared null and void.

The city's position was doubtless undermined by admissions that some $266 million from proceeds of the Coliseum sale had already been included in the FY 1988 budget before final approval of the sale. This gave the appearance that the greater density had been granted to balance the city's budget, rather than to promote the public interest. An equally damaging piece of evidence was the city's request for proposals, which stated that the purchase price offered would be "the primary consideration" and that the chosen developer "must apply for and use its best efforts to obtain the maximum 20 percent subway bonus," amounting to an increment of 448,500 square feet. (Ordinarily, the developer initiates the application to qualify for use of a zoning bonus.)

Although the city's architectural cognoscenti summarily panned Safdie's design, most agreed that the megalithic structure was the fault of neither the architect nor the developer. By insisting that density be maximized, the city all but ensured that the winning design would be too large. "Whether so big a building was the right response to this site, a question which the city, incredibly, never even asked itself," was not in itself the issue, writes architectural critic Robert Campbell. Instead, he says, the issue was "one of an elected government too lazy even to think about urban design." [24] The eight-person review committee did not include a single design professional. According to New York writer Carter Wiseman, architectural design considerations were apparently declared irrelevant in advance. He contrasts the 80-page book devoted to design guidelines for the Battery Park City competition with the 11-line paragraph for the Coliseum site. [25]

In fairness to the city, one competing project had substantially outbid Boston Properties. The city's final determination had largely been influenced by the promise that Salomon Brothers, Inc., a partner in the project and major tenant, would maintain its headquarters in Manhattan. The company had evidently threatened to move its operations out of the city if the proposal was rejected. Thus, the project was viewed as a critical economic development move for the city.

In the event, when the stock market bottomed out in October 1987, Salomon Brothers laid off some 800

employees and withdrew from the project. Zuckerman then hired David Childs, with Skidmore, Owings & Merrill's New York office, to create a totally different design.

In June 1988, New York City and Boston Properties presented a new proposal that would be 11 acres smaller and cost $98 million less than the former project, so that it would need no zoning bonus. Offering modest improvements over the original project, the new version was reduced in height from 925 to 850 feet, and the bulk was redistributed so that most of the building's shadow was concealed in the one already cast by the Gulf & Western Building.

Although the city initially appealed the case, it was eager to avoid further litigation and sought to reach a compromise with the Municipal Art Society. Following intense negotiation, a third plan was hatched, shortening the building by 175 feet and subtracting almost 700,000 square feet of floor area from the original proposal. Also, the city committed itself to providing 120 units of subsidized housing in the surrounding Clinton neighborhood, as well as community space in the new building itself. On May 4, 1989, the city's board of estimate approved the most recently proposed Columbus Center development.

Despite this agreement, a larger question remains: Is Judge Lehner's decision limited to the particular facts of this case—a violation of the precise standards for granting a subway improvement bonus under New York's Midtown Zoning—or does the decision have broader ramifications? That is, could it ultimately jeopardize the use of other bonus amenities offered by cities as part of their incentive zoning systems? At least, one important lesson of the case is to adhere to the bonus guidelines, especially when they are laid down in the zoning. Second-generation incentive zoning systems contain explicit standards for procedures and design criteria for awarding bonuses. Therefore, if zoning bonuses are awarded for public improvements either without the developers' incorporating a mandated design feature or without their hewing to the dictated procedures, then these agreements could well be thrown out by the courts. The Columbus Center case also illustrates the difficulties of mixing prestated, as-of-right incentive provisions (with explicit bonus criteria) with more flexible, negotiated arrangements.

Finally, the New York decision highlights the complications that invariably arise when a public entity participates in land ventures, as well as the potential hazards of public/private deal making. As Costonis remarks, when a public agency wears the hats both of protector of the public interest and of joint venturer with a developer, "troublesome conflicts of interest are inherent in the agency's split role, a point not lost on litigation-minded community groups displeased with the project approved by the agency." New York City's "cash sale" of a zoning bonus "presumably would not have been suspect if the city had not been a joint venturer with the bonus recipient."[26]

Kent Barwick, president of the Municipal Art Society, concurs: "I'm not nominating Mort Zuckerman for Man of the Year, but at least he's a developer who is behaving like a developer. . . . Our complaint is that the city is a government that's behaving like a developer."[27]

Whether a city can at once pursue its entrepreneurial interests and adequately protect the public welfare has yet to be decided. But according to the 1987 court decision, New York City in this case upset the delicate balance between competing public and private interests. New York made economic return the deciding factor, with scant attention to other public goals and land use considerations.

Notes

1. For an excellent review of incentive zoning, see Judith Getzels and Martin Jaffe with Brian W. Blaesser and Robert F. Brown, *Zoning Bonuses in Central Cities*, Planning Advisory Service Report no. 410 (Chicago: American Planning Association, 1988), p. 1.

2. City of New York Department of City Planning, *Midtown Development Review* (New York: author, July 1987).

3. Paul Goldberger, "When Developers Change the Rules during the Game," *New York Times* (March 19, 1989).

4. See Getzels and Jaffe, op. cit., p. 3.

5. William H. Whyte, *City: Rediscovering the Center* (New York: Doubleday, 1989), p. 244.

6. New York State, Office of the State Comptroller, *New York City Planning Commission: Granting Special Permits for Bonus Floor Area*, Report A-23-88 (September 15, 1988), p. MS-3.

7. Bernard Frieden, "Deal Making Goes Public: Learning from Columbus Center," in ULI's soon-to-be-published book on cities as the new deal makers.

8. Getzels and Jaffe, *Zoning Bonuses in Central Cities*, pp. 1–2.

9. Whyte, *City*, p. 253.

10. City of Chicago Department of Planning, *Density Bonus Calibration: A Comparison of Approaches and Model for Chicago*, Working Paper no. 1, Chicago Zoning Bonus Study (Chicago: author, September 1987).
Also, see Getzels and Jaffe, op. cit., for a thoughtful analysis of these models, pp. 16–21.

11. Getzels and Jaffe, op. cit., p. 19.

12. Quoted by Scott Maier in "How one high-rise grew up," *Seattle Post-Intelligencer* (April 18, 1988).

13. Peter Staten, "A Bonus Is a Bonanza," *Seattle Weekly* (July 1988).

14. Peter Steinbrueck, "Public Costs and Private Benefits," *CityWatch*, vol.1, issue 4 (March 1989), p. 304. *CityWatch* is published by Vision Seattle, which cosponsored CAP.

15. For more discussion of enforcement issues, see Getzels and Jaffe, *Zoning Bonuses in Central Cities*, p. 13.

16. Robert S. Cook, Jr., *Zoning for Downtown Urban Design* (Lexington, Massachusetts: Lexington Books, 1980), pp.153–154. (This book is now out of print.)

17. Quoted by Mark McCain in "Racing the Clock in West Midtown," *New York Times* (May 10, 1987).

18. John J. Costonis, "Law and Aesthetics: A Critique and a Reformulation of the Dilemmas," *Michigan Law Review*, vol. 80 (1982), pp. 363–364.

19. As noted by Getzels and Jaffe in *Zoning Bonuses in Central Cities*, p. 23.

20. See ibid., p. 9.

21. From a forthcoming ULI book on cities as the new deal makers. John J. Costonis's chapter is entitled "Tinker to Evers to Chance: Community Groups As the Third Player in the Development Game."

22. 137 Misc. 2d 832, 522 N.Y.S. 800 (S. Ct. 1987).

23. Mortimer Zuckerman in an interview (December 1987).

24. Robert Campbell, "New York: Quick Cash, Bad Planning," *Boston Globe* (September 8, 1987).

25. Carter Wiseman, "Cashing In on the Coliseum: The Battle over Dollars and Design," *New York* (July 29, 1985).

26. Costonis, "Tinker to Evers to Chance: Community Groups As the Third Player in the Development Game," in upcoming ULI book.

27. Cited by Richard F. Babcock in his paper "The City As Entrepreneur: Folly or Wisdom," presented at ULI's 1988 policy forum and planned as a chapter in the upcoming ULI book on city deal making.

CHAPTER 2

FOUR BONUSES IN CLOSEUP

Many of the specific bonus options available through downtown zoning regulations will be discussed in depth in the chapters that follow. Incentives for short-term parking and transit access, for example, will be covered in Chapter 10, "Parking and Transportation"; the sculptured rooftop bonus is featured in Chapter 5, "Zoning as Shaper of Building Design"; and density incentives for strengthening retail activity are examined in Chapter 7, "Retail Uses." The present discussion focuses on four bonus categories not covered in other sections of the book: artworks, visual arts space, and water features; employment and job training; human services; and daycare.

PUBLIC ART

ARTWORKS

Many downtown zoning regulations integrate requirements for public art into their incentive systems. Seattle's zoning requires artwork in the following bonused public spaces: shopping and public atriums, shopping corridors, parcel parks, residential parcel parks, street parks, rooftop gardens, hillside terraces, harborfront open space, performing arts theaters, and urban plazas. The city and county also mandate that 1 percent of all public funds appropriated for municipal construction be used for public artwork. Orlando, Florida, also requires a 1 percent set-aside for artwork, architectural enhancement, or special landscape treatment as part of its bonus system (see Insert 1).

Insert 1.
Orlando: The Public Art Requirement
(code excerpt)

Public Art Required—Wherever any intensity bonus set forth below is used in connection with any development, a set-aside shall also be required of at least 1.0 percent of total construction costs for works of art, architectural enhancement, or special landscape treatment. Said work of art, architectural enhancement, or special landscape treatment may be integral parts of the building, may be situated within or outside the building, or may be located in other public places where numbers of people may experience them. Said works of art, architectural enhancement, or special landscape treatment shall be reviewed, selected, and approved by the public art advisory board . . .

Incentive zoning systems in Cincinnati (see Insert 2), Bellevue, Washington, and Portland, Oregon, also offer public art as one of their bonus options. Whereas Cincinnati sometimes allows the artwork to be located indoors, Bellevue's code stipulates that any form of sculpture or other artwork must stand outside a building and "be displayed near the main pedestrian entrance to a building." In Bellevue, indoor amenities are not eligible for additional density awards.

Insert 2.
Cincinnati's Public Art Bonus
(code excerpt)

Sec. 2403.2.13
(a) In order to qualify for bonus floor area, public art shall satisfy all of the following criteria:
 i) Be one or more lasting works of art by an artist whose works have been exhibited in art museums or institutes.
 ii) Be permanently installed in an atrium, plaza, garden, small setback, sidewalk, building arcade, or skywalk that qualifies for bonus floor area, in a location approved by the director of city planning that provides general public view but does not materially hinder pedestrian traffic.
 iii) Be approved as aesthetically appropriate for the intended setting by the director of city planning.
(b) The bonus floor area for public art shall be proportionate to the value of the work:
 (i) The value of the work shall be authenticated by a certified bill of sale for the work of art. The value shall not include the cost of site improvements for the installation of the work.
 ii) The value of the public art shall be divided by five. The quotient shall be the public art bonus floor area in square feet—provided, however, [that] the maximum public art floor area bonus shall not exceed the building site size in square feet.
 iii) The work shall be installed prior to the issuance of the certificate of occupancy for the building.

In July 1988, Portland, Oregon, adopted a Percent for Art bonus as part of its new Central City Plan. If a developer commits 1 percent of overall project costs

Jonathan W. Frank; courtesy, City of Chicago Department of Cultural Affairs

"Untitled" by Pablo Picasso, Daley Civic Plaza, Chicago.

to public art, a floor area bonus equal to the site area of the project is granted. The bonus may be doubled by committing 2 percent: A public art commitment beyond 1 percent increases the floor area by 10 percent for each additional 0.1 percent of project costs for art, up to a maximum of 2 percent. The provision also holds that at least 25 percent of the project's art budget must be in the form of a cash contribution to a public art trust fund. (See Insert 3 for code language.) Developers may opt instead to pay the total art budget into the trust fund, which will be used to acquire and install works in strategic locations throughout the Central City. Because the purchase of an artwork may yield an attractive investment return, the city expects few developers to choose to pay into the fund.

Insert 3.
Portland, Oregon: The Percent for Art Program (code excerpt)

4. "Percent for Art" Bonus Provision. Projects which commit 1 percent of their total construction cost to public art may receive a floor/area ratio bonus of 1:1. Total construction costs must be as-

sumed to be the sum of all construction costs shown on all building permits associated with the project. Projects committing more than 1 percent of public art receive additional bonus floor/area ratio of 0.1:1 for each additional 0.1 percent of the project's total construction cost devoted to public art, up to a maximum total "percent for art" floor/area ratio bonus of 2:1. Projects utilizing this bonus provision must place at least 25 percent of the project's public art budget into [the] Central City Public Art Trust Fund, maintained by the metropolitan arts commission. Should a project's developers choose to, the entire amount of "percent for art" funds may be placed in the public art trust fund. The public art trust fund is used to purchase and install public art in the Central City. Works of art to be placed on the project site in satisfaction of a "percent for art" commitment must meet all the following criteria:

a. The process and budget for selecting the artist and for selecting and installing the specific works of art to be included in the project will be approved by the metropolitan arts commission;

b. Works of art to be placed in a project will be approved by the metropolitan arts commission;

c. Works of art will be placed on the outside of the building or at a location clearly visible and freely accessible by the public from the sidewalk during daylight hours: the location of each work of art will be approved by the metropolitan arts commission;

d. The public art provided may not also satisfy another provision of the city code, state, or federal law; and

e. Installation, future preservation, maintenance, and replacement, if necessary, of the public art provided to qualify for this bonus is assured by the property owner executing a covenant with the city . . .

City planner Michael Harrison, who wrote Portland's bonus provision, explains that locations identified as sites for new works of public art will form connecting public art walks, which will become "outdoor museums" as more works are installed. These art walks will later align with and tie into the general system of transit malls, pedestrianways, bicycleways, and open space corridors that link various sectors of the Central City.

Scottsdale, Arizona's city council passed a downtown improvement ordinance, effective July 1988, to see that developers of major downtown projects (planned-block developments exceeding 100,000 square feet) designate 1 percent of their building valuations for public art. The ordinance states that the artwork must be original and executed by a professional artist, as opposed to "off-the-shelf" work. The work may be placed either inside or outside a building, as long as public access is made available. Also, developers may contribute 1 percent of the project's value to the city's cultural trust fund, which will be used to sponsor public arts projects in the downtown.

For all private projects of 25,000 square feet or more, San Francisco requires "sculpture, bas-relief, murals, mosaics, decorative water features, tapestries, or other artworks [that are] permanently affixed to the building or its grounds, . . . but [that] may not include architectural features of the building." The 1 percent art contribution (1 percent of the hard construction costs) is part of the city's package of developer fees for housing, transit, open space, and daycare in the downtown. The art contribution, however, must actually be provided on a building and therefore, unlike the other fees, never passes through city hands. The city offers no in-lieu citywide art fund. The ordinance states that "works of art shall be installed prior to issuance of the first certificate of occupancy, provided, however, that if the zoning administrator concludes that it is not feasible to install the works within that time [but] that adequate assurance is provided, . . . the works will be installed in a timely manner. . . ."

San Francisco's public art provision also specifies that "a plaque or cornerstone identifying the project architect and the creator of the artwork . . . and the erection date shall be placed at a publicly conspicuous location on the building prior to the issuance of the first certificate of occupancy." The planning department has apparently been encouraged to limit the "creators" to living artists, prompting some critics to challenge the provision as a full employment act for San Francisco artists.

Some cities with art bonus provisions also call for public artwork for government projects, as in the U.S. General Services Administration's Art in Architecture Program. Started in 1963, this program states that 0.5 percent of construction funds for federal government buildings must be spent on art. Many state and municipal governments, including those of Portland and Seattle, have similar requirements for artwork on public buildings.

Another trend is to require artwork in redevelopment projects. One of the best-known examples is the $23 million Museum of Contemporary Art (MOCA) in Los Angeles—part of the $1.2 billion California Plaza redevelopment project atop Bunker Hill. Because the project was sponsored by the Los Angeles Community Redevelopment Agency, 1.5 percent of the total project budget had to be set aside for buying public art. Rather than randomly sprinkle the 11.2-acre site with individual sculptures, the city instead used the money for a first-rate modern art museum.

VISUAL ARTS SPACE

In a related civic effort, Hartford offers increased density for building a visual arts space or public arts space as part of its bonus for cultural/entertainment facilities. The visual arts space may "includ[e] but not [be] limited to exhibition halls and galleries" and should be "visible from and directly accessible to the

pedestrian circulation system." The space must also have appropriate seating, lighting, and security equipment. The bonus ratio, first set at 1 to 8, has been reduced to 1 to 4.

Under this program, a 3,600-square-foot private art gallery in one Hartford office project has earned some 28,200 square feet of extra commercial space for the developer. The city's cultural affairs commission stipulated that the gallery should feature living local artists.

WATER FEATURES

Although San Francisco simply categorizes "decorative water features" as part of its public art requirement, Bellevue and Portland treat public fountains as a distinct bonus selection. In Bellevue, the "fountain, cascade, stream, water sculpture, or reflection" must "(1) . . . be located outside of the building, and be publicly visible and accessible at the main pedestrian entrance to a building, or along a pedestrian connection; (2) . . . be maintained in a clean and noncontaminated condition; and (3) . . . be in motion during daylight hours." (See Insert 4 for Portland's provision.)

Insert 4.
Water Features in Portland
(code excerpt)

7. **Water Features or Public Fountains Bonus Provision.** Projects which commit a percentage of the total construction cost of the project to the development and maintenance of a water feature or public fountain will receive additional FAR. For each 0.1 percent of construction cost committed to development of fountains or water features, an FAR bonus of 0.1:1 will be granted, up to a maximum of 0.5:1. Total construction costs are defined as the sum of all construction costs shown on all building permits associated with the project. To qualify for this bonus, the water feature or public fountain must meet the following criteria:

   a. The design of the water feature or public fountain must be approved as part of the design review of the total project.
   b. To enhance the environment for pedestrians, the water feature or public fountain must be accessible by pedestrians from a sidewalk or from a plaza which is accessible from a sidewalk.
   c. The water feature or public fountain must be located outdoors.
   d. The fountain or water feature must be visible and accessible by the public from the sidewalks that provide access for pedestrians to the project.
   e. If public art is included in the fountain or water feature, the art object must meet all the approval criteria for the "Percent for Art" bonus.
   f. The fountain will be maintained by the building owners.
   g. The water feature must be designed to use water efficiently with a low water makeup rate. The water feature must recirculate water and be designed to reduce water loss due to evaporation and wind. A method of keeping the water clean must be provided.

h. The maintenance and continued operation of the water feature or public fountain, on private property, will be assured by the acceptance and recording of a covenant with the city . . .

MAINTENANCE AND REMOVAL

Two major concerns of zoning requirements and incentives for artwork are maintenance and possible replacement. Cincinnati's code explicitly states that

> The owner shall covenant . . . to maintain the public art for the life of the building. The work . . . shall not be removed without the express authorization of the director of city planning. The director may authorize temporary removal for exhibition elsewhere, for their protection, or for their restoration in event of damage. The director may authorize permanent removal if the work is replaced with work of equal or greater artistic merit and value. The owner shall keep the work sufficiently insured to restore or replace in the event the work is damaged or destroyed. The city shall be named an additional insured. Such restoration or replacement shall be with the approval of the director.

Seattle could have benefited from adopting equally stringent criteria for the removal of public artwork. When Seattle's Seafirst National Bank sold its headquarters building to JMB Realty of Chicago in 1983, it also put up for sale a major Henry Moore sculpture in the plaza flanking the entryway. The city's department of construction and land use claimed that the unilateral decision to sell was improper for the sculpture, which was part of a bonused plaza belonging to the public and, as such, needed the city's consent to its sale. Although the requirement that some bonus features must also contain artwork had not yet been enacted at the time the project was permitted, the city claimed the sculpture's location on a plaza bonused under the old code made it, by implication, part of the public domain.

The Seattle dispute was satisfactorily resolved, for the sale never went through and the sculpture still graces the plaza today. Nonetheless, the dispute raised important issues regarding the ownership, removal, and sale of public artwork, as well as the need to decide these questions in advance and spell out clear criteria in the regulations.

EMPLOYMENT AND JOB TRAINING

Another kind of bonus option is aimed at enhancing employment opportunities for low-income residents and promoting the development of human services facilities in the downtown.

HARTFORD

Hartford's bonus for employment and job training contains the following wording:

> Provision of employment and/or job training programs for Hartford residents, either as part of the construction phase or upon completion of a project, shall be in accordance with a hiring and employment agreement between the city of Hartford and the applicant.

> In determining the FAR bonus, each permanent job above twenty-five percent (25%) of the total employment in the occupancy phase of a project reserved for Hartford residents shall be equal to six hundred twenty-five (625) square feet of bonus floor area.

In other words, developers may earn an FAR bonus of 625 square feet (above a base FAR of 10) for each square foot of the amenity, up to an FAR cap of 6. Failure to meet the employment requirement results in the loss of the bonus award or substitute payment.

Contribution to the linkage trust fund for either housing or employment and job training is now $15 for each square foot of additional bonus floor area. This bonus caps at an FAR of 4 for payment in lieu of residential development, or at an FAR of 6 for employment. The fee went up from $5 to $15 a square foot in 1987, but even at the lower rate, no developer had contributed to the employment and job training fund. In Hartford, where the cost for an FAR square foot of commercial space is roughly $25, the higher fee still appears to be a bargain.

Lack of developer interest in the bonus feature has been blamed mostly on administrative difficulties. Employment during the construction phase is largely controlled by labor unions. Moreover, developers point out that a substantial portion of new downtown development is speculative, and that the unknown tenant mix prevents them from exercising the needed control either to enter into or to monitor a hiring and employment agreement. They also question whether such agreements can actually be enforced, particularly when a business declares bankruptcy or pulls out of a project for another reason.

On the other hand, a roughly equal amount of development to that spurred by speculation has been prompted by the insurance industry's seemingly insatiable appetite for larger facilities and new back-office space. In these cases, the tenants are known entities. This trend may be slowed by predicted cutbacks in the insurance industry, but in any event, the speculative factor alone would not inhibit developer contributions to the employment and job training fund. It has been suggested, however, that given the choice of furthering low-income housing or employment in a city wracked by severe housing shortages, it is politically more expedient to promote the former.

SAN FRANCISCO

San Francisco's Downtown Plan calls for local employment programs and "employment brokerage services" for downtown projects "where the gross square feet of new, converted, or added floor area for office [use] equals at least 100,000 square feet." The purpose is "to assure that adequate measures are undertaken and maintained to maximize the access of San Francisco residents to new jobs created by added office development in the downtown. The project sponsor must provide the employment brokerage services for the lifetime of the building." (See Insert 5 for the code criteria of the local employment program.)

Insert 5.
San Francisco's Employment Provision
(code excerpt)

Sec. 164. Local Employment Programs and Employment Brokerage Services in C-3 Districts.

(a) **Purpose.** This section is intended to assure that adequate measures are undertaken and maintained to maximize the access of San Francisco residents to new jobs created by added office development in the downtown.

(b) **Requirement.** For any new building or additions to or conversion of an existing building in C-3 Districts where the gross square feet of new, converted, or added floor area for office use equals at least 100,000 square feet, the project sponsor shall be required to provide employment brokerage services for the actual lifetime of the project, as provided in this subsection. Prior to the issuance of the first permit of occupancy . . . , the project sponsor shall: (1) prepare a local employment program to be approved by the director of planning, or his or her designee, and to be implemented by the provider of employment brokerage services; and (2) execute an agreement with the department of city planning, or its designee, for the provision of employment brokerage services and implementation of the local employment program. The local employment program shall be designed:
1. to determine the number and nature of jobs that will become available as a result of added downtown office development;
2. to publicize to San Francisco residents the availability of those jobs;
3. to work with local schools and job training programs to create a labor pool of San Francisco residents qualified to obtain jobs created by added downtown office development;
4. to work with employers in the building to encourage their hiring of qualified San Francisco residents;
5. to carry out other activities determined by the department of city planning, or its designee, to be reasonable and appropriate in meeting the purpose of this requirement.

(c) All such agreements required under this section shall mandate that the project sponsor shall abide by any existing applicable state or local programs and laws designed to both train and place in employment minorities and economically disadvantaged women, as defined in this section. For the purposes of this sec-

tion, the term "minorities" shall include, but not be limited to, blacks, Hispanics, Asians (including, but not limited to, Chinese, Japanese, Koreans, Pacific Islanders, Samoans, and Southeast Asians), Filipinos, and American Indians. For the purpose of this section, "economically disadvantaged women" shall include, but not be limited to, women receiving Aid for Families with Dependent Children (AFDC) or similar state or local aid. Where there are no such training and employment placement programs, or existing programs are found inadequate by the human rights commission, that commission may recommend to the director for consideration additional programs to fulfill the goals of this section.

BOSTON

As part of its linkage program, Boston requires its downtown developers to pay a $1-per-square-foot fee for job training programs. Since 1986, when the fee was enacted, nearly $300,000 has been committed, and another $1.1 million is expected. Developers may elect to give to a jobs trust fund or to start an on-site job training program to employ low- and moderate-income workers. (For more discussion of Boston's linkage system, see Chapter 11, "Housing.")

HUMAN SERVICES

BELLEVUE, WASHINGTON

Incentive zoning regulations in Seattle and Bellevue offer density bonuses for integrating nonprofit human services facilities into commercial projects. In Bellevue, the space for "nonprofit social services" must be "made available, rent-free, to charitable and social service organizations which provide emergency assistance, health services, referral services, or other specialized social services directly to the public," with the stipulation that this "space shall principally provide outreach functions, rather than administrative functions." Space may be provided on site or off site, and the maximum bonusable area is 5,000 square feet.

SEATTLE

Seattle's similar public benefit feature (see Insert 6) is intended to encourage the development of human services, including legal aid services, job training and counseling, food banks, and health facilities targeted at low-income downtown residents. The bonus obligation may be met in one of three ways: by provision of the human service facility on the site of the new project, by building it off site on a different downtown lot, or by contribution to the Downtown Health and Human Services Fund. The minimum bonusable area per lot is 1,000 square feet of interior gross floor area, and the maximum is 10,000 square feet.

If the human services space is built off site, in an existing building, the bonus ratio is about half that awarded for provision of the facility on site. Also, the bonus ratio varies with the location of the human services space within those downtown sectors named in the code. The largest award is given for space developed in new construction on the same site within the office sector. Less credit is granted when the space is sited within a retail or mixed/residential sector.

So far, no developer has paid into the trust fund or even applied for the human services bonus. Even at the highest rate of $70 per seven square feet of additional rentable office space, the trust fund option is less prohibitive than the cost of buying land in downtown Seattle. Reluctance to join in the program is ascribed to several factors. By far the greatest inhibitor is the general perception within the development community that providing legal aid services, health facilities, or food banks—operations whose names smack of street people and "undesirables"—will inevitably jeopardize financing prospects and marketing potential.

The city of Seattle claims that this perception is misguided and based on inaccurate information; it has launched a program to educate the business community about the use of the bonus. Planning officials maintain that the human services uses need not be incompatible with commercial development and note that some 90 human services facilities already operate within the downtown without apparent dire effects. The bonus obligation is not confined to drop-in premises. Facilities providing job counseling, legal aid, or psychological services, note city planners, generally harmonize with office uses.

Specific code requirements further block use of the bonus. For example, in the case of off-site construction, the requirement that a lien or deed of trust be placed on the property in which the facility is to be located burdens the wrong party, say critics. A similar requirement for the off-site daycare obligation deters use of that bonus, and the city is now looking into other mechanisms whereby the burden would be borne by the recipient of the bonus credit.

Another proposal entails tiering the human services bonus within the incentive zoning structure, as has been done with the low-income housing bonus. To build beyond a designated density, developers would have no choice but to meet the human services and housing bonus obligations or to contribute toward the construction of these uses. Seattle planning officials are also debating whether to expand the permitted off-site locations outside the downtown.

A suggestion has been made that the off-site option would prove more attractive if the bonus value were awarded at the same rate as the on-site obligation. But perhaps the matter is solely one of perception. Although daycare centers, like human services, also earn less commercial density when provided off site, daycare facilities are seen as project amenities. Any diminished value, therefore, is largely offset by the enhancement factor of the child care space.

BOSTON

New zoning regulations for Boston's Midtown Cultural District (a 27-block area between Back Bay and the financial district) provide density bonuses for the inclusion of community service organizations, community health centers or clinics, and temporary housing shelters in commercial projects. The 1989 ordinance names several criteria, among them a proviso that surplus density will only be granted if the board of appeal finds that "the proposed project and its massing are architecturally compatible with the surrounding area, in accordance with . . . urban design provisions" set out in the code and "is consistent with the Midtown Cultural District Plan and the general plan for the city as a whole."

DOWNTOWN DAYCARE

Proponents of placing daycare centers in downtown office towers often seem to be taking on a Sisyphean struggle. Few parents relish the prospect of lengthy commutes or awkward maneuvers on trains and buses with young children. And densely built-up downtowns lack the space needed for the outdoor playgrounds required by many state licensers. Furthermore, most building owners are unenthusiastic about giving prime ground-floor space to child care centers that pay little or no rent.

A strong argument in favor of office-based daycare is that employees in the building can visit their children during breaks or lunch hours. But if a building's daycare center is supported by a general city-administered fund backed by developer payments or by other parties besides the building owner, its clients will not necessarily be the people who work in the building. Another problem is that some parents still see urban environments as basically pernicious and unhealthy for young children. On the other hand, downtowns do offer the necessary number of working parents to support these centers.

Despite the several hurdles that must be surmounted, many cities are encouraging the building of daycare centers in their downtowns and are furnishing child care bonuses as part of their incentive zoning packages. Bellevue, Cincinnati, Hartford, Seattle, and more recently, Portland, Oregon, are giving additional density awards in exchange for building child care facilities within commercial projects. (See Inserts 7a, b, and c for examples of daycare bonuses in Portland, Cincinnati, and Seattle.) San Francisco compels developers to provide daycare facilities, and Boston recently set up a similar program. (Insert 8, taken from San Francisco's code, amplifies and clearly sets out the rationale behind that city's mandate.)

Insert 7.
Daycare Options in Three Cities

7a. Portland
(code excerpt)
2. Daycare Bonus Provision. Projects providing daycare within CX, CE, and/or RX Zones may receive a floor area bonus. For each one square foot of interior space developed and committed to use as a qualifying daycare facility for children, a bonus of three square feet of additional floor area will be granted. To qualify for this bonus, the daycare facility must meet the following approval criteria:
a. The daycare facility will be used for the purpose of daycare for the life of the building. The facility will be open during normal business hours at least five days each week and 50 weeks each calendar year.
b. The daycare facility will be maintained and kept in a good state of repair throughout the life of the building.
c. Future daycare use and maintenance of the daycare facility is assured by the acceptance and recording of a covenant with the city . . .

7b. Cincinnati
(code excerpt)
Sec. 2403.2.5 Daycare Center Bonus. In order to qualify for the allowance of floor area bonus, a daycare center shall satisfy all structural requirements imposed by code, ordinance, or regulation for children's daycare. Required exterior yard space may be provided off site, if approved by all agencies regulating children's daycare centers. The owner shall covenant to make the center available for a period of 40 years for the exclusive use and operation as a children's daycare center. . . . At the time of the building permit application, the applicant shall exhibit a letter of intent from a qualified daycare center operator who intends to operate a daycare center in the space provided.

7c. Seattle
(code excerpt)
B. Daycare
1. Intent
The intent of the daycare bonus is to provide a wide range of potential locations for daycare centers which serve downtown residents and/or employees.
2. The daycare center may be provided either on the same lot as the project using the bonus or on a different downtown lot.
3. Bonusable area
a. The minimum bonusable area per lot shall be 1,000 square feet of interior gross floor area.
b. The maximum bonusable area per lot shall be 10,000 square feet.
c. All exterior play area approved by the department of social and health services shall be eligible for a bonus, provided that the space is not already part of another bonused public open space.
4. Clientele—Basic Standards
The daycare center shall provide services at rates affordable to the range of income levels represented in the downtown workforce.

5. Leasing of space—Basic Standards
   a. The developer shall secure at least a five-year lease with the operator of the daycare center before a certificate of occupancy for the project using the bonus is issued.
   b. The developer shall finish the space with ceilings, walls, flooring, and utility connections.
   c. Any additional improvements beyond the minimum requirements may be provided either by the developer or the daycare center operator, as specified in the lease agreement.
   d. The daycare center shall not be charged rent, but may be required to pay a portion of the utility, insurance, and maintenance expenses for the space.

Insert 8.
San Francisco: Mandatory Child Care
(code excerpts)

Sec. 314. Child Care Requirements for Office and Hotel Development Projects. . . .
Sec. 314.2. Findings. The board hereby finds and declares as follows: Large-scale office and hotel developments in the city and county of San Francisco (hereinafter "city") have attracted and continue to attract additional employees to the city, and there is a causal relationship between such developments and the need for additional child care facilities in the city, particularly child care facilities affordable to households of low and moderate income.

Office and hotel uses in the city are benefited by the availability of child care for persons employed in such offices and hotels close to their place of employment. However, the supply of child care in the city has not kept pace with the demand for child care created by these new employees. Due to this shortage of child care, employers will have difficulty in securing a labor force, and employees unable to find accessible and affordable, quality child care will be forced either to work where such services are available outside San Francisco, or leave the workforce entirely, in some cases seeking public assistance to support their children. In either case, there will be a detrimental effect on San Francisco's economy and its quality of life.

Projections from the EIR for the Downtown Plan indicate that between 1984 and 2000, there will be a significant increase of nearly 100,000 jobs in the C-3 District under the Downtown Plan. Most of that employment growth will occur in office and hotel work, which [has] a predominantly female workforce.

According to the survey conducted of C-3 District workers in 1981, 65 percent of the workforce was between the ages of 25–44. These are the prime childbearing years for women, and the prime fathering years for men. The survey also indicated that only 12 percent of the C-3 District jobs were part-time, leaving up to 88 percent of the positions occupied by full-time workers. . . .

The scarcity of child care in the city is due in great part to large office and hotel development, both within the C-3 District and elsewhere in the city, which has attracted and will continue to attract additional employees and residents to the city. . . . At the same time that large office and hotel development is generating an increased demand for child care, it is improbable that factors inhibiting increased supply of child care will be mitigated by the marketplace; hence, the supply of child care will become increasingly scarce.

The Master Plan encourages "continued growth of prime downtown office activities, so long as undesirable consequences of such growth can be avoided," and requires that there be the provision of "adequate amenities for those who live, work, and use downtown." In light of these provisions, the city should impose requirements on developers of office and hotel projects designed to mitigate the adverse effects of the expanded employment facilitated by such projects. To that end, the city planning commission is authorized to promote affirm-

atively the policies of the San Francisco Master Plan through the imposition of special child care development or assessment requirements. It is desirable to impose the costs of the increased burden of providing child care necessitated by such office and hotel development projects directly upon the sponsors of new development generating the need. This is to be done through a requirement that the sponsor construct child care facilities, or pay a fee into a fund used to foster the expansion of and to ease access to affordable child care, as a condition of the privilege of development. . . .

REQUIRED DAYCARE

San Francisco. San Francisco was the first major city to require daycare facilities in or near new downtown commercial projects. Developers of office or hotel projects exceeding 50,000 square feet and located anywhere within the city or county must set aside 2,000 square feet of floor space or 1 percent of the total floor area, whichever is greater, for a child care center. The latter will be made available to a nonprofit child care provider. Two or more developers may share construction costs for an on-site facility in one of their projects or for a nearby facility off site. Alternatively, the developers of affected projects may give $1 per square foot of office and/or hotel space to a citywide fund to boost the supply of child care centers and cut the costs of child care for households of low and moderate income.

San Francisco's 1985 Downtown Plan also requires developers to carry out planning and brokerage activities to aid project occupants in getting child care services. (See Insert 9.) The developers/owners of major downtown commercial projects must supply building occupants with specified types of information on the availability of child care and must also collect data on the occupants' child care needs. Developers may contract out these obligations to a nonprofit child care resource or referral agency. Projects are actively encouraged "to adopt flextime or staggered-work-hours programs, job-sharing programs, parental leave policies, and dependent care assistance programs designed to accommodate the needs of working parents and their children." They are also urged "to promote and coordinate the development of transportation services assisting employees who choose either to bring their children to on-site care or who seek means of transporting their children to off-site care."

Insert 9.
San Francisco on Child Care Plans and Brokerage Services
(code excerpt)

Sec. 165. . . .
(a) **Purpose.** This section is intended to ensure that adequate measures are undertaken and maintained to minimize the child care impacts created by additional office employment in the downtown, in a manner consistent with the objectives and policies of

the Master Plan, by facilitating the development, expansion, and maintenance of affordable, quality child care programs and auxiliary services, the latter including, but not limited to, resource and referral services.

(b) **Requirement.** For any new building or additions to or conversion of an existing building in the C-3 District where the gross square feet of new, converted, or added floor area for office use equals at least 100,000 square feet, the project sponsor shall be required to provide on-site child care brokerage services for the actual lifetime of the project. For any new building or additions to or conversion of an existing building in the C-3 District where the gross square feet of new, converted, or added floor area for office use equals at least 50,000 square feet, the project sponsor shall be required to provide child care brokerage services for the lifetime of the project, by either: (1) providing such services on site, or (2) providing such services through a consortium of like-sized sponsors, where such services are made available within a radius of two city blocks from the sponsor's project, or (3) subcontracting with a child care brokerage service already serving a project within a radius of two city blocks from the sponsor's project. . . . The child care plan and child care brokerage services shall be designed:

(1) To promote the provision of on-site child care resource services and easily accessible child care referral services, using, to the maximum extent feasible, existing community agencies;

(2) To promote, where feasible, the development of on-site child care facilities, accessible and affordable to all segments of the community; to promote the development, expansion, and maintenance of off-site child care facilities accessible and affordable to all segments of the community;

(3) To promote and coordinate the development and use of open space for child care programs in the C-3 District;

(4) To promote and coordinate the development of transportation services assisting employees who choose either to bring their children to on-site care or who seek means of transporting their children to off-site care;

(5) To promote and encourage project occupants to adopt flex-time or staggered-work-hours programs, job-sharing programs, parental leave policies, and dependent care assistance programs designed to accommodate the needs of working parents and their children;

(6) To promote the development of parenting resources;

(7) To promote the development of data collection, to document the numbers of worker parents in the project workforce, number and ages of their children, supply of child care available to those parents, cost of available care, preferences for child care and need for special services; and coordinate such data collection with the data collection efforts of other project sponsors and the local resource and referral agency; [and]

(8) To carry out other activities determined by the department of city planning to be appropriate to meeting the purpose of this requirement.

(c) **Notice.** The agreement to provide child care brokerage services and the child care plan required by Subsection (b) shall each provide for periodic notice reasonably calculated to apprise all persons then employed in the office development who have children under their primary care of the availability of child care brokerage services and the existence of a child care plan. Such notice shall be given at least once during each calendar year, and shall state a place at which a copy of the child care plan for the development may be inspected during regular business hours. . . .

Three office projects approved in 1987 that were subject to the child care requirement are just now breaking ground. In addition, the San Francisco Redevelopment Agency has applied the child care requirement to some projects within redevelopment areas. So far, all developers have chosen to contribute to the city's Affordable Child Care Fund, for a total of about $1 million. The average contribution by the office projects is $250,000. These contributions, which will not be paid until the projects are ready for occupancy in 1991, will subsidize existing child care services or help establish new ones. With construction costs for child care space running some $125 to $200 a square foot, not to mention lost rents and ongoing expenses for property taxes, repairs, utilities, and so forth, it is not surprising that developers are choosing to pay the one-time fee.

Boston. The Boston Redevelopment Authority recently approved inclusion of a child care requirement for major commercial projects in the new zoning regulations for the city's Midtown Cultural District. The cultural district plan, passed for Midtown in March 1989, is the first permanent district plan completed since passage of Boston's 1987 Downtown Interim Zoning Plan. The Midtown regulations would obliterate what remains of the city's adult entertainment district, the "combat zone," in favor of office and residential development and a new cultural district.

Boston's child care requirement, which only applies to projects exceeding a height of 125 feet or an

FAR of 8, or both, calls for commercial projects between 200,000 and 500,000 square feet (excluding any floor area devoted to residential use) to include at least 4,000 square feet for a child care facility. For projects between 500,000 and 1 million square feet, the obligation is 8,000 square feet of daycare space, which may be embodied in two centers (one may be off site). Projects between 100,000 and 200,000 square feet must devote at least 2 percent of their gross square footage to a child care facility. Finally, projects exceeding 1 million square feet must proffer 12,000 square feet of child care space, which may be divided among three centers, two of which may be off site. Off-site centers are to be located in the Midtown district or in one of two adjacent residential sections.

There is no in-lieu fee option comparable to the one contained in the city's housing and job-training linkage programs for office projects. The specific regulations for the compulsory daycare centers have not yet been written, but undoubtedly the affordability of the centers and their availability to city residents will be top priorities. It is expected that daycare requirements will also be proposed for some of the downtown's 10 other planning districts.

BONUSABLE DAYCARE

Cincinnati. Cincinnati's daycare bonus provision, adopted in 1987, states: "The owner shall covenant to make the center available for a period of 40 years for the exclusive use and operation as a children's daycare center. The bonus floor area shall equal the net interior floor area made available for the exclusive use of the daycare center, multiplied [by 16]."

Several of Cincinnati's downtown projects contain child care centers; because no extra density was needed, however, none of these centers was approved under the bonus provision. Observers predict that the city's exceptionally generous as-of-right zoning (13 FAR) will impede use of the bonus system.

Hartford. In 1984, Hartford enacted a bonus provision for daycare centers or nurseries built in downtown projects. For each square foot devoted to a daycare facility—defined as a private or public establishment "enrolling young children for care, instruction, or recreation during or after school hours"—developers may add six feet of commercial space to their projects, up to an FAR cap of 1. Hartford's bonus guidelines do not address the issue of subsidy.

The first daycare center to be sited in the city's office core is planned for the ground floor of the 46-story 180 Allyn Street tower, a project with some

1,064,000 square feet of office space and 60,000 square feet of street-level retail. The project is scheduled to open in the second quarter of 1992. Approximately 90 spaces in the privately operated center will be reserved for children of the building's tenants, with half of the spaces kept for the children of Hartford residents. A 6,700-square-foot outdoor playground will occupy an adjacent site owned by a church.

Developer Joseph Friedman says he would have built the 5,000-square-foot facility regardless of the bonus award, which will allow him to add some 30,000 square feet to the project's second phase. Many of the city's primary tenants—especially insurance companies—are offering their employees child care credits, and the demand is mounting for child care services in the downtown. Friedman intends to use the amenity to help market the project. The center, which is located on a prime pedestrian strip midway between the newly renovated train station and the civic center, will be pulled out to the street and showcased with large storefront windows.

Seattle. In 1985, Seattle set up a daycare bonus that allows the bonusable center to be erected either on the lot that is using the bonus or on a different downtown lot. Bonus credits range from 3.5 additional FAR in renovations to 16 in new office towers. The minimum bonusable area per lot is 1,000 square feet, and the maximum is 10,000 square feet. The code says the center must offer services at rates affordable within the range of incomes earned by downtown workers and that the center shall not be charged rent, although it may have to pay a portion of the space's utility, insurance, and maintenance expenses. (See Insert 7c for the bonus criteria and ratios applied to daycare centers in Seattle.)

A number of daycare centers have been built or planned in several commercial projects downtown. Two of these were encouraged directly by the bonus provisions. The 44-story Pacific First Centre, with about 872,000 square feet of office space and 98,500 of retail space, is a project of Prescott Development Company. When completed in summer 1989, it will contain a daycare center on the third floor and an open play space on an adjoining landscaped rooftop. The approach to the facility will be via elevators and escalators serving a three-level shopping arcade.

Permitted before the city's 1985 rezoning, the project did not qualify for a specific daycare center bonus. However, Prescott's request for an alley closing triggered discretionary review by the city council, which attached several conditions to its approval, one of which was the provision of 150,000 square feet of public space. The 4,000-square-foot child care center and its 3,800-square-foot open playground will meet part of this requirement.

Pacific First Centre's daycare space will house 52 children, most of whom will be preschoolers from 2½ to 5 years old. Priority will be given to the children of employees in the building. The daycare operator, Pacific Montessori Children's Center, will assume responsibility for the buildout costs but will not be charged rent.

The first daycare center to be built under the city's incentive zoning regulations opened in September 1988 in the 1 million-square-foot Washington Mutual Tower. With somewhat fewer than 2,000 square feet, the center accommodates 22 infants and toddlers. Developer Jon Runstad of Wright Runstad & Company chose to build a facility smaller than the maximum bonusable one partly because he did not need the greater density. Operated by the YWCA, the center reserves 20 percent of its spaces at a nominal fee for the children of low-income workers and sets the fees on the remaining spaces on a sliding scale ranging from $280 to $570 a month for infants and $250 to $540 for toddlers. (The going rate for downtown infant care in Seattle is $565 to $675 and approximately $400 outside the downtown.) The turnkey space, which cost Wright Runstad about $500,000 to build, is provided rent-free. The company is also subsidizing utility, insurance, and maintenance expenses. Washington Mutual Tower tenants were given priority, and the 22 spaces were filled almost as soon as they were offered.

The state mandates 75 square feet of open outside play area per child for a given group at one time: thus, 10 children playing outdoors would need 750 square feet of open space. But the state will waive the open space requirement for children younger than 31 months, if adequate indoor space with appropriate equipment is available. The center in Washington Mutual Tower, restricted to children younger than 31 months, received such a waiver.

Fairly recent amendments to the state's building code allow child care centers to be built above street level, up to the third floor, if fire safety and health regulations are met. Although the daycare space in Washington Mutual Tower is located on the second floor, the exits are at grade, and therefore no waiver was needed. The same developer was granted an exemption for a center in another project, to be located on the second floor with a deck affording open space.

Thanks to the city's flexibility in permitting child care centers above ground level in commercial buildings, one center may be found on the roof of a parking garage in a space once occupied by a health club.

Seattle is investigating the use of city parks for open play areas, which must "adjoin" the child care facility or be accessible by a safe route.

Currently, Seattle is considering several amendments to the daycare bonus criteria. One would codify the already adopted policy of meting out 20 percent of the spaces to the children of low-income workers; at issue is whether to give building tenants some preference or to make the spaces equally available to all downtown workers. The provision for off-site daycare has never been used and is undergoing revision. Under the present system, a lien or deed of trust (equivalent to the center's value) is placed on the property where the off-site center will stand. If the center fails and is not replaced within six months, the lien falls due. It is widely agreed that this mechanism unfairly burdens the owner of the existing building rather than the developer, who is reaping the benefits of the increased density. The city is exploring ways of shifting the risk to the developer.

THE NUTS AND BOLTS

Any city contemplating bonuses for daycare has many issues to settle. So does a developer mulling over the inclusion of a subsidized daycare facility in a project—whether or not the primary motivation is to earn extra floor space.

What Is the Public Benefit? Cities considering daycare incentives first need to assess the potential public benefit. Some detractors claim that in those downtowns where the need for child care is critical and the demand is high enough, daycare facilities should be required, not bonused. Others question the efficacy of rewarding developers for adding an amenity they might have built anyway to attract or retain tenants: Daycare centers were built into several projects in Seattle that predated the 1985 code that gave bonuses for such centers. It has been suggested, however, that the code's listing of daycare as a public benefit and the ensuing public debate have served to educate concerned citizens, as well as the real estate and business community, about the need for child care facilities. In this way, the controversy has encouraged the voluntary construction of daycare centers in the downtown.

Cities must also define which "public" the daycare bonus is meant to benefit. Should bonused facilities serve people of all income levels? If so, the facilities will need to be subsidized. Should a building's tenants come first, or should the center's services be distributed equally among all downtown workers? When it comes to allocating the scarce spaces in daycare facilities developed for bonuses, some cities want their own residents to have priority over commuters from other jurisdictions.

The Regulatory Quagmire. A panoply of state and municipal regulations governs daycare facilities. Child care centers in Seattle, for instance, must conform to the stipulations of the state's department of social and health services and of several city agencies, including the department of licensing and consumer affairs, the department of construction and land use (which administers both the zoning and building codes), and the fire department. Requirements for daycare centers tend to be explicit and to cover everything from the placement of entryways, exits, and fire alarms to the size and location of interior and exterior play areas. Regulations typically require a center to be on the ground level and to have access to adjacent open space, thus placing formidable obstacles in the way of daycare centers in the downtown.

Local codes are often even more restrictive. They may limit child care facilities to the first floor where state building codes do not. Some cities may need to amend their building codes, as did Seattle and San Francisco, to allow centers on upper levels. San Francisco now permits child care space to occupy virtually any floor, as long as certain fire and safety precautions are taken; it also shows some elasticity regarding open space.

The licensing requirements for open space are usually more flexible for on-site infant and toddler (under two years old) daycare facilities than for child care centers. Whereas licensers typically demand that a percentage of open space adjoin a child care center, the open play area for infant daycare services often may be reduced or even waived. "Without some flexibility in the open space requirement," says Jon Pon, program manager in San Francisco's mayor's office of community development, "developers are not going to build on-site centers."[1]

A child care center aiming to comply with San Francisco's building code must qualify as a "licensed child care facility." To ensure licensability, the mayor's office of community development offers technical advice and serves as a liaison among state and local licensing departments, architects, and developers during the licensing application process. The latter generally takes six months. The mayor's office also helps developers write requests for proposals to select daycare providers.

Size. Various factors determine the optimal size for downtown child care centers, including the average size of projects being built and land and construction costs. Most state and local health codes prescribe a minimum amount of space that must be afforded each child. Downtown daycare facilities are generally smaller than those in the suburbs. At first, San Francisco required a minimum of 3,000 square feet, but later it amended the amount to 2,000, which is probably more in scale with the moderate-sized buildings now being encouraged under the Downtown Plan. A 2,000-square-foot center should accommodate 35 children.

Jon Pon notes that the minimum size has been reduced to give developers more leeway. For instance, if a developer's obligation amounts to 5,000 square feet of child care space, there are several alternatives: to build a 5,000-square-foot facility; to build, say, one with 2,000 and another with 3,000 square feet; to meet the entire obligation by giving to the Affordable Child Care Fund; or to build a 2,000-square-foot facility and meet the rest of the obligation through a contribution to the fund. Another reason for cutting the minimum requirement was to urge developers to provide facilities instead of contributing money.

Location. In Seattle and San Francisco, developers may build on or off site. San Francisco allows consortiums of developers whose projects are within one-half mile of one another to set aside space at one of their developments, or to provide a center elsewhere within a one-mile radius of their various sites.

Retrofits. Jon Pon reports that it has been nearly impossible to retrofit a child care facility once a project has reached completion and tenants have moved in. Although many businesses have attempted to construct new on-site child care centers in existing buildings, they have ultimately been discouraged by the many physical obstacles.

Contributions in Lieu of Facilities. From the developer's viewpoint, paying $1 a square foot (the current fee in San Francisco) into the Affordable Child Care Fund is infinitely easier than building a center that meets code specifications and negotiating with daycare operators. On the other hand, child care facilities may help a project attract and keep tenants—a good reason to choose the production option.

Although the developers of the five San Francisco projects so far affected by the child care obligation have indicated they will be paying into the fund, later projects may opt for production. Much of the building design on the first five projects had already been worked out before the child care obligation was imposed, and some projects had already lined up tenants. For them, the path of least resistance was to pay into the fund.

Abby Cohen, managing attorney for the Child Care Law Center in San Francisco, who helped draft the language of the city's child care regulations, points

Finally an office building so friendly you can bring your kids to work.

The catch of the day at The Brooklyn Cafe. "Global cuisine and Seattle's finest shellfish bar," says restaurateur Larry Hamlin. Photo: Chef Alvin Binueya and co-owner Jack Pederson.

Day care achieves new heights. Cooper Moore will go to day care where Mom works, at 1201 Third Avenue. "A first in Seattle's high-rise history," says Tema Nesoff, YWCA associate director.

Pacific Nautilus is one lease option you can exercise daily. David Bruce of tenant Perkins Coie can take the elevator to work out.

Bob's Shoeshine. An illuminating experience from Boris "Bob" Volinsky, the affable Ukranian.

The atrium overlooking the grand plaza. It's the perfect rendez-vous for espresso, casual dining or Roosevelt High School's 25th reunion. Photo: Diane Maxwell and Maureen McCormick of tenant Stewart Title.

Property Manager Neal Warner (center), Paige Carns and Jim Jackson are three members of the building management team at Wright Runstad & Company.

Shown above are just six of our many services at 1201 Third Avenue.

The building is now open. First tenants are in. And if you're lucky enough to be one in the future, picture all of this just an elevator away:

Umberto's pizza slices at Mel's Market. A business meeting box lunch from Estelle's Sandwich Kitchen. A Chicago Frankfurter from The Umbrella Club. A mocha from the 1201 Espresso Bar.

A cut and perm from the hair styling salon. A wash and wax from the car service in the garage. A spray of blooms from the florist.

The Wall Street Journal from FIGS sundries. "The Power of Ethical Management" at Beks Book-store. New wildlife stamps at the postal service. A real wildlife adventure arranged through the resi-dent travel agency.

For the full leasing story and the cook's tour, call friendly Kevin Kaywood, (206) 447-9000, Wright Runstad & Company.

At 65% leased, he's all smiles.

1201 Third Avenue
The Seattle building they talk about in Seattle.

Beyond the density bonus, developer Wright Runstad & Company gets extra mileage from this daycare center: it is promoted as one of the main building amenities in Wright Runstad's advertisements for Washington Mutual Tower (formerly 1201 Third Avenue).

out that the fund approach affords the city greater con-trol over the planning of facilities. The city can place a center strategically: where needs are most pressing, where it is convenient for its clients, and where open space is at hand.

A Center's Longevity. Most daycare bonus provi-sions dictate that the space must be kept as a child care center for a given time period. In Cincinnati, the period is 40 years. In Seattle, it is the life of the proj-ect, although the developer need secure only "a five-year lease with the operator of the daycare center be-fore a certificate of occupancy for the project using the bonus is issued." In San Francisco, the duration of the off-site obligation is 20 years, and a lease to any nonprofit provider must extend for at least three years.

San Francisco's daycare requirement also calls for annual evaluation. If the planning commission deter-mines,

after review of an empirical study, that the formulae . . . impose a greater requirement for child care facilities than is necessary to provide child care for the number of employees attracted to office development projects . . . , the planning commission shall refund that portion of

any fee paid or permit a reduction of the space in the of-fice development project dedicated for child care by a sponsor, consistent with the conclusions of such study. The planning commission shall adjust any sponsor's re-quirement and the formulae . . . so that the amount of the exaction is set at the level necessary to provide child care for the number of employees attracted to office de-velopment projects. . . .

Particularly where the daycare obligation is man-dated as an exaction, as in Boston and San Francisco, it becomes important to allow for periodic evaluation and formula adjustment to avoid legal challenges.

Liability. Another major issue, and one that is not directly addressed in daycare bonus regulations, is lia-bility. Some insurance underwriters have apparently stopped writing child care liability policies. Although a nationwide survey by Child, Inc., a private non-profit child care provider headquartered in Austin, showed that only 12 percent of providers had claims filed against them, with the average claim amounting to no more than $1,200, many insurance companies nonetheless have limited coverage, lowered policy limits, and raised premiums by as much as 200 to

1,000 percent.[2] For liability reasons, among others, developers are encouraged to contract with seasoned professional providers. Recognizing that they are not themselves in the child care business, most developers are turning over facility operations to for-profit or not-for-profit agencies.

Costs and Subsidies. The fire and building codes for daycare centers are normally stricter than those applied to routine commercial uses. Thus, the centers cost more to construct. Startup costs for a modest-sized child care service range from $200,000 to $500,000.[3] The Washington Mutual Tower's new 2,000-square-foot center accommodating only 22 children cost about $250 a square foot. A daycare center, especially on the first floor, cannot pay anywhere near the kind of rent an owner could get from other tenants. Daycare is a labor-intensive operation, and labor is relatively costlier in downtowns than in suburbs. As daycare is increasingly seen as an attractive amenity in commercial buildings, developers are realizing that child care centers are marketing tools. Accordingly, they often prefer to finish the spaces themselves with high-quality materials and special design features that cost more than those an operator might provide.

The dauntingly steep costs of building and running downtown daycare centers make unsubsidized facilities economically infeasible. Without subsidies, downtown daycare cannot compete with centers in suburbs, where land costs, rents, salaries, and operating expenses are frequently lower.

A developer subsidy generally takes one of two forms, forgone rent or additional tenant improvements. Seattle's code prescribes that bonusable daycare space be turnkey, with the developer finishing the "ceilings, walls, flooring, and utility connections." Beyond these minimum requirements, any other improvements must be specified in the lease agreement between developer and operator. Although the center is not charged rent, the operator may be compelled to pay its share of such expenses as insur-

ance, utilities, and maintenance. San Francisco's code is explicit: the space for the required child care facility will be offered to a "nonprofit child care provider without charge for rent, utilities, property taxes, building services, or any other charges of any nature."

City planner Peter Spitzner of Hartford says that a goal of his city's daycare bonus is to ease the entry of low-wage workers into the job market, as well as to facilitate such workers' keeping their jobs. The city's child care zoning incentive, however, has no developer subsidy obligations or income limits on the clientele of the bonusable center. These matters are left entirely to the developer and operator to negotiate in their lease agreements. Similarly, in Cincinnati, developers need not subsidize the centers they put into their projects.

In Seattle, the developer subsidy is meant not only to lighten the financial burden for the provider and thereby better ensure the success of the operation, but also to make the service more accessible to low- and moderate-income downtown workers. Without the developer subsidy, the operator in the Washington Mutual Tower project would be hard pressed to set aside 20 percent of the spaces for the children of low-income workers, even though the service gets funds from the city, the state, and the United Way.

Billy Young, child care coordinator for the city of Seattle, observes that the city wanted its bonus to bring more than "yuppie daycare." However, an essentially two-tiered system has evolved, catering mostly to the wealthy and the poor, with few middle-class subscribers.

Notes

1. Remarks at daycare session of the ULI Semiannual Meeting in San Francisco, November 1988.
2. Lisa Walker, "Guess Who's Minding the Kids? Day Care at the Office," *Building Economics* (August 1986), p. 24.
3. Startup costs as of 1986, reported in ibid., p. 19.

CHAPTER 3

DEVELOPMENT AND DESIGN REVIEWS

BACKGROUND AND BRIEF SURVEY

Jonathan Barnett once described an urban designer as "someone who [knows] the answers to a lot of questions that no one is asking." [1] Today, he says, more people are asking the questions. The recent proliferation of development review procedures, design review guidelines, and other regulatory tools reflects the rise of visual literacy and the growing broadbased concern for urban design quality. (Because the two procedures—development review and design review—are generally overlapping processes and sometimes even coextensive ones, they are discussed together in this chapter.) The growing concern for quality has been propelled largely by major shifts in the urban political context over the last 20 years. The environmental conservation movement has established, among other achievements, the format for the environmental impact statement—a detailed review of the potential adverse effects of a development proposal. The historic preservation movement, essentially grounded in mainstream architectural philosophy, has promoted and still promotes the tenet that new development should be sensitive to the existing physical fabric.

Also within the last 20 years, a newly influential force on the urban development scene has been the community-based approval process, which goes hand-in-hand with proactive citizen intervention. "The new urban design," writes John Morris Dixon, editor of *Progressive Architecture*, "reflects the political reality of organized community reaction to development." [2] The so-called community architecture movement subscribes to the theory that potential users, not just property owners, should in effect have the final say on project size and shape. Whereas the privilege of developing major buildings once hinged on agreement between a city and a developer, the current initiative, in

many instances, is more of a trilateral agreement wherein the public must also accede to the proposal.

Defining "the public" may be difficult, for the public is multifaceted and often encompasses residents, local merchants, preservation and arts groups, the homeless, and many other diverse groups. Nonetheless, it has become increasingly important to involve the appropriate publics at the earliest opportunity and to listen to their concerns and objections at the planning stage rather than later, in the courtroom.

One way to elicit early public reaction is to involve the public directly in the process of creating a new zoning plan and specifically in formulating the development review and design guidelines. Another way is to encourage public input during the development review process. For example, New York City's Uniform Land Use Review Procedure (ULURP) establishes a system of public review through citizen "community boards"; in this way, New York ensures that certain zoning changes, negotiated bonus awards, special permits, franchise awards, and other discretionary actions undergo prompt review by the community boards and borough boards, as well as by the city planning commission and board of estimate. Although their input is advisory, the 59 community boards wield significant influence over development decisions. In Los Angeles, in response to citizen demands for citywide growth control, the city council recently authorized community planning advisory committees, one for each of the city's 35 community planning areas. The committees will review and analyze the community plans and make recommendations on future development.

The rise of urban design literacy is also seen in the realization that "rental response relates directly to a building's recognition factor on the skyline." [3] Long-time proponents of design excellence have been joined by corporation heads and developers who, increasingly, view good design as good for business and believe that high-quality design helps buildings hold their value.

Babcock and Weaver, who link the amount of interest in design to the proportion of corporate headquarters in a city, write that "[a]rchitectural inspiration to produce results needs a patron, and the Medicis of this era are the corporate chief executives." [4] As a developer for many of these modern-day Medicis, Gerald Hines has often teamed up with some of the country's most prestigious practitioners of what Ada Louise Huxtable calls the High Modern Corporate style. [5]

Within the last decade, other developers of speculative office buildings have also discovered that good design may be a marketable commodity for corporations seeking prestige. "What really upped the ante," notes Charlotte architect Gerard "Joddy" Peer, "was corporate expectations. If you have a major corporation investing a lot of money, a developer feels comfortable hiring an architect of more repute and asking for more design character in the building." [6] Similarly, developer Daniel Friedman, who hired Skidmore, Owings & Merrill to design a downtown office high rise in Hartford, observes that "tenants look to the credibility of a building's architect, and [of] its design, as an extension of their own credibility." [7] Architectural writer Paul M. Sachner remarks that "enlightened spec-office developers are beginning to realize what city builders in the 19th and early 20th centuries knew all along: that the fiscal exigencies of the bottom line by no means preclude the time-honored architectural principles of firmness, commodity, and delight." [8]

It is important, however, to differentiate between dramatic or high-image buildings and good urban design, two distinct goals that may prove incompatible in practice. San Francisco's 1970s Urban Design Plan, for example, tried in part to deal with the proliferation of corporate-sponsored, high-image "look-at-me" buildings. Some planning and design professionals felt that these structures ignored basic urban design principles and detracted from the overall harmony and continuity of the cityscape. In like fashion, these same urban designers would be more apt to praise the residential buildings at, say, New York's Battery Park City, which unobtrusively blend into a unified whole, than some of the architectural tour de forces of Philip Johnson, for instance.

Finally, the rise in visual literacy is also evidenced in the heightened emphasis on urban design requirements as integral parts of the development review process. One method that is fast gaining support is that of treating the entire downtown as a distinct development review or design zone, with separate design elements required for it besides those for the rest of the city. Whereas design review traditionally has been reserved for projects needing some discretionary action or special permit, many cities now require such review for as-of-right projects, too.

Each city takes its own tack. As stated, some cities integrate design review criteria into the overall development review, whereas others treat design review as a separate procedure. Design guidelines are sometimes folded into the actual zoning code, sometimes published separately. The present discussion focuses almost solely on those development and design review procedures that are incorporated into zoning regulations and omits procedures that are exercised only as a matter of policy.

The development review process may involve several layers of separate reviews. In many cities, major projects are analyzed for potential environmental impacts and historic preservation consequences, as well as for architectural compatibility; these reviews are often written into the overall site plan review. Each of these reviews may trigger a distinct set of design criteria. Elsewhere, design review is a significant component of the local historic preservation ordinance. Alternatively, design considerations may form part of the environmental review for such effects as shadows, glare, sun access, and wind. Thus, in such cities as Pittsburgh and Seattle, neither of which has a design review requirement per se, downtown projects nonetheless must comply with a rigorous set of design standards imposed through the development review process. (The environmental impacts of tall buildings are the exclusive concern of Chapter 6.)

This blending of various development and design review approaches is an accelerating trend in downtowns nationwide. The remainder of this chapter looks at varied methods of design review, including special district guidelines, design criteria for incentive bonus features, design review as a means to density bonuses, and review of public projects. Studies of the overall development review process in Pittsburgh, Portland, Oregon, and Bellevue, Washington, conclude the chapter.

THE SPECIAL DISTRICT APPROACH

Many design guidelines were first devised to set apart and protect distinctive neighborhoods, primarily historic districts. Special regulations governing the scale and types of buildings, their responses to their contexts, and their use of particular building materials were written to preserve historic structures and neighborhoods. Design standards were later concocted for other special feature areas, such as retail, theater, arts, and waterfront districts.

Of New York's 34 special districts, the most famous are its theater and retail districts. Zoning for the Fifth Avenue Special District, for instance, demands that some three-quarters of the frontage along the Avenue be reserved for retail uses, that street walls rise to between 85 and 125 feet to preserve continuous street patterns, and that major new projects be set back from the Avenue.

Although no city has followed to the same degree New York's extreme example of fracturing its downtown into special districts, many cities apply disparate sets of regulations, specially sensitized to different parts of the downtown. Concerning retail, requirements or incentives for street-level shopping uses are typically reserved for development within the retail core, rather than throughout the city. Some downtowns also impose more stringent height limits in the retail sector, as in areas next to waterfronts. Curtailed building heights, which let in a modicum of sunlight and help diminish wind tunnel effects, enhance the quality of the pedestrian streetscape, which is all-important to a healthy retail climate. In addition, retail districts are often rich in historic structures, so that the height limits in the retail cores of Portland and Seattle, for instance, also work to encourage preservation of their downtowns' terra cotta–decorated buildings, as well as to promote retail.

Special district–type zoning regulations have spawned a myriad of design guidelines. Whether a city is protecting views of its capitol building with a capitol interest district (as are Washington, D.C., Austin, and Tallahassee) or preserving berthing for commercial fishing boats from the onslaught of gentrified wharfs (as is Portland, Maine, in its waterfront zone), special district zoning and its accompanying guidelines are tailor-made to encourage or discourage given activities or uses.

DESIGN REVIEW OF BONUS FEATURES

Another type of specialized design review process is that applied to bonus features within incentive zoning systems, such as those used in Cincinnati, Portland, Oregon, New York, Hartford, Bellevue, Washington, and Seattle. In the cases of Cincinnati and Seattle, where design review for private projects is minimal, the separate sets of bonus review criteria that must be met to earn the increased density func-

tion partly as design guidelines. As discussed earlier in this book, a rising dissatisfaction with the negligible public benefits gained from some bonus items has spurred cities to insert specific standards into their second-generation bonus systems.

HARTFORD

In 1983, city planners conjectured that mandatory design review would be the most incendiary issue of Hartford's new Downtown Development District zoning. Would projects be denied for failing to pass design review? Hartford's 1984 incentive zoning code did in fact create a five-member review board appointed by the city council, but it has advisory powers only. (The board's decisions can be overturned by the council, and have been on several occasions). The review board's authority was later expanded beyond the Downtown Development District to take in several neighborhood commercial districts as well.

The initial review criteria, as stated in the code, were quite general:

> Where reviewing a project . . . the board will determine whether the applicant has demonstrated that the project:
> (a) Creates an attractive environment that is in harmony with the . . . downtown district;
> (b) Is compatible with and enhances the design concept of adjacent buildings; and
> (c) Encourages an active and vital pedestrian environment.
> In making its determination, the board will consider criteria such as massing, height, materials, color, harmony and proportion of overall design, architectural style, siting, scale, and fenestration.

As project applications were submitted under the new code and developers proposed including bonus features to get more leasable commercial space, it quickly became clear that extra design review guidelines were needed. Architects and developers wanted the rules spelled out in advance, and investors wanted additional assurance that all projects would be judged by the same rules and that a long-range plan existed. Therefore, the review board issued a more detailed set of guidelines in 1986, with more explicit evaluation standards for the nine available bonus features. The stated goal of the guidelines is "to encourage design excellence expressing human scale, richness, and variety within the urban environment."

The new guidelines specify those precise elements that must be included to qualify for density bonuses. The special criteria the design review board is directed to consider in its review of bonus floor area make it crystal-clear that the bonus award is not automatic. The main design considerations, over and above the general requirement of a demonstrated need for the proposed benefit, are that the location affords maximum public exposure and that the design follows as closely as possible the criteria outlined in the supplementary bonus guidelines. Hartford's chief staff planner, Peter Spitzner, notes that in several intances, density credits have indeed been denied where the guidelines were not followed, and that the bonus guidelines have afforded the city greater control over the development review process.

In addition to design review, new projects in downtown Hartford must also undergo basic site plan review or bonus project review, if applicable. Whereas Hartford publishes its bonus guidelines separately from its downtown code, Cincinnati and Bellevue integrate theirs into the code language.

SEATTLE

Unlike Hartford and Bellevue, Seattle requires no comprehensive design review for private projects and has chosen instead to address many urban design issues through the vehicle of its full-blown bonus review system. At one time, the city considered and then rejected the idea of enacting administrative design review in the downtown, although design guidelines have been written for the three special districts within the downtown—the International District, Pioneer Square, and Pike Place Market.

Seattle's criteria for each of its 28 public benefit features function to some extent as downtown design guidelines. They are only triggered, however, when a developer applies for a particular bonus amenity to qualify for additional density, and therefore they operate on a piecemeal basis. Serving a quasi–design review function, the criteria for the public benefit features are exhaustively detailed.

The city's bonus system is explained in a comprehensive report referred to as *Director's Rule 11-85,* which is published separately from the code. Local architects and developers observe that the stupefying list of bonus guidelines at least informs them in advance of the exact criteria that must be met to qualify for bonus gains and thus makes the development review process relatively predictable. Although some of the bonus selections are subject to discretionary review, the system's across-the-board approach is seen by some proponents as preferable to the highly subjective design review programs used by some other cities.

Many of the bonus features and accompanying guidelines were inspired by Seattle's existing landmarks and successful urban spaces. The whimsical art deco cap topping the Smith Tower (1914), for example, was the prototype for the sculptured rooftop

bonus. And the hillclimb assist bonus, designed to aid pedestrians on sites abutting steeply sloping streets, was patterned after the escalator built into an earlier office tower to ease a demanding east/west climb.

DESIGN REVIEW ITSELF AS BONUS FEATURE

Various cities, including Bethesda, Maryland, Coral Gables, Florida, Cincinnati, and Boston, award greater density in return for submitting to design review. Bethesda, which has evolved from a sleepy suburb of Washington, D.C., into a bustling urban office center, encourages dense development around the local subway station and allows much greater densities for those projects submitting to design review and following a set of design guidelines. The process is akin to the special review procedures and site-specific design reviews for planned unit developments.

CORAL GABLES, FLORIDA

In the mid-1980s, Coral Gables adopted a unique architectural review ordinance that promotes the use of the Mediterranean style for new construction and renovation of commercial projects and apartment buildings. In this context, the "Mediterranean style" refers to classical architectural traditions, including colonial, Spanish, Venetian, and Italianate design. The purpose of the ordinance is to "enhance the image of the city by providing a visual linkage between contemporary development and the city's unique historic thematic appearance."

Those projects within the Mediterranean Overlay District that comply with the architectural review may earn greater density or height allowances. For example, the number of apartment units permitted under the city's zoning regulations may be hiked up to 25 percent. Existing structures not originally designed in the Mediterranean style may, with appropriate renovation, earn one extra square foot of floor area for each six square feet of gross renovated floor area. Projects applying for bonus allowances must also provide such amenities as retail at the ground floor, pedestrian courtyards, arcades and loggias, underground parking, and landscaping beyond the minimum code requirement.

Projects applying for bonuses also must follow the city's Mediterranean style guidelines and undergo review by the municipal board of architects. The guidelines hold up as models several existing structures built in the Mediterranean style and include a list of general stylistic characteristics, including tile roofs, textured stucco exteriors, arcades and loggias, wrought-iron detailing, and ceramic tile accents.

CINCINNATI

In downtown Cincinnati, design review is one of the bonus options under the city's 1987 incentive zoning scheme. The bonus is equivalent to a 20 percent increase in density. Whereas design review is voluntary as a bonus option, it is mandatory under three circumstances: 1) for parking garages included in mixed-use projects or for parking facilities that constitute the major part of a building, 2) for large-scale projects in which the total bonus floor area exceeds one-third of the base building floor area, and 3) for projects in which a developer wants to deviate from bonus criteria spelled out in the code.

Design review was apparently one of the most hotly contested features of the new code and was challenged by the business and development community, as well as by the city's economic development department. Although Cincinnati's urban design review board, which is appointed by the city manager and reports directly to the director of economic development, had routinely subjected major downtown projects to design review under the old zoning, the economic development department vehemently opposed mandatory review and adoption of design guidelines. (Design guidelines were only implemented for parking structures.) The department preferred to continue negotiating design quality on a project-by-project basis and was loath to have its hands tied when the city's heretofore freewheeling design review approach was codified.

Therefore, although design review is an integral part of Cincinnati's downtown development review process, the system has its quirks. For instance, although the design review responsibility is clearly ascribed in the code, the urban design review board is never actually named, nor are its composition and specific powers. This deliberate omission was undoubtedly intended to preserve the flexibility of the old code's modus operandi. The reasoning seemed to be that the advisory design review would be more effective and the board would wield (or retain) more clout if reference to it remained ambiguous in the new zoning regulations.

Babcock and Weaver describe this kind of behavior as "the say-nothing approach" to zoning. It rests on the belief that "procedure checks power. To the extent that the administrative structure and the standards governing it can be nebulous, the power of those who control the process is enhanced."[9]

The Rector Place neighborhood at Battery Park City, New York.

DESIGN REVIEW FOR PUBLIC PROJECTS

Although in-depth discussion of public agency design guidelines exceeds the scope of this book, brief reference should be made to one of the most talked-about urban designs of the decade—Battery Park City in New York. This unprecedented 92-acre planned community, standing on a landfill site (most of which resulted from the digging of the foundations for the World Trade Center), juts into the Hudson River along Lower Manhattan. The roaring success of the project's design program has been traced, in part, to the inventive master plan and accompanying design guidelines prepared by Cooper Eckstut Associates. The plan and guidelines require architects to mold the exteriors of residential buildings into a fluid street wall with masonry on the first two stories, brick on the walls above, nonrectangular rooflines, and prominent cornice edges.

The residences in Battery Park City are interspersed with carefully defined public open spaces. Although some of these landscaped areas are rather formal, any New Yorker would feel at home with the sidewalks' hexagonal pavers and with the traditional black iron fences. The guidelines were modeled after "New York's durable successes—the romantic office towers of Lower Manhattan and the finely textured buildings of the city's older neighborhoods,"[10] such as Central Park West and Riverside Drive, thus creating an instant identity. For instance, the highly urbane personality of Rector Park at Battery Park City generally echoes that of Gramercy Park.

Rector Place was the first residential neighborhood to be completed under the guidelines for Battery Park City. These specify such details as locations of lobby

Rector Park, which looks to Gramercy Park for its concept.

T.J. Lassar

entrances, curb cuts, and sidewalk dimensions, in addition to the general heights and shapes of buildings. Architects were also told where balconies were permitted (sparingly, on upper floors only), what the entrances should look like, which colors and materials to use generally, and the like. Although many architects view the guidelines as creating a necessary order, some say a few design elements are too strict. Specifications for lobby entrance locations caused disruptive layout problems inside some buildings. Equally unpopular was the requirement on certain streets for covered shopping arcades—a rule that has spawned undesirably dark, shadowy retail areas.

Criticism also has been leveled at the state-created Battery Park City Authority's seeming lack of flexibility in putting the guidelines to work. The authority's review process requires, for instance, a sign-off at every stage of a building's design, making it extremely difficult for architects to change any early decisions after the schematic and design development stages. On the other hand, what makes this "despotic system" work, says Paul Goldberger, is that "it has been managed by remarkably enlightened despots."[11]

EVALUATION OF DESIGN GUIDELINES

Deftly written guidelines can undoubtedly help clarify planning goals and diminish some of the uncertainty many design review procedures pose for prospective developers. However, unless the guidelines are integrated into the zoning or incorporated by reference, cities should not assume compliance with design directives that are only advisory.

Design guidelines may be particularly useful during the first phase of a new zoning system, helping educate developers and architects about the requirements and incentives. Hartford architects said they were confused about what they had to do to qualify

for various bonus items until the planning department issued a set of guidelines for the amenity features. Likewise, Bellevue supplements its performance-based design criteria, which are generally described in the code, with detailed separate design guidelines. These more explicit guidelines focus on those development types deemed most needed in the Bellevue downtown—namely, projects on the pedestrian corridor and on the street edge.

Increasingly, cities are supplementing written design standards with visual aids and guidebooks. In Charlotte, the illustrations are woven into the fabric of the zoning text. Portland, Oregon, publishes a separate book of its downtown design guidelines that examines the various issues each guideline addresses and includes many photographs, historic maps, and engravings for clarification. Other cities illustrate the design approaches that should be avoided.

An additional consideration is the age-old internal taffy pull between the desirability of flexibility and the need for clarity and certainty. The most detailed specifications cannot guarantee design excellence. Furthermore, too much detail may stymie the best solutions. Although design requirements must be specified, the good intentions and skills of the developer and architect ultimately matter more than the literal wording of the requirements. (See section on legislating design in Chapter 5, "Zoning As Shaper of Building Design.")

Christopher Duerksen cautions against guidelines that concentrate mainly on detailed building design and notes that "[u]nless the community desires buildings of a distinct architectural style, it may be well advised to set general parameters to control height and other specific characteristics (such as requiring distinctive rooflines) and leave the actual building design in the hands of the developer's architect."[12]

Writing about Nantucket's historic district guidelines, Jonathan Barnett states that although the guidelines "are clear[,] . . . go right down to details of building materials [, and] can prevent egregiously incompetent buildings," they may "also screen out unconventional and inventive designs." He notes that architect Robert Venturi, who has designed several houses on the island, has had a number of run-ins with the local historic districts commission of sufficient intensity to cause his firm to refuse any future projects on the island.[13]

LEGAL CONSIDERATIONS

When formulating design guidelines, cities also need to consider the legal ramifications. The more detailed the design standards, the less vulnerable they will be to possible constitutional due-process or void-for-vagueness challenges in state courts. Design review systems are rife with vague, broad-sweeping phrases such as "will not adversely affect," "will be compatible with," and "must be harmonious."

Aesthetic zoning has come of age since the U.S. Supreme Court's decision in *Berman* v. *Parker*.[14] The Court, in approving urban renewal in the nation's capital, endorsed the use of aesthetic regulation as a valid exercise of the police power. Many states now base the constitutionality of their aesthetic standards, including those used in design and historic preservation review, on a broad reading of the general welfare clause of the police powers provision. It should be noted, however, that only a minority of jurisdictions now sanction aesthetics alone as a legitimate public purpose, and the majority rule is that aesthetic motivation must be coupled with other factors such as economic considerations.[15]

Courts also carefully scrutinize architectural review standards that call for some similarity and compatibility or, alternatively, that ban cookie-cutter development with anti-lookalike regulations.[16] The first type of regulation prohibits wayward departures from the prevailing design standards in the area, whereas the second type legislates against monotony.

Whereas many courts mandate such strict review standards, a minority of state courts, like those of Illinois and New Jersey, require that aesthetic land use regulation be achieved only through "objective" criteria and are inclined to prescribe only those "subjective" standards aimed at ensuring design compatibility. In *Morristown Road Associates* v. *Mayor and Common Council and Planning Board*, for example, a New Jersey court struck down an ordinance dictating that new development must "harmonize with existing buildings," on the grounds that it neither adequately limited the administrative decision process nor set clear criteria for judicial review.[17]

One solution is for ordinances to state explicitly that a structure must be harmonious with reference to such specific items as materials, colors, gradelines, and cornice edges.

Similarly, in incentive zoning systems, bonus design standards are sometimes highly subjective and need interpretation. What, for instance, should be made of the requirement that a plaza should promote "a high level of activity" or be "publicly accessible"?[18]

Even apart from the potential legal difficulties, vague, overly broad design review criteria may be notoriously difficult to administer and enforce. For example, vague criteria used for development review of

projects taller than 45 feet in Portland, Maine's downtown waterfront zone—"will be compatible in scale, bulk, and massing with neighboring buildings," "will not unduly obstruct or adversely affect significant public scenic views," and "will not obscure natural or manmade prominent visual landmarks"—defy precise interpretation and therefore are hard to enforce. One criterion has indeed been the subject of a legal dispute.

DEVELOPMENT AND DESIGN REVIEW CASE STUDIES

PITTSBURGH

Zoning for Pittsburgh's downtown, the Golden Triangle, calls for discretionary, or "project development plan," review for almost every new structure downtown and for all additions or alterations costing more than $50,000. Although the city has no design review per se, various design elements are incorporated into the overall development application process. Once the zoning administrator determines that all objective requirements of the code are met, the planning commission reviews the project, using the 14 general review criteria (see Insert 1). These criteria run the gamut of topics, including corridor view protection, access to public transport, traffic generation characteristics, provision of parking loading areas, open space functions, and architectural relationships with surrounding buildings. Design review, therefore, is an integral part of the downtown zoning ordinance and of the development review process.

Insert 1.
Pittsburgh's General Development Review Criteria (code excerpt)

(1) Provision of parking and loading areas and proposed vehicular access in relation to street capacity, . . . functional classification, and land use patterns;
(2) Traffic generation characteristics in relation to street capacity, classification, and existing and projected traffic volumes;
(3) Pedestrian traffic generation, proposed pedestrian circulation facilities, and patterns;
(4) Access to public transportation facilities;
(5) Use characteristics of proposed development, provisions for maintenance of retail facilities and [for] continuity in applicable C5 Subdistricts;
(6) Use characteristics of proposed development and provision for residential uses in applicable C5 Subdistricts;
(7) Preservation of historic structures;
(8) Architectural relationships with surrounding buildings, including building siting, massing, facade treatment, materials, proportion, scale, color, maintenance of street walls, parapet and fenestration treatments, and design of building tops;
(9) Microclimate effects of proposed development, including wind velocities, sun reflectance and sun access to streets, existing buildings, and public, urban, and usable open space;

(10) Protection of views and view corridors;
(11) Location, development, and functions of urban open space;
(12) Location, development, and functions of usable open space;
(13) Barrier-free design [access for the handicapped];
(14) Preservation of significant features of existing buildings.

For many years, the city used zoning-sanctioned site plan review for downtown projects, but review powers were narrowly limited to curb cuts, open space requirements, and the like. Under the expanded project development plan review, in place since 1983, more explicit site requirements than those in the general criteria are left open until an actual project is proposed.

The specific elements of each of the 14 review criteria are worked out, project by project. The open space standards are the only criteria with written guidelines: Pittsburgh has a mandatory 20 percent open space requirement. The open space guidelines (detailed in Chapter 8, "Open Space and Street-scapes") have been written into the seven "urban space standards" for the Golden Triangle.

Once a proposal is submitted, development review guidelines are completed within about 30 days. The code does not require that a developer come in for preliminary review. However, if developers fail to meet early with the city, they will miss those often crucial preliminary signals about specifics and may jeopardize the success of their projects.

Pittsburgh's administrative review provides scant opportunity for community participation measures like public hearings. Because there is virtually no residential constituency in the compact downtown, this omission has not posed a major problem. In a larger, more populated downtown, of course, it becomes more important to have some procedure for inviting public input.

One of the strengths of the city's development review process, according to Deputy Planning Director Paul Farmer, is that the "significant public interest issues are laid out in advance on a site-by-site basis, making for a process of negotiation rather than confrontation." For major projects, site-specific plans and design criteria are issued by the planning department (which staffs the planning commission) as early as possible, preferably before an architect is hired. As of June 1987, some 80 projects had undergone development review, and formal site-specific plans and expectations had been prepared for eight others. Historically, many cities have reserved site-specific review for larger projects, but in Pittsburgh, both private and city-initiated land-sale projects are subject to the same development review process, with similar design

guideline procedures for public and private developers.

Urban designer Jonathan Barnett has consulted with the city for almost 10 years and has helped draw up some of its more comprehensive reviews, such as the one undertaken for the PPG Industries headquarters. Barnett characterizes the review criteria as

performance specification[s], describing the urban design and planning problems that need to be solved and the nature of a satisfactory resolution, without spelling out how the building should be designed. In this way, the city is on record from the beginning of the project concerning the issues that are of greatest importance to the public interest, but an arbitrary design strait jacket is not created.[19]

PPG Place, covering the equivalent of two city blocks, consists of a 40-story tower and five attendant buildings. It uses a castellated architectural motif and is sheathed entirely in 1 million square feet of the trademark reflective glass. The project was to be located south of Market Square, a public park. However, the project's impact on the sunlight available to neighboring public open spaces was one of the city's review criteria, and architect Philip Johnson's original design involved a tower that would have blocked all sunlight from Market Square between the hours of noon and 2:00 p.m. Here was a prime example of a conflict between the goals of urban design and those of dramatic high-image architecture. Although Johnson purportedly trashed the review criteria, the tower was reconfigured and moved to the west to preserve sunlight in the square. Barnett ascribes the major redesign to the fact that sun access was one of the development review elements.[20]

According to Barnett, the ad hoc development review process that appears to allow Pittsburgh "to exercise an undefined amount of discretionary authority"[21] is reined in, to some extent, by the spelled-out review criteria. Once the major design decisions have been made according to the individualized review criteria, the city's power to raise new issues or impose later requirements is limited.[22] Moreover, the planning commission's final decision must "include a description of the specific site improvements and developments and development characteristics upon which its approval is conditioned." These conditions are binding on the applicant, whose only recourse is a court appeal.

It has been pointed out that this seemingly highly discretionary review process counterbalances Pittsburgh's relatively permissive zoning and generous FAR limits. Two downtown districts with maximum FARs of 13 have no explicit height limits, while the remaining three districts, with maximum FARs of 7.5, have height limits based on a series of inclined planes to preserve river views. Until 1983, computation of the project site area was based on adjacent street center lines, so that major projects in the core could effectively achieve as-of-right FARs of 17. (Since 1983, the FAR has been based on the actual lot size instead of the street center line, reducing allowed densities.)

The site-specific criteria for every major downtown project are part of the public record, as is the commission's final written decision granting approval or disapproval. Out-of-town developers and architects who have never participated in Pittsburgh's review procedure are encouraged to examine these documents. But although the planning commission's philosophy has not changed over the past 10 years, no guarantee exists within the highly discretionary system that yesterday's reasoning will be applied to any of tomorrow's projects.

PORTLAND, OREGON

Theoretically, close attention to architectural quality and urban design is more likely in downtowns with competitive real estate markets, and aggressive regulatory systems are more effective in jurisdictions where development demand is high. In Portland, however, despite the sometimes sluggish economy, urban design matters have often generated sustained interest and have generally held a high priority.

Unlike the Gold Rush speculators who set the boom/bust pace for development in San Francisco and Seattle, the second sons of New England's Brahmin families, who helped settle Portland, established a fairly conservative approach to growth. Portland architect Greg Baldwin says Portland never joined in the furor of speculative office building that swept through many cities in the last decade; after all, "everything in Portland is earned."

Portland's architectural legacy bears the rich imprint of New England design. Many Portland architectural icons were designed by Bostonian or Boston-trained architects. These landmarks include the terra cotta–fronted Meier and Frank department store and the Portland Hotel, now demolished, which once stood on the site of Pioneer Courthouse Square. Pietro Belluschi, the doyen of Portland architecture, sustained the cross-fertilization between the two cities and purchased the Portland firm of Whidden and Lewis, then sold it to Skidmore, Owings & Merrill when he took over as dean of MIT's school of architecture. Robert Frasca, partner in one of Portland's

leading architectural firms, Zimmer Gunsul Frasca (ZGF), in turn studied under Belluschi at MIT.

Compared with the development climate in some cities, particularly those located in the Southwest and in oil-dependent states, Portland's relatively low vacancy rate for class-A office space is enviable. Yet the city has only managed to pull itself out of the recession within the last several years. During the lean years of the early 1980s, however, Portland did manage to implement one of the country's most comprehensive urban design review systems.

Portland's Design Zone overlays the entire downtown, and virtually all new projects must address the 22 design guidelines. These standards focus primarily on the relationships between buildings and their contexts, including streetscapes and adjacent buildings. In 1988, the Design Zone was expanded to cover all areas within the Central City Plan. The guidelines are intended to implement the following goals:

1) Enhance the existing character of Portland's downtown;
2) Promote the development of diversity and areas of special character within the downtown;
3) Provide for a pleasant, rich, and diverse pedestrian experience; and
4) Provide for the humanization of the downtown through promotion of the arts and excellence in design.

The 1972 Downtown Plan was translated into zoning in 1979, and the guidelines were implemented a year later. Michael Harrison, the city planner who drafted the guidelines in 1977, attempted to create a system that would learn from and build on its past. Harrison says that although urban design issues were taken seriously in the mid-1970s, the development review process of the time was hopelessly fragmented. Major development proposals provoked heated debates over design issues and generated endless hours of testimony, which only started all over again with each new project.

Design Guidelines. Adopted in 1980, the 22 guidelines are tiered in order of importance. For example, maintaining the integrity of the downtown's 200-foot-long blocks, which make for extraordinarily legible streets, is a high priority and is listed as the first guideline: "Preserve the present grid pattern typical of downtown Portland's public right-of-ways [sic] and the ratio of open space to buildings that it produces." The design principles are illustrated with maps, historic engravings, and photographs of old and new buildings.

Each guideline is amplified by a short discussion of the pertinent issues. In the case of the tight block system, this discussion reads:

> Portland's small blocks and frequent streets provide greater open space, light, air, and more direct pedestrian travel than is typically available in city centers. When the ground floors of new development projects are allowed to occupy more than a single block, these characteristics of the downtown are lost.

Although a frequently stated principle is that large development sites afford greater flexibility, Portland's tight blocks have not seemed to stifle building creativity and have functioned more as an asset and a challenge than a constraint. One writer notes that there is a "miniaturizing ethos" to Portland's 200-foot-long blocks, and that the expansive north/south avenues "strategically orient downtown buildings toward the sun." [23]

According to Michael Harrison, although the guidelines are qualitative rather than quantitative, they are applied literally. In addition, many of them reinforce and overlap with specific code requirements for the Downtown Development Zone. For example, Portland's 1982 skywalk policy, which severely limits new overhead connections, is buttressed by the design guidelines addressing view protection and structures over the rights-of-way. Likewise, the code provisions that mandate a percentage of retail uses at the ground level on some downtown streets and that prohibit blank walls are strengthened further by those guidelines dealing with maintenance of the street wall, differentiation of the ground level from the upper floors, and provision of secure, comfortable stopping places for pedestrians. One guideline, entitled "Corners That Build Intersections," focuses on the importance of corner treatment at intersections. For instance, when a project stands at the intersection of two pedestrianways, the guideline encourages retail entryways at the corner, where the retail will be more visible and thus more marketable.

When Portland officials set about the task of implementing the 1972 Downtown Plan, they briefly considered but ultimately dismissed the idea of using bonus incentives to achieve certain design amenities. They rejected the bonus route because they thought some design considerations so important they should be mandated via code provisions; furthermore, design guidelines should apply to each and every project instead of changing with the vagaries of the market. (In 1988, however, the city did adopt an incentive zoning scheme with passage of the Central City Plan, which covers the downtown.)

According to Greg Baldwin, one of the virtues of Portland's design guidelines is that they distribute more evenly the burden of compliance. In some cities, the design review process puts the city in a defensive position, whereas in Portland, developers must take the initiative and demonstrate that their proposals meet the intent of the guidelines.

Another virtue noted by Baldwin and other Portland architects is the flexible way the city interprets both the guidelines and the design-related code provisions. For example, the requirement to break up blank walls with views into retail, office, or lobby spaces may be met in some circumstances by substituting an artwork. In the same way, the height limit and the 75 percent required building line on designated streets are subject to adjustment and, in rare situations, to exemption. The goal is to meet the intent, not the letter, of the code. The city has also occasionally waived some of the design guidelines on a given project and considered alternative design solutions, if it could be demonstrated that the alternative approach carried out more closely the intent of the city's downtown design policy.

The Guidelines and the Public Sector. The city's design guidelines apply to both public and private projects. Some jurisdictions exempt city-initiated projects from zoning requirements and design review. But projects sponsored by the Portland Development Commission (PDC), as well as by other city and state agencies, must comply not only with the special development guidelines written by the PDC for the individual renewal districts, but also with the downtown zoning provisions and design guidelines.

RiverPlace. The PDC-sponsored mixed-use development called RiverPlace, the first phase of a 10-acre project in Portland's South Waterfront Renewal District, was subject to review under both sets of design guidelines. The Seattle-based Cornerstone Columbia Development Company won a competition to develop the project in 1985.

One major design concern shared by both the PDC and the city's design commission was the site's high visibility from freeways, bridges, and downtown office towers. Therefore, rooftop variety, with no flat roofs permitted on structures of fewer than five stories, became one of the controlling design standards. The successful mélange of gabled and other sloping roof types emphasizes the project's largely residential character and confirms the overall neighborhood theme. In addition, the round-arched dormers and peaked roofs of the RiverPlace Athletic Club make for a recognizable profile on the sloped site.

City design goals that proved harder to accomplish in RiverPlace were those requiring maintenance of the

T. J. Lassar

Privacy and security concerns had to be weighed in planning the pedestrian paths leading from the public spaces throughout RiverPlace, Portland, Oregon.

integrity of the 200-foot blocks and of north/south and east/west pedestrian access routes. Reinforcing "active pedestrian-oriented uses on the north/south avenues" is one of the city's design guidelines. However, construction of connecting pedestrian paths throughout the multiblock RiverPlace—which crammed hotel, residential, restaurant, marina, office, and retail uses into an inordinately tight triangular site—raised privacy and security concerns. A compromise was reached by building an east/west pedestrian path cutting through the project to the public esplanade along the Willamette River. Unfortunately, gates close off this path in the evening. The sole north/south connection is the city-built walk extending the length of the esplanade, a favorite haunt of strollers.

Apparently, the only real disagreement between the two review processes came over the issue of covered moorage in the marina. The PDC conjectured that owners would want to shelter their expensive boats, while the city design commission said the exposed moorage would enhance the marina's image. The city won out, and high demand for the prime location has compensated for any loss engendered by the open moorage.

Former PDC Project Manager Brian McCarl emphasizes that although the city's design policy was closely followed in the execution of the project, other considerations probably mattered more at the project selection stage. The developer's management capability, previous experience with similar projects, financial strength, and development team composition were among these concerns. McCarl says Portland is not interested in staging beauty pageants.

In theory, the PDC considers the city's guidelines in advance and inserts them into its own project guidelines, thereby meshing the two reviews. But because the PDC functions in part as an advocate for private developers, it does not have the same degree of commitment to the city guidelines as do the design commission and the planning bureau. Herein lies a potential tension between the design review conducted by the city and that done by the development commission.

Development Review Process. Preapplication review is the trend nationwide. Most planning departments urge developers and architects to discuss informally their preliminary plans with the city at the earliest possible date. In Portland, a preapplication conference is part of the mandatory review procedure. At the conference, developers, planning staff, and representatives of varied city departments and neighborhood organizations outline the issues and flag potential problems. Once a formal application is submitted to the planning bureau, it is circulated to all interested city agencies, which must respond by a given date. The agencies' input is combined in a staff report, written by the planning bureau.

Major projects warrant public hearings, and staff reports must be available to the public at least 10 days before the hearings. Also, the staff report must address each of the design guidelines. Harriet Sherburne, former vice president of Cornerstone Columbia Development Company, comments that not only has Portland gone further than most cities in stating precise design guidelines, but it also budgets sufficient funds to hire adequate staff to interpret and implement them. Three full-time staff members and one part-time staffer work on design review issues citywide. The fee charged for design review partially supports the staff. About 200 downtown projects undergo design review each year; of these, some 30 go to hearings.

The citizen-member design commission, with its one liaison person from the planning commission, issues a decision within 10 days of the hearing. Although the staff report's recommendations are often dispositive, the commission need not base its decision on the report. The commission's decision is final but appealable to the city council and then to the courts.

An additional level of review is that conducted by the hearings land use officer. Much as in Washington State, the Portland hearings officer reviews most so-called discretionary decisions—partial waivers or exemptions from code provisions, variances, and conditional use permits, including permits to build structured parking garages on surface lots within the downtown. As part of the overall design review, the design commission makes the first determination on compliance with code requirements, such as the reservation of a percentage of a building's ground floor for retail use and the blank wall limitation. The commission also wields the authority to grant departures from these requirements. But most major projects in downtown Portland call for some form of discretionary review by the hearing officer (these reviews generally concern parking issues).

Harriet Sherburne, who is a member of Portland's design commission, characterizes Portland's review process as "remarkably speedy." Total review time for RiverPlace, from preapplication conference to public hearing, was six weeks, probably the average review time in Portland. Sherburne ascribes Portland's accelerated review time partly to the explicit design guidelines, which announce in advance the city's expectations and goals. Local and out-of-town architects generally agree that the effective review procedures, combined with the clearly phrased guidelines, inject a welcome modicum of certainty into Portland's development application process.

The Capital Web and Civic Design. During the heyday of the urban renewal era, Edward J. Logue, first New Haven's director of redevelopment and then Boston's, worked out an outrageously successful system in both cities to leverage local capital projects and generate unprecedented sums of federal investment. David Crane, Boston's former planning director, translated this strategy into the theory of the capital web, whereby "public investment became the framework for controlling the location and timing of all investment in an area." [24]

Urban designer Jonathan Barnett could be describing Portland's use of the capital web in its approach to civic architecture and municipal investment when he writes that "[i]f public investment policies are viewed strategically, as a means of carrying out urban design objectives as well as providing the solution to immediate problems, the design of the city can be greatly enhanced." [25]

Portland has relied heavily on public capital improvements to stimulate private investments and to upgrade building design and has spelled out this connection in its 1972 Downtown Plan. For instance, architect Greg Baldwin talks about the "shaping power" of transportation; indeed, Portland's transit mall has generated an estimated 2 million square feet of public/private space within the last 15 years. Much of this space otherwise might have been built in the suburbs without the transportation improvements. A mixed-use project, Pacwest Center, somewhat re-

moved from the heart of the retail core, extended the bus transit mall to its own doorstep, complete with the attendant improvements—brick pavers, street fixtures and furniture, planters, and landscaping. Another major office tower, One Financial Center, made similar improvements in order to link with the light-rail line.

As previously noted, the city development agency conforms for the most part with the code and design guidelines in city-sponsored projects. As a result, Portland's civic buildings are unusually lively and extroverted. The ZGF-designed Justice Center, which houses the municipal courts, jail, and police department, incorporates a restaurant, delicatessen, hair salon, and camera shop on the ground floor, in addition to public art displays. Even public parking garages sport retail space at the street level. Built on a public park across from the ill-famed Portland Building (which turns its back on the park, a garage dominating its entryway), the Justice Center attempts to serve a wider public and create a rapport with its surroundings.

Robert Frasca observes that the city's involvement in and commitment to quality in architectural design should not be underestimated. The city knows the precedent-setting function of municipal buildings and so tries to imbue them with a civic character through the use of superior materials, thoughtful design, and public art throughout. In spurring private building through its public investment in the downtown, Portland has succeeded in leveraging design excellence. This phenomenon Frasca calls the "peer pressure of good design."

BELLEVUE

"They used to call it Car City. Strip Commercial. The land of endless asphalt, no sidewalks, and boredom. The quintessential suburban city of the '50s." [26] Today, however, Bellevue, Washington, an erstwhile suburb of some 85,000 people, is making an all-out effort to turn its downtown into an intensely urban place.[27] Neal Peirce remarks that "of all America's big suburbs-turned-city, Bellevue seems to be making the most conscious pitch for quality." [28]

This pitch for excellence is reflected in the rigorous citywide administrative design review (ADR). The totally administrative procedure is conducted by planning department staff with no presentations to boards or public hearings. The public, however, is formally notified of major proposals via large billboards, and all residents, even renters, within a 400-foot radius of the proposed site are notified by mail. Any project failing to meet any of the design review criteria or guidelines must make accommodating changes to obtain a building permit. As in Portland, the final decision is appealable, first to the city council and second to the courts.

Since the design review process has been in place, more than 300 projects have undergone reviews in the last eight years, with only six appeals. Initially, some 50 to 60 projects a year were subject to a full-scale review consuming anywhere from two to 11 months. Happily, amendments to the review procedure have helped speed recent projects through a more abbreviated process.

Whereas the practice in some cities is to provide staff review for small projects but to send larger ones to a board, Bellevue has opted exclusively for professional staff review, conducted by architects, landscape architects, and experienced design professionals, all hired specially for this purpose. This staff also determines whether the bonus design criteria have been met and whether a proposed amenity will actually benefit the public. The director of the design and development department makes the formal decision, usually one of approval with conditions. So far, the director has only denied one project.

Bellevue began requiring design review for some areas in 1980. More comprehensive design review procedures were set up under the city's 1982 land use code, which aimed to inject the suburban sprawl with such urban-vernacular elements as density, animated public open spaces and streets, and pedestrian features. The code eliminated archaic setback standards, confined larger, denser projects to the downtown core, and cut the parking requirements in half. Several urban design refinements, however, did not sprout full-grown in the 1982 code. In fact, the design criteria enacted under the code (see Insert 2) proved too vague, and more specific guidelines had to be written later. For example, detailed design guidelines for building/sidewalk relationships and for development on the Major Pedestrian Corridor and in major public open spaces were added. Tailor-made sets of design guidelines were also developed for the downtown's special districts.

Insert 2.
Bellevue's Original Design Review Criteria
(code excerpt)

A. Site Design Criteria
   1. Vehicular circulation and parking
   2. Pedestrian circulation and amenities
   3. Wind and sun
   4. Open space
   5. Light and glare
B. Downtown Patterns and Context
   1. Natural setting and topography
   2. Landscape design
   3. Views
   4. Building height and bulk
   5. Transitions
   6. Patterns of activity

Guidelines for Building/Street Relationships.
The street-edge guidelines, which have been incorporated by reference into the land use code, categorize streets according to the amount of projected pedestrian use and state the requisite edge conditions for each category. They take into account such elements as retail and commercial uses; transparent windows; street walls; multiple entrances; ground-level differentiation; canopies, awnings, and arcades; paving; seating; artwork; and landscaping. (See the section on Bellevue's pedestrian corridor in Chapter 8, "Open Space and Streetscapes.")

In 1983, the city implemented design guidelines for its Major Pedestrian Corridor, which, when completed, will serve as the city's main street, linking the retail hub with the high-rise financial district. The corridor's guidelines, designed to forge this east/west, retail/commercial connection, address such issues as primary and secondary movement paths, corridor walls, massing of abutting structures, continuity, vegetation, and pedestrian amenities. (Inserts covering Bellevue's pedestrian amenity guidelines appear in Chapter 8.)

Design review in Bellevue is not confined to strictly visual considerations. Like Portland, Oregon, Burlington, Vermont, and other downtowns across the country that use comprehensive design review systems, Bellevue addresses in its ADR the broader development issues, such as wind and glare impacts and mitigation measures for each, accessible open space areas for the handicapped, pedestrian activity patterns, and protection of public views.

The ADR is but one element of Bellevue's final staff report. The report also entails review for compliance with the city's comprehensive plan, plus zoning and environmental impact assessments—separate reviews that overlap to some extent. For example, the environmental assessment deals with vehicular circulation and parking issues (design review criterion 1) in addition to light access and glare (criterion 5). The city's position is that the specific design guidelines and environmental assessments reinforce the more general design criteria.

Bellevue's System Assessed. What can be learned from studying the development and design review techniques used by Bellevue? An informal "cost/benefit analysis" balancing the points that seem to be the most workable with those that have caused difficulties may prove useful.

On the plus side, the city's chief urban designer, Mark Hinshaw, maintains that the design standards and accompanying guidelines for building/sidewalk relationships and major open spaces guarantee some degree of quality. This assurance allows developers some certainty about the caliber of future buildings.

John Nordby, who heads Wright Runstad & Company's Bellevue development activities, applauds one precedent set by the ADR process. Under the ADR system, developers can read the city's evaluations of past projects (in the staff reports) and better understand the city's design priorities and interpretation of specific criteria.

Another strength of Bellevue's system is that, like Portland's design guidelines, Bellevue's design criteria are mostly performance-based and provide a good deal of flexibility. Of course, the system can be no more flexible than the review staff. Jeffrey Soehren, architect of Rainier Bank Plaza, a Wright Runstad project, cites one situation that shows the city's flexibility and willingness to consider alternative design solutions. The code stipulates certain design features on heavily used pedestrian streets, but Soehren's design for Rainier Bank Plaza called for altering some of these requirements. The slope on one street made it awkward to install pedestrian seating or put in clear windows, canopies, awnings, or arcades, as recommended by the guidelines. To soften the street wall, Soehren instead suggested a series of cascading granite walls with contrasting finishes. The city in turn worked with an artist chosen by the developer to create a motif to inscribe on a number of the granite panels. The city and the architect agreed on designs depicting the fruit gardens that once had flourished on the building site. The inscribed images complement the fruit motif on the light standards designed for the downtown transit mall.

These successful negotiations between the city and a developer illustrate a point stressed by interviewees for this book who had experience working with Bellevue's development review system: It is essential, they say, to approach the design and development department as early as possible to discover exactly what the city wants. Two development firms, each of which has built several projects in downtown Bellevue, both emphasize that the review process was far shorter and smoother on their second projects. By that time, both firms had learned to talk with the city at the inception, before spending much time and money in pursuing any given design scheme.

As stated earlier, Bellevue's more detailed guidelines were developed several years after the 1982 code requirement for design review. And, some observers say, none too soon. Indeed, some architects and developers have remarked that in the beginning, before any guidelines had been devised or imposed, they really did not know what the city wanted before meeting with staffers and asking. Moreover, they were not convinced that the city itself knew what it wanted. This criticism probably is more directly related to the newness of the system and the need to work out the bureaucratic kinks than to an inherent flaw in Bellevue's design review process.

Other problems may ensue, opponents maintain, from the workings of the public/private revolving door. This phenomenon is hardly unique to Bellevue. However, the city's recent history of vesting many of the design review powers within a few individuals raises questions. Potential weaknesses of administrative design review systems—staff turnover and discontinuity—could become pitfalls in Bellevue, where much of the design review responsibility devolves upon a few, some say too few, individuals. Although developers and architects generally have been impressed by the level of expertise and overall competence of Bellevue's staff, they express concern that the development review process might be seriously disrupted in the event of staff turnover, particularly the departure of a key design staffer. Such a person is Mark Hinshaw, who, as city architect and chief designer, has made a fundamental imprint on the city's urban landscape.

"Education" is another issue. As discussed above, developers who have built several projects in downtown Bellevue say the second time around is far speedier than the first. On the second round, both public and private parties have been educated on the earlier projects. Local developers have learned the ins and outs of the city's review approach and have profited by them. But what about out-of-town developers and architects? Are they discouraged from participating in an interactional system, whereby much of a building's design is hammered out in the give-and-take of meetings between city and builder? Do developers want to spend their time steeping themselves in the intricacies of Bellevue's demanding code and their energy in negotiating with the planning department?

Yes and no. Some developers, particularly those who have never worked in Bellevue, are put off by the ADR and have taken their work elsewhere. Others welcome the chance to work within a system that is seemingly flexible and open to new design solutions. Developers across the board, however, complain of the lengthy review time; they suggest that schedules with set time limits for both project applications and city responses be made part of the code, as they are, for instance, in Portland.

DEVELOPMENT AND DESIGN REVIEWS: AN EVALUATION

This section is not a chapter summary. Nor is it a how-to guide for beginning zoners. Rather, it is a way of asking what emerges from a backward glance at the systems described in this chapter? What are the distinguishing points among the review techniques, and what, parenthetically, are some of the lessons learned?

MANDATE/INCENTIVE CHOICE

The first step in devising or judging a development review process is deciding between mandatory and voluntary procedures. This decision will doubtless be influenced by the prevailing economic market. It is generally agreed that aggressive urban design controls need competitive development markets to compensate for any disincentives posed by regulations. John Morris Dixon writes that the design review "process works only where a profitable market can be demonstrated. Unless the scheme appeals to developers, urban design guidelines can have little effect, and the planners may have to shift to a strategy of incentives . . ." [29]

For this reason, it is unsurprising that San Francisco, which adopted one of the country's most aggressive systems of urban design requirements, did so at a time when its office vacancy rate was close to 2 percent (although the rate had climbed considerably higher by the time the plan was finally enacted in 1985). In contrast, Cincinnati, whose current building renaissance is newly earned, is skittish about mandating design review. Instead, the city offers it as a bonus: developers may earn 20 percent more density by submitting to design review.

COSTS AND DELAYS

A second consideration is cost. Participation in the San Francisco "beauty contest," for instance, costs an estimated one-quarter of a million dollars for architectural fees alone. One developer who withdrew from the first competition in 1986 and then won approval for his project in the 1987 contest estimated the miscellaneous soft costs directly attributable to the permitting and design review process in general at $4 million. Development review costs in some cities are augmented by their required tests for the environmental effects of buildings, such as shadows, glare, lack

of sun access, and wind created at the pedestrian level. These tests may also carry a substantial price tag. (See Chapter 6, "Environmental Impacts of Tall Buildings.")

Time delays are a cost factor. Each added layer of development review, whether it be for design, environmental concerns, or increased density, may prolong the time required to complete the review process. In cities like San Francisco and New York, where assessment of the potential environmental effects of development proposals is mandated by state law, the length of the review period is legendary.

Under New York's Uniform Land Use Review Procedure (ULURP), citizens and other interested parties can review proposals for projects seeking discretionary density bonuses and certain other forms of zoning relief. This often makes for a protracted review period. In fact, a 1988 study by the New York Office of the State Comptroller reports that a developer requesting a special permit would have to wait an average of 447 days before receiving approval. [30]

The actual culprit in New York, however, is not the ULURP, which sets out precise time limits not to exceed a total of 120 days. Much of the delay occurs during the precertification period, when city agencies typically demand further information. Apparently, many project amenities are also negotiated during the precertification phase, which is largely exempt from comment and public review. [31]

Postponements and escalated costs can also result from overlapping requirements imposed by different city departments, which cause needless duplication. This criticism has been raised in those cities with formal, state-mandated environmental quality acts, like New York, San Francisco, Bellevue, and Seattle. Bellevue, like Seattle, has tried to excise from the environmental review process those review criteria that were eventually codified in the zoning. But the effort to streamline the various reviews and procedures is an ongoing one.

It is generally agreed that preapplication review procedures are useful for cutting review time. Whether the procedure is mandated, as in Portland, or voluntary, as in Pittsburgh, architects and developers benefit from consulting with the city at their first opportunity. In this way, they may identify the city's expectations before sinking large sums into design plans. Preapplication meetings are most important when they involve either out-of-town developers, who need to be initiated into a city's review process, or a new zoning system, in which glitches may need to be worked out.

Another method of shrinking review time is to set formal review guidelines for both the city and the developer. Developers in Bellevue, for instance, have objected to the absence of stated time limits for the city's administrative design and environmental reviews. But fixed time limits are only effective if there is enough staff to handle the workload. The amount of staff workload, which is largely controlled by project sizes and building activity, is most important in jurisdictions with broad review procedures. (Here, the amount of work may influence a city's decision whether to opt for a lay design review board or an administrative staff review. Bellevue, which subjects some 50 to 60 projects a year to a comprehensive review, has chosen to institute an administrative design procedure rather than create a citizen-appointed lay review board. Other considerations influencing this choice might be the availability of funds and the caliber of the staff.)

AMOUNT OF DISCRETION

A third consideration in shaping a city's review program is the extent of discretion—at once the virtue and the drawback of any development review system. Discretionary review systems offer greater flexibility, so that design responses may be tailored to the unique characteristics of a site. But such systems also may prove highly unpredictable and subject to abuse either by an overly demanding municipality or by a developer who takes advantage of a weak market. An excessively discretionary review process also may be open to legal challenge.

Therefore, "the design control process," writes zoning attorney Robert Cook, "must . . . tread the narrow line between the Scylla of overly rigid certainty and the Charybdis of easily abused flexibility."[32] New York's special district approach was devised to get around its ossified zoning code; however, the attendant lengthy negotiation process and unfettered discretion have often been thought just as onerous as the rigid code.

Subject to the vicissitudes of public administration, design and development review systems are only as good as the staff. It is as simple as that. Some bureaucrats are exceptionally competent, other less so. In a system well served by able individuals, flexibility and discretion will afford greater leverage to developers. But in a jurisdiction where staff members are few or lack knowhow, limiting discretion is preferable.

Excessively discretionary review systems can be effectively reined in through the use of firm, detailed development review guidelines. Also, the processes of fleshing out policy issues and of formulating guideline language can be used as consensus-building

mechanisms to help a community identify shared goals and decide whose values it wants to promote.

The level of specificity of review guidelines will generally depend on the review process. For example, Seattle, which has no formal design review for most private projects, addresses design issues through its incentive zoning system. The city's remarkably detailed criteria for all of its 28 public benefit features double as design guidelines for the downtown, in what has sometimes been called a "cookbook" approach. Taking a quite different route, Portland and Bellevue have inserted formal administrative design reviews into their development review processes. In these two cities, the review guidelines are not nearly so detailed and may be more flexibly interpreted.

EARLY PARTICIPATION

A final step, possibly the most valuable one, is that of involving interested parties from the beginning of the rezoning effort and of listening and responding to their input. Many cities actively solicit the opinions of key business, environmental, housing, preservation, and other activist citizen groups, engaging the groups directly in determining procedures and guidelines.

The advantages for developers and architects of participating in the creation of a new review system should not be underestimated. Wright Runstad & Company, for instance, found it infinitely worthwhile to join in formulating Seattle's 1985 Downtown Plan and in drafting the implementing zoning and guidelines. The company was a member of the technical advisory committee that helped judge the many zoning proposals for Seattle's downtown, and also helped write the design guidelines for development on Bellevue's Major Pedestrian Corridor. As a result, the members of the Wright Runstad development team have become extraordinarily enlightened about Bellevue's and Seattle's zoning and urban design matters as they adroitly navigate the interstices of the labyrinthine code requirements.

Clearly, the rewards of early and direct involvement are several. The most obvious reward is the chance to influence the direction and implementation of the regulations, the better to control one's own destiny.

Notes

1. Jonathan Barnett, *Urban Design As Public Policy* (New York: Architectural Record Books, 1974), p. 19.
2. John Morris Dixon, editorial in *Progressive Architecture* (March 3, 1988), p. 9.
3. Ada Louise Huxtable, *The Tall Building Artistically Reconsidered: The Search for a Skyscraper Style* (New York: Pantheon Books, 1982), p. 68.

4. Clifford L. Weaver and Richard F. Babcock, *City Zoning: The Once and Future Frontier* (Chicago: American Planning Association, 1979), p. 61.

5. Huxtable, op. cit., p. 50.

6. Richard Maschal, "Charlotte Ups the Ante," *Architectural Record* (July 1988), p. 104.

7. Paul M. Sachner, "Three Cities on Spec," *Architectural Record* (July 1988), p. 98.

8. Ibid.

9. Weaver and Babcock, *City Zoning*, pp. 134–135.

10. Carter Wiseman, "The Next Great Place," *New York* (June 16, 1986), p. 37.

11. Paul Goldberger, "Public Space Gets a New Cachet," *New York Times* (May 23, 1988).

12. Christopher J. Duerksen, *Aesthetics and Land-Use Controls*, Planning Advisory Service Report no. 399 (Chicago: American Planning Association, 1987), p. 16. See primarily Section 2, pp. 5–16, for Duerksen's excellent examination of design review and legal considerations.

13. Jonathan Barnett, "Designing Downtown Pittsburgh," *Architectural Record* (January 1982), pp. 90–106 and 124.

14. 348 U.S. 26 (1954).

15. See Samuel Bufford, "Beyond the Eye of the Beholder: A New Majority of Jurisdictions Authorize Aesthetic Regulations," *University of Missouri-Kansas City Law Review*, vol. 48 (1980), pp. 125–166.

See also Roger A. Cunningham and Daniel R. Mandelker, *Planning and Control of Land Development*, 2d ed. (Charlottesville, Virginia: The Michie Company, 1985), pp. 603–605.

16. For additional discussion, see Cunningham and Mandelker, op. cit., pp. 629–635.

See also Duerksen, *Aesthetics and Land-Use Controls*, pp. 12–13.

17. 394 A.2d 157 (N.J. 1978).

18. See Judith Getzels and Martin Jaffe with Brian W. Blaesser and Robert F. Brown, *Zoning Bonuses in Central Cities*, Planning Advisory Service Report no. 410 (Chicago: American Planning Association, 1988), p. 5. See also pp. 14–15 for a treatment of legal issues and incentive zoning.

19. Jonathan Barnett, "Urban Design Survival Tools," *Urban Design International*, vol. 5, no. 1 (Spring 1984), p. 39.

20. Recounted by Barnett in his *Introduction to Urban Design* (New York: Harper & Row, 1982), p. 216.

21. Barnett, "Designing Downtown Pittsburgh," p. 91.

22. ———, "In the Public Interest: Design Guidelines," *Architectural Record* (July 1987), p. 119.

23. Gideon Bosker and Lena Lencek, *Frozen Music: A History of Portland Architecture* (Portland, Oregon: The Press of the Oregon Historical Society, 1985), p. 87.

24. Barnett, *An Introduction to Urban Design*, p. 226.

25. Ibid., p. 223.

26. Neal Peirce, "Can a Boring 50s Suburb Become a Classy 90s City?," *Sarasota Herald-Tribune* (December 29, 1985).

27. See William H. Whyte's discussion of Bellevue as one of the "semi-cities" in *City: Rediscovering the Center* (New York: Doubleday, 1989), pp. 307–309.

28. Peirce, "Can a Boring 50s Suburb Become a Classy 90s City?"

29. John Morris Dixon, editorial in *Progressive Architecture* (March 1988), p. 9.

30. New York State, Office of the State Comptroller, *New York City Planning Commission: Granting Special Permits for Bonus Floor Area*, Report A-23-88 (September 15, 1988), p. MS-6.

31. Telephone interview with Steven Spinola, president, New York's real estate board (March 1989).

32. Robert S. Cook, Jr., *Zoning for Downtown Urban Design* (Lexington, Massachusetts: D.C. Heath and Company, 1980), p. 157. (This book is out of print.)

CHAPTER 4

DESIGN REVIEW OVERDOSE, SAN FRANCISCO–STYLE

Most persons think that a state, in order to be happy, ought to be large; . . . [yet] if the citizens of a state are to judge and distribute offices according to merit, they must know each other's characters; where they do not possess this knowledge, both the election to offices and the decision of lawsuits will go wrong. When the population is very large, they are manifestly settled at haphazard, which clearly ought not to be. . . . The best limit of the population of a city, then, is the largest number which suffices for the purposes of life, and can be taken in at a single view.

–Aristotle, *Politics*

Following years of debate over the so-called Manhattanization of San Francisco's downtown, the board of supervisors, by a 6-to-5 vote, enacted the Downtown Plan into zoning in 1985. The ordinance adopting the plan runs to 139 pages—the size of complete zoning codes in many cities. It sets out one of the most ambitious zoning systems ever enacted by an American city. The notorious development fees for open space, transit, child care, public art, and housing, in addition to the stringent shadow restrictions and height and bulk limits, receive attention in other chapters of this book; the present chapter focuses exclusively on the city's experiences with its design review process.

THE 1985 GROWTH CAP

The most fiercely contested feature of San Francisco's plan is the much-hyped office rationing system. Although the planning department believed that the plan's aggressive regulatory restraints would adequately control the market and redirect commercial growth to strategic parts of the downtown, the mayor's office introduced the idea of a limit on high-

The increasingly Manhattanlike skyline of San Francisco.

rise development as a means of securing approval of the plan from the board of supervisors. The first interim growth cap was written into the plan and enacted with it in 1985. The cap limited large-scale office development for three years to 2,850,000 square feet, which averages out to 950,000 square feet a year, less than the square footage in many individual Manhattan office towers.

THE ECONOMIC CLIMATE

It has been suggested that developers raised little resistance to the interim cap because they were too busy putting up projects that had been grandfathered-in before the plan. Moreover, with so much commercial space permitted between 1981 and 1983, preceding the 1983 recession, there was a general consensus by 1985 that the market was overbuilt and would probably remain so for some time; therefore, 950,000 square feet of new commercial space a year seemed not unreasonable.

Historically, absorption rates in the city have been strong, ranging from 1.5 to 2 million square feet on the average and generally comparable to the annual rate of construction. During the early 1980s, however, San Francisco, like many other cities, underwent a surge in speculative office development. The cap, then, came on the heels of a major local building boom (fueled in part by the city's low vacancy rate and high rents), and amid an abundance of investment capital generated through retirement funds, foreign capital seeking safe havens, and favorable tax laws.

During the mid-1980s, the downtown's annual rate of office growth doubled, then tripled. This trend combined with the drop in demand to increase the office vacancy rate to an unprecedented 16 percent by 1986. The city's current soft office market, however, is not attributable solely to overbuilding. Extremely low vacancy rates in the early 1980s pushed rental rates up into the $40-per-square-foot range, prompting several significant corporate decisions to relocate to the suburbs. The results of these relocations, however, did not become evident until the mid-1980s, when the new quarters were completed. Net absorption in 1985 was a negative 900,000 square feet; absorption had also been depressed in 1984 and dropped again in 1986. The consequent surplus of space caused a drop in rental rates, so that there were far fewer relocations in 1987 and 1988. According to projections, this cycle will repeat itself by the early to mid-1990s, with rental rates escalating and major relocations resuming in the late 1990s (based on decisions made in the first half of the decade).

PROPOSITION M (1986)

Although the accelerated rate of approval in the early 1980s was related more directly to new financing mechanisms and the greater availability of capital than to the city's planning process, nevertheless slow-growth activists felt betrayed by the Downtown Plan and called for stricter limits. Promoted by grass-roots groups such as San Franciscans for Reasonable Growth and the Coalition for San Francisco Neighborhoods, the voter initiative called Proposition M passed in November 1986. Five earlier initiatives calling for similar limits had already been voted down. Essentially, Proposition M shrinks permitted new downtown office development by half. It does this by allocating half of the 950,000-square-foot cap to "pipeline" projects—those projects that secured permits after November 29, 1984 (when the planning commission made the Downtown Plan part of the master plan), but that were approved before passage of Proposition M. Thus, until the pipeline projects are built, newly proposed projects over 25,000 square feet are now limited to a total of 475,000 square feet per year, of which 75,000 square feet must be reserved for office buildings between 25,000 and 49,999 square feet. Whereas the 1985 plan sets a three-year limit on the office rationing system, Proposition M makes the cap permanent unless changed by the voters.

Detractors call the proposition a "meat ax approach" to growth control. On the other hand, proponents claim the permanent annual cap was necessary to compensate for the unbridled approval rate, which accelerated after adoption of the Downtown Plan. Not until the pipeline projects, whose permits were grandfathered-in, have been fully written off will 950,000 square feet again be available for newly proposed projects on a yearly basis. This is not expected to occur until the late 1990s. With about 4 million square feet of new office space under construction and 3.5 million approved, the city has a total office inventory of some 65 million square feet of net rentable area, with 40 million in the downtown alone. Vacancy rates vary according to location. Whereas rates in prime locations north of Market Street are projected at 10 percent, they may be as high as 18 to 20 percent on the less desirable sites south of Market, where development has purportedly been encouraged by the Downtown Plan.

Although the office high-rise cap was bootstrapped onto the Downtown Plan, it is effective citywide and comes into play when any office project exceeds 25,000 square feet. Any square footage of the quota not allotted in a given year may be carried over. As

71

the city's planning director, Dean Macris, says, "This is the first plan anywhere to prescribe both the rate of growth and the standard of quality for new development." [1]

According to *New York Times* architectural critic Paul Goldberger, the office limitation program, or growth cap, "intended to strengthen the plan, . . . has instead virtually overwhelmed it, coming to control the whole process of building in downtown San Francisco and changing it in a way that has implications for the very nature of municipal planning in the United States. For what San Francisco created was, in a sense, the first quota system for city planning." [2] Michael McGill, spokesman for the citizens' business coalition, says the cap assumes that a "building is guilty until proven innocent." [3]

THE BEAUTY CONTEST

In determining which projects to approve under the quota, the planning department is directed to consider seven criteria, including consistency with master plan objectives and policies, suitability of project location and contextual impact, effect on employment, market need, and design quality. The mechanism for evaluating design quality is known as the "beauty contest." To judge it, a panel of nationally recognized architectural experts is appointed for each competition to advise the planning department.

Developers and architects were outraged when not one of the projects competing in the first (1986) review received approval. Of the five projects that entered the competition (two of which later dropped out), the architectural review board said that although the Downtown Plan had evidently "raised architects' consciousness about a series of design issues, . . . none of the projects fully demonstrate[d] the plan's potential to produce better buildings. None [was] brilliant and none [was] an awful embarrassment."

Noting that the 1986 office vacancy rate in San Francisco was approaching 16 percent, the planning department questioned the benefit of adding more office space and gave preliminary approval to only one of the entries. That project's strength, according to the department, was its provision of additional back-office space in the Civic Center vicinity, which contains a heavy concentration of government operations. The city commissioners, however, ultimately rejected all three of the proposals that had not dropped out.

Some critics contend that the commissioners' decision was influenced largely by politics. With Proposition M on the ballot at the time, the commissioners hoped that their decision to disapprove all of the projects would help assuage the slow-growth lobby. The

Roger Lewis, from his Washington Post column, "Shaping the City," 6/13/87

plan backlashed, for the city's apparent betrayal of the building community virtually assured passage of Proposition M. Pass it did, although by a mere 4,500 votes. Enraged and demoralized by the city's position, developers had no incentive to fight for the integrity of the Downtown Plan and put up scant resistance to Proposition M.

At the time of the second (1987) review, the city's office vacancy rate hovered at 17 percent. Nevertheless, the city commissioners approved three moderate-sized office towers in the second competition. Five projects, seeking a total of 1.2 million square feet, vied for 800,000 square feet, the available allotments for 1986 and 1987. Critics claimed that tenancy ultimately was a more important criterion than design quality in the 1987 judging: instead of making market need one of the dispositive criteria, the city asked for evidence of lease commitments. Unsurprisingly, one of the winning projects will house the headquarters for the San Francisco Federal Home Loan Bank, which allegedly threatened to leave town if its headquarters were not approved under the 1987 quota.

Although the other two approved projects were speculative buildings, one will contain a local institution, the Wells Fargo Bank. The second speculative building, consuming some 147,500 square feet of the quota, was rated "excellent" by the architectural review board. The two rejected projects were advised to improve their designs and reenter.

In the spring 1989 contest, three of the four competing projects were holdovers from past years, two of which were approved. In contrast, 15 proposals were submitted for a recent redevelopment project. One reason for this discrepancy in developer interest is that although port, state-sponsored, and city redevelopment projects are counted into the annual cap, such projects are exempt from the beauty contest. It is anticipated that two such projects will soon be approved, effectively consuming the cap allocation for the next three years.

Apart from the market conditions, another reason for the dearth of interest in the design competition is the high risk factor. The upfront costs are high, and the probability of approval is low. Although the planning commission recently approved three of the four 1989 contestants, until then no project had been approved for two years. In the 1989 contest, four projects, totaling more than 1 million square feet, vied for the mere 892,721 square feet of office space available in that year's allocation.

Costs for competing in the beauty contest have been estimated at a quarter of a million dollars. The architectural competition is one of the last development approval hoops, and developers must first incur expensive environmental assessments, legal and accounting fees, and steep land carrying costs, with almost no guarantee their projects will ever proceed. Charles I.M. Graham, executive vice president of London & Edinburgh Trust, developer of a 25-story office project that withdrew from the first competition and was approved in the 1987 contest, estimates that his architectural fees amounted to about $150,000 per contest and that the miscellaneous soft costs directly attributable to the permitting and design review process over a four-year period came to $4 million. Graham also notes that developers have no choice but to use premium materials, so that the cost of the skin alone for this 150,000-square-foot project exceeded $5 million. (For further information on this project, see the section on sun access in San Francisco in Chapter 6, "Environmental Impacts of Tall Buildings.")

San Francisco economic consultant Alan Billingsley predicts the city will only see new development interest when the projected returns on a building are high enough to justify playing in this dicey market. He notes, further, that if land prices are bid downward in the future to lower the upfront costs and raise the potential return on investment, developers may be more willing to enter the fray. As of this writing, however, almost no land sales have transpired in downtown San Francisco since 1984. It is thought that landowners prefer to hold onto their land in the hope that Proposition M will be repealed and the city will eventually ease up on permit approvals, rather than sell at the current market value, depressed as it is by the risk factor. Therefore, the three holdovers in the 1989 contest, says Billingsley, were simply trying to salvage some value of the land they bought before Proposition M.

THE MINI-CONTEST

Proposition M requires that 75,000 square feet of the total yearly cap be reserved for office structures smaller than 50,000 square feet, necessitating a second design competition. Proposals for smaller projects are presented separately but to the same architectural review board. San Francisco architect Jeffrey Heller, who won approval in 1987 for one of his projects in the smaller competition, notes that the evaluation procedures for the two design contests are identical and that the hefty costs incurred by participating in the beauty contest are far more difficult for smaller projects to absorb. As a result, only one project has competed in the review for smaller buildings, and there is now a surplus of unused square footage in this allotment.

EVALUATION

"To a critic of the excesses of development that have plagued most American downtowns, San Francisco would appear to be the promised land. Here, the planners and the voters, not the real estate developers, hold the power." [4] Concurring, Planning Director Dean Macris notes: "In this city, if a bad building goes up, they don't blame the architect, they blame the planning department." [5] Paul Goldberger warns that the city's quota system has "opened up a Pandora's box of problems." [6] One frequently voiced criticism is that the imposition of the growth cap has unduly politicized the plan; indeed, according to Jeffrey Heller, the design review process "uses the architect as a whipping boy and as a subterfuge for what are essentially political decisions." [7]

Although the city has made a valiant effort to ensure premier-quality design, in practice the highly discretionary review process often defers to conflicting interests, such as lease commitments (preferably to single local entities), job opportunities for local residents, and participation in the city's development rights transfer program for historic preservation, housing, and open space.

On this point, some observers claim that the importance given in the 1987 competition to documented evidence of signing up a major tenant with economic appeal undoubtedly favored development in less risky, established areas; the effect was to undermine the plan's original policy of shunting future office development away from the financial district and toward the less congested area south of Market Street. The choice of three projects that would all be located within a two-block radius of the financial district's core, contrary to the Downtown Plan, was contested by the disapproved projects, which would have been built south of Market Street. An additional sore point was that the three projects, combined, called for demolition of some 800 parking spaces in a section where parking was already scarce.

George Williams, assistant planning director, said that in the 1989 beauty contest, projects proposed for the South-of-Market district would be given priority. Not surprisingly, the three winners are located south of Market, and the disapproved project is north of Market.

Another issue is the efficacy of planning departments' engaging in financial feasibility and market analyses of development potential. Zoning has always been used as a growth management tool to encourage or discourage development in particular areas. But a planning department's conducting extensive assessments of a city's office market and then denying all significant new office development for the year because of market considerations is sui generis. Asserting that it should be free to take whatever economic risks it wants, the development and business community has pointed out serious flaws in the city's economic analysis.

For example, the city's endorsement of the one project in 1986 was based on its strategic location and potential for providing back-office space in an area with a high concentration of government operations. Back offices are the routine, often computer-based operations of corporations and large service firms. Back-office jobs, largely clerical and data-entry positions, are generally low-paying and held by women and minorities. Further investigation (since the city's endorsement of the 1986 winner for having an apparently strategic locale) has shown, on the contrary, that back-office development is highly elastic in its siting choices. Its major concerns are low-cost space and large enough floor plates to enable an efficient layout of bullpen clerical areas and computer networks. Unlike corporate headquarters, back-office users are unconcerned with window-facing perimeter space and theoretically could locate in any part of town.

Moreover, economist David E. Dowall maintains that "back-office jobs have become San Francisco's new bedrock employment base, replacing the traditional blue-collar manufacturing jobs once so predominant in the city . . . [and] the coup de grâce for back-office operations within the downtown may well turn out to be the office space development cap." [8] The cap, besides limiting new construction, sends office rents skyward, forcing back-office operations out of the city and penalizing their mostly female and minority personnel. Furthermore, the 1987 competition showed a bias toward dividing the 475,000 square feet among several projects, rather than giving it all to a single large one. (Some critics point out that the former choice is more politically expedient because it pleases more, or displeases fewer, developers.) This bias further impedes the opportunity for back-office construction, which generally requires floor plates exceeding 20,000 square feet.

A 1985 study by the Center for Real Estate and Urban Economics at Berkeley predicted that the office rationing cap would raise office rents and lower employment, income, and property tax levels. The real beneficiaries, the study said, would be the then-current owners of office buildings. In addition, a few developers each year would achieve exceptional positions from which to market high-priced space. [9]

Although these predictions may yet be borne out, the temporarily stalled development market probably has more to do with the rigors of the design competition—in addition to earlier overbuilding, high vacancy rates, and relocations out of the city—than with the actual restraints imposed by the cap. Despite diminished building interest in the downtown, however, the city's economy is exceptionally strong, as reflected in the 30 percent increase in home prices in 1988. And the corporate relocations are the results of significant growth, as well as of the shortage of available space in the early 1980s.

With vacant office space being absorbed at a rate of 1.6 million square feet a year, and with only 475,000 square feet being built annually, "we're going to work through the inventory pretty fast," says George Williams.[10] The constraints of the cap may soon be felt. At such a time, the business and development community may very well exercise its political muscle to raise the limit.

One irony is that the growth lid is inhibiting, or at least markedly delaying, implementation of the Downtown Plan. With less than 500,000 square feet permitted in one year, probably for the next 10 years—amounting to no more than one mid-sized and perhaps one smaller building a year—the impact of the various requirements for employment training programs, open space, historic preservation, and other public benefits is and may remain negligible. By adopting the office limit, the city has all but capped its own revenues for the office/housing linkage program at about $2.5 million a year.

Also, many opponents claim that the cap transmuted permits for the "old dogs" (approved before the new zoning and thus exempt from the new design requirements) into gold, virtually assuring that they would be built. Especially valuable were permits for sites in the office core, as well as in other parts of the city where the new zoning would have a heavy impact.

Others ask, has the Downtown Plan really improved the quality of building design? As stated above, of the projects that competed in the first design review in 1986, the architectural review panel found that "none of the projects fully demonstrate[d] the plan's potential to produce better buildings. None [was] brilliant." Paul Goldberger wrote of the projects recommended for approval in the following year's beauty contest: "None was particularly impressive as a work of architecture. They . . . all turned out to be tame examples of the postmodern style, cautious little buildings that struggle[d] not to offend." [11]

San Francisco developer Tom Swift says of highly regulated markets, in which political realities dictate many of the solutions, that "the natural design process in a building is the real loser. This, unfortunately, will mean there probably aren't going to be any bad buildings, but no real great ones either." [12]

Planning Director Dean Macris comments: "What we hadn't foreseen was that there would be a tendency to seek out national firms, and not take any risk with architecture." [13] In the 1986 competition, all the rejected submissions were the work of local firms. In the 1987 review, two national firms—Kohn Pedersen Fox and the partnership of John Burgee and Philip Johnson—designed two of the four approved projects.

WILL THE DOWNTOWN PLAN PLAY IN OTHER CITIES?

In San Francisco, where required development fees for housing, transit, public art, open space, and daycare add anywhere from $15 to $18 a square foot to construction costs, the city has firmly established the principle that real estate development is not a right but a privilege. However, it is instructive to recall that most of these fees (except for the prior fees for housing and transit) were conceived in the early 1980s as part of the Downtown Plan, at a time when the city was caught up in a building spree and office vacancy rates were no higher than 2 percent. Indeed, in 1980,

the city's office vacancy rate was lower than 1 percent, and rents for first-class buildings were second only to New York's.

Dean Macris maintains that the package of fees affects only residual land values, for it is charged back against land prices. Developers say instead that the fees are ultimately passed on to users through higher rents, outpricing potential rentals for small businesses and back-office users.

When, like many other cities, San Francisco experienced unprecedented office vacancy rates in 1986 and 1987 and witnessed the exodus of major financial institutions and corporate headquarters out of the downtown, some of these firms stayed in the region and moved to the suburbs. But some moved to Los Angeles. Nationwide mergermania also toppled some of the city's corporate Goliaths. This change in the economic climate has been blamed on a number of variables, including the short supply of architecturally suitable space (large floor plates) in the downtown, the substantial addition of suburban office space, the widespread perception that the city has a negative attitude toward business and industry, and the fiercest set of development controls of any major city. The San Francisco Planning and Urban Research Association (SPUR) reports that San Francisco "has lost its status as a major financial center to Los Angeles [partly] as a result of the dramatically larger population that exists in Southern California, which attracts more retail banking facilities to serve it. But Los Angeles is also attracting other financial and business services in recognition of its status as the largest port on the West Coast, as well as its number-one rank among American cities in manufacturing." [14]

One would think that all of these obstacles would effectively discourage developer interest in San Francisco. So they have, to some extent. At the same time, though, the artificial constraints on supply and demand within a highly regulated development system will ultimately enhance the value of downtown real estate. Salomon Brothers, Inc., reports that this type of market will be eminently attractive to investors:

> With many real estate markets glutted, institutional investors have sought out zoning-induced supply-constrained markets. Buildings in these markets are protected from competition and thus tend to achieve higher rents and occupancy levels. The quasi-monopoly values are capitalized into building prices. [15]

In fact, the hottest development activity in San Francisco now is acquiring older existing buildings (especially those 20 to 30 years old), renovating them, and extracting attractive rents. These buildings are then sold to institutional or foreign investors at aggressive cap rates.

And despite the complaints about excessive regulation, the Downtown Plan at least spells out rules with which the development community can work. Tom Swift of Gerald D. Hines Interests states that the main difference between the city's development review process and that of two other highly regulated major markets—New York and Boston—is the fact that it is "known": "You may not like it, you may want to argue with it, you may wish it were different, but at least, it's relatively known." [16]

Although the plan is the subject of close scrutiny by planning departments across the country, most cities are more interested in stimulating and sustaining growth than in rationing it. For that reason, other downtowns would probably be imprudent to adopt equally restrictive growth caps on office development (although Seattle recently passed a similar downtown building limit, as described in Chapter 1, "Incentive Zoning"). And the current high office vacancy rates nationwide may well render moot the issue of commercial growth caps in most downtowns. However, many cities might find it useful (as many already have) to look to the San Francisco plan—first, for its strong dose of firm, explicit zoning guidelines for density, height, and architectural character; and second, for its innovative approaches both to enlivening streetscapes and public spaces and to preserving its sumptuous inventory of older structures. It is unfortunate that the boldest urban design plan adopted by any major American city was derailed from the very start.

Notes

1. Statement made at a session of ULI's November 1988 Semiannual Meeting in San Francisco.

2. Paul Goldberger, "When Planning Can Be Too Much of a Good Thing," *New York Times* (December 6, 1987).

3. Statement made by Michael McGill, executive director of the San Francisco Planning and Urban Research Association (SPUR), at the National Policy Council session of ULI's November 1988 Semiannual Meeting in San Francisco.

4. Ibid.

5. Quoted by Goldberger, op. cit.

6. Ibid.

7. Comment made in phone interview (March 1989). (Heller is a partner in the San Francisco architectural firm of Heller & Leake.)

8. David E. Dowall, cited in the article "Endangered Species," *Urban Land* (August 1986), p. 9. Adapted from a longer version of the article, published as *Back Offices and San Francisco's Office Development Growth Cap*, Working Paper no. 448 (Berkeley: Institute of Urban and Regional Development of the University of California, March 1986).

9. Study conducted by the Center for Real Estate and Urban Economics, University of California, Berkeley, in 1985. Cited by Douglas R. Porter in "Downtown San Francisco's New Plan," *Urban Land* (February 1986), p. 35.

10. Cited by William Trombley in "Downtown San Francisco Joins Slow-Growth Ranks," *Los Angeles Times* (August 3, 1988).

11. Goldberger, "When Planning Can Be Too Much of a Good Thing."

12. Statement made at a session of ULI's October 1987 Semiannual Meeting in Los Angeles.

13. Cited by Paul Goldberger, "For San Francisco, 'Cure' Is Worse than High-Rise 'Disease'," *New York Times* (December 5, 1987).

14. Report by the San Francisco Planning and Urban Research Association (SPUR), no. 234 (April 1987), p. 2.

15. David Shulman, *An Uneasy Look at "First Lutheran and Nollan,"* a July 27, 1987, report by the bond market research division of Salomon Brothers, Inc.

16. Statement made at a session of ULI's October 1987 Semiannual Meeting in Los Angeles.

CHAPTER 5

ZONING AS SHAPER OF BUILDING DESIGN

We "live in a single world culture," writes architectural critic Robert Campbell, and without design guidelines, every city in the world will soon resemble every other city.[1] For this reason, cities like San Francisco are self-consciously legislating images of themselves. San Francisco "decided it was a white city, a city of pointed tops, a city of ornamented surfaces,"[2] and mandated those particular physical characteristics in its Downtown Plan.

Recognizing this auxiliary power of zoning, the urban design team of Andres Duany and Elizabeth Plater-Zyberk bear it in mind when drawing up guidelines for residential projects throughout the country. In doing so, they look to design elements of 18th- and 19th-century American town plans, and at the same time actively seek contracts to rewrite the local zoning codes. Because they realize that the person who draws up the code may wield more power over building design than the architect, they treat "zoning laws . . . the way Latin American revolutionaries once hungrily eyed radio stations: take 'em over and you've almost won."[3]

Similarly, Jonathan Barnett observes that, while the lawyer, surveyor, and municipal engineer consider "their primary task to be, not control over design but over more abstract considerations of public health and welfare," nonetheless they have "[u]nintentionally . . . determined the basic design framework of the American city through a combination of local zoning regulations and the street pattern. . . ."[4]

Since their inception, development regulations have shaped the physical appearance of the city, either intentionally or unintentionally. Architect François Mansart's gambrel roof, for example, was said to have gained popularity in 17th-century Paris as a means of circumventing a law that taxed building owners according to the structure's number of stories. The double-pitched roof, with its lower slope much steeper than its top portion, neatly disguised two floors, and owners were taxed for only one story.

Scott R. Thomas; New York Affairs, vol. 8, no. 4 (1985), p. 108

This view (35th Street looking west across Sixth Avenue) shows how the setback requirements of the 1916 Zoning Ordinance shaped the space above the city.

In this country, New York City is, "[m]ore than most American cities, . . . a physical representation of its zoning."[5] Much has been written about the way the setback requirements in New York's 1916 zoning transformed the sleek, straight towers of the early skyscrapers into the familiar pyramidal masses, or ziggurats. Hugh Ferriss's evocative charcoal drawings of abstract skyscraper forms illustrated the possibilities of the 1916 zoning envelope and the maximum mass permitted by the new law. To protect streets from being turned into dark canyons, the regulations established height districts, limiting the height a building could rise to (in proportion to the street width it fronted on) before it had to be stepped back.

Another of New York's tower rules allowed a proportion of a building—up to 25 percent of the lot area—to rise without setbacks if the tower was sufficiently separated from the street. These were apparently the only height and bulk limits. The setback requirements were passed at a time when two major U.S. urban health problems were rickets and tuberculosis, whose incidence was said to be aggravated by insufficient natural light in buildings. Thus, the requirements were motivated alike by health and design considerations.

Just as New York's first zoning regulations spawned the characteristic tiered "wedding-cake" skyscraper, so the city's 1961 Zoning Resolution proved to be a powerful shaper of the urban landscape. Although built three years before the adoption of the 1961 code, the svelte glass-and-bronze Seagram Building, with its flat granite plaza, was looked to as a tangible expression of the new tower-in-the plaza form. A "sky exposure plane," plus a new set of bulk shaping rules, replaced the height districts. To meet the need for larger floor plates, the tower was allowed to cover more of the lot area, the limit rising from 25 to 40 percent. The 1961 zoning revision also fostered a new method for controlling density—the use of the floor/area ratio. Plazas proliferated under the 20 percent density bonus awarded for creating each urban open space within certain permitted districts.

In order to maximize floor area under the 1961 zoning constraints, developers built to the outer limits of the zoning envelope. Market forces combined with the emerging popularity of the international style to produce the austere, rectilinear high rises that soon dominated many urban skylines. "It is hideously expensive to build high," notes former architecture critic for the *New York Times* Ada Louise Huxtable. But because "almost anything is possible technologically today—the architect designs and the engineer makes it stand up—even the basic structure is subject to economic determination. . . . [Therefore,] within the market calculations, the modern skyscraper is squeezed into the mold made by zoning laws and building codes. Ultimately, the design of the tall building is a

Scott R. Thomas; New York Affairs, vol. 8, no. 4 (1985), p. 55

This view of Manhattan emphasizes the varied building silhouettes fostered by the city's major zoning revisions.

product of investment economics and urban politics." [6] A major cost-saving attraction of the skyscrapers was the uniform floor plates, which eased installation of elevator equipment and HVAC systems.

The notion that zoning regulations fuse with economics to produce a particular building configuration is often raised in the context of height limits. The strict height cap in Washington, D.C., for example, is routinely blamed for the city's uninspiring shoebox-style office buildings, which until recently dominated the commercial core. The tight building envelope enforced by the height limits, say some developers, gives them no choice but to fill out every available square foot. This rationale is dismissed, however, by the many commentators who attribute much of the city's charm and uniqueness to the height constraints.

It has also been suggested that zoning is used deliberately to promote or discourage architectural styles. For example, the postmodern style, which burst upon the country some 10 years ago, rebels against the severities of the international style and resurrects architectural elements from earlier periods. Meantime, many downtown zoning revisions, redolent of historicism, are also encouraging the architectural trappings of bygone times, including cornices, beltcourses, and nonrectangular rooflines. A prime example is New York's 1982 Midtown Zoning, a throwback, some say, to the stepped-back ziggurat style espoused by the city's as-of-right 1916 ordinance.

In like fashion, the San Francisco Downtown Plan urges the building of light-colored, richly surfaced structures with bay windows, setbacks, and articulated rooflines, in an apparent overt rejection of the international style. It is no accident that the first three major projects to win approval in the city's design competition were freighted with historical associations and distinctly postmodern. Planning professor Richard Tseng-yi Lai writes that the ordinance's "specifications governing architectural decoration and fenestration not only promote designs reminiscent of older, prewar buildings about the city but give virtual code endorsement to the current fashion of postmodernism. As Macris [San Francisco planning director] is quoted as saying: 'We think it is time for a departure from the international style.' " [7]

The keystone of the Battery Park City (New York) design guidelines is their historical reference to the early 20th-century masonry-clad office towers and apartments of the Upper West Side in Manhattan, with their stone bases, midheight beltcourses, and stepped-back penthouses. The guidelines require that the exteriors of residential buildings be molded into a fluid street wall with masonry on the first two stories, brick on the walls above, prominent cornice edges, and nonrectangular rooflines.

But do these style choices derive entirely from zoning concerns? How big a part does taste alone play? The use of regulations to promote particular architectural styles raises the perennial cause-and-effect conundrum; it would be misleading to attribute exclusively to zoning controls a trend that may be largely a matter of fashion.

Those zoning provisions aimed solely at controlling environmental effects—blockage of sunlight, shadows, street-level pedestrian winds, and view corridor obstruction—may also influence architectural design. For instance, San Francisco's sunlight ordinance, Proposition K, virtually mandates year-round, all-day sun access for all city-owned parks and open spaces. In the case of one 350,000-square-foot office project that competed in the 1987 beauty contest, compliance with Proposition K resulted in a loss of 10 stories. The sharp reduction from 25 to 15 stories called for a dramatic shift in architectural approach and many reworkings of Philip Johnson's original scheme.

Robert Venturi's design for Seattle's new art museum was similarly affected by that city's 1985 downtown zoning regulations. The mandatory setback provisions to preserve views of Elliott Bay, West Seattle, Mount Rainier, and the Olympic Mountains markedly altered Venturi's original intention, which was to hold together the building wall as one unified mass and build out to the property lines. Rather than break up the facade for the view corridors, Venturi chose to set back the entire structure some 30 feet. In the process, he created a "hillside terrace," an open space on a steeply sloped street that qualifies as a bonusable public benefit feature. The 150,000-square-foot limestone structure, banded by a pattern of granite, marble, and terra cotta on the ground floor, is slated for completion in 1990.

Today's building designs also bear the marks of zoning provisions that regulate the bases of high-rise structures. In a considered effort to arouse visual interest and strengthen streetscape continuity in the downtowns, many cities are writing zoning provisions that directly influence massing, selection of building materials, proportions of facade openings, designs of structured parking lots, and facade organization. In much the same way, transparency requirements, blank wall limits, and mandated build-to lines (street walls flush with lot lines) reflect the increased attention to building/sidewalk relationships and to the appearance of the building base.

The 1987 amendments to Charlotte's Uptown Mixed-Use District ordinance, for example, require that the base of a high-rise building (over five stories) be clearly differentiated from the upper stories and offer "design elements that will enhance the pedestrian environment. Such elements as cornices, beltcourses, corbelling, molding, stringcourses, ornamentation, changes in material or color, and other sculpturing of the base as are appropriate must be provided to add special interest to the base." The code also states that special attention must be paid to the windows within the base. "Band windows are discouraged"; instead, recessed "windows that are distinguished from the shaft of the building through the use of arches, pediments, mullions, and other treatments are encouraged." (An illustration in the section on ground-floor design in Chapter 8, "Open Space and Streetscapes," demonstrates this concept.)

SCULPTURED ROOFTOPS

Just as zoning regulates the design of building bases, so it controls roof configurations. The close connections among zoning, building appearance, and the use of design regulations to foster an architectural style are underscored by the plethora of zoning provisions for sculptured rooftops.

Fed up with the legions of flat-topped edifices that dominate their skylines, some cities are using zoning regulations to encourage variety in roofline design. Although San Francisco is the only downtown actually to require "party hats" on new office towers, zoning incentives in other cities have inspired a panoply of angled, pyramidal, curved, and pointed building tops.

and Chippendale furniture, while other Johnson-Burgee office towers, featuring gables, pinnacles, and superscaled steeples, mirror the medieval Gothic style. Some of the new buildings have domes. Others have sharply angled tops, like New York's Citicorp Building. Some, like Portland, Oregon's KOIN Center, are topped by pyramids.

PARTY HATS IN SAN FRANCISCO

The urban design element of San Francisco's 1985 Downtown Plan addresses the appearances of individual new buildings, as well as their cumulative impact on the city's skyline. According to the plan, the city should present a textured, finely scaled skyline:

> In general, the texture of San Francisco, when viewed from close up or from afar, is one of small-scale buildings covering the hills on a grid street pattern, punctuated by green space and occasional larger significant structures, such as churches, schools, and hospitals. The collective mass of office buildings in the financial district has become the most prominent significant component of the skyline. . . . The bulkiness and repetitive boxiness of many recent structures have obscured the fine-scale sculptured skyline of pre–World War II San Francisco. To create a new sculptured skyline, new buildings must have generally thinner and more complex shapes.

The downtown ordinance, which calls for leaner, "more finely detailed buildings," sets up bulk controls that taper buildings at both their lower and upper levels, and requires more expressive, modulated building tops. To soften benching—the tendency to build to the height limit, particularly in districts where height is restricted to less than 400 feet, creating a monotonous skyline of building tops all in a row—the code encourages tapered buildings and allows some exceptions from the height restrictions. Up to 10 percent of allowable height may be added for undertaking additional bulk reduction in upper floors to create a "more slender . . . profile and sculptured building termination."

Tapered buildings also promote purely environmental objectives. They allow more sunlight into the streets and decrease ground-level wind velocity, thus enhancing pedestrian comfort.

INCENTIVES FOR ROOFTOP VARIETY

Rather than requiring that saucy building tops festoon their skylines, many cities work toward rooftop variety through various design review procedures. Bellevue, Washington's administrative design review process includes provisions for "encourag[ing] slen-

Cities have long been in the business of controlling the uses of roofs—the placement, for example, of mechanical equipment or, more recently, television antennas and satellite dishes. But regulating the shapes of building towers is a relatively new idea. It would be an oversimplification, however, to trace the phenomenon of ornate tops on new buildings exclusively to downtown zoning revisions. After all, corporate heads have long recognized that prominent signature roofs lend a certain cachet to their headquarters, and developers know that rental response often relates "directly to a building's recognition factor on the skyline." [8] Through the commercial successes of the Transamerica Building in San Francisco, the RepublicBank Center in Houston, and the AT&T headquarters in New York City, corporations are discovering the benefits of having an identifiable silhouette within a skyline.

Ever-shifting architectural tastes also shape roofline design. Resurrected by the postmodern style, history is "respectable again," writes Ada Louise Huxtable, and "is being mined for nostalgia, novelty, and innuendo." [9] The notorious split pediment of Philip Johnson's AT&T Building, for instance, recalls for some the 18th-century charm of Georgian architecture

T. J. Lassar

Rooftop interest was a high design priority for RiverPlace (foreground) and KOIN Center (background), Portland, Oregon.

der towers, particularly at upper levels," and for using a "high quality of design for all buildings . . . affording a silhouette against the sky." Portland, Oregon, is now considering adding sculptured rooftops to its more than 20 design guidelines for the Central City.

Rooftop design is particularly important for projects with high visibility from above, that is, from hills or nearby office towers. For example, one of the major design issues for RiverPlace, a mixed-use development on the west bank of the Willamette River in downtown Portland, was the site's visibility from nearby freeways, bridges, and office towers. Rooftop variety became one of the controlling design standards; no flat roofs were permitted on structures with fewer than five stories. The mixture of gabled and other sloping roof types underscores the project's essentially residential character and bolsters the overall neighborhood theme. And the peaked roofs and rounded-arch dormers of the athletic club give the project a recognizable profile.

A new building's contribution to the skyline is also a design criterion in Burlington, Vermont. The downtown zoning code states that "[t]raditionally, Burlington's values are expressed and reflected in its skyline. Future buildings shall be thoughtfully shaped in relationship to their position in the skyline and sympathetic to surrounding 19th-century vernacular architecture. The impact of rooftop form shall be carefully considered. Alternatives to flat roofs shall be encouraged."

In Seattle, sculptured building tops figure as a general public benefit for which additional density and/or height may be awarded. Surplus floor area is granted

for the total amount of area by which each upper-story floor is reduced, with a maximum set at 30,000 square feet. Although the bonus is not limited to full-block development, the amount of floor area reduction required on upper floors to qualify for the award makes it likely that only buildings with large floor plates will apply for the bonus.

The first building to take advantage of Seattle's sculptured top bonus was the 55-story Washington Mutual Tower, completed in 1988. The project was designed by Kohn Pedersen Fox, working with McKinley Architects of Seattle. The pinkish-beige, stepped-back structure, clad in Brazilian granite and sporting a wedding-cake cupola, undoubtedly was inspired by the architecture of the 1914 terra cotta–clad Smith Tower and other nearby art deco buildings. This test of the city's 1985 zoning ordinance, in which "the code shaped the building, and the building shaped the code," [10] revealed several glitches that needed to be ironed out of the code. One of these was the original formula for the sculptured rooftop bonus. Jon Runstad, the tower's developer, had to submit more than a dozen rooftop designs before the city finally agreed to award the gain, amounting to 45,000 square feet. The city has since changed the formula to alleviate this problem. (See Insert 1 for the formula, standards, and guidelines.)

T. J. Lassar

Art deco–inspired Washington Mutual Tower (center) breaks up the monotony of Seattle's skyline.

1. Intent

   Sculptured building tops are intended to promote visual interest and variety in the downtown skyline. They have the greatest impact in areas of downtown where the tallest buildings are permitted. A sculptured building top which modifies the silhouette of a building by reducing the area of the top floors reduces the appearance of the overall bulk of the building to produce a more interesting building form. As buildings increase in height, the more visible upper portion is shaped to appear increasingly slender and more ornamental. Mechanical equipment on the roof will also be enclosed and integrated into the design of the building as a whole.

2. Bonusable area

   a. The bonusable area shall be the sum of all reductions on qualifying floors, plus a 10,000-square-foot automatic reduction granted [under] the provisions of Subsection 3.

   b. In order to qualify for a bonus, reductions in areas of floors to create the sculptured building top shall occur within the upper 30 percent of the total occupiable height of the structure.

   c. The maximum total reduced floor area eligible for a bonus shall be 30,000 square feet.

3. Reduced floor area

   Basic Standards

   a. The minimum reduction in building area within the upper 30 percent of the total occupiable building height, measured from the lowest street elevation, shall be as follows:

      (1) The area of the highest enclosed floor shall be no greater than 80 percent of the area of the floor at the 70 percent height elevation.

      (2) The minimum reduction in floor area between the highest occupiable enclosed floor and the 70 percent level shall be achieved through floor area reductions on no less than two floors.

      (3) The maximum vertical dimension between any two floors on which area is reduced shall be 90 feet.

      (4) No single reduction on a floor shall be less than 5 percent of the gross floor area of the floor below.

   b. In addition to the minimum reduction in 3a. above, all occupiable floors in the upper 30 percent of the structure reduced by at least 5 percent in area from the floor below shall qualify for calculation of bonusable area.

   Design Guidelines

   c. On the floors reduced to create the sculptured building top, the perimeter walls shall be set back from the floor below on at least two sides of the structure for a total length equal to approximately half of the perimeter dimension of the floor below. The depth of the setback shall generally be no less than three feet.

   d. All mechanical equipment, equipment spaces, penthouses, and other rooftop features above the last occupiable floor shall be enclosed. The design and materials of mechanical enclosures shall be architecturally integrated with the sculptured building top and the balance of the entire building.

   e. The area of enclosures of mechanical equipment higher than 25 feet above the last occipiable floor shall not exceed 65 percent of the floor area at the 70 percent level and shall have at least one setback in conformance with b. above or other modulation of the enclosure to add interest and create a more slender building silhouette.

Unhappily, the bonus's still excessively complicated formula may make it too costly to use. A developer who recently applied for a permit under the new zoning chose not to apply for the bonus, to avoid paying an architect to submit numerous alternatives.

Some critics remain unconvinced of the wisdom of encouraging sculptured roofs in Seattle and question the value and efficacy of awarding extra density for this amenity. Their claim is that ornamental building tops are very much de rigueur and will be built regardless of the density award. Jon Runstad seems to agree with this view. He acknowledges that the distinctive rooftop design for his postmodern Washington Mutual Tower was selected mainly for aesthetic reasons rather than bonus value.

Paul Goldberger notes that, although the Washington Mutual Tower is not the tallest building in the city, in every other way it is "downtown Seattle's most prominent building [and is] likely to become the symbol of a skyline that has not had a tall structure strong enough to serve as an icon since the quirky, amiable Space Needle went up in 1962." [11]

ZONING AS SHAPER OF SAN FRANCISCO'S URBAN FABRIC

San Francisco's urban design system has been simultaneously acclaimed as a bold experiment, "the first modern planning analysis of any major American municipality to assess comprehensively the urban form and character of the city as a whole," [12] and assailed as "an example of design review run amok." [13] Some commentators note that the 1971 Urban Design Plan, which was largely translated into the 1985 Downtown Plan, "[m]ore than any other municipal zoning . . . dictate[s] all but the final design of architectural development," [14] so that the city "no longer has planners, it has design czars." [15]

More specific than the 1971 Urban Design Plan, the 1985 code revision sedulously assesses, block by block, and in some cases building by building, the visual character and function of San Francisco's downtown. The Downtown Plan, which aims to "create an urban form for downtown that enhances San Francisco's stature as one of the world's most visually attractive cities," portrays "a white city spread over the hills" with a texture of "small-scale buildings . . . , punctuated by green spaces and occasional larger significant structures." Moreover, its "visual appeal . . . is based on its topography—its hills and ridges and their relationship to the ocean and bay—and on the scale of existing development. This scale is by and large a light-toned texture of separate shapes blended and articulated over the city's topography."

To reinforce the scale of existing development, the 1985 ordinance cuts heights in the retail core, which previously ranged from 240 to 500 feet, to 80 feet; reduces FAR limits in the densest commercial areas, which previously ranged from 9 to 14, to 6 to 9; and imposes strict setback requirements. (See Insert 2 for the amount of space required between towers on new development.) The plan also requires the preservation of 251 "significant" buildings and provides incentives to retain 183 other buildings that are less historically important but that nonetheless contribute to the historic and architectural integrity of the downtown.

Insert 2.
San Francisco: Separation between Towers
(code illustration)

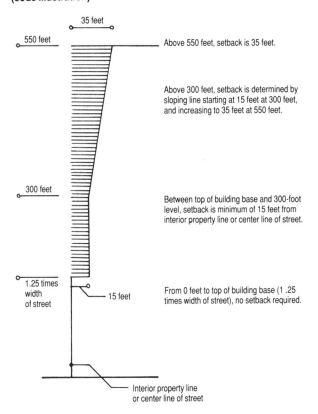

35 feet

550 feet — Above 550 feet, setback is 35 feet.

Above 300 feet, setback is determined by sloping line starting at 15 feet at 300 feet, and increasing to 35 feet at 550 feet.

300 feet

Between top of building base and 300-foot level, setback is minimum of 15 feet from interior property line or center line of street.

1.25 times width of street — 15 feet

From 0 feet to top of building base (1.25 times width of street), no setback required.

Interior property line or center line of street

The code also permits the transfer of unused development rights (TDRs) from significant and "contributory" buildings. Significant buildings may be demolished only for public safety or economic reasons (if a building's TDR value is so minimal that it retains no substantial remaining market value). Alterations to these buildings must be reviewed according to the U.S. Secretary of the Interior's standards for rehabilitation, and owners must maintain the structures. Although the code does not mandate preservation of con-

tributory buildings, these structures must be rehabilitated and maintained as landmarks before TDRs may be sold. [16]

The 1985 Downtown Plan expunged most of the city's bonus provisions, so that developers must rely instead on the TDR mechanism to gain density. To achieve maximum density, developers must buy TDRs from historic buildings or open space. (The only other means of acquiring any extra density is through an inclusionary housing provision.) By purchasing TDRs, developers may push FARs within the office core, which range from 6 to 9, to as high an apex as 18 in some areas; thus, a strong incentive exists to use the TDR option. Compare San Francisco's approach to that taken by Hartford, for example. The latter treats historic preservation as but one of many bonus selections offered on the incentive zoning menu. Building conservation must therefore compete with other public amenities such as open space, daycare, and ground-floor retail to reap greater densities for developers.

San Francisco's planning department undoubtedly added muscle to its historic preservation program by making it part of the downtown ordinance. Indeed, the city's historic preservation code ranks as one of the most aggressive in the country. But the office rationing system, which places a lid on building citywide (as discussed in the previous chapter), has gone hand-in-hand with the high office vacancy rates of recent years to quell developer interest and thwart significant use of the TDRs.

The regulations for historic preservation, bulk control, setbacks, spatial separation between towers, tapered building forms, and sculptured rooftops work together with those code sections encouraging greater articulation of building surfaces through the use of deep-set windows, beltcourses, cornices, and pilasters to shape the physical design of new development. Because bay windows, for instance, are regarded as among the city's distinctive architectural features, the code dictates that building overhangs be modulated by multiangled glazed units to reinforce the bay window tradition. And to maintain the rowhouse character of many downtown blocks, building facades exceeding a designated width must be divided visually. [17]

Like other cities, San Francisco tries to animate the pedestrian streetscape by promoting architectural variety at ground level. The plan imposes certain fenestration requirements inhibiting the use of dark opaque glass and reflective glazing. (See Chapter 6, "Environmental Impacts of Tall Buildings.")

San Francisco also demands that buildings exceeding 25,000 square feet in the commercial district incorporate public art amounting to at least 1 percent of construction costs or, in the case of city-sponsored projects, 2 percent. "Said works of art may include sculpture, bas relief, murals, mosaics, decorative water features, tapestries, or other artworks permanently affixed to the building or its grounds . . . but may not include architectural features of the building. Artworks shall be displayed in a manner that will enhance their enjoyment by the general public." The code also states that "a plaque or cornerstone identifying the project architect and the creator of the artwork . . . [shall be] placed at a publicly conspicuous location on the building prior to the issuance of the first certificate of occupancy."

San Francisco is not alone in requiring that a portion of a building's construction costs be earmarked for public art. (See Chapter 2, "Four Bonuses in Closeup.") A more common practice, however, as followed by such cities as Hartford, Cincinnati, and Orlando, is to treat public art as one of the bonus amenities within an incentive zoning package.

San Francisco has another code provision governing building design that is unique to its Downtown Plan. Developers must construct two scale models of projects proposed for the commercial district that exceed 40 feet in height. One model must show the building at a scale of one inch to 100 feet; the other must depict the block in which the building is located at a scale of one inch to 32 feet and include all the buildings on the block and those on the streets surrounding it. The dimensions for these models have been carefully scaled to fit into the larger model of the entire downtown that is housed at Berkeley's Environmental Simulation Laboratory. The cost for the two models runs roughly from $25,000 to $30,000.

The proposed project, as depicted in the models, is photographed from as many angles as possible to imitate the variety of views seen in the real world. The models are tested for accuracy of color, shape, texture, detailing, and lighting factors. Proponents and opponents of the project have equal access to the facility, where they may verify the dimensions of the building, as well as those of neighboring structures.[18]

CAN YOU LEGISLATE DESIGN?

Finally, San Francisco's urban design system raises the basic question of whether architecture can be successfully legislated. The short answer is, "You bet! Just go to San Francisco." Legislating good design, however, is another matter. Paul Goldberger asks the same question about the recent zoning provisions for Times Square, requiring New York builders to use an-

imated supersigns on new office and hotel development. Describing the new Times Square zoning as "something of a shotgun marriage between real opposites"[19]—a merger of corporate formality with theater-district flamboyance—Goldberg questions this attempt to institutionalize the neon chaos of Times Square and to keep alive through legislation a style that, until now, has been spontaneous and casual.

The general consensus seems to be that highly prescriptive regulatory schemes and comprehensive design review programs generally do no more than weed out the worst. They are not guarantees of architectural excellence. Mediocrity, on the other hand, generally discourages attacks. This issue was hotly debated at a 1987 architecture conference sponsored by the *San Francisco Examiner*. As architectural historian Sally Woodbridge commented, "When someone comes along and designs a totally banal office building, it's very hard to fight it. Have you ever tried to attack a mediocre building? There's nothing you can say."[20]

Another difficulty is that because regulations generally lag several years behind aesthetic tastes, one is essentially taking "ideas that are about five years old, . . . now universally considered to be good, and . . . say[ing] that's what we want to see built. Then along comes someone like Michael (Graves or Michelangelo) who wants to do something brand new. It will take five years to be accepted. In the meantime, there will be a whole bunch of clone architects doing knock-offs."[21]

More architectural styles have been discarded in the 20th century than in the previous 500 years put together.[22] Can zoning codes be sufficiently flexible and prescient to accommodate and anticipate such frequent shifts in design tastes?

Because building design is subject to the vagaries of fluctuating tastes and trends, the recent entrant, or "alien" structure, that threatens our sense of order and stability may very well be transmogrified over time into a city's "icon." This is one of John Costonis's main arguments in his book *Icons and Aliens*. As Costonis notes, when the Eiffel Tower was first erected in 1899,

it was scorned as the "dishonor of Paris" by Gounod, Prudhomme, and other members of the Committee of Three Hundred (one member per meter of the tower's height). Implored the group: "Is Paris going to be associated with the grotesque mercantile imagings of a constructor of machines . . . ?" Yet the tower still stands, now as the beloved signature of the Parisian skyline and an officially designated monument to boot.[23]

Almost 100 years later, I.M. Pei's new addition to the Louvre is provoking similar debate.

Likewise, New York's brownstones are now the pride of many neighborhood districts. But in the eyes of 19th-century writer Edith Wharton, they were loathsome buildings clad in a "chocolate-colored coating of the most hideous stone ever quarried [and set within a] cramped, horizontal gridiron of a town . . . hidebound in its deadly uniformity of mean ugliness."[24] Other examples of aliens that have ended up as icons are New York's Flatiron Building and Guggenheim Museum, and perhaps the Transamerica Building.

Costonis delights in recounting the ironies that

came with a mid-1980s proposal to place a postmodern Michael Graves addition atop Marcel Breuer's "new brutalist" Whitney Museum in New York City. Breuer, of course, had earlier enraged preservationists with his proposal to place an international-style office tower atop the Beaux Arts Grand Central Terminal. The villain in that controversy, Breuer became the hero in the Whitney Museum spat because his building was now the icon threatened by Graves's alien.[25]

Some critics also question whether some of the new zoning design tools intended to add architectural variety and visual interest are not producing instead the opposite results. Incentives to build sculptured rooftops, for example, have inspired a medley of angled, pyramid-shaped, and pointed building tops. Might not the uniform skylines formed by the box-topped international-style buildings merely give way to a new brand of monotony—a parade of lookalike stylized rooftops?

Similar reservations have been expressed about the bulk and massing controls in Seattle's 1985 incentive zoning code. The ordinance establishes a system of view corridor setbacks on certain street segments to preserve views of Elliott Bay, West Seattle, Mount Rainier, and the Olympic Mountains. Opponents say the view corridor constraints produce similar zoning envelopes and may eventually promote a cookie-cutter aesthetic. Setback requirements prevent building out to the corners, so that in order to maximize a structure's footprint, an architect must move the center of gravity to the center of the block. The tendency, therefore, is to take down any existing smaller structures not designated as historic and to build one megabuilding on the block. One Seattle architect noted that although the bulk restrictions differ for each of the downtown districts, the resulting floor plates are remarkably alike.

From the very start, Seattle's American Institute of Architects (AIA) chapter was skeptical about adopting view corridor constraints and noted that in a ma-

Roger K. Lewis, from his Washington Post column, "Shaping the City," 1/28/89

ture urban area such as Seattle's downtown, many of the theoretical view planes have already been disrupted by existing buildings.

Despite San Francisco's ambitious efforts to ensure design quality through its rigorous architectural review process, the winning projects in 1987—"cautious little buildings that struggle not to offend," as described by one critic[26]—are hardly remarkable. The local AIA chapter claimed the beauty contest encouraged a "painting by the numbers" approach to architectural design. The competition is so fierce and the compulsion to please so overwhelming that architects are loath to risk any design exceptions.[27]

Finally, many architects both inside and outside San Francisco are uncomfortable about mandating a given design style for a robust and changing downtown. They warn that, in its drive to create an urban scene based on prevailing aesthetic tastes, San Francisco may have opted for a Disneylandish stage setting of contrived architecture. According to Robert Campbell, by self-consciously legislating an image of itself, "San Francisco admittedly has turned itself into San Franciscoland. It is becoming, to some extent, a representation of itself. But what's the alternative, worldwide uniformity?"[28]

As more cities reevaluate their downtown zoning systems, they too may attempt to shape the character of their centers and, more importantly, determine whose design values they want to put forward. These difficult decisions will inevitably be somewhat arbitrary. But it's better, states Campbell, "to be Bostonland than not to be Boston at all."[29]

Some urban designers assert, in opposition, that public intervention should be directed mainly toward influencing the design of the public space infrastructure; the streets, sidewalks, and urban spaces that provide the base for private development need more controlling than the appearances of individual buildings.[30] Some designers go further and claim that the best climate for nurturing good architectural design is one in which public intervention is minimal.

When asked which cities are most conducive to building great buildings, architect Eugene Kohn responded, "Chicago and Philadelphia." The development and design review systems in these cities happen to rank among the more flexible, highly negotiable, and discretionary review processes in the country. In addition, Kohn attributes Chicago's fertile building climate to the city's architectural heritage. Chicago cabbies are just as likely to point out the local architectural landmarks as they are to boast about their baseball teams. A veritable crucible of distinct architectural styles, Chicago has always attracted some of the country's most notable architects, who must work hard to satisfy a city that is consummately knowledgeable and critical about matters of building design. In cities like Chicago, where design excellence is already part of the city's collective unconscious, the most effective design regulations may very well be those that impose the least restraint on the creative process.

Notes

1. Robert Campbell, "Should Boston Adopt a San Francisco Plan?," *Boston Globe* (April 5, 1987).
2. Ibid.
3. Patrick Pinnell, "Back to the Future," *Museum & Arts* (March/April 1989), p. 81.
4. Jonathan Barnett, *An Introduction to Urban Design* (New York: Harper & Row, 1982), p. 60.
5. Michael Kwartler, "Zoning As Architect and Urban Designer," in *Real Estate Development and City Regulations*, a special issue of *New York Affairs*, vol. 8, no. 4 (1985), p. 104.

6. Ada Louise Huxtable, *The Tall Building Artistically Reconsidered: The Search for a Skyscraper Style* (New York: Pantheon Books, 1982), p. 99.
7. Richard Tseng-yi Lai, *Law in Urban Design and Planning: The Invisible Web* (New York: Van Nostrand Reinhold Company, (1988), p. 339.
8. Huxtable, op. cit., p. 68.
9. Ibid., p. 20.
10. Scott Maier, "How one high-rise grew up," *Seattle Post-Intelligencer* (April 18, 1988).
11. Paul Goldberger, "Proud of Its Height, a New Tower Rules over Seattle," *New York Times* (November 27, 1988).
12. Lai, *Law in Urban Design and Planning*, p. 334.
13. Ed Zotti, "Design by Committee," *Planning* (May 1987), p. 24.
14. Lai, op. cit., p. 335.
15. Paul Goldberger, "When Planning Can Be Too Much of a Good Thing," *New York Times* (December 6, 1987).
16. See Richard J. Roddewig and Cheryl A. Inghram's comprehensive discussion of TDR programs operating throughout the country in *Transferable Development Rights Programs*, Planning Advisory Service Report no. 401 (Chicago: American Planning Association, 1987). The San Francisco discussion is on pp. 11–12.
17. See Lai, *Law in Urban Design and Planning*, p. 335.
18. See Peter Bosselmann, "Experiencing Downtown Streets in San Francisco," in *Public Streets for Public Use*, ed. Anne Vernez Moudon (New York: Van Nostrand Reinhold Company, 1987), pp. 218–220.
19. Paul Goldberger, "New York Times Square Zoning: Skyscrapers with Signs," *New York Times* (January 30, 1987).
20. Reported by Bradley Inman, "Designs for the City," *San Francisco Examiner* (November 29, 1987).
21. Ibid.
22. As claimed in a letter to the editor in *Architectural Record* (October 1988), p. 4.
23. John J. Costonis, *Icons and Aliens: Law, Aesthetics, and Environmental Change* (Urbana and Chicago: University of Illinois Press, 1989), p. 64.
24. Cited by Costonis, ibid., p. 25.
25. Ibid., p. 109.
26. Goldberger, "When Planning Can Be Too Much of a Good Thing."
27. Letter (April 23, 1986) from the AIA's San Francisco chapter to the president of the planning commission, urging the commission to dismiss the evaluation of the design review panel in the first competition.
28. Campbell, "Should Boston Adopt a San Francisco Plan?"
29. Ibid.
30. See Jonathan Barnett, *Urban Design as Public Policy* (New York: Architectural Record Books, 1974), p. 186.

CHAPTER 6

ENVIRONMENTAL IMPACTS OF TALL BUILDINGS

We shape our buildings, and afterwards our buildings shape us.

–Winston Churchill

A frequent component of the development and design review process is review for environmental impacts. In many downtowns, buildings must comply with regulations designed to protect environmental values—light access, shadow limits, reduction of winds affecting pedestrians, and view protection. One trend is to require analysis and documentation of a proposal's "microclimatic effects" as part of the development approval process. For example, one of the 14 criteria of Pittsburgh's so-called project development plan review for downtown buildings is "microclimatic effects of proposed development, including wind velocities, sun reflectance, and sun access to streets. . . ." Hartford, Connecticut, requires wind and shadow studies at both the preliminary and final application stages for buildings in the downtown, and projects taller than 50 feet in downtown Charlotte, North Carolina, must conduct sun studies to determine shadow patterns for development approval.

Microclimatic impacts are often incorporated into design review. Protecting solar access, minimizing shadows, and reserving views of Lake Champlain and the Adirondack Mountains are design review criteria for projects in downtown Burlington, Vermont. Likewise, corridor view protection is one of the essential design review guidelines in Portland, Oregon.

This chapter deals with those environmental or microclimatic impacts of tall buildings most commonly addressed in the project approval procedures of downtown zoning regulations. Traffic impacts and associated mitigation measures are examined in Chapter 10, "Parking and Transportation."

BACKGROUND

Recurrently, review for environmental impacts is regulated through specific zoning provisions as well as through federal, state, and municipal laws. In many cities, environmental review is mandated by a state environmental act modeled after the 1969 National Environmental Policy Act (NEPA). Based on the premise that "each person should enjoy a healthy environment," NEPA enunciates a national goal of "ensur[ing] that presently quantified environmental amenities and values . . . be given appropriate consideration in decision making, along with economic and technical considerations" and requires federal agencies to "utilize a systematic, interdisciplinary approach which will insure the integrated use of the natural and social sciences and the environmental design arts in planning and decision making which may have an impact on man's environment. . . . "

The Act also directs the Council on Environmental Quality to respond "to the . . . social, aesthetic, and cultural needs and interests of the nation. . . . " John Costonis writes that the Act "broadcasts the convergence of environmental and aesthetic values," a linkage that is "also featured in the 'little NEPAs' of the states." [1] During the 1970s, many states enacted these NEPA clones, mounting what some commentators have called "a quiet revolution in land use control." [2] The California Environmental Quality Act (CEQA) was passed in 1970 and was followed by state environmental acts in Connecticut, Hawaii, Montana, New York, North Carolina, South Dakota, Virginia, Washington, Wisconsin, and Puerto Rico. It "was the adoption of [these] state statutes that applied environmental impact analysis to the general run of day-to-day land use decisions." [3]

Although some states initially limited the definition of environmental impact to "physical impacts," the scope of environmental reviews as written into most state laws and empowered through municipal regulations is generally a broad one. It covers a myriad of concerns, ranging from the impacts of surface water movement, erosion, view blockage, light, and glare; to their effects on historic and cultural preservation;

to such issues as vehicular traffic, housing, public services and utilities, parks and other recreational facilities, sewer capacity, and distribution of growth; and to aesthetic and urban design considerations.

For instance, in 1986, New York State's highest court ruled on the environmental impact statement (EIS) of a luxury high-rise condominium in Chinatown. Under New York City's environmental quality review (CEQR) and the state's environmental act, the project was remiss for failing to consider adequately whether it would "accelerate the displacement" of local low-income residents and businesses in the neighborhood or "alter the character of the community."[4] The court indicated that the term "environment" covered more than the physical environment, and that cities must note, among other social and economic results, the effects of the proposed action on population and community character. Moreover, developers must mitigate any secondary displacement consequences of the construction of luxury housing in low-rent neighborhoods like Chinatown.

The general procedural approach imposed by state environmental acts begins with a study to determine possible significant environmental impacts. Then, if such impacts are identified, preparation of an environmental impact statement must follow, with a public review and comment period and with a showing that adverse impacts have been mitigated or alternatives adopted to the extent "practicable" or "feasible." This description is deceptively simple, however. In practice, the process is fraught with complexities and ambiguities. Most states, for example, limit environmental review to so-called "discretionary," as opposed to "ministerial," decisions. The issuance of a building permit for a project that complies with the permitted as-of-right zoning is generally treated as a ministerial act. However, the Washington State Supreme Court held, in *Polygon Corporation* v. *City of Seattle*,[5] that a building permit for a project that meets the underlying zoning standards may nonetheless be denied on a finding of adverse environmental impact based on urban design criteria (excessive size and view blockage) or economic considerations (devalued neighboring residential property).

The purpose of the introductory discussion above has been mainly to stress how thoroughly environmental impact analysis permeates the permit application process; indeed, in many jurisdictions, it has become the *Weltanschauung* of development review. The "environmental neurosis," as Jonathan Barnett labels it,[6] is indeed the prevailing mind-set in many regions. Moreover, even if the state has not passed an environmental act, some cities nevertheless incorporate environmental assessment requirements into their development approval processes.

One continuing concern is the overlap, and sometimes duplication, between EIS requirements and development review in those states with environmental policy acts. In Seattle and Bellevue, Washington, for instance, the intention is to excise those items from environmental review that are later codified in the zoning. However, despite numerous streamlining efforts, developers in New York, California, and Washington generally criticize the unnecessary duplication that adds to the already burdensome time delays and costs entailed in their respective development and environmental approval processes. Some Washington State developers also indicate that the costliest requirement of environmental review is meeting the conditions for traffic mitigation, which must be agreed on before a building permit is issued. These conditions generally take the form of upfront fees to be borne by the developer, for lenders are loath to step in until all approvals have been secured.

LIGHT ACCESS

Simultaneous sensations of flooding sunshine, extensive openness, and a chunk of blue sky reaching down almost to eye level are so rare in Manhattan outside a park or a penthouse that I glanced up toward the sun to see how long the sunshine part of this could last.

This is one kind of celestial calculation that many New Yorkers learn to make automatically; it amounts to an astronomical equivalent of looking at a parking meter or checking the fuel gauge on a car's dashboard—only, instead of looking at an arrow moving through a semicircle on top of a parking meter to see how many minutes you've got left before the "EXPIRED" sign flips up, you look up at the sun to find out how big a piece of open sky it can still arc through before a building somewhere on the skyline blocks it and throws a shadow over you.[7]

There is nothing new about using zoning to preserve light. When the 1922 Standard State Zoning Enabling Act was published, two major U.S. urban health problems were rickets and tuberculosis; the incidence of both diseases is aggravated by insufficient light in buildings. The need for naturally lit building interiors diminished with the invention of artificial lighting, ventilation, and cooling and heating systems. However, the development of other engineering techniques, such as elevators and curtain-wall construction, meant the erection of sky-annihilating structures that fundamentally altered the character of downtown streets, sidewalks, and parks.

Controls for solar access in low- to moderate-density development are familiar features in suburban zoning. By setting standards for site planning and landscaping, or by stipulating solar easements, these controls usually protect access to sunshine for buildings with active or passive solar technology. Solar access is an equally important component of many downtown zoning ordinances, but the concerns are quite different. Downtown controls affecting light and shadow protect people, not buildings, and the issue is enhancing pedestrian comfort rather than conserving energy.

Charlotte, North Carolina's 1987 Uptown Mixed-Use District (UMUD) ordinance, which covers the downtown, requires analysis of the influences of any proposed new construction over 50 feet tall on nearby buildings, urban open spaces, and pedestrian areas. The analysis must include sun studies "to determine the shadow patterns that will be cast by the proposed building at 9:00 a.m., 12:00 noon, and 3:00 p.m. at the equinoxes and solstices." (See Insert 1 for an illustration from the ordinance.)

Insert 1.
Charlotte's Shadow Controls
(code excerpt)

Building Height, Setback, and Shadow Patterns

In accordance with Section 3053.6.4 of this ordinance, all new construction over 50 feet in height must provide a microclimate study that analyzes the impact of the new project on surrounding buildings, urban open spaces, and pedestrian areas. This analysis should include, but not be limited to, sun studies to determine the shadow patterns cast by the proposed building.

As illustrated here, a taller building will need to be located a greater distance from the property line in order to cast a minimum shadow of 20 feet onto any adjacent residentially zoned parcel.

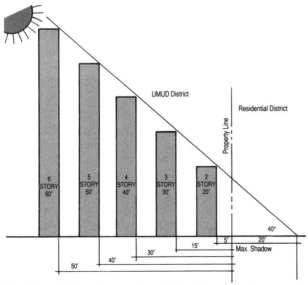

This diagram is illustrative, and the setback distances from the property line are approximated.

Charlotte's sun access regulation affords even greater protection for residential properties next to the downtown and sets a maximum height. "No structure, fixture, or other objects on a lot abutting residentially zoned land may be situated so that it casts a shadow at a distance greater than 20 feet across any property line on September 21 between the hours of 9:00 a.m. and 3:00 p.m. Eastern Standard Time."

Likewise, regulations for Boston's Midtown Cultural District state that within planned development areas,

Each proposed project shall be arranged and designed in a way to assure that it does not cast shadows for more than two hours from 8:00 a.m. through 2:30 p.m., on any day from March 21 through October 21, in any calendar year, on any portion of the Shadow Impact Areas depicted [on map] that are not cast in shadow during such period on such days by structures existing as of the effective date of this article, or would not be cast in shadow during such period on such days by structures built to the maximum sizes permitted. . . .

Many regulations are far less precise in describing solar access goals and shadow limits. For example, one of the design review criteria in Bellevue is to "[e]nsure that the form and placement of buildings consider desirable year-round conditions of sun and shade in surrounding open spaces and public areas." Similarly, Burlington, Vermont's downtown design review, which calls for shadow diagrams, states ambiguously: "New buildings and additions to existing buildings shall be shaped to reduce substantial impacts of shadows on public plazas and other publicly accessible spaces."

An additional light impact issue is the use of reflective surface building materials and the ensuing glare. In parts of downtown Austin, Texas, the city prohibits the use of mirrored glass or other glare-producing surface building materials. Mirrored glass is defined as any glass with a reflectivity index greater than 20 percent. Bellevue permits a maximum reflectivity of no more than 29 percent, and developers must "mitigate light and glare impacts upon major public facilities, streets, and major public open spaces." In Charlotte, the maximum reflectivity value is 36 percent, "as measured under the applicable provisions of federal specifications."

One objection to the use of highly reflective materials as cladding for downtown office structures is that such materials are essentially opaque: their effect is akin to that of building a blank wall, which contributes nothing to the streetscape. Concern about glare is also related to automobile safety. In Seattle, slow-downs and massive traffic snarls on a freeway leading into town were ascribed directly to the reflected light from a new Hilton hotel. During morning rush hours in the winter, glare from the glass-walled hotel shot straight into drivers' eyes. The city council responded in 1978 with legislation compelling developers to mitigate potential adverse impacts from light and glare.[8]

When used in densely built settings, reflective glass also tends to raise the temperature. Several suits have been brought by building owners in Texas over the extra air-conditioning load caused by reflections from glass buildings.[9]

NEW YORK'S SOLUTION

New York is one of two cities that have adopted the country's most ambitious solar retention regulations. (The other is San Francisco, covered in the next subsection below.) Indeed, New York City's 1916 Zoning Ordinance, the first comprehensive zoning system promulgated by a major U.S. city, contained a "sky exposure plane" provision devised to encourage sun penetration into windows and preserve views of the sky. The result was the familiar ziggurat, or wedding-cake, architecture with uniform street walls and upper-story setbacks.

This effective bulk control system, however, was steadily eroded by the city's practice of granting height and setback waivers for providing indoor public amenities, as permitted under the 1961 Zoning Resolution. Developers wishing to maximize their building envelopes constructed atrium-type spaces and thus sought relief from the bulk and height controls. Such tinkering thoroughly undermined the effectiveness of any sky exposure plane. Furthermore, height and setback rules were relaxed for some projects involving transferable air rights for landmark structures.

New York's great building boom in the 1960s, coupled with these incentive zoning provisions, steadily deprived Midtown Manhattan of sunlight, so that "by mid-afternoon, the great bulk of Midtown was in shadow."[10]

The 1982 Midtown Zoning introduced a two-tier system of height and bulk regulation. According to the rules of the "prescriptive tier," buildings must comply with stipulated street-wall heights and daylight angles, measured from the center of the street. Taller buildings must be set back farther to avoid breaking the sun access plane. A system of trade-offs, called "encroachment and compensation," allows for design flexibility. For a building found to encroach into the space above the plane, compensation must be provided or a bulk reduction made elsewhere on the site. The rules vary. For instance, additional compen-

sation is needed on corner sites, where the projected impacts from encroachment are thought to be greater.

Whereas the first option is an as-of-right one, the second approach, or "performance tier," measures effects and thus permits greater design diversity, says one of the primary crafters of the two-tier system, Patrick Ping-Tze Too, New York City's principal urban designer. Under this alternative approach, building proposals are judged on a daylight evaluation chart, or Waldram diagram, a device first used in England that measures the amount of daylight a proposed building would block as viewed by a person on the street. Proposals failing to meet the more traditional setback requirements may now be built if they achieve the requisite scores of the daylight evaluation chart.[11]

Rather than having to conform to a setback curve that relates buildings to angles of visibility from the street, a structure is gauged according to the amount of "sky" left unobstructed.[12] The diagram is divided into a number of squares that represent equal units of the sky. When a proposed building is plotted on the diagram, it earns a score based on the number and location of the squares—the increments of sky—that are blocked by the building mass. Scoring rules vary with street width, so the level of acceptable daylighting performance is based on the existing urban context.

Although administering the performance approach was at first a burden for city staff, the system has become easier to work with over time, especially with the increased availability of computer models, as developed by the New York office of Skidmore, Owings & Merrill. To its credit, the system has not been blamed for excessive permitting delays.

T.J. Gottesdiener, architect with Skidmore, Owings & Merrill, says that shadow studies generally have not been a problem in New York: "You either pass or fail." When the 1982 zoning regulations were first proposed, Jonathan Barnett noted they signaled a return to the traditional as-of-right or "rulebook system," in which light and air for neighboring buildings were the primary considerations.[13]

PENUMBRA UMBRAGE IN SAN FRANCISCO

Surrounded on three sides by water, San Francisco is a city where wind, clouds, and fog are climatic constants for much of the year. Sunlight preservation and shadow reduction, therefore, were addressed in the city's 1985 Downtown Plan. Several provisions aim to prevent new buildings from casting new shadows on selected streets and open spaces during times of peak pedestrian use. For example, sidewalks on the north side of Market Street must remain sunny after

11 a.m. from March 21 to September 21, which limits street-wall building heights to 119 feet. Behind the street wall, a building may rise higher as it gets farther back from the street, up to the limit of the "sun access angle plane" (see Insert 2). The phrase "sun access angle plane" clearly echoes the concept of the "sky exposure plane" contained in New York's 1916 code.

Insert 2.
San Francisco: Sun Access to Public Sidewalks (code excerpt)

Sec. 146. . . .

(a) *Requirement of Sunlight Access on Certain Streets.* In C-3 Districts, in order to maintain direct sunlight on public sidewalks in certain downtown areas during critical periods of use, new structures and additions to existing structures on parcels which abut on the side of a street identified below shall be required to avoid penetration of a sun access plane, defined by an angle sloping away from the street above a stipulated height at the property line abutting the street, as follows:

(b) *Exception.* An exception to the requirements of Subsection (a) may be granted. . .where (i) the penetration of the plane does not create shadow because of the shadow already cast by other buildings, or (ii) the shadow created by the penetration of the plane is deemed insignificant because of the limited extent or duration of the shadow or because of the limited public use of the shadowed space.

The ordinance lists designated streets, with sun access angle planes for each and maximum street-wall heights. Even buildings located on a street not specifically listed in the ordinance "shall be shaped, if it can be done without creating an unattractive design and without unduly restricting the development potential of the site in question, so as to reduce substantial shadow impacts on public sidewalks. . . . "

San Francisco's 1985 Downtown Plan contains an additional shadow limitation provision:

New buildings and additions to existing buildings . . . shall be shaped, consistent with the dictates of good design and without unduly restricting the development potential of the site in question, to reduce substantial shadow impacts on public plazas and other publicly accessible spaces. . . . In determining the impact of shadows, the following factors shall be taken into account: The amount of area shadowed, the duration of the shadow, and the importance of sunlight to the type of open space being shadowed.

The Onset of Proposition K. Known as the sunlight ordinance, Proposition K, which was passed as a citizen initiative in June 1984 and enacted into law the following January, virtually mandates year-round, all-day sun access for approximately 70 open spaces and parks within the jurisdiction of the city's recre-

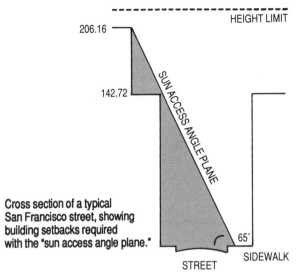

Cross section of a typical San Francisco street, showing building setbacks required with the "sun access angle plane."

Source: San Francisco Downtown Plan (code illustration).

ation and parks commission. Fourteen of these public open spaces are located in the downtown. Certain exemptions are made for shadows cast by buildings less than 40 feet tall. The regulation's major bailout language is an exemption for "shading or shadowing" where "the impact would be insignificant." In 1989, the city planning commission enacted criteria for determining significant shadows; however, for four years, the shadow ban prohibited new buildings from casting *any* shadows on existing city-owned parks or open spaces, or on those designated for acquisition by the city.

"The passage of Proposition K," remarks Patrick Phillips, "throws something of a monkey wrench into the city's solar planning works. . . . " [14] Regarding the 14 downtown properties managed by the city parks department, the measure is unforgiving and contravenes the more moderate stance of other code provisions, such as the one that considers the effects of the shadow controls on development potential and building design (discussed above). The reason for this apparent contradiction is that Proposition K, which arose out of a voter-approved initiative in June 1984, supersedes the Downtown Plan.

The Genesis of Proposition K. Peter Bosselmann, director of the Environmental Simulation Laboratory at the University of California at Berkeley, has been conducting sun studies for San Francisco since 1981. In that year, he was asked to evaluate the shadow effects of a proposed 132-foot condominium on a small playground in Chinatown. His team merged pictures of a variety of building envelopes reaching the then-allowed height of 160 feet with photos of the playground taken with a fisheye lens. The resulting photomontages revealed the effects of the proposed development on the sky exposure: sunlight on the playground during late afternoon would be diminished just when children would be likeliest to use it, namely, after school hours.[15]

Bosselmann's studies involved using the sky simulator, or "artificial sky," developed at Berkeley. The facility copies a range of outdoor sky and sun conditions for testing architectural scale models. Electronically controlled light sources within its dome reproduce the light distributions expected from clear and overcast skies and also test skies of uniform luminance. As well as simulating light from the sky, the model has a computer-driven sun that can introduce direct sunlight into the equation. The sky simulator allows designers to make both quantitative and qualitative evaluations of daylight in their building designs.

Beyond testing sunlight availability for public parks and plazas, the facility analyzes the performance of architectural devices to control daylighting, glare, or solar heat gain and validates newly developed computer models for predicting interior illumination.

In response to the studies conducted by Bosselmann's team, the planning commission passed a resolution curbing heights in the area of the playground, and the board of supervisors later upheld the resolution in interim zoning that reduced the heights from 160 to 50 feet. Bosselmann states that this resolution departed from the traditional method of defining building heights according to contour lines. Rather, building heights were "to follow 'cutoff' planes based on the path of the sun, called 'solar fans'."[16] Bosselmann also notes that in the early stages, San Francisco planners studied the two sun access measurement techniques in New York's 1982 Midtown Zoning, but rejected them as being too complicated.[17]

The planning commission then ordered solar fans for all open spaces in the downtown. By this time, however, the much-politicized "Sun for Open Spaces" movement had gathered such momentum that the city was pressured into ordering more comprehensive studies to evaluate tall buildings' effects on sun, wind, and temperature during different seasons and at different times of day.

When the results of Bosselmann's studies, conducted over a four-year period, were published, work on the Downtown Plan had reached a critical stage, and environmental advocates pushed the issue of sunlight in parks and squares onto the 1984 primary ballot. The initiative passed by more than 60 percent. As an amendment to the city charter, Proposition K ex-

ceeded the intentions of the planning department and seemed to take on a life of its own.

Proposition K requires shadow measurements for nearly every daylight hour, unlike the city's environmental impact reporting procedure, which generally limits analysis to four designated days of the year at 10:00 a.m., 12:00 noon, and 3:00 p.m. The city has had to allocate more than $200,000 toward designing a three-dimensional data base and computer system for simulating shadows on the affected parks and squares. Parcel-specific data must be compiled within a one-foot accuracy range and must also account for preexisting shadows.

So far, Peter Bosselmann and his team at the Environmental Simulation Laboratory have compiled data bases for the 14 downtown parks and squares covered by the ordinance. Some 1,000 buildings already cast shadows on these spaces. Data bases still need to be worked up for some 56 additional public spaces elsewhere in the city.

As administered by the city, Bosselmann's computer modeling system theoretically gives developers advance notice of the shadow constraints on their potential projects. However, for projects conceived before the advent of Proposition K and designed without the aid of these computer projections, the effects of the all-or-nothing shadow ban have often been draconian. In addition, although Proposition K's ambit is limited to city-owned parks and plazas, considerable political pressure exists to extend its protection to privately owned public spaces.

The Shadow Ban in Action. The first significant test of the city's sunshine law was a 24-story office tower at Pine and Kearny Streets, across from the headquarters of the Bank of America. Proposed by developer Walter Shorenstein, the building would have shadowed the adjacent St. Mary's Square in Chinatown. In fact, any building on that site exceeding six stories probably would have violated the shadow constraints.

Three weeks after Proposition K was passed, the project architects, Skidmore, Owings & Merrill, produced an alternative design six stories shorter and proposed expanding the park so there would be no net loss of sunshine. Shorenstein rebuffed the suggestion that the city purchase the site for a public park but proposed swapping a piece of it for exemption from Proposition K. Rejecting his revised design and subsequent proposal, the city refused to approve the shadow-creating structure. Persevering, Shorenstein announced in May 1985 that he would construct a six-story parking garage on the site. Today, the site is still vacant.

Proposition K also left its imprimatur on two projects approved in the 1987 office development limitation program that has come to be known as "the beauty contest." (See Chapter 4, "Design Review Overdose, San Francisco–Style.") The larger of the two is the speculative office tower at 235 Pine, in the center of the financial district. Extensive shadow studies indicated the building would shade a small portion of St. Mary's Square, three blocks away, for three minutes in the early morning on 20 days out of the year. To make matters worse, a year after this problem had been broached, expansion of the roof of a parking garage located beneath the square called for more shadow testing. The results dictated that the building's height drop 52 feet, to 25 stories.

Charles I.M. Graham, executive vice president of London & Edinburgh Trust, developer of the project, says the approval and appeal process took four years but that only part of the delay could be blamed on Proposition K. The land for 235 Pine was originally bought for $9 million. As much again was spent on, first, the net carrying costs over the four-year approval period ($5 million) and, second, the miscellaneous soft costs directly attributable to the permitting and design review process ($4 million). Thus, the land and associated approval costs came to about $120 a rentable square foot for this 150,000-square-foot project.

As Graham says, "If developers know the rules before undertaking project evaluation and feasibility studies, we can assess the extent of the restrictions." Downtown San Francisco's stringent building cap, within the context of an extremely competitive market, leaves developers small latitude to challenge the shadow proscriptions; generally, they simply work around the constraints. But "rules brought in halfway through are especially cruel." Graham notes, however, that the influence of the shadow limits on his project (the 52-foot loss) was not catastrophic: "After all, the project is going up."

Paul E. Zigman, president of Environmental Science Associates, Inc., of San Francisco and Los Angeles, which has conducted many of the environmental reviews on San Francisco's downtown building designs, says that shadow testing can cost the developer anywhere between several hundred dollars and $30,000. The price depends on the building's location in relation to the open space and the sun's path. A building placed on the south side of a designated plaza, for instance, would likely suffer considerable shadow problems.

A second survivor of the 1987 design competition, 343 Sansome Street, was even more dramatically changed by the city's shadow limits. The 24,000-square-foot site for Gerald Hines Interests' third project in downtown San Francisco was bought in 1983 for $1,000 a square foot.

Philip Johnson, who consulted with John Burgee Architects, designed the original 350,000-square-foot, 25-story office project in conformance with the 1985 Downtown Plan. (See illustrations on next page of the tower as proposed.) The plan had slashed the prevailing FAR in the area from 14 to 10; a later amendment reduced the FAR to 9. Tom Swift, Hines Interests' executive vice president, reported at the 1987 ULI Semiannual Meeting in San Francisco that the various upfront development fees imposed by the plan for art, housing, open space, transit, and child care added $18 per square foot to project costs and translated to $2 per square foot in rental rates. Swift characterized the plan as reasonable: "You could learn to live with it . . . whether you liked it or not." Then Proposition K came along "like a bad dream."

Studies showed that impermissible shadows might be cast on several downtown parks, as well as on Maritime Plaza, a public open space in the financial district. To comply with Proposition K, seven stories were eliminated. But seven were not enough. Even the reduced design violated the shadow ban, if only, according to Swift, by shading an air vent in Maritime Plaza. Three more stories had to be lopped off.

The sharp reduction from 25 to 15 stories necessitated a drastic shift in architectural approach and numerous reworkings of the design. According to Swift, "because permits are so difficult, if not impossible, to secure in downtown San Francisco, land becomes . . . illiquid. We had no choice but to go ahead and develop the project."

The de facto height limits created by Proposition K are generally far more severe than those set out in the San Francisco Downtown Plan. Although the planning commission recently implemented criteria for determining when shadows are "insignificant" under Proposition K, these criteria are highly restrictive. For example, new shadows are permitted on only three of the 14 downtown parks. The amount of new shading allowed on Union Square may not exceed 1/10 of a percent of the existing shaded area. Although the criteria were derived from the date bases computed by Bosselmann's team, some critics question whether the system is accurate enough to make such precise determinations.

Another criticism of Proposition K is that it fails to distinguish materially between shadows cast at different times of the day. Whereas most downtown parks and public open spaces are used most heavily during

Courtesy, Gerald Hines Interests

343 Sansome Street, San Francisco, before (model at left) and after first redesign to accord with Proposition K's sun access rules. The redesign was complicated by the inclusion of a historic building (center, both photographs) into the new project.

midday lunch hours, the ordinance contains no tiering mechanism reflecting use variations. Instead, all shadows are treated as if they had identical impacts.

As a potential constraint on the building envelope, Proposition K heavily influences land costs. It is increasingly common for prospective buyers to undertake extensive shadow analysis before making major investments.

TESTING THE WINDS

- In 1982, financial analyst Rose Spielvogel stepped out of a steel skyscraper in New York and shat-

tered her shoulder when a gust of wind swept her into a concrete planter. Her $6.5 million claim against the building's architect, owner, and builder and against the city of New York is still wending its way through the courts.

- The opening of Boston's 60-story John Hancock Tower at Copley Square was delayed for five years, in part because of winds that created severe twisting and blew out half of the building's 10,344 windows.

- In 1983, a Canadian family filed a $3 million suit against the city of Toronto for injuries sustained when careening winds swept them off a jogging track. Elevated on a two-story podium at the base of Toronto's City Hall, part of the track was actually blown off the podium.

In the early 1970s, when the Hancock Tower was designed, the science of testing for the effects of wind was relatively crude by comparison with current sophisticated technology. Neither engineers nor building codes had taken into account the combined effects of gravity and wind. Far more worrying than the perils of plummeting window glass during the tower's construction, however, was the discovery that given certain wind conditions, the Hancock Tower might even collapse. Although potential wind damage is not strictly a modern concern, the present popularity of svelte, soaring structures sheathed in lightweight steel and glass exacerbates the problem.

Wind engineer Jack Cermak observes that today's "vertical steering rods" penetrate the atmospheric boundary layer, causing air of differing temperatures and layers to mix unnaturally and profoundly transforming wind speed. Like a fluid, wind pours over and around buildings, creating turbulence on the ground and at the corners. One of the more routine wind hazards is created when the wind strikes a tower and gushes downward over the slick building slab till it hits the ground, sending powerful updrafts across streets, sidewalks, and urban plazas. This has been dubbed the "Monroe effect," after a well-known photo showing Marilyn Monroe standing on a subway grate with an airborne hemline.[18]

Although wind testing is not new (the Empire State Building underwent a fairly unsophisticated tunnel analysis before construction in 1930), testing for the wind impacts that a building causes, rather than the other way around, is a recent concern. Whereas wind testing facilities once focused almost entirely on struc-

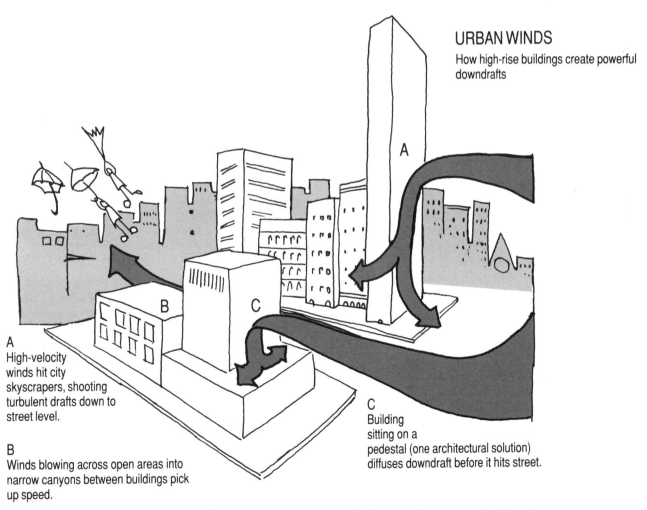

URBAN WINDS
How high-rise buildings create powerful downdrafts

A
High-velocity winds hit city skyscrapers, shooting turbulent drafts down to street level.

B
Winds blowing across open areas into narrow canyons between buildings pick up speed.

C
Building sitting on a pedestal (one architectural solution) diffuses downdraft before it hits street.

Source: From diagram accompanying Scott Armstrong, "Taming the fury of man-made wind," *Christian Science Monitor* (January 15, 1985), p. 23.

tural testing of wind effects on a building's cladding and frame, current testing procedures also evaluate air movement across landscapes, cities, and around buildings for its effects on human comfort in the outdoors.

ZONING FOR WIND EFFECTS

In the case of very tall structures, building codes have typically enumerated explicit performance standards for permissible wind loads, deflections, and peak accelerations. Thresholds for sidewalk-level winds, however, are rarely spelled out. They tend therefore to be more subjective, notes T.J. Gottesdiener.

The lack of comprehensive objective standards has not deterred cities from passing regulations to protect the pedestrian from prevailing winds. Although the Canadian cities of Calgary, Edmonton, and Toronto took the lead in passing legislative limits on street-level winds, wind tunnel testing is now de rigueur in cities throughout the United States. In Charlotte, North Carolina, Seattle and Bellevue, Washington, Boston, Denver, Hartford, Pittsburgh, and many other downtowns, buildings exceeding certain heights must undergo wind testing. In some downtowns, such as Bellevue, Washington, and Portland, Maine, pedestrian wind impact analyses are part of the design review process. New York City and San Francisco require wind impact analyses, both in their zoning ordinances and in their state environmental laws.

Although more and more downtown zoning ordinances are regulating the wind effects of tall buildings, particularly their impacts on the quality of the street-level pedestrian environment, few contain threshold limits. San Francisco is the exception. To date, San Francisco has imposed the most explicit and most rigorous constraints on street-level wind. Since 1974, the city has required wind studies of new highrise buildings as part of its environmental impact review, and in 1985, specific wind comfort standards were put into the Downtown Plan.

The plan sets the parameters for the comfort level of wind speed in areas of "substantial pedestrian use" at 11 miles per hour and in "public seating areas" at seven miles per hour. Between the hours of 7:00 a.m. and 6:00 p.m., ground-level wind currents are not permitted to exceed the limits in either category more than 10 percent of the time, year-round. Exceptions may be granted only when it can be shown that 1) compliance with the constraints would produce an unattractive, ungainly building and restrict the development potential of the site, and 2) noncompliance would be minimal and of short duration. The 1985 Downtown plan includes a table graphically describing the varying consequences of wind on pedestrian comfort (see Insert 3).

One 18-story office tower proposed for a particularly windy site in San Francisco reportedly underwent more than 20 design variations. Only one design alternative met the code wind criteria, but city staff deemed it aesthetically unacceptable. Eventually, a design exceeding the wind comfort limits at one of its measurement locations was approved.

Wendy Lockwood, senior associate with Environmental Science Associates, points to the toughest component of San Francisco's limits on wind effects. In her opinion, it is the code provision demanding that, when the existing wind created by surrounding development exceeds the comfort criteria, a proposed building must be designed to reduce overall wind speed until the criteria are met. This provision effectively forces the unlucky latecomer to bear more than a pro rata share of the mitigation burden for preexisting conditions.

San Francisco land use attorney Tim Tosta notes, however, that because street-level winds can be alleviated in most situations by using appropriate mitigation measures, the possible loss in square footage is usually not devastating. For this reason, Tosta regards the constraints on wind impacts as far less onerous than Proposition K, the year-round shadow ban.

The 1989 regulations for Boston's Midtown Cultural District state:

Buildings are to be designed to avoid excessive and uncomfortable downdrafts on pedestrians. Each proposed project shall be shaped, or other wind-baffling measures shall be adopted, so that the proposed project will not cause ground-level ambient wind speeds to exceed the standards in Table B of this section. [See Insert 4.]

Table B

Activity Area	Effective Gust Velocity[1]	Permitted Occurrence Frequency
Limit for All Pedestrian Areas	13.8 m/sec (31 mph)	1.0%
Major Walkways—especially Principal Egress Paths for High-Rise Buildings	13.8 m/sec (31 mph)	1.0%
Other Pedestrian Walkways—including Street and Arcade Shopping Areas	11.2 m/sec (25 mph)	5.0%
Open Plazas and Park Areas; Walking, Strolling Areas	6.3 m/sec (14.1 mph)	15.0%
Open Plazas and Park Areas; Open Air Restaurants	4.0 m/sec (9 mph)	20.0%

[1] For the purposes of the above standards, "effective gust velocity" is defined as meaning hourly wind speeds + 1.5 root-mean-square of the fluctuating velocity component, measured at the same locations over the same time interval.

WIND TESTING TECHNOLOGY

Jack Cermak heads Colorado State University's Fluid Dynamics and Diffusion Laboratory, as well as the Fort Collins consulting firm of Cermak Peterka Petersen, Inc. The firm, which analyzes the microclimatic impacts of tall buildings, houses two wind tunnels that mimic conditions in the boundary layer—the lower 1,000 to 2,000 feet of atmosphere affected by the earth's surface friction. The wind tunnels simulate the natural wind over models of the built environment to predict wind effects at full scale. To produce a reliable simulation, a combination of flow conditioning devices in the upwind portion of each tunnel creates a mock boundary layer of varying speed and turbulence that characterizes the terrain around the model. The patterns of wind flow are made visible with smoke and drifting particles, and wind speeds, turbulence, and pressures are measured with a range of electronic sensors.

Only a handful of such testing facilities exists in Canada and the United States: the Fort Collins facility, the Canadian National Research Laboratory in Ottawa, and the boundary-layer wind tunnels at the University of Western Ontario and University of California (Berkeley and Davis campuses). Many of these facilities predict the effects of wind on pedestrian comfort as well as on the structural soundness of a building. Some also measure potential air pollution dispersal and evaluate building energy efficiency.

Cermak generally recommends examining wind impacts on building cladding and structure when a building's width-to-height ratio exceeds 1 to 5. Working from the architect's drawings, Cermak's team members make a model of the proposed building from styrofoam, balsa wood, or lucite, typically on a scale of 1 to 500. They also reconstruct some 2,000 square feet of the built environment of the project. (Knee-deep in "Pittsburgh," with "San Francisco" only a few yards away, Cermak and his team work in the land of Lilliput. Storing these model cities is no simple task. His firm warehouses approximately 7,000 square feet of built environments.) The cityscape model is then mounted on a 360-degree turntable in the wind tunnel, where the effects of wind gusts, as generated by 50-horsepower motor-driven fans, may be examined from all directions.

Some of the project models are shot with tiny holes hooked up to gauges that measure pressure points on the building. Computers tabulate the results. Other models are mounted on delicate springs and dampers and sway as they would under outdoor conditions. This "aeroelastic" test, used for determining structural soundness, is reserved for unusually wind-sensitive structures, those with width/height ratios approaching 1 to 7. Another technique is to inject a white chemical smoke into the built landscape and photograph the spiraling eddies. Working with helium bubble machines or styrofoam beads, wind testing consultants use these tracking devices to make flow visualization videos. The videos are in turn used to inform architects and developers of the test findings and to recommend appropriate mitigation means.

MITIGATION MEASURES

San Francisco's baseball stadium, Candlestick Park, dubbed "the cave of the winds," was a major source of embarrassment to city officials. A record seven errors made during the 10th inning of the 1961 All Star Game were attributed in part to capricious winds, which nearly swept Stu Miller off the pitcher's mound. Cermak's Colorado State University group determined that the stadium stood at the vortex of two competing wind flows, which formed a whirlwind on the field. Moreover, the horseshoe shape of the upper stands aggravated the problem. Studies showed that if the stadium had been built one playing field to the north, where gusts were less treacherous, the wind problem could have been avoided. Cermak recommended three mitigation measures: building a partial dome roof opening to the northeast; constructing a porous screen above the upper stands; or extending the upper stands to form a closed oval completely encircling the stadium. The third alternative, the least effective but also the cheapest, was put in place and has cut the wind problem to some extent.

Likewise, wind tunnel testing done in San Francisco's Yerba Buena Center in 1971 helped avert a downwash problem that would have been created by an open walkway beneath a 375-foot tower. These tests also foresaw pollution problems that would have ensued if fumes had swept into the central plaza from the exhaust stacks of the underground parking garage. Cermak's group advised that the open space be eliminated beneath the tower, that the plaza be covered with a transparent skylight just below roof level, and that the height of the smokestacks be quadrupled.

Other solutions to wind problems caused by high-rise buildings include placing the main tower on a podium, which helps deflect winds rushing down the building's surface and effectively raises wind flow above the sidewalks; using tree canopies or shrubbery screens as wind baffles; covering main entries with awnings or marquees; and avoiding placement of entries on corners. (See Insert 5.) Tiered, wedding-cake, rounded, and otherwise sculptured building tops also help blunt wind impacts. Admittedly, the technique of covering walkways with tree canopies or other durable vegetation barriers may be difficult to use in those downtowns where light is scarce.

Insert 5.
Charlotte: Microclimate Planting Solutions
(code suggestions)

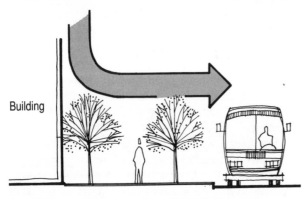

A double row of street trees can be planted at the base of tall buildings and along the edge of the sidewalk to divert and reduce the speed of strong winds moving down the face of the structure. Awnings and canopies can provide similar wind protection.

Fred Bauman, development engineer at the University of California's wind testing facility at Berkeley, notes that a building's aerodynamic shape, location, and relationship to neighboring structures may also be critical. Depending on the prevailing winds, a tall building in the vicinity could easily influence the wind's effects on a nearby structure. Bauman also cautions against placing open walkways in locations subject to great differentials in air pressure. This situation is more apt to occur in areas with mild climates, where buildings typically feature open arcades leading to sky-exposed courtyards. High-pressure gusts may build up on the windward side, then travel through the arcade to the low-pressure interior courtyard, where blasts of high winds erupt. One mitigation technique involves placing vegetative baffles within the arcade, thereby slowing the wind. Another method entails reducing the air pressure differential by covering the central courtyard with a canopy or dome or by transforming it into an atrium.

VIEW PROTECTION: A CAPITOL IDEA

View corridor protection, like sun access policy, has evolved out of state environmental protection legislation. A good example is Washington State's Shoreline Management Act of 1971, a public-trust doctrine mandating public access and view corridors to the water from designated streets through stringent height limits on waterfront development. View protection may also be a requirement of city environmental impact regulations. Cincinnati's hillside protection ordinance is partly intended to preserve prominent hillsides' views of major streams or valleys, and partly to ensure stability of hillside structures and environmental quality of new construction. The ordinance imposes environmental assessments before building permits may be obtained in any of the city's environmental quality districts. In like fashion, Austin has set aside five hill-country roadway corridors to protect scenic views and urge orderly and environmentally sensitive development along these corridors.

Capital cities, including Austin, Denver, Lincoln, Sacramento, Tallahassee, and Washington, D.C., preserve views of their capitol buildings and environs with height and setback provisions in their downtown zoning ordinances. In fact, although view corridor protection is generally a citywide concern, many other cities' downtown ordinances contain their own view protection provisions. A municipal ordinance in Rochester, New York, protects views of the city's Eastman Theater; Pittsburgh preserves its river views; Denver, Burlington, Vermont, and Portland, Oregon, protect their mountain vistas; and Seattle mandates a series of setbacks within view corridors of Elliott Bay, West Seattle, and the Olympic Mountains.

A new wrinkle is the protection of views as gained from roads, streets, and highways. As Christopher J.

Duerksen notes, "because driving is the leading form of outdoor recreation, there is renewed interest in creating and protecting scenic roadways and entryways to cities and towns." [19] Austin protects views of its capitol dome as seen from moving cars. The "Capitol of Texas Highway Corridor" and "Red Bud Trail Corridor" are but two of the city's 26 corridors preserving views of the capitol.

VIEW PROTECTION MECHANISMS

Among techniques for protecting scenic vistas are: height limits and mandatory setbacks established through special districts, overlay zones, or view protection corridors; site plan and planned development review; and massing and bulk requirements. These mechanisms typically are implemented through zoning, but they need not be. Denver's mountain view ordinance, for instance, is part of the city's building code. The simplest technique is a mandatory cap on building heights. This is the approach taken in Washington, D.C. To preserve views of the Capitol's dome and other public buildings and monuments, Congress passed the Building Height Limitation Act of 1910. The Act set a citywide building height cap of 130 feet for commercial sectors and 110 feet for residential areas, with some exemptions on Pennsylvania Avenue.

Until recently, no building in Philadelphia could rise above 491 feet, the height of William Penn's statue atop City Hall. This arbitrary ceiling (about that of a 40-story building) was founded on no more than a "gentleman's agreement" that the tallest building in the city should be its city hall. Developers tacitly respected the height cap until 1985, when the proposed Liberty Center shot through the limits. Despite an enormous civic outcry, the city approved the project and relaxed the gentleman's agreement.

"Peek Protection." Denver's mountain view preservation ordinances, developed in the mid-1960s, are designed to protect panoramic vistas of the Rockies as seen from selected parks and public spaces and to create a series of overlay zones with custom-tailored height limits. Based on a system of view planes, height increments are permitted at 100-foot intervals from reference points throughout the city. Five distinct zones make up the Capitol/Civic Center Building Height Control District, which aims to protect mountain views from the capitol's grounds, as well as capitol views from elsewhere.

Austin uses two mechanisms to protect capitol views. Its Capitol Dominance Zoning District is an overlay that limits heights within one-quarter mile of the capitol to 653 feet above sea level and permits proportional increases depending on a structure's distance from the capitol. A second method, used in the 26 Capitol View Corridor Zones, is based on a comprehensive formula of trigonometric projections. This more complex method grew out of an exhaustive study that identified 60 major corridors and assessed the expected economic impact of protecting each. (See Insert 6.)

Insert 6.
Capitol View Preservation in Austin:
The Height Calculation Formula
(code illustration)

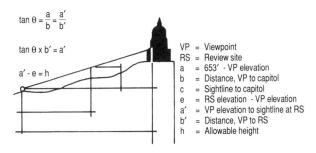

$$\tan \theta = \frac{a}{b} = \frac{a'}{b'}$$

$$\tan \theta \times b' = a'$$

$$a' - e = h$$

VP = Viewpoint
RS = Review site
a = 653' - VP elevation
b = Distance, VP to capitol
c = Sightline to capitol
e = RS elevation - VP elevation
a' = VP elevation to sightline at RS
b' = Distance, VP to RS
h = Allowable height

The less complicated formulas used in Lincoln, Nebraska, and Tallahassee, Florida, also work by projecting angles from their capitol domes to various sites.

View Preservation as Review Component. Alternatively, view protection may function as part of the site plan and planned development review processes. For instance, in Burlington, Vermont, any structure taller than 35 feet must undergo site plan review, and the design review board and planning commission must consider these criteria:

Views of Lake Champlain and the Adirondack Mountains are Burlington's most precious physical assets. All future development along the east/west corridors must seek to preserve this view, minimize obstruction, and extend access to the view for adjacent sections of the community.

Similarly, in Portland, Oregon, and Bellevue, Washington, view protection is integrated into the design review process as one of the standards that new development must meet.

Review criteria for special districts may also act as view protection mechanisms. Preserving vistas of rivers, bays, lakes, or oceans is typically one of the criteria for approving new development in waterfront districts, as in Wilmington, Delaware, Norfolk, Virginia, and Portland, Maine.

Massing and Bulk Controls. Pittsburgh, San Francisco, and Seattle use these tools to reinforce their appointed view corridors.

PITTSBURGH

Pittsburgh uses an inclined plane system, with a series of height limits and setbacks in two downtown areas flanking the Monongahela and Allegheny Rivers. Heights are staggered according to a building's proximity to the rivers; floor areas are shrunk according to a city-mandated formula. Height limits based on these inclined planes range from 180 feet adjacent to the rivers to 450 feet inland. Additional code provisions concern related issues of design flexibility and transition in scale. (See Insert 7.)

Insert 7.
Pittsburgh's Inclined Plane System
(code excerpt)

(c) C5-C Golden Triangle District C.

. . .

(3) Height. For the use listed [above], the height of any structure hereafter erected or enlarged is controlled by floor/area ratio and shall not exceed a maximum height determined by the following:

   A. Monongahela River Side.
   Structures or portions of structures shall not penetrate an inclined plane determined by straight lines connecting points one hundred and eighty feet (180') above established street grade on Fort Pitt Boulevard and three hundred and eighty-five feet (385') above street grade on Third Avenue, calculated at the property lines.

   B. Allegheny River Side.
   Structures or portions of structures, other than those containing residential uses, shall not penetrate an inclined plane determined by straight lines connecting points one hundred and eighty feet (180') above established street grade on Fort Duquesne Boulevard and four hundred and fifty feet (450') above street grade on Liberty Avenue, calculated at the property lines. . . .

   C. In order to reduce the bulk of buildings on the skyline above 300 feet, . . . the total floor area for all floors at or above 300 feet shall be reduced by the following [formula]:

   Total floor area at or above 300 feet = (base floor area) (number of floors) x (reduction factor from table below)

   1. Base floor area equals average floor area of all floors or portions of floors above 100 feet in height and below 300 feet in height;

   2. Number of floors for purposes of the calculation above shall be those floors or portions of floors at or above 300 feet which have a floor area no less than 50 percent of the floor area of the floor immediately below. Floors not meeting this requirement may be constructed and shall be counted as part of the total project floor area; however, no floor or floors above a floor not meeting this requirement

shall be used in determining the floor elevation of the top floor for purposes of the table below;

   3. The reduction factor used in the calculation above shall be determined in the table below by the floor elevation of any portion of the top floor as established in (2) above and by the corresponding reduction factor from (4) below:

   4.
Floor Elevation above Street Grade (Feet)	Reduction Factor (Percent)
440	59.5
430	61.5
420	63.6
410	65.9
400	68.2
390	70.7
380	73.3
370	76.1
360	79.0
350	82.0
340	85.6
330	88.6
320	92.2
310	96.0
300	100.0

   D. In order to provide design flexibility for structures which utilize the entire height allowed by the inclined plane, any structure or structures in a unit group development may penetrate a portion of the inclined plane only if an equal amount of building bulk is reduced below the inclined plane and only if the maximum height of the structure or structures occurs at that portion of the site covered by the highest portion of the inclined plane.

   E. In order to provide a transition in scale from new structures to existing structures on the boulevards fronting on the rivers, development on sites next to existing structures which exceed the height limitation created by the inclined planes may exceed the height limitation by 50 percent of the extent to which the existing structure exceeds the height limitation, providing that any portion of the new structure above the inclined plane achieve a minimum setback of 20 feet from property lines along Fort Pitt Boulevard and Fort Duquesne Boulevard.

PORTLAND

View protection issues are sometimes addressed in skywalk regulations. Portland's skywalk ordinance contains a view corridor map with different standards depending on whether a proposed overhead connection blocks a "visual focal point" lying on a primary, secondary, or tertiary view corridor. (Portland's view corridor map is reproduced in Chapter 9, "Skywalks.")

SAN FRANCISCO

View conservation was apparently one of the animating forces behind the stringent height and bulk controls in San Francisco's 1985 Downtown Plan. According to Peter Bosselmann, the fight against the "Manhattanization" of the city began over the issue of view blockage.[20] In 1980, as part of the work for the new plan, growth projections were made for the next 20 years. A team from Bosselmann's environmental simulation laboratory was called in to analyze the environmental impacts of this projected growth, particularly those impacts on sun access, wind speeds, and view corridors. Via simulated models, films enabled viewers to "previsualize" the effects of several development options.

Bosselmann assessed the effects of future development on both long-range and middle-range views and tested them against the city's master-planned goal of a skyline shaped like a "downtown hill." His studies showed that views from certain "elevated points to the south of downtown showed an abruptly rising plateau instead of the gentle slopes expected on the 'downtown hill'."[21] Middle-range views taken from publicly accessible points in the downtown also demonstrated a general noncomformance with the city's design policy, which required downtown development to gradually step down in height to level with the heights of existing buildings in the neighborhoods.

The Sim Lab team also studied before-and-after eye-level views of streets in those areas of expected growth concentration. Its studies showed that the massive tower walls of new hotel and office structures would dramatically alter the retail-lined neighborhood streets, where most buildings were no taller than 70 to 100 feet. Bosselman concluded that the urban-design master plan of 1971 did not contain specific enough guidelines for judging environmental impacts on the skyline and streetscapes.

Bosselmann's before-and-after film studies, made over a six-year period for the San Francisco Department of City Planning, were shown on public television to educate citizens about the proposed Downtown Plan. The telecast films are thought to have contributed to the plan's adoption in 1985. According to one planning commissioner, "It was the simulation films that let us see what would happen to the city if we stayed with the old zoning—and what kind of zoning we need to get the city we want."[22]

The resulting height and bulk controls in San Francisco's 1985 zoning—probably the most restrictive in the country—are mapped according to individual districts and public focal points. Heights in the retail district, for example, were cut from a range of 240 to 500 feet to a peak of 80 feet; and FARs in the densest downtown sectors, which previously ranged from 14 to 9, were reduced to 9 to 6.

The code's approach to the "benching" phenomenon reinforces its programs for massing and bulk control. Benching results when the tendency to build to the height limit, particularly in height districts capped at less than 400 feet, causes a "visible lining up of building tops," a monotonous skyline. To soften existing benching, the code encourages tapered buildings. It allows some exemptions (up to 10 percent) from the height restrictions for making additional bulk reductions in upper towers toward a "more slender . . . profile and sculptured building termination." (For further discussion of San Francisco's attack on benching, see the section on sculptured rooftops in Chapter 5, "Zoning As Shaper of Building Design.")

SEATTLE

Seattle uses a system of view corridor setbacks on certain street segments to ensure views of Elliott Bay, West Seattle, Mount Rainier, and the Olympic Mountains. Depending on location, the maximum elevations above sidewalks, minimum distances from street property lines, and setback depths are prescribed for upper-level setbacks.

As of this writing, only one building—the Washington Mutual Tower, designed by the New York firm of Kohn Pedersen Fox—has been built to comply with the 1985 zoning revisions, including the view corridor requirements. The code calls for upper-level setbacks at intervals of 25 and 35 feet beginning at 20 feet from the street property line. The project's lead local architect, Pat Gordon, states that the massing decisions were reached independently of the code and the setbacks would have been made anyway. Other Seattle architects note, however, that the corridor constraints tend to center a building on a block with uniform setbacks, thus encouraging similar zoning envelopes around it.

View corridor setbacks have also significantly affected Robert Venturi's design for Seattle's new art museum. Setback constraints interfered with Venturi's original intention to hold together the building wall as one unified mass and build out to the property lines. Rather than break up the facade for the view corridors, Venturi chose to set back the entire structure some 30 feet. In the process, he created a "hillside terrace," a bonusable public benefit feature that makes for open space on a steeply sloping street. The 150,000-square-foot limestone structure, banded by a pattern of granite, marble, and terra cotta on the ground floor, is due for completion in 1990.

Unhappily, one difficulty in imposing view preservation constraints on a mature urban area like Seattle's downtown is that many of the theoretical view planes have already been disrupted by existing buildings.

A NOTE ON LEGAL CONSIDERATIONS

One advantage of yoking view protection to environmental impact assessment, as is done in many jurisdictions with state environmental policy acts, is that it roots in solid ground what might otherwise be seen as mere aesthetic zoning. Although aesthetic zoning has come of age, a few state courts are nonetheless reluctant to endorse aesthetic appeal as the sine qua non for a zoning regulation. Therefore, a city is usually prudent to underscore the environmental and economic benefits of view corridor protection. Economic justifications—promoting retail and tourist activity and thus boosting the city's overall economy—are clearly named in the "Purposes" sections of Austin's and Denver's preservation ordinances.

Companion state legislation may add muscle to municipal view preservation ordinances. Because the sites of capitol buildings often lie within state jurisdictions, legislatures can reinforce scenic and capitol view ordinances with matching state laws. This is the case in Austin, where the state has passed separate enabling legislation.

Both Austin and the state of Texas authorize the use of transferable development rights (TDRs) as a mitigation measure for developments affected by the height restrictions. When the TDRs were authorized, a very brief time limit (one month) was set for certifying those development proposals eligible for TDRs. By January 1986, the city had certified 15 projects, comprising slightly more than 3 million square feet. The air rights, which could be transferred to two areas in the central business district, had to be used within three years, but as of December 1988, no transfers had been made. The three-year time limit may yet be extended, but this move would require legislative action.

DIFFERING POINTS OF VIEW: A COLORADO CASE

In December 1986, the Colorado Supreme Court upheld Denver's mountain view preservation ordinance, which limits building heights to between 30 and 250 feet in some 10 percent of the city.[23] The complainant in the case, Landmark Land Company, sought to develop a 21-story office building, as the site's zoning would have allowed. The view preservation ordinance, however, restricted building heights in southeast Denver's Southmoor Park to 42 feet.

One of the arguments made by the developers was that the height restrictions in Southmoor Park were a subterfuge disguising the city's real motive—growth management. Allegedly, the 1982 ordinance amendment that extended mountain view protection to Southmoor Park had been instigated by neighbors abutting the Landmark project, who had earlier tried to downzone the area.

The Colorado court, however, refused to question legislative motives. Because the mountains were a fundamental part of Denver's "unique environmental heritage," the court held that protecting the right to see the distant scenery was a legitimate exercise of the city's police power, whether or not Landmark Land Company, Inc., was deprived of the maximum return on its property. Landmark asserted that the amendment to the mountain view ordinance effectively devalued their land by at least 60 percent and that this amounted to an unconstitutional taking of private property. Thus, the claimants appealed to the U.S. Supreme Court, but the Court refused to consider the case.

More recently, the Denver City Council passed a citizen-initiated ordinance preserving the downtown skyline as viewed from Sloan Lake Park, which borders the lake, three-quarters of a mile long. This is evidently the city's first view protection measure to conserve a view of the entire city center. The ordinance permits buildings up to 35 feet high in the affected area and sets elevation limits for the tops of taller structures.

Meanwhile, the Colorado court decision could influence other "scenic right-of-way" disputes. One much-publicized example is PortAmerica, a giant $1 billion mixed-use project along the Potomac River in suburban Washington, D.C. Although the citywide 110-foot height limit did not apply directly, the city fathers feared that the project, to be built only seven miles from the downtown and to include a 52-story World Trade Center, would encroach on the capital city's low-rise skyline and its vistas of federal monuments. Members of Congress introduced legislation to levy a tax of $1 million on every foot of a building exceeding a 140-foot height limit. Also, the Federal Aviation Agency contended that the building's height posed a hazard for aircraft using National Airport.

A delay of more than a year, and millions of dollars of additional legal and consultant fees, prompted developer James T. Lewis to redesign the project. Philip Johnson and John Burgee scaled back the World Trade Center complex to a 22-story octagonal tower flanked by six 10-story office buildings.

EVALUATION: COSTS AND OTHER REALITIES

These sophisticated studies of potential environmental impacts come with a price tag. Paul Zigman,

San Francisco environmental consultant, has assessed many of that city's downtown office towers. As mentioned earlier, Zigman sets the range of costs for shadow studies at several hundred dollars to $30,000. Likewise, the typical charges for wind testing run from $5,000 to $6,000 for a specific design feature, and it is often necessary to run several separate tests. Fees for the more extensive atmospheric boundary-layer wind tunnel tests are considerably higher. According to Jack Cermak, the rigid-model testing costs about $30,000, and the aeroelastic structural analysis, in which the models are mounted on springs and dampers to duplicate outdoor conditions, will typically run another $30,000. Some of Cermak's more elaborate projects—for instance, those that entailed modeling the entire city of Seattle or major segments of Los Angeles—have proved much costlier.

Fred Bauman notes that higher expenses are incurred whenever alternative designs are considered. Each alternative calls for separate measurements: In the case of one 18-story office tower in San Francisco that underwent more than 20 design variations, the wind testing costs alone were daunting. Expenses may be defrayed somewhat if the developer provides an architectural model of the project and the several square blocks surrounding it. Bauman warns, however, that many architectural models cannot withstand the high wind speeds simulated in the wind tunnels.

Builders might balk at the expense, but wind effects analysts and many of their clients agree that the chance to repair otherwise inalterable mistakes generally overrides any additional costs and time delays incurred by testing. In contrast, the mitigation measures for alleviating shadows are far less effective, and the ramifications of meeting the constraints of San Francisco's virtual all-or-nothing shadow ban are far more drastic. Hence, developers are less charitable in their opinions on sun-blockage testing.

The costs of state-mandated environmental impact assessments are borne by the private developer. So are the costs of initial testing for wind, shadows, and sun access, as required by a raft of downtown zoning codes. Moreover, lenders are loath to undertake big risks until after approvals have been granted, so that these testing fees are paid for upfront. To developers, the time delays and uncertainties frequently wrought by the testing requirements are often far more onerous than direct testing costs. Paul Zigman notes that processing an environmental impact review (EIR) in San Francisco may take up to four years, although two years is the norm.

The most expensive EIR done in San Francisco to date—costing Santa Fe Pacific Realty Corporation more than $3 million—was recently issued for the 325-acre, multibillion-dollar Mission Bay redevelopment project, which will be built out over the next 25 years. Because the environmental impacts of the colossal project will ramify throughout the city, the planning department apparently delayed holding the next office design competition until the EIR was completed. It has been suggested that the city deliberately uses EIRs funded by the private sector to expand its own environmental information inventory. Indeed, Paul Zigman observes that San Francisco uses the process of environmental assessment to aid in city planning. Environmental reports developed by the private sector provide data that often are converted into planning policy.

Testing for the impacts of tall buildings, however, raises yet another cost issue: the cost to the city of developing and administering the programs. Peter Bosselmann's Environmental Simulation Laboratory at Berkeley did background studies on San Francisco's shadow ban over a four-year period. The fees, which amounted to more than $90,000, were paid for by private foundations and by the city's planning commission. And with the passage of Proposition K, which far surpassed the city's original intentions, San Francisco had to specially allocate some $200,000 for computer modeling of the 70 city parks and public squares affected by the stricter shadow ban. The city must administer the modeling system, which in theory gives developers advance notice of the shadow constraints on their projects. Although the $200,000 is a one-time expense, the system also demands a high level of expertise and much staff time in administration.

Two-hundred thousand dollars is modest compared with some of the fees cities have paid for the drafting of environmental impact statements. New York City, for example, spent roughly $1 million for the EIS done on the $2 billion redevelopment plan for Times Square. Therefore, cities like San Francisco and New York are equipped or, perhaps more accurately, accustomed to navigating their ways through the environmental review maze. It is no accident that the same New York City law firms that specialize in zoning matters and steering developers through the complicated ULURP process also broker the environmental review process. More often than not, "an EIS is an invitation to a lawsuit."[24]

Administrative demands like these might well strain the lesser budgets, more modest staffs, and less sophisticated planning capabilities of smaller cities. Yet downtowns throughout the country are increasingly addressing the microclimatic impacts of tall

Pechard; Environmental Simulation Lab, Berkeley

Lilliputian scale model of San Francisco. Peter Bosselmann is shown seated at left, William H. Whyte seated in center, and Donald Appleyard at right.

buildings in their zoning codes. The limits contained in New York's daylight evaluation chart for measuring sun access, or the maximum thresholds in San Francisco's Downtown Plan for wind speeds and sun blockage are extremely exacting. But, it should be remembered, the criteria for environmental impacts as set forth in most downtown zoning codes are far less specific. This situation gives both developers and city staffs inadequate guidelines and affords the city greater discretion.

A developer in Bellevue doubts that the city staff had enough expertise to intelligently evaluate the conclusions of a private consultant's wind tunnel testing report, particularly as the project in question was one of the first to undergo the wind testing requirement. In Portland, Oregon, a developer succeeded in acquiring much greater density after bringing in consultants to show that the project at issue did not in fact block a disputed view corridor; the latter had apparently been miscalculated by the city. Such discrepancies are probably the norm. They are among the many wrinkles found in new planning techniques or evaluation methods and are usually ironed out through experience.

Perhaps one difficulty is that many municipal zoning constraints for wind, shadow, and view impacts have been derived from state requirements for EISs. These in turn have been modeled after the requirements in the National Environmental Policy Act, which totally neglects to set any standards for acceptable or unacceptable environmental impacts.[25] This absence of precise standards means that for major development in Manhattan, where the environmental impact statement required by the city's environmental quality review (CEQR) repeatedly delays projects by more than a year, "the last EIS typically becomes the floor for the next one."[26]

THE IMPORTANCE OF ENVIRONMENTAL SIMULATION

Few techniques accurately measure or predict the anticipated impacts of new development. Given this deficiency, the ability to describe the experiential effects of full-scale rebuilding on the urban environment, a "rarely found skill among professionals," becomes largely a matter of guesswork.[27] For more than 20 years, Peter Bosselmann has been using the technique of previsualization in his Sim Lab movies to project the experiential effects of proposed development alternatives. Donald Appleyard pioneered this technique when he headed the same environmental simulation laboratory. Much like Cermak and his wind effects analysts, who build Lilliputian scale-model cities, Bosselmann's team fashions cardboard stage sets of buildings, streets, neighborhoods, pedestrians, signage, and trees, complete with moving cut-out photographs of crowds. With these aids, he predicts visually the effects of new development on sun access, on the perceived scale of surrounding buildings, on traffic flow, and on open spaces.

Built to the same scale as model railroads—one-sixteenth of an inch to one foot—Bosselmann's simulated developments incorporate the standard fixtures of model train sets. Buildings are made interchangeable to test for alternative development patterns. To test possible changes in the San Francisco skyline, for instance, the Bosselmann team used a model of the city first created in 1935 as a WPA project. With constant updating, this model can show past, present, and future skylines.

The technique is identical to that used by *Star Wars* filmmaker George Lucas to depict imaginary worlds of the universe. The camera, suspended from a gantry crane to minimize vibrations, runs along a track. The filmed sequences are shot through a periscope with a mirror and a wide-angle (60-degree) lens.

Besides collecting specific data, the Sim Lab films have been used to recommend zoning changes. As previously discussed, Bosselmann's films analyzing aspects of San Francisco's zoning were broadcast on public television and widely believed to have influenced city commissioners and citizens alike to pass the Downtown Plan.

In 1985, after Bosselmann's San Francisco studies had been completed, his team studied more than 20 sites around New York's Times Square, where $2 billion worth of development is planned. In contrast to the EIS done for this area in 1984, which cost almost $1 million, the sim film was finished within two months with a total budget of $25,000. The film ulti-

Apparatus for creating simulation films.

mately recommended a package of specific zoning changes for preserving the raucous, gaudy experience of the area. The city has implemented some of the suggested changes. In 1987, the board of estimate voted a zoning requirement to preserve the glitz around the square, mandating a 50-foot setback at approximately the four-story level (at 50 feet) to accommodate the giant neon signs. A sign's size must be directly proportional to the length of the frontage of each new project, at a rate of 50 square feet of signage for every foot of Times Square frontage. In exchange, buildings are permitted to rise higher than the 50-foot setbacks.

Also in response to Bosselmann's recommendations, the city has adopted an amendment requiring new buildings in the theater subdistrict to dedicate 5 percent of their space to entertainment-related uses like rehearsal halls and cinemas.

The advanced simulation techniques just described would be particularly useful to those downtowns devising incentive zoning systems. City staff could use the films to visualize and anticipate the effects of given bonus alternatives; in truth, they could discover how a certain block, district, or entire downtown would look and "feel" if developers took advantage of the full bonus potential.

Notes

1. John J. Costonis, "Law and Aesthetics: A Critique and a Reformulation of the Dilemmas," *Michigan Law Review*, vol. 80 (1982), p. 362.
2. Fred Bosselmann and David Callies, in *The Quiet Revolution in Land Use Control* (Washington, D. C.: Council on Environmental Quality, 1971), give an account of some pioneering state environmental regulations.
3. Jean O. Melious, "The Environmental Quality Act's Substantial Impact on Zoning," *Land Use Law & Zoning Digest*, vol. 39, no. 6 (June 1987), p. 4.
4. *Chinese Staff and Workers Association* v. *City of New York*, 502 N.E. 2d 176 (N.Y. 1986).
5. 578 P. 2d 1039 (1978).
6. Jonathan Barnett, *An Introduction to Urban Design* (New York: Harper & Row, 1982), p. 17.
7. Tony Hiss, "Experiencing Places," Part II, *The New Yorker* (June 29, 1987), p. 76.
8. See William H. Whyte, *City: Rediscovering the Center* (New York: Doubleday, 1989), p. 259.
   His chapter entitled "Sun and Shadow" (pp. 256–266) presents a review of light access issues.
9. Ibid., p. 272. See also the intriguing discussion of "bounce light" on pp. 267–275. Whyte notes that the "same big bad buildings that are cutting off light to one area can reflect it to another. The potentials for such bounce light should be explored; so, too, should spotlighting techniques for redirecting the sun into dark places that never had it before." (p. 266)
10. Ibid., p. 256.
11. Barnett, *An Introduction to Urban Design*, p. 112.
    Whyte also discusses the two-tier system (in *City*, cited above, on pp. 264–265).
12. Ibid., p. 112.
13. Ibid., p. 111.
14. Patrick Phillips, "Sidewalk Solar Access: Downtown Zoning for Sun and Light," *Urban Land* (February 1985), p. 36.
15. For Bosselmann's account of the studies, refer to his article "Experiencing Downtown Streets in San Francisco," in *Public Streets for Public Use*, ed. Anne Vernez Moudon (New York: Van Nostrand Reinhold Company, 1987), p. 210.
16. Ibid., p. 210.
17. Ibid., p. 207.
18. See Scott Armstrong, "Taming the fury of man-made wind," *Christian Science Monitor* (January 15, 1985).
19. Christopher J. Duerksen, *Aesthetics and Land Use Controls*, Planning Advisory Service Report no. 399 (Chicago: American Planning Association, 1986), p. 17. View protection is treated on pp. 17–22.
20. See Bosselmann, "Experiencing Downtown Streets in San Francisco," p. 205.
21. Ibid., p. 205.
22. Quoted by Tony Hiss in "Experiencing Places," Part II, p. 75.
23. *Landmark Land Company, Inc.* v. *City and County of Denver*, 728 P. 2d 1281 (1986).
24. Scott R. Thomas in *Real Estate Development and City Regulations*, a special issue of *New York Affairs*, vol. 8, no. 4 (1985), p. 7.
    See also Rae Zimmerman's "Environmental Impact and Real Estate Development," in the same issue, pp. 132–144.
25. Jonathan Barnett examines the influence of environmental impact analysis on urban design in *An Introduction to Urban Design*, pp. 15–26.
26. Statement made by New York zoning attorney Robert S. Cook, Jr., in phone interview (March 1988).
27. Hiss, "Experiencing Places," Part II, p. 74.

CHAPTER 7

RETAIL USES

THE CHALLENGE

For three decades, ending in the early 1980s, planners and others concerned with reviving down-at-the-heels retail cores watched in dismay as commercial uses atrophied and pedestrians vanished from the sidewalks. Nevertheless, civic leaders and land use experts worked tirelessly to pump new life into the moribund downtowns and stop the debilitating drain to the suburbs.

Thus, when office development was spurred by a booming service sector in the 1980s, the influx was at first embraced as the ticket to survival for many downtown economies. Public regulations were seldom allowed to impede or even modify such development.

In time, however, in the cities where more and more button-down-style corporate office blocks rose to greater and greater heights, increasing disenchantment set in. The implantation of faceless, impenetrable towers whose offices and bank lobbies usurped first-floor commercial space meant that the street activity allied with them also disappeared. Although the burgeoning service industry was injecting new economic life into downtowns across the country, there was a growing perception that something was missing—retail shopping, people on the streets, and "triangulation" (the process by which some external stimulus prompts strangers to interact).[1] In short, those qualities were lacking that traditionally have made downtowns vibrant community centers.

The city officials, planners, and businesspeople interviewed for this book expressed shared goals and were generally working to transform their downtowns into 18-hour activity centers with healthy retail cores, sidewalks jammed with pedestrians, cultural and entertainment opportunities, and downtown residents. The markets for entertainment, cultural, and residential uses must, in many instances, be imported to the downtown area. But office workers who are already downtown create a ready-made retail market, albeit a time-limited one. Therefore, the logical first step for revitalizing the downtown core is to bring active uses to the street level to support the retail sector. The phenomenon of the inner-city festival marketplace, touted by James Rouse, has underscored the importance of concentrating retail activity to achieve a critical mass.

It should be remembered, however, that the economic engine of downtown is not really shopping but office development. The symbiotic relationship between the two uses is critical to achieving a healthy retail core.

OVERVIEW OF RETAIL ZONING MECHANISMS

The most frequently used zoning tool to bolster downtown retail is a mandate that a percentage of street-level retail be built into new development. Since 1987, Cincinnati's Downtown District regulations require that "at least 60 percent of certain building frontages shall be exclusively devoted to retail uses." Other zoning definitions for retail use include pedestrian-oriented frontage, commercial uses, or personal services businesses. Because the goal is to generate interest and pedestrian activity on the first floor, many code definitions specifically exclude banks, travel agents, or airline ticket counters. Some codes also limit the percentage of nonpedestrian consumer-oriented establishments that may be permitted to satisfy the ground-floor retail requirement. For example, in Sacramento, such uses as stockbrokers, optometrists, attorneys, and employment agencies may not occupy more than 50 percent of the ground-floor area of major projects.

The various definitions for retail use reflect the range of differing public policies being promoted in the downtowns. For instance, Bellevue, Washington's pedestrian-oriented frontage requirement, which includes retail shops, groceries, drugstores, department stores, and hardware stores, shows Bellevue's efforts to transform the downtown into a neighborhood for the convenience of the people living and working in and near it. Similarly, San Francisco's 1985 code explicitly encourages businesses that meet the convenience-shopping and service needs of less affluent downtown workers and local residents; the city offers strong incentives for retaining small-scale ground-floor retail shops, services, and restaurants in downtown buildings.

Because thriving retail cores depend on a critical mass of continuous activity, those cities with retail zoning mechanisms generally mandate the retail uses, rather than taking the incentive approach, which would result in isolated commercial pockets. It is not uncommon, however, to offer density bonuses for providing additional ground-floor retail in excess of the requirement. Moreover, some cities with retail requirements exempt the amount of floor area occupied by these uses from the total FAR count.

Although the retail mandate usually affects only new development or major renovations, in Orlando, Florida, the requirement also applies to existing buildings and is triggered by a change in occupancy.

Most cities with retail zoning confine the requirement to designated streets, generally those with the heaviest pedestrian activity lying within or close to the retail core. Likewise, where greater density is available for providing extra ground-floor retail, the award is generally made only if the commercial use faces onto a pedestrian corridor or public space or connects with the established retail district.

Another technique is the special retail zoning district. For instance, in 1971, New York created its Fifth Avenue Special District primarily to preserve the street's famous retail trade, which was giving way under tremendous real estate pressures to more lucrative office rentals.

THE HISTORIC PRESERVATION CONNECTION

Height and FAR limits are also used in many downtown retail cores. They are usually combined with other regulatory tools, mainly historic preservation ordinances, to preserve older structures. These regulatory techniques tend to reduce development pressures and enhance the economic viability of smaller historic buildings, which often are concentrated in the retail

area. These older structures frequently house commercial uses on the first floor and promote a healthy diversity in the downtown, mixing large and small, new and old.

The retail/historic preservation connection, however, garners mixed reviews. Seattle developer Richard Clotfelter questions whether some techniques for preserving historic structures may not ultimately contravene the goal of strengthening retail. He points out that because merchandising patterns have changed, it is no longer necessary to stock the extensive inventories that had called for facilities with deep building dimensions; downtown retail tenants now prefer depths of 60 to 80 feet and widths of 25 to 30 feet, difficult dimensions to achieve in many of the historic structures in Seattle's retail sector. The city's older terra cotta buildings, for example, are generally quite deep, sometimes 110 to 120 feet. Clotfelter also notes that a policy of preserving low-density development in the retail core may attenuate the critical mass needed to support the retail activity.

On the other hand, Madison Avenue (from about 59th Street to the mid-70s) has lately undergone a meteoric ascent to one of the world's premier shopping streets, perhaps eclipsing Fifth Avenue. This climb has been attributed in part to the area's designation as a historic district in 1981. Although some newer structures have been built, the five-story brownstone—20 feet wide, with 10 brownstones to the block—is the basic module, setting the form and character of the Avenue.[2]

Unlike may other parts of Manhattan, Madison Avenue enjoys real estate values deriving from the existing older structures rather than from the land. This gives building owners an incentive to undertake extensive repairs and renovations. Skyrocketing rents have pushed out many old-time retail tenants, while the names of the street's new tenants "read like a compendium of international opulence: Emilio Cavallini, Godiva, Movado, Floris of London, [and] Pilar Rossi. . . ."[3] Some of the longstanding apparel stores, which previously occupied prime street-level space, are moving to the second floor, where rents have not yet soared into the stratosphere.

The Madison Avenue bonanza, however, may have limited application to other cities. The lavish shops lining the Avenue tend to draw an exclusive, largely international clientele. And because many of the shops are European, the tenants are used to working within awkwardly designed interiors that are excessively deep. Moreover, the low density of the preserved streetfronts reinforces the continental allure of the Avenue. To the extent that downtown shopping is marketed as entertainment, setting the stage becomes part of the economic strategy, and one way to prepare an effective stage set is to save the older structures and the original streetscapes.

Needless to say, those cities aggressively working to boost their retail economies are not relying only on the regulatory means described above. Many communities are undertaking ambitious public/private ventures and supplying an assortment of tax breaks, write-downs, subsidies, and other incentives in exchange for increased public involvement and benefit. Some cities are also enacting special benefit and local improvement districts, as well as centralized retail management (CRM) programs, also called merchants' associations.

Under CRM programs, independent downtown business owners cooperate to further their joint interests, much as they would in a mall. Centralized retail management typically involves the creation of a public/private entity to coordinate functions such as marketing, security, business hours, promotion, maintenance, street improvements, parking, and leasing.

DEFINING THE MARKET

A fundamental merchandising principle is that retail follows its customers, so that any program to revitalize downtown retailing should first build on the existing market. The market for downtown retail is generally far more diverse than that for other retail types.

Downtown festival marketplaces, for instance, which typically depend on tourists, represent a kind of extraregional specialty center. In cities like Boston, Chicago, and San Francisco, tourism is a tremendous retail draw. On the other hand, convenience retail types, such as shoe repair shops, delis, and hardware stores, serve the downtown residents who can walk to these shops, and these retail uses function together much as commercial neighborhood shopping centers. In contrast, old established department stores may very well have a regional draw. However, in most downtowns, the largest retail market by far is the universe of office workers, although this market only exists within a limited time frame.

Because downtown retail typically encompasses several categories, the downtown retail function is multilayered. As a result, some traditional retail strategies may prove ineffective. Nonetheless, downtown retailers must recognize each of the existing market segments, as well as potential or desired markets, and ensure that their merchandising practices address each segment. The marketing programs and approaches to tenant mix, as well as to decisions affecting shop size,

business hours, and location, vary according to retail type.[4]

Unlike in a suburban mall, where a single owner generally controls locational decisions, retail tenants in the downtowns have a far harder time securing optimal space. Retail locations within malls, for example, are predictable to a large extent: It is no accident that the better jewelry stores stand next to the high-end women's apparel shops or that a pharmacy is often positioned next to a barber shop, which in turn stands next to a beauty salon. This deliberate matching of consumer behaviors and needs with specific retail placement is harder to achieve outside the controlled environment of a self-contained shopping center. But independent downtown merchants should consider adopting this strategy, which has also worked effectively in vertical downtown shopping complexes.

One instance in which the placement of downtown retail uses may be particularly important is that of parking garages. As discussed in other chapters of this book, some cities require that downtown parking garages provide a percentage of street-level retail uses. Those uses that have worked best are convenience stores, including dry cleaners, food shops, and photo development services. Customers may drop off their dry cleaning on their way to work or buy food on their way home.

Finally, the health of downtown retail is also inextricably tied to related transportation and urban design issues, to environmental quality, and most importantly, to the quality of the pedestrian's trip through the downtown. Portland, Oregon, acknowledges this interdependence. The city's zoning reveals a panoramic vision, weaving together provisions for transportation, urban design, environmental quality, and pedestrian interest, all of which concerns promote a more active retail function.

PORTLAND: THE COMPLETE RETAIL APPROACH

Since the early 1970s, Portland has used a wide range of zoning tools to shape its downtown development and specifically to boost its retail economy. Although zoning is not solely responsible for the city's vibrant downtown environment, it has certainly played an important part. In 1975, for instance, Portland adopted the Downtown Parking and Circulation Policy as part of its zoning code; a parking space limit of some 40,000 spaces was imposed in the 500-block downtown, in partial response to the Federal Clean Air Act. At the same time, the city encouraged greater use of public transit and in 1977 began a bus transit mall on a half-mile stretch along two major downtown arteries. The light-rail transit line, MAX, opened nine years later. Portland architect Greg Baldwin talks about the "shaping power of transportation," in particular the salutary effect of the light-rail system on adjacent properties. According to Baldwin, "Retail sales have increased by 20 to 40 percent in adjacent properties, and the value of private construction on nearby parcels [has] exceeded the system's entire capital costs by five to seven times." [5] (Portland's transportation approach is described more fully in Chapter 10, "Parking and Transportation.")

Augmenting this transportation policy, Portland adopted a skywalk policy in 1982. The policy severely limits new connections and effectively channels most pedestrian traffic to the street level. (See Chapter 9, "Skywalks.") The city also states that retail and personal-service businesses must be the predominant ground-floor uses within the retail core, with the stipulation that at least 50 percent of that space must be devoted to uses other than banks, loan offices, travel agencies, or other ticket agencies. The areas of applicability were more than doubled under the zoning revisions of the 1988 Central City Plan, which extends the retail requirement to the transit mall and historic districts. In its so-called blank wall provision, Portland mandates that at least half a building's frontage must have windows at the ground level— although sometimes this requirement has been waived for substituting artwork.

These provisions also extend to public projects, so that the Justice Center, housing the municipal courts, jail, and police department, integrates a restaurant, delicatessen, hair salon, and camera shop into its ground floor, as well as public art displays. Even public parking garages include the requisite retail space.

Portland's attention to downtown's retail function has resulted in a dramatic revival of shopping. Fifteen years ago, retailing was fading fast, marked by the threatened departure of two major department stores. Today, the sidewalks in front of Nordstrom in Pioneer Courthouse Square are jammed. Ridership on the light-rail has exceeded all expectations, and Saturday is the busiest shopping day.

Although this was not the case in the mid-1970s, when ground-floor retail was first required, Portland office developers now treat retail space as a basic marketing tool that helps set the image for the rest of the building. (See Chapter 10 for a look at the relationship between retail and transit in Portland's office development.)

During the second half of the 1980s, the city has steadily increased its portion of the regional retail market. Even though Lloyd Center, a regional shopping center built in the late 1950s, was at first seen as a threat to the retail core just two miles away across the Willamette River, it is now regarded as sharing the same market as those downtown stores serving the region's high-end shoppers. The light rail, which stops at Lloyd Center, further strengthens this connection. Melvin Simon & Associates, Inc., will soon renovate the mixed-use office and shopping complex. Nearby, a new convention center is under construction, due for completion in 1990.

RETAIL CONTINUITY

BASIC CONCERNS

One important reason for mandating a percentage of retail uses at the street level, rather than merely promoting active uses through incentives, is to establish retail continuity. Uninterrupted commercial activity makes for a synergy between the individual retail uses, which in turn generates pedestrian activity and attracts shoppers. Thus, continuity is deemed essential to the viability of any retail core.

In contrast to many European cities, such as London and Paris, where nearly every block is filled in, downtowns in this country are all too often pockmarked with gaping parking lots that seriously disrupt both a neighborhood's design unity and its continuity of retail-store frontage. Therefore, many contemporary U.S. zoning codes prohibit as-of-right surface parking lots in the downtown (as explored in Chapter 10, "Parking and Transportation"). Cities are also passing regulations banning long expanses of blank walls and demanding that a portion of a building's street-level frontage contain a percentage of clear glass. (Blank wall and transparency requirements receive closer attention in the next chapter, "Open Space and Streetscapes.") For the same reason, some cities are requiring that the first floor of structured downtown parking facilities contain retail uses and are promulgating design guidelines for these facilities. (Coverage of design guidelines for parking garages may be found in Appendix A.)

It is now generally acknowledged, too, that the once-popular incentive for plazas, first created with New York's 1961 Zoning Resolution and then multiplying throughout the country, also severely fragmented continuous retail activity at street level. This was one of several reasons why many city planning departments decided either to abandon or to redefine the plaza bonus (see the next chapter).

Other zoning mechanisms for strengthening retail continuity are height limits and mandatory build-to lines in the retail core. In the country's preeminent shopping area, New York's Fifth Avenue Special District, street-wall frontages of building facades on Fifth Avenue must extend to the lot line and reach a minimum height. Different setback requirements were once used to distinguish between the east and west sides of the Avenue, but current regulations place a uniform maximum height on the lot-line facade.[6] (A later section of this chapter further discusses this special district.)

ORLANDO AND STREETFRONT CONTINUITY

The Approach. Orlando takes a twofold zoning approach to bolstering downtown retail. The city names an obligatory retail set-aside area within the historic retail core. The second, incentive-based approach urges the incorporation of a retail element into both new and existing projects.

The retail requirements are determined by the percentage of lineal feet of leasable street frontage in a given building. The frontage excludes such elements as lobby entrances and driveways, and the leasable space must measure a minimum depth of 18 feet from the facade of a building. Uses meeting the requirement are retail, personal services, entertainment services, and restaurants, whereas banks, savings institutions, and radio and television stations do not count (see Inserts 1, 2, and 3).

Insert 1.
Orlando's Ground-Floor Retail Requirement
(code extract)

First 50 Percent Mandatory in Certain Areas—Within the area(s) shown in Figure II-6, it shall be mandatory that at least 50 percent of ground-floor street frontage shall consist of eligible commercial uses in every new development as well as the reoccupation of existing development, and the available bonus shall be awarded for such frontage. Additional street frontage and bonuses available for such frontage elsewhere in the AC-3A District shall be at the option of the applicant.

Location of Mandatory Ground-Floor Retail—Where a structure has frontage on both Orange Avenue and a side street, the 50 percent mandatory ground-floor retail shall be provided on Orange Avenue, unless the retail space occupies a corner of the structure, in which case the ground-floor retail may occupy 25 percent of the Orange Avenue frontage and 25 percent of the side-street frontage.

Orientation toward Street—All business sites counted toward satisfying the standards of this bonus shall be so oriented as to promote and strengthen pedestrian activity on the pedestrian street or mall which they abut. The DDB development review committee and the planning official must find in their review of the proposed development that such pedestrian activity is promoted and strengthened.

Insert 2.
Orlando: The Ground-Floor Commercial Use Map
(code illustration)

Figure II-6

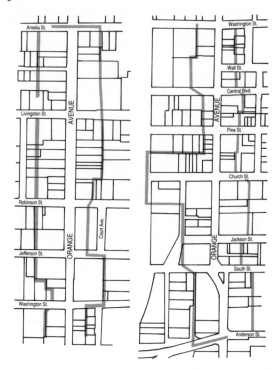

Insert 3.
Orlando on Ground-Floor Commercial Uses
(code extract)

Section 58.2222. . . .

NOTE: This bonus is only available to developments having frontage on primary or secondary pedestrian streets, or malls, designated by the streetscape requirements of Article III, Part 2F, Figure III-6. The bonus encourages commercial uses to be located on these pedestrian streets.

Bonuses for ground-floor commercial use shall be awarded only where the street-level lineal building-site frontage on all primary and secondary pedestrian streets and malls abutting the development is occupied by commercial uses conforming with the following standards:

Bonuses Available—
For at least 50 percent of leasable street frontage* (mandatory in area shown in Figure II-6) [map] . . . . 1.0 FAR
For at least 70 percent of street frontage* (optional). . . . . 1.5 FAR
For 90 percent of street frontage* (optional) . . . . 2.0 FAR
* Exclusive of lobby entrances and driveways.

NOTE: For existing buildings, the appropriate reviewing authority may approve minor deviations from these percentages, when literal compliance is impossible.

*Eligible Uses—*Only uses in the following land use categories may be counted toward satisfying minimum street frontage standards for this bonus:

(a) Light retailing (except banks and savings institutions)
(b) Personal services
(c) Entertainment services (except radio and television studios)
(d) Eating and drinking establishments

Minimum Depth from Building Facade—All business sites counted toward satisfying the standards of this bonus shall extend a minimum of 18 feet in depth from the building facade.

Under the retail set-aside requirement, at least 50 percent of the ground-floor street frontage on designated sections of Orange Avenue and Church Street must consist of retail uses. This mandatory set-aside is perhaps more aggressive than similar approaches taken by other cities, in that Orlando's requirement applies to existing structures as well as new construction. In existing buildings, the retail requirement is triggered by a change in occupancy. Once a nonconforming use is terminated, a conforming retail use must replace it. The aim is to reinforce retail continuity. With the eventual phasing-out of nonconforming uses, gaps will gradually fill in, and a majority of retail uses will return to the street level. Otherwise, gaps caused by preexisting nonconforming uses and long-term leases might remain indefinitely.

Besides in the historic retail district, the city also encourages retail development throughout the downtown. Developers building on primary and secondary pedestrian streets outside the mandated area must also comply with a 50 percent retail set-aside, entitling them to a bonus of 1 FAR. Provision of 70 percent or 90 percent of retail street frontage reaps further bonuses of 1.5 or 2 FAR, respectively. Without these bonuses, the maximum FAR in the downtown is 3.

Reactions to the Program. One glitch in the scheme showed up in the application of the retail requirement to corner buildings in downtown Orlando. Property owners complained they were penalized by having to put in double the amount of commercial uses for corner buildings. Interpretation of the zoning has been modified, and corner buildings need only provide commercial uses on Orange Avenue, the main downtown artery, which has the heaviest pedestrian flow.

Developers also have objected to the fact that the commercial-use definition excludes banks. In the case of one new project, a local bank, now located at the 100 percent corner (the intersection of Church Street and Orange Avenue), is expanding its headquarters into a connecting new building. At first, the city insisted the existing bank lobby contravened the retail requirement, but it eventually agreed to accept a lower ratio of ground-floor commercial uses.

Some developers also have indicated that whereas first-class retail space in the central core is leasing in as high a range as $30 to $40 (the high range for class-A office space in the city is projected at the low to mid-20s), commercial space in some buildings on the periphery of the retail core is harder to lease and sometimes needs substantial subsidy. Until sufficient critical mass is built up on the peripheries, these developers maintain, the 50 percent mandatory retail requirement is unrealistic and is aimed at the future, rather than the present, market. Therefore, it has been suggested that the percentage of mandatory commercial use be adjusted to account for lesser demand in areas outside the retail core. The city's position, however, is that the depth of the space that must be allocated to commercial uses—a minimum of 18 feet—is quite shallow, so that a newsstand, flower stand, dry cleaner, or other strictly service retail use accommodating a building's own occupants would easily comply.

ANALYSIS OF RETAIL ZONING TECHNIQUES

LOOKING AT THE MARKET

In any attempt to stimulate retail development through zoning, it is first essential to determine the realistic market for retail space and for certain mixes of store types. Because downtown retail tends to be multifunctional, homing in on the precise market and mix is no easy task. Nevertheless, some general retailing principles still apply. The basic rule—that retail follows the customers—must serve as the guide when formulating a downtown retail strategy. Marketing efforts should first be directed to the primary retail customer, who in many downtowns is the office

Roger K. Lewis, from his Washington Post column, "Shaping the City," 1/14/89

worker. In such a market, convenience and service retail, such as bookstores, flower and gift shops, barber shops, copy stores, and restaurants mainly targeted at the building tenants, generally has the best chance of succeeding. Specialty and destination retail uses—women's or men's clothing boutiques, antique shops, or art galleries, which often depend on strong tourist support or require importing customers to the downtown—are more suited to retail environments that are already robust.

Downtowns should also do extensive market analyses to ascertain the optimal commercial mix. City officials and planners might look to those standards now followed by the retail industry. The Urban Land Institute has compiled data on shopping center composition by tenant classification.[7] Within neighborhood shopping centers, for example, the percentage of gross leasable area devoted to food uses is 34.3 percent and to jewelry, 0.5 percent. On the other hand, the percentage of space devoted to jewelry in a super regional shopping center (of which the downtown equivalent might be a festival marketplace) would be much higher, at 3 percent. Likewise, while building materials and hardware uses take up 2.7 percent of leasable space in neighborhood centers, that amount drops to 0.2 percent in super regional centers.

THE SCOPE OF RETAIL REQUIREMENTS

Cities should be realistic about confining their retail zoning efforts to an appropriate geographic area. One common approach is to categorize streets. Seattle, for instance, uses eight downtown street categories, which seem largely to have been determined by analyzing pedestrian traffic flow. The categories include access streets, several classes of pedestrian streets, principal transit streets, street parks, and undeveloped streets. Active ground-floor uses are generally required on those streets where pedestrian activity is now concentrated or where it is expected or desired. Developers, however, routinely complain that cities are overly ambitious about forcing retail and that they extend the requirement beyond the boundaries of the retail core. Naturally, retail space on the periphery of the core and separated from other retail uses is harder to lease. The boundaries of a retail use mandate can always be expanded at a later date, and it is preferable to concentrate the retail uses rather than to produce disparate pockets or diffuse activity throughout the city.

A related issue is the size of the retail requirement in relation to the overall zoning envelope. For example, one of the most controversial provisions of the District of Columbia's downtown SHOP overlay district is a requirement that new office construction and major renovations devote 20 percent of their space to retail, arts, and service-related uses—roughly four times the amount currently included in the typical commercial project in downtown D.C. Banks, other financial institutions, and travel agencies may occupy no more than 20 percent of the ground-floor space. In a downtown where the zoning envelope is severely circumscribed by strict height caps and a maximum FAR of 10, this requirement (amounting to about 2 FAR) means that some retail inevitably will be pushed up to the second floor, and some driven underground. These are locales historically shunned by retailers and shoppers alike. Dubbed by Washington developers the "Shop till You Drop" district, the area covered by the retail requirement comprises 18 downtown blocks.

During the 1980s, Washington, D.C.'s downtown lost more than 3 million square feet of retail, much of which was apparently pushed out by office development. The SHOP district was enacted in 1989 to help retain some 1.2 million square feet of retail space (of which some 658,600 is contained within three department stores) within the core. As an inducement for a fourth department store or similar retail facility to come to the downtown, the overlay grants density bonuses beyond those granted by the preferred uses requirement, and allows development rights transfers (TDRs) outside the district to several designated receiving zones. (See Insert 4 for excerpts from the SHOP district's zoning rules.)

Insert 4.
Washington, D.C.'s Downtown SHOP District
(code extracts)

1700 **General Provisions**
1700.2 Specific purposes [of the SHOP district] include:
  (a) To create the most concentrated area of retail, service, arts, and entertainment uses in downtown.
  (c) To strengthen the character and identity of the district by means of physical design standards which ensure the following:
     (1) New buildings constructed to the property line and primarily oriented to the street;
     (2) Continuous retail, service, and entertainment uses of the ground level of buildings, with ample display windows and frequent store entrances to the outdoor pedestrian circulation system;
     (3) A pedestrian environment with ample sidewalks interrupted by a minimum of vehicular driveways; and
     (4) A sensitive design relationship between new and older buildings.
1701 **Use Provisions**
1701.1 Each new or altered building shall devote not less than either 1.5 or 2.0 FAR equivalent [depending on the building's location as spelled out in Subsection 1701.1 (b)] to retail and personal

service uses listed in Section 1707 or the arts uses listed in Section 1708.

1701.3 Not less that fifty percent (50%) of the gross floor area of the ground level of the building shall be devoted to the preferred uses; provided that not more than twenty percent (20%) of the required ground-level space shall be occupied by banks, loan offices, other financial institutions, travel agencies, or other ticket offices.

1702 Design Standards

1702.3 Not less than fifty percent (50%) of the surface area of the street wall at the ground floor of each building shall be devoted to display windows and to entrances to commercial uses or to the building.

1703 Development Flexibility and Bonuses

1703.2 If a building provides gross floor area for preferred uses in excess of the required 1.5 or 2.0 FAR equivalent specified in Subsection 1701.1, the excess square footage may be used in one of the following ways:

(a) The excess floor area devoted to preferred uses may be linked by combined-lot development with another lot within the SHOP district and thereby count toward the preferred use requirement of the other lot, pursuant to Section 1704 [entitled "Combined-Lot Development"]; or

(b) The excess square feet of gross floor area equivalent devoted to preferred uses may be used to increase the gross floor area of the building for all permitted uses on a one-to-one (1:1) ratio.

1703.3 A building which provides preferred uses in excess of the required 1.5 or 2.0 FAR equivalent, and which includes [a department store, a legitimate theater, or other specified uses, such as a performing arts space or a minority business], may count the floor area devoted to such use or uses at the bonus ratio of [1:3 for a department store, 1:2 for a legitimate theater, and 1:0.5 for the other specified uses] for the purpose of earning surplus density.

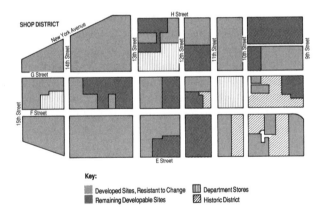

SHOP DISTRICT

Key:
- Developed Sites, Resistant to Change
- Remaining Developable Sites
- Department Stores
- Historic District

ENFORCEMENT

According to Matthew Terry, director of the design and development department in Bellevue, Washington, one of the main difficulties of administering a retail zoning requirement is enforcement. In Bellevue, both the active ground-floor use requirement and the voluntary pedestrian-frontage incentive are enforced for the life of a project, even if a particular retail use changes. Other cities with incentive zoning for ground-floor retail, like Hartford, only require that the retail

use remain in place for a given number of years. In Hartford, the period is 20 years. On the other hand, when a city mandates a percentage of active street-level pedestrian use, the duration is generally for the life of the project.

Terry attributes much of the enforcement difficulty to transitional problems. In cities like Hartford and Bellevue, where retail activity in the downtown office core was until lately either waning or nonexistent, the retail zoning requirements are forcing the market. Until sufficient retailing mass has been reached, with supporting public amenities to attract pedestrians, the retail uses in the first phase of a development will likely require some form of private subsidy. How, then, does a city mandate something that within 10 or 15 years will be a reasonable requirement but which at present is no more than a wish?

Part of the transitional dilemma is a matter of education. Peter Spitzner, chief staff planner in Hartford, notes that when the city's downtown zoning was first implemented, the development community tended to think that credit would be automatically awarded for providing any of the available bonus features. They needed to be educated about the requirements of the Downtown Development Plan, as well as the bonus design guidelines, and to understand that only those amenities that actually benefited the public would be eligible for increased density. They needed to learn that a restoration or remodeling project that destroyed existing retail would not automatically earn credit for retail uses when merely replacing the space that had been destroyed.

Fortunately, once developers grow accustomed to using ground-floor retail as an amenity to enhance the value of their commercial projects, the retail zoning requirement is no longer viewed as a "stick." In Portland, Oregon, which has required active ground-floor uses on pedestrian streets for a longer time than most other cities (since 1974), the requirement has been internalized into the development process and is part and parcel of doing business in the city.

Another enforcement problem arises because most retail regulations do not address the issue of existing nonconforming uses. Clifford Weaver and Richard Babcock note that the zoning provisions for New York's Fifth Avenue Special District do not apply to the existing nonconforming uses, which in 1979 constituted as much as 45 percent of the street frontage and which undermined the goal of continuous activity at the street level.[8] For this reason, Orlando, Florida, goes one step further than most jurisdictions and extends the retail requirement to cover cases in which a nonconforming use moves out or a lease comes up for renewal.

An additional factor is changes of tenancy. If the first retail tenant was unsuccessful and moved out of a space, a city could theoretically prevent a nonretail tenant from occupying the space, though it might have to resort to legal measures.

QUALITY CONTROLS

An allied problem to that of general enforcement arises when marginal retail uses meet the technical requirements of the code but not the spirit. For instance, such uses as orange juice stands, key duplication booths, or computer firms are not the caliber of retail that Bellevue envisioned for its prime downtown locations. Yet, in cities like Bellevue, where the downtown is still suffering the growing pains of adolescence, such marginal uses are going in where former retail tenants have failed. The space might otherwise have stood empty. If we grant that a city can require that a certain ratio of street-level commercial space be retained for active retail uses, then controlling the quality and character of the uses is more complicated.

It must be emphasized, however, that in most instances, developers of new Class-A downtown office buildings seek out good-quality retail as an amenity-enhancing feature to attract tenants and to contribute to the project's overall image.

Hartford land use attorney Dwight Merriam suggests the notion of a "retail executory interest" (in an analogy to probate law). Under this kind of provision, an office building would have to include space on the ground floor that later was convertible into retail uses. This space could be devoted to office use until such time as it was determined that the market could support retail, when the space would have to be converted to the latter. One snare in this plan is that it might prove prohibitively expensive to retrofit office space (though maybe not any more so than subsidizing the space for years). Another pitfall is the likelihood that, this way, the retail market might develop more slowly, if at all, because it was not forced from the start.

Marginal retail uses may pose a problem within highly competitive retail markets, too. For instance, tourist-oriented discount electronics shops are willing to pay exorbitant rents for prime locations to take advantage of tourists on Fifth Avenue or on Times Square. Such shops, which are proliferating along the prime stretch of Fifth Avenue, are regarded as a blight by upscale merchants like Rolex, which owns its 11-story building at Fifth Avenue and 53rd Street, and by other office-building owners who want prestigious retail tenants to enhance the value of their upper office floors.

The problem here is that the owners of the smaller buildings located between the larger office structures in this part of Manhattan generate most of their revenue at the ground-floor level; thus, they will likely accept the highest offer from a retail tenant. Some of these less desirable tenants take leases in office buildings in which either the landlord has lost control of the ground-floor level by granting a master lease to a separate realty concern, or the lease dates back to the financially troubled era of the mid-1970s, when landlords welcomed any retailer willing to pay the rent.[9]

COMMERCIAL CONCENTRATION

Retail zoning regulations can be used to control the placement, as well as the type or mix, of retail. The most direct method for exerting this form of control is simply to limit the size of the space. This is done in the Worth Avenue District in Palm Beach, Florida, where retail-related uses may not exceed a maximum GLA of 2,000 square feet. The purpose of the district is "to preserve and enhance an area of unique quality and character oriented to pedestrian comparison shopping and providing a wide range of retail and service establishments . . . serving the short-term and long-term needs of townpersons. . . . " An additional purpose of the limit on GLA is to "reduc[e] the problems of parking and traffic congestion determined to result from establishments of a region-serving scale."

The Worth Avenue District zoning was also intended to address the problem of "commercial over-concentration," the displacement of businesses providing the smaller neighborhood market with convenience goods by establishments that serve a citywide or regional market.[10] Commercial displacement is the product of a strong retail climate, where the economics tend to support regional luxury shopping tastes at the expense of neighborhood retail goods and services.

The term "neighborhood convenience goods" generally refers to hardware stores, groceries, and shoe repair shops, which are threatened by an influx of antique shops, women's clothing boutiques, or gourmet food stores. In the case of Worth Avenue, one of the wealthiest shopping streets in the world, however, the neighborhood retail consists of high-end apparel shops, boutiques, photo studios, and specialty food establishments that are threatened by regional plazas, malls, and department stores. Although the Worth Avenue District was designed to protect the rich and famous, the methodology is equally applicable to Mom-and-Pop stores.

Under traditional categorical zoning approaches (those using straight office, retail, or residential districts), the concentration of uses is determined by the market. Because traditional zoning techniques are ineffective in dealing with commercial overcrowding, a few cities, notably Berkeley and San Francisco, employ a novel system of use quotas to secure the optimal mix of neighborhood commercial establishments. Sometimes referred to as "quantitative zoning," this technique is the opposite of traditional Euclidean zoning, wherein the existence of a particular use creates a presumption that more of that same use will be permitted in the vicinity.

Although the few existing use quota systems were specifically framed for neighborhood commercial districts outside the downtown, this still-rare zoning technique might be applicable to downtown sectors that serve similar neighborhood functions and that also suffer from commercial overconcentration. As one planning official notes about Washington, D.C., "The downtown doesn't need any more Benettons [or other luxury shops]; what's needed are more grocery stores and hardware stores that downtown residents can easily walk to."

William H. Whyte writes about this problem as it exists in downtown Boulder:

> One time I went looking for aspirin in Boulder, Colorado. It was a most attractive downtown. On the pedestrian mall, there were people ambling about, some sunning on the grass, some reading, one playing a guitar. There were nice outdoor eating places. There were many shops. I could buy books and records, handcrafted leather goods, oil paintings. There was a gazebo with homemade ice cream. But no aspirin. Not one store stocked it. . . . At length I did what millions of Americans do. I got in the car and drove to the shopping mall.[11]

BERKELEY

Berkeley's use quota ordinance for the Elmwood Commercial District was implemented in 1984 to "maintain a scale and balance of retail goods and services in the district to compatibly serve the everyday needs of surrounding neighborhoods . . . [by] controlling the number and size[s] of uses, which have increased in number at the expense of district commercial diversity." The ordinance limits the number of women's apparel shops to six; full-service restaurants are limited to seven; establishments selling "gifts, jewelry, and/or arts and crafts" are limited to 11 and must not exceed 1,500 square feet. In 1987, the California legislature nixed the city's commercial rent control law, but the Elmwood use quota ordinance remained in place.

The city's most recent attempt to discourage "gourmet ghettos" was made in the university shopping neighborhood, where use quotas were enacted last year for the Telegraph Avenue Commercial District.

SAN FRANCISCO

In the 1980s, San Francisco has experimented with various quantitative zoning schemes and passed several interim ordinances setting explicit numerical limits for retail businesses in established neighborhoods. The city no longer uses a strict numerical approach. But San Francisco's 1985 Neighborhood Commercial Rezoning establishes use thresholds for 200 neighborhood commercial districts outside the downtown. In these districts, restaurants, bank branches, and bars have squeezed out older, neighborhood-based businesses. Most of the districts limit restaurants and bars, for example, to no more than 25 percent of the total retail frontage. New bank branches and financial services offices must be separated by 300 feet from similar offices.[12]

Depending on the fabric of the neighborhood, new or expanding uses may not exceed a maximum size without securing a conditional use permit. For example, new retail uses in the Pacific Heights/Union Street Neighborhood Commercial District may not go over 2,500 square feet by right. This limit was imposed to discourage the practice of combining several storefronts and to halt further violations of the district's close-grained Victorian character.

No significant legal challenge has been brought against either Berkeley's or San Francisco's use quota system. Chicago zoning attorney William McElyea warns, however, that if the city's underlying motive appears to be that of protecting existing businesses from competition, the courts are apt to find that the quota systems are an illegal restraint of trade. This finding raises numerous antitrust questions, as well as issues of the proper use of the police powers. Courts are also likelier to overturn such systems when the percentages of permitted uses have been set arbitrarily, on an ad hoc basis.[13]

RETAIL ZONING CASE STUDIES

NEW YORK CITY

The impetus behind New York's first zoning act in 1916 has been ascribed in part to efforts to protect Fifth Avenue retailers from the onslaught of the garment industry, which was steadily marching up Manhattan. Merchants feared encroachment by the "rag trade" and the possible effects on the district's wealthy clientele. Therefore, it is unsurprising that one of the first cities to implement zoning requirements for street-level retail was New York City.

The Fifth Avenue Special District was created in 1971 primarily because the street's famous retail trade, under tremendous real estate pressures, was giving way to more lucrative office rentals. High-end retail shops were being supplanted by banks, brokerage firms, and ticket offices, often accompanied by large expanses of blank walls and contributing little to the pedestrian activity at the ground floor. In 1971, retailers occupied only 55 percent of the frontage along Fifth Avenue between 34th and 56th Streets, whereas banks and travel agencies took up 21.4 percent.[14] Airlines, particularly those owned by foreign governments, were undismayed by the area's steep rental rates and were moving in at an alarming pace. During this same period, two department stores—Best & Co. and DePinna—announced their decisions to sell out to real estate interests, and it was because Fifth Avenue was losing its cachet that the 1971 zoning was implemented.[15]

Jaquelin Robertson—then director of the Urban Design Group, part of the planning commission, and later of the mayor's office of Midtown planning and development—headed up the study for the special district plan, one of the country's first examples of mixed-use zoning for a downtown office district. The Fifth Avenue Special District had several objectives: to support 24-hour activity, encourage retail activity at ground level along the Avenue and covered pedestrian spaces in the interior, eliminate the need for parking in the area and curb cuts fronting Fifth Avenue, encourage residential building in Midtown Manhattan, and strengthen the vitality of the street wall along the Avenue.

Zoning for the special district was partly mandatory, partly incentive. The district zoning required a minimum of 1 FAR for retail, starting on the ground floor. Some of the retail could be placed on upper levels, a provision that invites vertical retail complexes. Within 50 feet of the Fifth Avenue street line, banks and airline offices were limited to no more than 15 percent of the total linear frontage. The city also devised requirements to enhance retail and design continuity—street-wall frontages of building facades had to be built out to the lot line to a minimum height of 85 feet. Although the special district zoning distinguished between the east and west sides of the Avenue, more recent regulations place a uniform 125-foot height maximum on lot-line facades.[16]

Bonuses were made available for providing more than the required retail space and for adding other public amenities, including covered pedestrian spaces and through-block connections. The hope was that the ampler density offered by these bonuses would attract new department stores or boutique complexes to replace the two department stores that had decided to move.

The most controversial aspect of the special district zoning was the use of density gains for hotel and residential construction within the district. Olympic Tower, built 14 years ago by Tishman Speyer, was the first building constructed under the Fifth Avenue Special District zoning regulations and took advantage of almost every available bonus. The 52-story mixed-use project, with 28 floors of condominiums, 19 floors of office space, and about 40,000 square feet of retail, achieved an FAR of 21.6. Floor area increased by 14 square feet for each square foot of covered pedestrian space alone.

Public reaction to the quality of development that went up under the Fifth Avenue Special District zoning was mixed. "Evidently," writes Jonathan Barnett, "the original assumption behind the Fifth Avenue district, that the Avenue was vulnerable to redevelopment, was a correct one. A situation was foreseen and planned for; but none of the buildings constructed has completely lived up to the intentions of the district."[17] Roberta Brandes Gratz writes of Olympic Towers: "The city got a pedestrian arcade few pedestrians know exist, interior retail space left unrented, an interior public area with a waterfall that rarely runs and lights that are seldom lit."[18] In contrast to Trump Tower, where the retail design was an integral part of the development, Olympic Tower had included poorly designed retail space as no more than a means of acquiring additional density.

The public outcry against the gargantuan scale of new development in the area in part influenced the city to make certain adjustments to the zoning. The chance to gain greater density by providing retail in excess of the requirement was eliminated. Responding to criticism that the vertical shopping complexes in both Olympic and Trump Towers siphoned away street activity and storefront retail, the planning department also did away with the bonus for interior public spaces in the 1982 Midtown Zoning.

HARTFORD

Retail History. In the early 1980s, the city's premier department store, G. Fox and Company, which was losing some $3 million a year, threatened to lease out much of its largely underused space or possibly to pull out of the downtown altogether. General confidence in the downtown's ability to support a viable retail market had probably reached an all-time low. The threatened exodus of G. Fox and Company helped galvanize the business community to undertake a comprehensive assessment of the downtown retail market. In 1983, a ULI Panel Advisory Service report evaluated Hartford's retail development strategies. It noted the precipitous decline in total downtown retail sales in the previous 11 years, from $1.124 billion in 1972 to approximately $117 million in 1982.

At about the same time, local office developer Richard H. Gordon was assembling land on the site of the city's 100 percent block, across from the Old State House. This was the site that ULI's advisory panel had identified as pivotal to the overall plan to boost downtown retail. The panel's proposed plan used the classic barbell shape: A recommendation was made to make a single entity of the three main downtown retail components: 1) the Main/State Street retail block (including part of Gordon's project), 2) the Civic Center Mall, and 3) the Pratt Street retailers. As one of the pioneers of speculative office development in downtown Hartford, however, Gordon wanted to stick to what he knew best—office building. Moreover, a prospective insurance-company tenant had indicated that it would need most of the ground floor of Gordon's project for office space.

The potential departure of G. Fox and Company and the proposed development of the 100 percent block underscored the fragile state of health of Hartford's downtown retail. There also appeared to be a consensus that the retail problems could not be addressed in isolation but were inextricably tied to the larger zoning regime, which needed to be overhauled.

The business community's initial involvement in the zoning effort, notes Richard Bradley, former executive director of the downtown council, grew out of a perceived need to resurrect retail activity in the downtown. The downtown council had raised funds for a market study, for the ULI panel evaluation, and for the subsequent zoning rewrite. Although the local business and development community was actively involved in the retail evaluations and zoning overhaul, out-of-town developers and expertise were also brought in. In this way, the retail-potential assessments would not be skewed by the self-fulfilling prophecies of the local development community.

Anthony Caruso, executive vice president of Hartford's downtown council, observes that the business community's interest in retail development was two-pronged: It wanted to improve the appearance and image of downtown for business recruiting purposes, and it hoped to use retail development as a leveraging tool to revive the center. Retail shopping had

steadily dwindled there; in contrast, a regional shopping center called West Farm Mall, located in the northwestern Hartford suburb of Farmington, was capturing one of the highest sales rates per square foot in the country. The city's earliest downtown retail strategy, then, was to tap into the same market as patronized the high-end West Farm Mall.

This initial marketing approach was used for the shops at the Civic Center, one of Hartford's first downtown retail development efforts. The shops were targeted at the suburban homemaker. According to Bill Russell, senior vice president of Aetna Realty Investors, which developed the shops, the latter were promoted as boutiques offering uniquely high-quality merchandise unavailable in the regional shopping malls. This first strategy failed, however, and had to be rethought.

Thus, the second phase of retail programming in the Civic Center was aimed instead at the expanding market of downtown office workers. Managed by Aetna Realty Investors, the second-generation Civic Center shops, featuring two local department stores and a sports store, among others, apparently required subsidies in the beginning, although they are now carrying their own and a waiting list exists for prospective leases. Although rents tend to be steeper in the downtown and service costs are correspondingly higher, several mall shops have opened branches at the Civic Center to establish a presence downtown.

A main source of development interest and capital in the city has been and continues to be the consolidation and expansion of insurance companies, and in this regard Hartford resembles a company town. More recently, the city is also becoming a regional banking center. As a company town, however, certain paternalistic vestiges persist that tend to impede downtown retail activity. One example is the company cafeteria. These heavily subsidized cafeterias are regarded as "perks," and executives hesitate to eliminate them in a town where a severe labor shortage means vigorous recruiting efforts.

A cafeteria became an issue in the Metro Center project in Hartford's downtown. The Metro Center was originally supposed to comply with the city's retail requirement. But because this was one of the early projects affected by the 1984 code, the city agreed to waive the requirement, and the prime retail space will be occupied instead by a cafeteria for an insurance-company tenant. Later development phases will have to make up for the loss of the retail component.

The ULI panel report and other studies routinely suggested expanding the downtown workers' lunch hour, giving employees the option to eat elsewhere or at least to run errands at midday. Lunch hours at some companies have evidently been extended from half an hour to 45 or 60 minutes. Some companies have also joined an "Eats Program," whereby employees are given food vouchers to use at downtown restaurants.

Other impediments to retail development in downtown Hartford have included those that typically plague downtowns throughout the country, mainly perceptions that security was inadequate and that transient parking facilities were scarce or inconvenient. In addition, the development of upscale regional malls has effectively siphoned off business to the suburbs.

Retail Zoning. Ultimately, G. Fox and Company decided to remain downtown. In 1983, it announced its intention to spend $10 million more on its flagship downtown location. Its threatened exodus, however, had underscored the need to upgrade downtown retailing. Having by the early 1980s reached a consensus that the retail renaissance would need a major zoning overhaul, the business and development community agreed to a six-month moratorium, as recommended by the planning department. During this time, a new zoning code and downtown development plan would be drafted. Business interests pledged to support the rezoning, as long as it did not stunt growth. The zoning rewrite was accomplished within a record 90 days.

The resulting 1984 zoning for the Downtown Development District states that one of its main purposes is "[t]o retain and promote the establishment of a variety of retail consumer and service businesses, so that the needs of the area's residential and working population[s] will be satisfied. . . . " Toward this end, the city instituted the following retail requirement:

35-5.44 (a) Uses mandated. For all buildings, at least fifteen (15) percent of the floor area of those floors which front on or connect to the pedestrian circulation system, as shown in the Downtown Development Plan, shall be used for uses that are designated as retail trade under the Table of Permitted Uses. . . . The retail trade use shall front on the pedestrian circulation system as shown in the Downtown Development Plan. The council may waive this requirement, or reduce the required percentage of retail trade uses, if it specifically finds that no requirement or a lesser percentage . . . [would not contravene the "purposes" section of the downtown zoning]. The applicant shall covenant to ensure the continued use of such retail trade use for at least twenty (20) years. . . . Such covenant shall be recorded on the land records and run with the land.

Retail or "trade uses" typically include vendors of apparel and accessories, automotive products (gas stations), food, groceries, liquor, and jewelry, and exclude banks and travel agencies.

Hartford also offers a retail bonus for "pedestrian-oriented retail uses," which is awarded at a rate of 1 to 3 and caps at 2. The bonus is only granted if the space abuts the pedestrian circulation system and is visible to pedestrians. In other words, it must in fact benefit the public.

Projects Affected by the Retail Zoning. The first project to come in under the requirement for "pedestrian-oriented retail uses" was a 12-story speculative office project, the Metro Center. The proposed retail uses, such as a restaurant, quick printing shop, and dry cleaner, would have provided services to the building occupants. After the project was approved, however, CIGNA Corporation committed as a tenant at the 11th hour and wanted most of the available ground-floor space for a company cafeteria. CIGNA was also concerned about potential security complications entailed by the retail uses. Because the downtown zoning was new, and this was the first project required to provide the retail uses at grade, the city was perhaps too lenient and permitted the developer to delay provision of these uses until the project's second phase.

The city was also flexible in applying the retail requirement to a 17-story office building in the financial district. The main tenant, Mechanics Savings Bank, which served as the Hartford/regional headquarters for Bank of Boston, Connecticut, needed most of the ground floor for its lobby and service facilities. Because the project was peripheral to the main retail spine, the planning department waived its specification of 15 percent retail; in the latter's place, a visual arts space will adjoin the main lobby entrance.

A Project Caught in the Middle. Office developer Richard Gordon was a vociferous opponent of the retail requirement and understandably so, for one of his projects, State House Square, was caught in the middle of the zoning changes during the six-month moratorium. Because of the project's location, deemed pivotal to the retail core's revival, Gordon was strong-armed into providing more than the mandatory 15 percent retail. With uncanny prescience, Gordon had successfully pioneered large-scale office towers far in advance of the city's downtown development boom (as described in Chapter 1, "Incentive Zoning"). Left to his own devices over State House Square, Gordon would merely have built the perfunctory service retail for his office tenants.

The conflict over the 700,000-square-foot State House Square is similar to ones played out in other downtowns that have undergone major zoning revisions. The pending projects, those caught in the pipeline, may be forced to comply with features that look forward to the new zoning and subjected to a review process from which the "bugs" have not yet been exterminated. According to Gordon, the design reconfigurations and consequent permitting delays, brought on mainly by the zoning rewrite, cost him some $10 million.

To mitigate the harsh impact of the new retail and design requirements on State House Square, the city helped defray capital costs with an incentive package consisting of a $3.3 million UDAG, earmarked for the proposed glass retail pavilion; $2.5 million for landscaping, bricking over, and other public improvements; and $6.38 million in tax breaks. In midproject, Hartford apparently expanded the initial retail requirement from 77,850 to more than 110,680 square feet. Furthermore, Gordon had to negotiate with the city for a permanent easement for the site of the retail pavilion.

The Gordon-owned Ashley Management Company took over leasing and management from James W. Rouse's Enterprise Development Company, under whose direction the festival market–style pavilion—now called simply the Pavillion—was originally designed. According to Gordon, Rouse anticipated charging as much as $40 a square foot for store space, plus $20 for expenses and maintenance charges. A 2,000-square-foot store in the Pavillion would have to pay $120,000 a year—nearly twice the cost of space in other downtown locations, like Civic Center Mall and Richardson Shops.[19] But Enterprise failed to secure the upscale tenants needed to support the hefty rents and pulled out.

Ashley Management emphasizes that the Pavillion is not the salvation of Hartford and characterizes it as a milestone for, rather than a keystone in, the downtown's retail redevelopment. Pavillion tenants, enjoined to remain open till 9 p.m. on weeknights, are doubtful about attracting evening patrons and claim that evening business hours are the riskiest aspect of leasing a store in the complex. It is hoped that other retail uses, as well as the two downtown department stores, will adopt similar hours, although evening hours may eventually be scaled back at the Pavillion in any case.

Although committed to furthering the commercial success of his project, Gordon remains skeptical about the downtown's ability to support retail and to compete with the regional malls. It is his opinion that "downtown Hartford shouldn't try to be something it is not."

Retail in Recent Projects. Ironically, Richard Gordon is developing another office project with a significant retail component on the north side of Pratt Street,

the city's historic retail corridor. Aetna Insurance Company, a general partner, will lease 170,000 of the total 245,000 square feet of office space, and Aetna Property Services will manage the 90,000 square feet of retail space throughout the project.

At present, Pratt Street supports some 30,000 square feet of retail space, housed within a series of bedraggled shops. The proposed 11,483 square feet of additional retail will bring in some 34,450 square feet in bonus density. Because Pratt Street connects the downtown's two main retail spines and forms the barbell that is thought crucial to the downtown's retail regrowth, the project was assiduously scrutinized for pedestrian circulation elements and streetscape improvements.

The plan is for a pedestrian mall with controlled vehicular traffic; a portion of the street improvements is being financed through a program to sell brick pavers at $45 apiece. Independent studies prepared by Cesar Pelli and Associates and by Halcyon, Ltd., have recommended building a transparent skywalk connecting the second-level retail to the shops in the Civic Center. If built, this skywalk will link Aetna's retail interests throughout the retail core.

The retail requirements in this project, however, were not nearly as problematic as those in State House Square. If new retail is to succeed in Hartford, the most likely location is on Pratt Street. Furthermore, Aetna Property Services is no newcomer to retail management and leasing.

Halcyon's Pratt Street study outlined merchandise concepts and retail programs, design alternatives, and public space activities. Cesar Pelli and Associates completed an earlier master plan and is the architect for a megaproject on the south side of Pratt, to be developed by the Society of Savings, together with Gerald Hines Interests. The 45-story tower will contain nearly 1 million square feet of office space and 33,400 square feet of retail. Although the two Pratt Street projects are being developed separately, it is hoped that they will eventually be centrally managed, with uniform hours, maintenance, and security.

CHARLOTTE, NORTH CAROLINA

The 1987 amendments to Charlotte's Uptown Mixed-Use District ordinance, the zoning for its downtown, were specifically directed at boosting retail activity in the city's shopping core. Just as the insurance industry generally dominates Hartford, so do banking and financial institutions shape development in downtown Charlotte. For example, two regional financial establishments, First Union Corporation and NCNB Corporation, which rank among the 20 largest banks nationwide, are significantly altering Charlotte's urban landscape. As primary tenants in much of the downtown's recent development, banks have typically located their lobbies and service functions on the first floor and generally squeezed out most commercial uses. The remaining street-level retail has steadily deteriorated. As local architect Joddy Peer states, "The death of streetfront retail is basically the result of Charlotte's main economic strength—banking." [20]

Historical Background of Retail Amendments. Charlotte's population of 450,000 supports more than 50,000 downtown workers. The regional population is 1.1 million, with most of the downtown workforce commuting from outlying counties. Downtown office development is strong. In 1988, the downtown contained 6.4 million square feet, and by 1991, 4 million square feet of announced projects will bring an additional 2.4 million. In the mid-1980s, the city spent some $8 million on street improvements to create the Tryon Street Mall, an 11-block project that was meant to act as the city's main street. Despite efforts to promote and market the transit/pedestrian mall through special municipal service districts, though, the idea failed to ignite and the mall was woefully underused.

In 1985, the Uptown Mixed-Use District ordinance was up for review. (The ordinance's sunset provision calls for review of the zoning every two years, at which time interested parties may submit suggestions and comments to the Charlotte-Mecklenburg Planning Commission.) In 1985, the Central Charlotte Association, a division of the city's chamber of commerce, wanted to require that all new development provide 100 percent retail uses, excluding banking uses, on the first floor. The association brought in representatives from a New York consulting group, Project for Public Spaces, to evaluate existing pedestrian patterns along the mall and recommend improvements. It was generally agreed to take the mandatory, rather than incentive, approach because the city had nothing to give away: Charlotte's downtown has no height or FAR restrictions, and parking limits are more liberal than in the nearby suburbs.

The Charlotte Uptown Development Corporation (CUDC), a quasi-public organization that represents government, banking, and real estate interests, decried the 100 percent retail requirement. CUDC claimed it would effectively drive a large chunk of the city's primary tenants—banks and financial institutions—to other cities. Another criticism was that the present market could not support the retail uses, which would thus need major subsidies.

The planning department pushed for a 75 percent retail requirement, and a compromise was reached at

50 percent, so that any new large-scale project must devote half of its net first-floor area to retail activities. Retail is defined broadly, to encompass more than the sale of merchandise; it also includes "personal and business services, restaurants, galleries, and similar uses, but not financial institutions" (see Insert 5).

As a result of vigorous lobbying by the business community, this requirement may be reduced by up to 25 percent if separate street entrances are built for the retail space. Moreover, an "optional review" provision allows certain exemptions from the retail mandate if a developer persuades the city council that the project in question is unique. If the exemption is approved, however, the developer is committed to maintaining the agreed-upon substitute uses for the life of the project; any future change, even if it is by-right, calls for separate approval.

Developers' Opinions. W. Kent Walker is president of Charter Walker, the firm that has joined with a bank-led partnership to develop the mixed-use project called NCNB Corporate Center. The corporate center will comply with the recent zoning amendments. The $300-million city-block development will comprise an office tower of at least 1 million square feet, a hotel, a three-level atrium with approximately 40,000 square feet of retail space, and a $35-million performing art center, to be developed in partnership with the city. Although the project is located at the Square on the Tryon Street Mall and will connect with one of the department stores, Walker is having to incorporate more retail than in his opinion is economically feasible. The requirement, says Walker, is unrealistic, at least for the time being: there is at present an inadequate market for high-quality retail in the downtown. The two downtown department stores have cut back extensively on their selling floors. According to Walker, a market exists for superior men's clothing, but women shoppers prefer to make their serious purchases in the suburbs on weekends, when they are not confined to their lunch hours.

Although the mandated retail is limited to certain streets, the development community maintains that the market is being artificially imposed on some areas on the periphery of the retail core, and urges that the designated area be further reduced.

The retail requirement is reinforced by other sections of the downtown ordinance aimed at animating the streetscape and bolstering pedestrian activity. Examples are the various standards for street tree planting and transparency, not to mention the detailed guidelines for the design of the bases and entrances of high-rise buildings. (See Chapter 8, "Open Space and Streetscapes.") The city also tries to invigorate first-floor retailing by controlling new connections to its overhead skywalk systems (as covered in Chapter 9, "Skywalks").

SEATTLE

The fact that Seattle's retail core survived the exodus to the suburbs can be ascribed partly to geographical accident. Because the downtown is surrounded by water and hills, the competitive regional shopping centers were forced to locate farther away from the downtown than was typical in other cities, thereby preserving the downtown as a centralized market. The exception to the rule is Bellevue Square, the suburban regional shopping center located only 10 miles away on the eastern shore of Lake Washington.

Although Seattle's present population of 492,000 is a stable one, overall tourist, trade, retail, and business activity is growing. During the last seven years of the 1980s, the city has enjoyed the highest absorption rate of leased office space in its history. In 1988, close to 1.5 square feet of commercial space was absorbed in the downtown.

Some major anchors have operated in the downtown for more than 40 years, and local commitment has traditionally been strong. With the completion of the $100-million Westlake Center in 1988, the city now contains some 4.5 million square feet of retail, with most of it concentrated in the core. The long-awaited public/private project developed by the Rouse Company and Koehler McFayden of Seattle,

Westlake Center features a 24-story office tower, small park, and three-story shopping mall with some 125,000 square feet of retail space. Work has been coordinated with progress on the $400-million Metro transit tunnel, which runs beneath the project and will be completed in 1990.

Retailers were particularly worried that construction for the bus tunnel, which had transformed much of the area into a combat zone, would severely disrupt retail activity in the core. Mobilized by the prospect of tunneling and the projected dire effects on retailing, the Seattle Downtown Association, representing the city's business community, formed a local improvement district (LID) in the retail core in 1987. Although it was predicted that the tunnel construction would cause retail sales to plummet by as much as 25 to 30 percent, by the summer of 1987, following creation of the LID, retail activity had stabilized.

Retail Zoning. Although Seattle's retail core is quite healthy, it is still seen as fragile. One of the motivating goals of the city's 1985 Land Use and Transportation Plan was to reinforce and concentrate retail activity on the 12 city blocks composing the retail spine. From the very start, the Seattle Downtown Association was involved directly in the city's rezoning efforts and worked on the plan for four years. Land use attorney Judith Runstad, former president of the Seattle Downtown Association, notes that although "the business community was initially reluctant to see regulations imposed in the core, it recognized that the area couldn't be taken for granted, and in the end, self-enlightenment overrode business self-interests."

Zoning goals in the retail core were twofold: to sustain and strengthen retail vitality and to preserve those smaller, older terra cotta buildings located in the area. The preservation efforts were largely spearheaded by the city's urban design watchdog, Allied Arts, so that the 1985 FAR and height limits are far more stringent than those for the office core.

Under the old zoning, the FAR limit in the retail core was 10, with bonuses ranging from 2 to 10 additional FAR. The area had no height limits. Under the 1985 zoning, the base FAR is 5, although that portion of the ground floor set aside for retail is exempt from the FAR count up to a maximum of 1.5 (which supports the elevation of lobbies off the first floor). By using various bonuses, it is possible to increase the FAR in most situations to 7.5. Whereas construction in the area once exceeded 400 feet, in 1985 the height limit became 240 feet.

Most recently, the citizen-sponsored Citizens Alternative Plan (CAP), which captured 62 percent of the votes in a May 1989 election, further curbed development in the retail core. CAP reduces the base FAR in the retail core from 5 to 2.5, and the maximum height is now generally 85 feet. The fulfillment of certain bonus obligations, such as provision of a department store or performing arts facility, however, permits somewhat more liberal density and height limits. But buildings may not be taller than 150 feet or exceed an FAR of 6. (CAP is described more extensively in Chapter 1, "Incentive Zoning.")

In parts of the city where retail continuity and street activity are especially important—the core, the Pioneer Square Historic District, the Pike Place renewal area, and the International District—retail and service use is obligatory for at least 75 percent of the street frontage. Downtown streets are categorized by their pedestrian circulation patterns, and those streets with heavy pedestrian use must also meet the retail requirement. In the core area, no more than 20 percent of the ground floor may be devoted to banks, airline ticket offices, travel agencies, or similar uses. There are no minimums for depth or square footage.

Retail and Retail-Related Bonuses. Increased density is available for providing various retail-related features, including retail shopping, shopping corridors, and shopping atriums (see Inserts 6 and 7). The retail shopping bonus is only available after the mandatory retail requirement is met; customer service offices like airline ticket agencies, travel agencies, and branch banks are ineligible.

Insert 6.
Seattle's Retail Shopping Bonus
(code extract)

1. Intent
    The intent of the retail shopping bonus is to generate a high level of pedestrian activity on major downtown pedestrian routes and on bonused public open spaces. While retail shopping uses help ensure that major pedestrian streets are active and vital, a limit to the amount eligible for a bonus is set in each zone, in order to maintain the dominance of the retail core as the center of downtown shopping activity.
2. Bonusable area
    The maximum bonusable area per lot shall be 0.5 FAR or 15,000 square feet, whichever is less.
3. Eligible uses—Basic Standards
    Retail sales and service uses and entertainment uses shall be eligible for a retail shopping bonus. Customer service offices such as airline ticket agencies, travel agencies, and branch banks shall not be eligible.
4. Street orientation—Basic Standards
    Bonused retail shopping uses should be located close to the sidewalk in order to add to street interest and activity. Bonused shopping uses shall meet the access and location requirements for required street-level uses for the zone in which they are located, as well as all facade transparency and blank wall limitations for Class I pedestrian streets in the zone.

5. Hours of operation—Basic Standards
    Bonused uses shall be open to the public at least five days a week for at least six hours per day.

Insert 7.
Seattle's Shopping Corridor Bonus
(code extract)

1. Intent
    Shopping corridors are intended to provide weather-protected through-block pedestrian connections and retail frontage where retail activity and pedestrian traffic are most concentrated downtown. Shopping corridors create additional "streets" in the most intensive area of shopping activity, and are intended to complement streetfront retail activity. The location and size of shopping corridors are limited to avoid the creation of a pedestrian network independent of pedestrian movement along the street. Shopping corridors that connect avenues and are generally located in the middle of the long blocks in the retail core area will provide additional retail frontage and improve pedestrian circulation without detracting from sidewalk activity. Where possible, shopping corridors should be aligned with existing pedestrian crosswalks or entries to other pedestrian corridors on adjacent blocks.
2. Bonusable area
    a. The maximum bonusable area shall be 7,200 square feet.
    b. The bonus value of the corridor may be increased by 25 percent when the corridor meets the provisions of Section 7 below.
3. Area and dimensions—Basic Standards
    The corridor should provide a pleasant space for pedestrian movement and shopping and should be designed so the connection between avenues is apparent.
    a. The minimum height of the corridor shall be 12 feet, except that open overhead walkways which cover not more than 5 percent of corridor area may have a height clearance of 10 feet.
    b. The maximum width of the corridor shall be 30 feet, with a minimum width of 20 feet that is free and clear of all obstructions, including columns.
4. Location and access
    Entrances shall be highly visible from the street, accessible, and inviting. It should be clear to pedestrians that the corridor provides a through-block connection.
    Basic Standards
    a. Shopping corridors shall connect two avenues.
    b. No more than two shopping corridors shall be bonused on a block.
    c. Entrances to the corridor must be at the same grade as the sidewalk. Level changes between entrances shall be permitted to accommodate changes in existing grade.
    Design Guidelines
    d. The minimum distance from any street property line which is parallel to a corridor should be 120 feet, and the minimum distance between corridors should be 60 feet. These dimensions shall be measured along the avenue property line from the inside face of the corridor walls.
    e. Entrances shall have a minimum height of approximately 12 feet and shall be the full width of the corridor. Entrances may be completely open, or may be enclosed with clear, transparent doors and glazing.
5. Retail requirements and hours of operation—Basic Standards
    a. Because shopping corridors should function as retail streets, frontage equivalent to at least 75 percent of the perimeter of the shopping corridor shall be occupied by uses which qual-

ify for the retail shopping bonus (Section F). These uses shall have entrances directly onto the corridor.

b. Because they are an element of pedestrian circulation, shopping corridors shall be open to the public from at least 7:00 a.m. to midnight, seven days a week. The uses required in Subsection 5a above shall be open to the public at least five days a week for at least six hours per day.

6. Facade treatment and furnishings

The facades and furnishings of shopping corridors should be designed to enhance shopping and add to pedestrian comfort; however, the design and location of furnishings, art, and kiosks should not detract from the corridor's principal function as a through-block connection.

Basic Standards

a. Art shall be incorporated as part of the corridor, as set forth in the general conditions of this rule.

b. Temporary kiosks, displays, art exhibits, and retail use of the corridor may be permitted, provided that use, access, and circulation through the space by the general public is not obstructed. Temporary structures are those that are movable or designed to be easily dismantled. In no case shall any temporary use of the space reduce the circulation path to a width of less than 10 feet.

Design Guidelines

c. The same transparency requirements and blank wall limitations that apply to Class I pedestrian streets in the zone in which the shopping corridor is located should be applied to the corridor walls.

d. Approximately one lineal foot of seating, either permanent or movable, shall be required for every 60 square feet of bonused corridor area. The arrangement of seating should not obstruct pedestrian movement through the space.

7. Additional bonus for natural light

The quality of the corridor area can be improved through access to daylight through skylights or clerestory windows. The bonus value of the entire shopping corridor shall be increased by 25 percent when the corridor meets the following provisions for natural light, additional height, and landscaping.

Basic Standards

a. Natural light may be provided as follows:
   1. At least 25 percent of the roof area above the corridor shall have skylights; or
   2. A minimum of 40 percent of the perimeter dimension of the corridor shall have clerestory windows a minimum of four feet in height; or
   3. A combination of Features 1 and 2 above may be provided.

b. When the additional bonus for natural light is used, 25 percent of the total length of the corridor shall be at least 18 feet high, and the minimum height of the remainder of the corridor shall be at least 12 feet . . .

c. A minimum of 15 percent of the corridor shall be landscaped and include seasonal plantings.

As discussed in Chapter 3 ("Development and Design Reviews"), the Seattle's bonus system also serves a design review function, and detailed design guidelines must be followed for many of the bonus selections. For instance, the guidelines for the shopping corridor bonus stipulate: "Approximately one lineal foot of seating, either permanent or movable, shall be required for every 60 square feet of bonused corridor area. The arrangement of seating should not obstruct pedestrian movement through the space." In addition, the bonus value may be increased by 25 percent by filling the corridor with skylights or clerestory windows. (Refer back to Insert 7 for design guidelines for lighting within shopping corridors.)

A bonus is also available for incorporating into a commercial project a major department store (80,000 square feet or larger). This one-time bonus permits exceeding the FAR and height limits, pushing the allowable FAR up to 11 and the height to 400 feet (under CAP, the new limits are 6 FAR and 150 feet).

It is also possible to bank the extra density for a later phase or use it on another site. However, a transfer site must be on one of several key blocks. Unlike the other retail bonuses mentioned above, which are automatic as long as the guidelines are met, the department store bonus is treated as a conditional use, subject to the discretionary review of the city council.

Another retail-related bonus is the one furnished for performing arts theaters. This bonus, like the special public benefit feature for department stores, is also discretionary. Use of the feature allows lifting the height lid from 150 to 400 feet, and the FAR from 6 to 11 (pre-CAP rates). The seating area for the live theater must contain at least 200 seats, and the facility must offer all the necessary support areas. Under one of the special review criteria, the theater should be located where it "will contribute to an active pedestrian environment and . . . help promote other related retail and entertainment uses."

Design guidelines for the bonus feature are intended to enhance pedestrian access and interest. For example, it is recommended that lobby areas located along the streetfront be given transparent walls, and theater street frontage should be limited to no more than 25 percent of the total street frontage of the lot, or 60 feet, whichever is less. Although the theater may be built above or below street level, direct access should be provided to the lobby from the street or from a bonused public open space.

Development within the Retail Core. Richard Clotfelter, the president of Seattle-based Prescott Development Company, is involved in several major projects in the retail core. He notes that whereas it once was economical to build on two lots, today it only makes sense to build on at least four lots. He attributes this change largely to the ground-floor retail requirement, which takes up space that would otherwise be used for loading, access, and cuts for arcades and covered atriums. Typical floor plates in the downtown are running 20,000 to 21,000, although those in most older projects are considerably smaller.

Clotfelter is considering applying for the department store bonus for the second phase of his Century Square Tower. The curved-glass-topped 28-story office tower, bordering the southern end of Seattle's retail core, opened in 1986 and houses some 52,000 square feet of retail space. Although the location is ideal—close to the three existing department stores and the new Westlake Center—the economics are rough.

According to Clotfelter, the site for the second phase of Century Square Tower theoretically could accommodate an FAR of 12. However, because of the potential for casting a shadow on Westlake Park, which is proscribed by the city's zoning and environmental review, that portion of the project next to the park cannot rise much higher than three floors. Therefore, Clotfelter will most likely bank and transfer the TDR credits to another site within the permissible three-block area. In Clotfelter's opinion, the value gained from the department store bonus is insufficient to cover the value that is offset to the sending site. The bonus would also be more valuable, he maintains, if it were transferable to a larger receiving area. Although an office tower atop a 90,000-square-foot department store would be economically feasible, a 10-story project could not adequately carry the department store.

Richard Clotfelter has also been negotiating with a local theater group and intends to use the bonus for performing arts theaters in another major Prescott Development mixed-use project, slated for construction in the retail core.

Downtown construction in the 1980s has run close to 1 million square feet per year on the average, with absorption running from 800,000 to 1 million square feet. Although close to 1.5 million square feet was absorbed in 1988, as more projects come on line there will inevitably be more turnkey jobs and discounts. Clotfelter says the 1988 vacancy rate for office development within the retail core, at 9 percent, was less than that for the overall downtown office market, at 12 to 14 percent, a fact that confirms the marketing advantage of mixing commercial and retail uses.

With four major projects entering the retail core within the near future, the vacancy rate will likely rise. A three-year absorption period is predicted for projects in the core. But severely curtailed building heights in the retail sector have magnified the pressure to proceed immediately with those projects that have already won approval, despite this extended absorption period. Similarly, the construction of these vested projects has been spurred by the shadow issue; the shadow ban prohibits casting shadows on *existing* public parks. For this reason, those vested projects planned for the retail area had a real incentive to build before Westlake Park was constructed.

BELLEVUE

Most cities spotlighted in this book are experimenting with innovative zoning approaches to boost or impede certain existing activities, or to promote given goals in their older downtowns. Bellevue, in contrast, is largely starting with a clean slate. Once the butt of Seattle cocktail-party jokes, portrayed as "Car City," and strewn with gas stations, strip commercial centers, sprawling office buildings, and other indicia of suburbia, Bellevue has changed suddenly and deliberately.

Work on a new downtown plan was begun in 1978, and in 1982 the city passed a radically revised land use code to achieve an intense, concentrated commercial core. The downtown was totally redefined as a 144-block area. Development was directed into the downtown, where FARs can go as high as 10.1 in some locations, while the FAR for any building outside the downtown is limited to 0.5. In exchange for providing various public amenities under the code's incentive system, heights of 300 feet or greater were permitted in the core. In addition, parking ratios were strictly circumscribed, setback mandates were removed, and an ambitious program of zoning rules and incentives aimed at making the downtown a distinct urban neighborhood was launched. Based on these policies, the city rejected a proposal for a mammoth shopping mall planned for a site several miles from the downtown.

Besides the zoning changes, which spawned a new breed of downtown office towers to fill out the 600-foot-long superblocks, several other factors have also contributed to the dramatic transformation of the 440-acre downtown. These include demographic shifts, corporate locational decisions, and transportation constraints.

Located 10 miles east of Seattle across Lake Washington at the intersections of Interstates 90 and 405, Bellevue is part of the "greater Eastside" suburban expansion, extending from Renton to Bothell and including Mercer Island. This expansion currently outstrips that of commercial development in Seattle. With a population of 85,000 and a service area of more than 300,000, Bellevue is the fourth largest city in the state. Downtown employment, now at 22,000, is projected to double by the year 2000. Seattle banks, accounting firms, and law offices have opened branches in Bellevue, and the city is the hub of a more-than-$1-billion high-tech industry.

Four years after the code was adopted, commercial space within the core had more than doubled. The roughly 8 million square feet of commercial space now standing, most of which has been developed within the last five years, consists of 6 million square feet of office and 3 million of retail, with another 1 million square feet of commercial space in design. More than one-third of the existing retail space is sited within Bellevue Square, a 1.2-million-square-foot regional shopping center west of the core. All told, allowing for projects under construction, it has been estimated that more retail space exists today in Bellevue than in Portland, Oregon.[21]

John Nordby, who has directed the development of several major office towers in downtown Bellevue for the Seattle-based Wright Runstad & Company, reports that Bellevue's retail market is highly competitive (in 1987, retail was leasing at Bellevue Square for between $25 and $35 a square foot). However, Nordby notes, retail space in commercial buildings less than four blocks away from Bellevue Square was renting at less than $10 a square foot and, in some instances, required subsidies by the building owners.

Office projects more than 20 stories tall have been built along 108th Street, referred to as Bellevue's Wall Street. And although overbuilding in the early 1980s saddled the city with high office vacancy rates and generous rent discounts, some Bellevue projects apparently now command higher rents than their Seattle counterparts. Most of the newer buildings are 80 percent occupied.

Retail Zoning Requirement. As part of its program to create a downtown neighborhood catering to pedestrians rather than cars and to the convenience of people living and working there, the city requires that new construction and substantial remodeling provide amenities on the ground floor. The requirement may be met with a landscape feature, arcade, marquee, awning, sculpture, or water feature, or with what is called "pedestrian-oriented frontage." This term is defined as, but not limited to, "specialty retail stores, groceries, drugstores, shoe repair shops, cleaning establishments, floral shops, beauty shops, barber shops, department stores, hardware stores, apparel shops, travel agencies and other services, restaurants, and theaters." Banks and financial institutions are excluded from the definition.

Pedestrian-oriented frontage is also one of the bonus features in the city's amenity incentive system. For this feature, credit is only awarded when the amenity is placed where active pedestrian use is expected or encouraged. Explicit design criteria stipulate that the pedestrian-oriented frontage 1) "must abut a sidewalk, plaza, or arcade"; 2) "must be physically accessible to the pedestrian at suitable intervals"; and 3) "must be visually accessible to the pedestrian at the sidewalk, plaza, or arcade level" (see Insert 8).

Insert 8.
Bellevue: Street Frontage That Invites Pedestrian Activity (code extract)

Section 20.25A.030.C

Amenity	Design Criteria
1. Pedestrian-Oriented Frontage Building frontage devoted to uses which stimulate pedestrian activity. Uses are typically sidewalk-oriented and physically or visually accessible by pedestrians from the sidewalk. Uses which compose pedestrian-oriented frontage include, but are not limited to, specialty retail stores, groceries, drugstores, shoe repair shops, cleaning establishments, floral shops, beauty shops, barber shops, department stores, hardware stores, apparel shops, travel agencies and other services, restaurants, and theaters. Banks and financial institutions are not pedestrian-oriented uses.	1. Pedestrian-oriented frontage must abut a sidewalk, plaza, or arcade. 2. A pedestrian-oriented use must be physically accessible to the pedestrian at suitable . . . intervals. 3. Pedestrian-oriented uses must be visually accessible to the pedestrian at the sidewalk, plaza, or arcade level.

To specifically spur development of major grocery stores in the downtown, the city created a retail food bonus. A retail food store is defined as "a self-service retail enterprise which sells food, beverages, and household goods for consumption off the premises." Only stores having a minimum gross floor area of 15,000 square feet are eligible. This bonus applies even if the store does not front on the street, in contrast to the bonuses for "pedestrian-oriented frontage."

Retail Zoning and Development. In many ways, Bellevue Square *is* retail in Bellevue. Built in the 1950s, the regional shopping center has undergone several expansions and modernizations. The most recent remodeling took place in the early 1980s. The Square anchors the western end of the Major Pedestrian Corridor, with Koll Center at the easternmost end. The approximately 1.2 million square feet of retail space consists of four department-store anchors linked by a covered mall that offers an assortment of smaller retailers. With some 30,000 shoppers a day, Bellevue Square captures the burgeoning Eastside market, as well as many Seattle shoppers, and boasts one of the highest sales volumes per square foot on the West Coast.

Caught amidst the city's rezoning efforts, the project had to meet some of the requirements of the 1981 code. Like all other development on the Major Pedestrian Corridor, the project had to comply with the pedestrian frontage requirement on Bellevue Way. This street runs past the entryway to The Bon department store, an entrance that also serves as the main "door" to the mall.

From the city's viewpoint, the hermetically sealed mall's inward-facing stance contributes nothing to pedestrian interest. This is a particularly serious omission, given the amount of regulatory attention that is focused on the pedestrian corridor. (See Chapter 8, "Open Space and Streetscapes.") Because shoppers approach from their cars, street-level uses on the fringes of the mall's parking lot are overlooked, and the mall sucks in potential pedestrian traffic.

When advised that part of the first-floor entryway of The Bon department store had to be devoted to competing smaller retail uses, store officials threatened to pull out of the lease. Bellevue Square's owner and developer, Kemper Freeman, Jr., reports that it has proven difficult to lease out the space, and he has been hard pressed to attract retail of a comparable quality to that in the rest of the mall. Store officials were equally put out by the requirement that windows at the street level be transparent, for some merchandise inevitably would be damaged by direct sunlight.

Freeman is currently developing a 1.7-million-square-foot project, Bellevue Place, diagonally across from Bellevue Square. The first phase, a hotel/office/retail complex with a 21-story office tower, opened in 1988. The development also contains a 30-story Hyatt Regency hotel and a three-level, glass-enclosed winter garden given over to retail uses. Another office high rise, a residential tower, and an arts center are planned for a later phase. After fulfilling the ground-floor amenity requirement, Bellevue Place gained some 123,000 square feet for providing extra pedestrian-oriented frontage. Freeman is also considering adding a grocery store, which would earn yet greater density.

Once the pedestrian corridor has been developed with retail-related uses lining the perimeter, and once it has connected Bellevue Square with the financial center, destination shoppers from the Square are expected to spill over into other parts of the downtown. (See Insert 9 for map.) The corridor, however, will be developed in segments, depending totally on private development, and completion of a continuous pedestrian link will not likely be achieved in the immediate future. (For more information on the corridor, refer to Chapter 8.) Until that time, most of the retail uses in

the financial core will continue to be specialty shops and service-related businesses (delicatessens, dry cleaners, florists, and quick print shops) catering to employees in the immediate vicinity. With the exception of some restaurants, these uses will not remain open in the evening. Restaurants already offering after-work service have had difficulty in attracting evening patrons.

Because the city demands that retail space qualifying for bonus credit be leased before a final certificate of occupancy can be issued, developers are aggressively courting retail uses. One developer bought the inventory of a bookstore moving from Seattle and subsidized the operation for the first six months. Likewise, the retail in the first phase of Koll Center, a 27-story, 495,000-square-foot office/retail tower abutting the eastern end of the pedestrian corridor, is also subsidized, and full rent will only be charged when the building is 85 percent leased. Recognizing that the retail leasing requirement is hard to meet during this early stage of the downtown's development, the city has shown some flexibility in enforcing the leasing schedule.

Insert 9.
Downtown Bellevue and Its Pedestrian Corridor (code illustration)

■ Boundary of high-rise core district
▬ Pedestrian Corridor
■ Boundary of downtown

Because of the need to subsidize the retail space, at least for the present, and because of the expense of preparing the frontage space, the pedestrian frontage feature is apparently one of the costlier requirements of the city's zoning. One developer said he could triple his net simply by putting in a lending institution instead.

IN SUMMARY

In the past, one of the greatest obstacles to the development of ground-level retail has been the prevailing corporate mind-set. According to this preconception, retail uses were incompatible with pricey, properly majestic office lobbies and sullied a building's pristine image. Times have changed in many cities, where retail is now viewed as an amenity and a prestigious selling feature, even for fashionable mixed-use office/retail complexes. This attitudinal shift undoubtedly was influenced by cities' demands that office buildings benefit a larger public, not only commercial tenants, and that they provide more street-level retail.

As stated earlier in this chapter, the cardinal rule for retail is that it follows its customers. It is nearly impossible to create a retail market in a downtown where none exists, but one can build on existing markets. Those downtowns blessed with sizable residential populations or with a strong tourist draw can boost ready-made retail markets. On the other hand, in many downtowns, the market is mainly defined by the universe of office workers. Retail thrives on the propinquity of other retail, as well as of cultural and entertainment facilities.

In those downtowns with major tourist and residential populations, retail space can reap a profitable return, sometimes more than the highest-priced office space. In such places, it might be argued that the market should dictate and that retail zoning is unnecessary. For example, as mentioned above, many downtowns bar relatively nonactive retailers, such as airline ticket offices and banks, from occupying prime ground-floor premises. Coincidentally, though, deregulated airlines have recently found such space in some cities too costly anyway and have moved to cheaper space on upper floors. In San Francisco, some banks also are moving to the second level, to save costs in a highly competitive banking environment.

On the other hand, an overly ambitious retail requirement may generate a glut of retail space. Developers routinely complain that cities force retail beyond the levels the market can support. In San Francisco, for instance, a mix of factors—the reduced density of new office projects, the loss of downtown employment through major corporate relocations, and an aggressive retail space requirement—has contributed to a glut of retail space in the downtown. In most cases, cities can avoid this problem by doing comprehensive market analyses, taking into account the relationship between the density of office employment and the retail space required.

At the same time, vacant retail space may be the fault of poor design rather than market forces. For this reason, many cities bolster their retail zoning mandates with design standards. These may include specifications for frequent entryways connecting directly to the sidewalk, encouragement of windows with clear glass or display space on the first floor, and limits on inward-gazing arcades and atriums. All of these features are meant to make the retail uses more visible and accessible. In addition, office developers, who often have no merchandising experience, might find it useful to hire retail consultants to work with their architects in the earliest planning stages to ensure that their retail space works.

Vacant retail space can also result from inadequate marketing. Not all landlords will make the effort to effectively promote retail when their primary interest is office.

Because office-block developers generally want the type of retail that lends cachet to their projects, nonchain uses (frequently minority and small, displaced businesses) are not actively courted. For the same reason, swanky office projects may be loaded with shops selling Belgian chocolates or designer socks, which are seen as enhancing a building's prestige, when what is really needed is a full-service dime store or drugstore.

In contrast to the earliest zoning controls, which mainly sought to keep the status quo, the new interventionist regulations are deliberate strategies to effect changes in the downtown. Because these strategies are often tied to commercial development, office developers are apt to resist those measures that seem to be forcing the market. Retail zoning tactics, however, must not only reflect existing market truths. They must also reveal a city's vision of its future and look forward to what is possible.

Notes

1. See William H. Whyte's discussion of "triangulation" in *City: Rediscovering the Center* (New York: Doubleday, 1989), pp. 154–155.
2. Ibid., p. 82.
3. Mark McCain, "A New Generation Joins Madison Avenue Boutiques, "*New York Times* (December 13, 1988).
4. Refer to ULI et al., *Dollars & Cents of Shopping Centers: 1987* (Washington, D.C.: Urban Land Institute, 1987), pp. 274–276 (under the heading "Shopping Center Composition by Tenant Classification").

5. Cited by Gideon Bosker and Lena Lencek in "Portland As an Urban Theme Park," *Architecture* (November 1987), p. 52.

6. Richard Tseng-yi Lai, *Law In Urban Design and Planning* (New York: Van Nostrand Reinhold Company, 1988), p. 326.

7. See ULI et al., *Dollars & Cents of Shopping Centers: 1987.*

8. Clifford L. Weaver and Richard F. Babcock, *City Zoning: The Once and Future Frontier* (Chicago: American Planning Association, 1979), pp. 127–128.

9. See Mark McCain, "Prestige Tenants Battling Tourist-Oriented Stores," *New York Times* (April 24, 1988).

10. William D. McElyea has explored use quota systems as correctives for the problems of commercial overconcentration in "Use Quotas for Achieving Well-Balanced Neighborhood Commercial Districts: A Question of Local Authority," *Ecology Law Quarterly*, vol. 14, no. 2 (1987), pp. 325–364.

11. Whyte, *City*, p. 322.

12. Ed Zotti, "San Francisco Rezoning Study," *Planning* (March 1989), p. 13.

13. For a legal analysis of quantitative zoning, refer to McElyea, op. cit., pp. 335–364.

14. According to Weaver and Babcock, *City Zoning*, p. 127.

15. As recounted by Robert Ponte in "Manhattan's Real Estate Boom," *New York Affairs*, vol. 8, no. 4 (1985) (a special issue subtitled *Real Estate Development and City Regulations*).

16. See Lai, *Law in Urban Design and Planning*, p. 326.

17. Jonathan Barnett, *An Introduction to Urban Design* (New York: Harper & Row, 1982), p. 110.

18. Roberta Gratz, "New York's Zoning Predicament," *Planning* (December 1979).

19. According to Mark Pazniokas and Pamela Klein in "Shopping center to open on scale less ambitious than was planned," *Hartford Courant* (May 14, 1987).

20. Joddy Peer, statement made at ULI's seminar on downtown zoning held in June 1987.

21. As reported by John Carlson, "We Got Problems, Too," *Seattle Weekly* (July 6, 1988).

CHAPTER 8

OPEN SPACE AND STREETSCAPES

INTRODUCTORY REMARKS

The street is a room by agreement.

– Louis Kahn

"Great buildings are not, in and of themselves, any guarantee of great cities," writes Paul Goldberger. "But great streets almost invariably make for civilized and comfortable cities."[1]

The sense of the street as a "public room," in which the semi-enclosed outdoor space stands for more than a void between buildings and functions as a place in its own right, is part of the appeal of great cities like Paris and London and of many sought-out urban neighborhoods in this country. Napoleon was said to have called the Piazza San Marco in Venice the finest drawing room in Europe. But any street is potentially a room, and the more time we spend in it, the more "intensely roomlike it becomes."[2]

Neotraditionalist architect Andres Duany, who employs the town planning principles of an earlier century, claims that in the historic Georgetown section of Washington, D.C., for example, "people will pay $400,000 to $500,000 for a house with small rooms, bad plumbing, and parking two blocks away; it has to do with the beautiful street in front of it."[3]

In addition to the buildings, then, those other elements of the built environment that shape the design character of the downtown are the open spaces, streets, sidewalks, and the myriad of smaller components—paving, plantings, street hardware, and lights. The real significance of Battery Park City in Manhattan, according to Goldberger, is "the message this large complex sends about the importance of the public realm."[4] In this 92-acre housing and office complex, developed by the state-created Battery Park City Authority, parks, waterfront promenades, streets, and public art are as important as the individual buildings. "Instead of plopping buildings down in open space, Mr. Cooper and Mr. Eckstut laid out traditional

T. J. Lassar

Esplanade at Battery Park City, New York.

streets connecting to a system of parks and a riverfront promenade, and required all buildings to conform to this larger urban design. The result [notes Goldberger] is a place, not a project."[5] Moreover, "making public places is what New York is really about," says Eckstut.[6]

Recognizing that their image and potential marketability are inextricably tied to the quality of their major public spaces, cities have been employing some of the country's most talented designers to organize buildings around downtown streets, public parks, squares, and waterfront esplanades. Many cities have also invested in downtown streetscape improvements or constructed pedestrian and transit malls as methods of stimulating private investment.

Often, this strategy has proved remarkably effective. Portland, Oregon, architect Greg Baldwin notes the salutary effect of Portland's 1987 light-rail system: "Retail sales have increased by 20 to 40 percent on adjacent properties, and the value of private construction on nearby parcels [has] exceeded the system's entire capital costs by five to seven times."[7]

San Antonio's River Walk, Denver's Sixteenth Street Mall, and Charlotte's Tryon Street Mall are similar examples of streetscape capital improvement projects where cities have effectively leveraged public money to generate private investment. The infusion of public funds is generally funneled into high-risk investment areas, such as undeveloped waterfronts, old rail yards, or ailing retail cores.

In more recent times, however, many fiscally strapped cities have been looking for new ways to finance infrastructure and public space improvements and are turning over much of the responsibility for building downtown public spaces to private developers. (In this regard, the process used to develop Battery Park City is the stunning exception rather than the norm.) One means of shifting the responsibility to the private sector is to zone public spaces. This chapter will examine some of the zoning techniques for expanding public space opportunities within the downtown.

Charlotte and San Francisco require developers to provide some open space within downtown commercial projects. San Francisco office developers must also contribute to a separate downtown park fund. Other cities, including Seattle and Bellevue, Washington, Cincinnati, Hartford, and Portland, award additional density for urban plazas, retail arcades, rooftop gardens, and parcel parks.

Cities are also more concerned about the quality and usability of their open spaces and have adopted explicit standards covering the design and maintenance of urban plazas. The centerpiece of Bellevue's downtown land use ordinance is its Major Pedestrian Corridor, which links the financial core to the city's retail hub. This corridor, to become Bellevue's main street, will be built virtually without public monies. It will be constructed incrementally by those developers with projects sited on the corridor alignment.

The recent flurry of open space zoning regulations reflects a renewed interest in the so-called public realm, a belief in the public's legitimate stake in the way cities develop and change: after all, cities by their very nature are public places, as well as individual clusters of private property. The most famous apostle of this concept, Robert Moses, had a notorious career as New York City's parks commissioner, construction coordinator, and planning commission member, as well as chairman of the Triborough Bridge and Tunnel Authority, state power commission, and state parks council, among other agencies. Moses's career attests to "his unwavering commitment to the idea of the public realm. Moses believed in public places—in the idea of public parks, public beaches, public open space, public housing." [8]

Once limited primarily to parks, tree-lined boulevards, sidewalks, and streets, the concept of the public realm has been expanded to include some privately owned areas, such as building lobbies, atriums, and skywalk connections, which, through their relationships to the streetscape and impact on the urban fabric, also function as public territory and as such are grist for the regulatory mill.

OPEN SPACE

PLAZA PERILS

New York City's urban plaza bonus has been widely imitated throughout the country; it is probably the most scrupulously studied zoning bonus feature to date. As the major bonus amenity in New York's 1961 Zoning Resolution and later amendments, the urban plaza is regarded by some commentators as the most significant urban design element of the city's early incentive zoning effort and, according to Jonathan Barnett, came "to have an excessively important role in the design of the city." [9]

Additional floor area of up to 20 percent in certain high-density commercial and residential areas was permitted in exchange for building a plaza. The use of the plaza bonus exceeded all expectations and spawned the generation of the international-style "tower-in-a plaza" paradigm, as inspired by Mies van der Rohe and Philip Johnson in their famed 1958 Seagram Building. "More than any other building, the Seagram design would serve as the new architectural vernacular for office skyscrapers, and the 1961 Zoning Resolution, with its 40 percent tower coverage provision and plaza and arcade bonuses, made the tower form almost irresistible." [10]

This tower-in-the-plaza planning fad, which John Costonis has described as "planning's Murphy's Law of unintended consequences," [11] produced "scores of 'bargain-basement Mies buildings'—cheap, bland imitations of the original; disruption of formerly uniform street walls by redundant, windswept plazas; and buildings that are discordant in scale and bulk with their neighbors and with the streets on which they front." [12]

In addition to the design criticism, namely, that many of these wind-bedeviled, unused spaces irreparably fragmented the streetscapes and isolated new buildings from their surroundings, their value as public amenities was also challenged. The rationale for the plaza bonus was that the "density-ameliorating" characteristics would more than compensate for the loss of light and air, the increased congestion, and the costs of providing the municipal services needed for the extra density. This quid pro quo would justify the bonus of 2 or 3 FAR and the ability to exceed the maximum FAR of 10 or 15. Critics noted, however, that whereas developers were reaping substantially more rentable space, the public gain was often negligible, if not nonexistent. The as-of-right plaza bonus "proved almost embarrassingly successful," [13] and according to William H. Whyte, "over the next decade, with no exceptions, every developer who put up an office building took advantage of it." [14]

In 1978, attorney/planner Jerold Kayden completed an economic analysis of the plaza bonus. [15] Kayden calculated that between 1961 and 1973, commercial developers put up some 7,640,556 square feet of additional commercial space in return for providing plazas, the costs of which amounted to roughly $3,820,278. In fact, figuring the average net capitalized value per square foot at $23.87 (a conservative estimate), Kayden calculated a bonus value of $186,199,350. In other words, for each dollar spent on plaza construction, developers gained almost $48 worth of extra space. [16]

Kayden also concluded that the as-of-right plaza bonus, which added more than 7 million square feet of floor area, aggravated the high office vacancy rates and deterioration in rents during the city's fiscal crisis in the mid-1970s.

Because the first zoning provision for the plaza bonus contained no definable standards or design guidelines, most of these spaces, "either through ignorance or indifference about what design characteristics made a plaza usable, or because the owner wanted to discourage public use to avoid maintenance, liability, and image problems," were designed as if to say "keep out." [17]

Recognizing that most of the plazas being built met the letter but not the spirit of the zoning, New York City hired urbanologist William H. Whyte to study plaza use and recommend appropriate design improvements. For more than a decade, Whyte had been observing and recording people in their natural urban habitats. He and his team studied plazas throughout the city and their use or nonuse. They sedulously cataloged precisely those elements that characterized the more successful urban open spaces, such as Paley Park, one of New York's first vest-pocket parks, and the Seagram Plaza.

Working with time-lapse films, photographs, and extensive interviews, Whyte frequently concluded the obvious, namely, that "people tend to sit where there are places to sit. If you want to seed a place with activity, put out food; and trees ought to be related much

more closely to sitting spaces than they usually are." [18] He noted, however, that although people speak of seeking an "oasis" or a "retreat" or of "getting away from it all," what "attracts people most, it would appear, is other people. . . . " [19]

On the basis of these findings, Whyte advised that the city develop specific design guidelines governing site location; climate conditions, including sun access, temperature, and wind; security; and comfortable seating. Whyte's observations and conclusions prompted New York City's Urban Design Group to develop a comprehensive set of detailed plaza design standards, which were enacted into legislation in 1975 and 1977.

Since that time, the open space standards have been substantially refined and expanded, so that now the criteria for urban plazas take up almost 20 pages in the 1982 Midtown Zoning. These criteria cover location and orientation, as well as circulation and access. Sunken plazas, not easily visible or accessible from sidewalks and all too often bereft of sunlight, are verboten.

The 1982 zoning, which reduces the bonus value from 3 to 1 FAR, defines an urban plaza as a "continuous open area which fronts upon a street or sidewalk widening and is accessible to the public at all times for the use and enjoyment of large numbers of people. Unless specifically permitted, . . . no part of an urban plaza may be closed to the public." The 24-hour public use requirement has been modified, so that the more recent plazas are typically gated in the evening, and movable chairs and tables may be stored away at closing time.

The code also lists explicit requirements for seating, planting and trees, paving, lighting, maintenance, and accessibility for the handicapped. In addition, as a means of informing the public of the specific features of each plaza, a plaque must be displayed listing its features and stating the name, address, and phone number of the person charged with maintenance. (See Inserts 1a, b, and c for code language.) Cities throughout the United States, as well as some cities in Japan and Taiwan, have been influenced by New York's prototype legislation and have adopted explicit plaza design standards.

Insert 1.
New York's Urban Plaza Bonus
(code excerpts) [1]

1a. Circulation and Access
   1. To facilitate access to an urban plaza, within 10 feet of a *street line* or sidewalk widening, along at least 50 percent of each *street* frontage of such urban plaza, the surface of the urban plaza shall be at the same elevation as the adjoining public sidewalk. Along that portion of the *street* frontage which has direct public access from a sidewalk or sidewalk

widening, comprising at least 50 percent of the length of such *street* frontage, an urban plaza shall have no obstruction of any kind for a depth of at least 20 feet from the *street line*. For the remaining 50 percent of the frontage, no walls or other obstructions may be higher than 36 inches above the *curb level* within 20 feet of the *street line*.

2. The level of an urban plaza shall not at any point be more than three feet above or three feet below the *curb level* of the nearest adjoining *street;* however, an urban plaza with an area of 10,000 square feet or more may additionally have a maximum of 15 percent of its area at an elevation more than three feet above or three feet below, but not more than either five feet above or five feet below *curb level* of the nearest adjoining *street*.

3. Where there is a grade change of at least 2.25 feet in 100 feet along a portion of a *street* fronted upon for a distance of at least 75 feet by an urban plaza with an area of 10,000 square feet or more, the level of such urban plaza may be at any elevation which is not more than either five feet above or five feet below *curb level* of the nearest adjoining *street*. Along the length of frontage not required for access, no wall higher than three feet above the level of the urban plaza may be constructed.

4. A covered portion of an urban plaza . . . may be closed to the public from 7:00 p.m. to 8:00 a.m.

1b. Seating

There shall be a minimum of one linear foot of seating for each 30 square feet of urban plaza area, except that for urban plazas fronting upon a *street* having a grade change of at least 2.25 feet in 100 feet or for through-block urban plazas, there shall be a minimum of one linear foot of seating for each 40 square feet of urban plaza area.

Not more than 50 percent of the linear seating capacity may be in movable seats which may be stored between the hours of 7:00 p.m. and 8:00 a.m. Seating shall be in accordance with the standards set forth below:

1. Seating shall have a minimum depth of 16 inches; however, seating with backs at least 12 inches high shall have a minimum depth of 14 inches. Seating 30 inches or more in depth shall count double, provided there is access to both sides.

2. Seating higher than 36 inches and lower than 12 inches above the level of the adjacent walking surface shall not count toward meeting the seating requirements.

3. The tops of walls including but not limited to those which bound planting beds, fountains, and pools may be counted as seating when they conform to the dimensional standards in Subparagraphs (1) and (2) above.

4. Movable seating or chairs, excluding seating of open air cafes, may be credited as 18 inches of linear seating per chair.

5. Steps, seats in outdoor amphitheaters, and seating of open air cafes do not count toward meeting the seating requirements.

6. Seating for any use within an urban plaza is subject to applicable articles and amendments of the New York City Building Code.

7. For the benefit of handicapped persons, a minimum of 5 percent of the required seating shall have backs.

1c. Plaques

A plaque or other permanent *sign* with a *surface area* not less than two nor more than four square feet shall be displayed in a prominent location on any urban plaza for which a bonus is granted. Such *sign* shall indicate the following:

1. The number of trees required on the urban plaza and *street* trees required on the *street* sidewalk area.

2. The number of movable chairs required on or adjacent to the urban plaza.

3. The name of the owner and the person he has designated to maintain the urban plaza and that person's address and a telephone number where he can be reached between the hours of 8:00 a.m. to 7:00 p.m.

4. The symbol for a city planning commission–certified urban plaza.

5. The International Symbol of Access and the statement: "This urban plaza is accessible to the physically handicapped."

6. The statement: "To ensure compliance with requirements regarding this urban plaza, a bond has been posted with the Comptroller of the City of New York."

---

[1] All italics in New York inserts are original.

OPEN SPACE IN PITTSBURGH

In 1965, Pittsburgh became the first major U.S. city to impose an open space zoning requirement throughout the entire downtown. The downtown ordinance has virtually no bulk requirements, so that the open space mandate works in much the same way as setbacks to preserve light and air.

The open space requirement applies to all new projects within the downtown (the Golden Triangle) and amounts to 20 percent of the ground-level lot area. In one downtown redevelopment district, where dense development is encouraged within a parklike setting, the requirement is 60 percent. Within this area, Gateway Center, the nation's first publicly sponsored, privately financed redevelopment project built according to the popular post–World War II planning ideal of a city in a park, was developed with a series of open spaces.

Architect Jonathan Barnett, who has worked as a consultant to the city for the past decade, notes that "Pittsburgh's planning policy is to look for . . . strategic opportunities where an investment in public open space will reinforce and redirect private development." [20] According to Barnett, "One of the most effective actions of the first Pittsburgh rebuilding program was the creation of Mellon Square." [21] The project involved clearing a city block and constructing an underground parking garage topped by a park. Property values shot up on the park frontages, where two corporate headquarters—those of Alcoa and U.S. Steel (later called Mellon Bank)—chose to locate. [22]

Although the open space requirement was put in place as early as 1965, the year of the city's second code revision, specific standards were not written until 1983. It has been suggested that the effort to implement open space standards gained initial support from the late Mayor Richard S. Caliguiri, who had previously directed the city's parks department. Using the techniques of William Whyte, the city evaluated the availability of sitting areas, trees, landscaping, and other amenities and used time-lapse photographic studies to evaluate the actual use of the spaces. In 1982, the planning department issued the study, which showed that some of the spaces developed under the 1965 code were sorely underused; the need for exact guidelines was underscored. To this end, quantitative standards were adopted in 1982 and incorporated into the 1983 code revisions (see Insert 2).

Insert 2.
Pittsburgh: Open Space Standards for the Golden Triangle (code excerpt)

(1) One tree (six-inch caliper minimum at time of planting) for every 1,000 square feet of required open space, to be planted in at least 250 cubic feet of soil; 3 feet 6 inches minimum depth; to be located within open space.
(2) A minimum of 25 linear feet of seating for every 1,000 square feet of required open space which shall be more than 12 inches and less than 30 inches in height and not less than 16 inches in depth. Seating more than 28 inches in depth and accessible from two sides shall count double. Movable chairs shall count as 2½ linear feet.
(3) At least one-half of the required open space shall be at street grade.
(4) At least one-quarter of the required open space shall be either provided as water or landscaped with groundcover, shrubs, or flowers.
(5) One water tap for every 10,000 square feet of each landscaped open space.
(6) One garbage receptacle for every 5,000 square feet of each physically separated open space.
(7) Spaces less than 6 feet wide may be counted as usable open space at the discretion of the planning commission.

Apart from setting the standards, the code revisions call for attention to existing and projected pedestrian volumes and circulation patterns; location, size, and character of existing open spaces in the vicinity; surrounding land use patterns; and relationships to public transportation policy and plans within the Golden Triangle. Open space must be accessible to the public during business hours and contain "specified amenities and development features designed to encourage use and enjoyment."

Fortunately, given the high density of downtown Pittsburgh, the open space requirement gives the city greater development review control, as well as flexibility. The process of negotiating over the design and location of the open space serves to some extent as a type of design review.

The Current Code Provisions. Since 1983, Pittsburgh's land use code has distinguished between urban open spaces and usable open spaces, the latter term being applicable to residential projects. In both instances, the space "may be located on the same zoning lot for which the space is required" or on an adjacent lot. Under unusual circumstances, funding is permitted in lieu of the open space obligation:

> On small sites where the required open space would result in areas of limited public usefulness, in locations where required open space would be adjacent to existing large open spaces, and in specific locations such as historic districts or other areas where the adopted plans and policy documents applicable to the district indicate that open space is not desirable, the commission may approve the payment of funds in lieu . . . , which payment shall be used by the city for the acquisition and development of open space elsewhere in . . . [the downtown]. The amount of such payment shall be based upon the [cost] of the land which would otherwise be incurred by the applicant for development of that space. . . .

So far, only one project has paid into the escrow fund ($500,000 in lieu of a 2,200-square-foot open space); these monies will be used to finance the open space improvements in a later development phase.

The code also sorts out those urban open spaces designed to facilitate pedestrian circulation or relieve pedestrian congestion from those that provide passive recreation. It further stipulates that when a development site lies next to a bus stop or transit station, the open space must provide access to the facility, as well as waiting areas for the transit riders. The earlier code requirement that a space be continuously available has been amended so that the area may be locked up and gated in the evening. As a result, the quality of the fixtures used in the spaces—fountains, benches, lights, artwork, and the like—is markedly higher than it once was.

Open air restaurants and ice skating rinks may fulfill a portion of the obligation, provided the relevant standards are met and the remainder of the open space is available for use without charge.

Open Space Bonus. A density bonus is awarded for urban open space built in excess of the requirement. In the downtown high-density redevelopment area, the bonus award may reach 60 percent. The bonus award is proportional to the extra open space provided. For instance, an increase in open space from 20 to 30 percent of the lot area would permit an increase of 50 percent in floor area, within the FAR limits set out in the zoning regulations.

The 1983 zoning revision also supplies density awards for interior open spaces, if the following standards are met:
• Entrances must be at least 20 feet wide and clearly visible from adjacent sidewalks or open space;

Indoor public space: Winter Garden at Battery Park City.

- Minimum and maximum height requirements must be met;
- The transparency requirement for walls of interior and exterior spaces must be met;
- Natural light sources or a glazed roof must be used;
- The space must function as a through-block passage accessible to the general public and contain seating; and
- The space must provide public toilet facilities and drinking fountains.
- To meet the requirement, a space may alternatively provide:
  - food services,
  - handicapped accessibility, or
  - an observation deck, viewing area, or permanent not-for-profit art gallery.

In developing the standards for the interior open space bonus, the planning department looked to other cities' successful interior spaces that combined cultural uses, such as New York's Whitney Museum Annex in the Philip Morris Building. The planners also observed successful spaces in Pittsburgh's own projects, such as the glassed-in winter garden at the PPG complex and the major public space in Oxford Center.

The code requires a maintenance agreement: "A legally binding agreement, in a form acceptable to the city, shall be executed for each urban open space provided and approved under the requirements of this ordinance. This agreement shall include provision for the permanent maintenance of the urban open space by its owner."

Retrofits. In the mid-1980s, Westinghouse waterproofed its underground garage. The renovation expense exceeded $50,000, so that Pittsburgh's open space requirement was triggered. Westinghouse had to completely redesign the existing open spaces, which were built before the city had implemented its standards. Located in the Gateway Center redevelopment area, where the open space requirement is 60 percent, the project underwent extensive landscaping improvements, including the addition of more than 1,000 feet of seating.

Impressed with the quality of these new public spaces, several downtown developers consulted with the planning department and voluntarily retrofitted older spaces in compliance with the new standards.

VARIED ZONING APPROACHES TO OPEN SPACE REGULATIONS

Charlotte, North Carolina. In downtown Charlotte, new office buildings must provide public open space proportionate to their bulk according to the following schedule:

Lot Size (Square Feet)	Open Space Required (1 square foot/gross square feet of floor area for office use)
0–20,000 sq. ft.	1 sq. ft./200 sq. ft.
20,001–40,000 sq. ft.	1 sq. ft./150 sq. ft.
above 40,000 sq. ft.	1 sq. ft./100 sq. ft.

A maximum of 30 percent of this required urban open space may be provided on an enclosed ground-floor level, provided the enclosed space meets all other requirements of these provisions. If a property line of the site is within 200 feet of the property line of a publicly owned and usable open space, then up to 50 percent of the required urban open space may be provided on an enclosed ground-floor level, provided the enclosed space meets all the requirements. The 200 feet shall be measured along the public right-of-way line.

The regulations for the Uptown Mixed-Use District (UMUD), which apply to the downtown, address such open space issues as accessibility to the street, provision for the handicapped, seating, trees, food, amenities, and upgrading of existing plazas and spaces.

The code's maintenance provision states that "the building owners, lessee, management entity, or authorized agent are jointly and severally responsible for the maintenance of the urban open space area, including litter control and care and replacement of trees and shrubs."(See Insert 3 for the precise urban design guidelines.)

Insert 3.
Charlotte's Urban Open Space Rule
(code excerpt)

2. *Accessibility to the Street.* Eighty-five percent (85%) of the total urban open space must be accessible to and visible from the street, but in no instance more than three feet above or below the level of an adjoining right-of-way. Walls higher than three feet are not allowed along that portion of the frontage that is needed for access to a required urban open space. Required entryways and steps must be at least 15 feet wide. Steps must have a maximum riser height of six inches and a minimum tread of 12 inches.

3. *Provision for the Handicapped.* All urban open spaces must conform with Section 11 of the North Carolina State Building Code, the Handicapped Section.

4. *Seating.* There must be at least one linear foot of seating for each 30 square feet of open space. Seating must be 16 to 24 inches high. In the case of a ledge which rises because of a grade change, the portion of the ledge between 20 inches and 36 inches high can count as seating. Seating must have a minimum depth of 15 inches. Ledges and benches which are sittable on both sides and are 30 inches deep will count double. The rims of planters which are flat and sittable can count as seating if they have a minimum depth of eight inches, a maximum height of 36 inches, and are not blocked by protruding shrubbery. Movable chairs will count as 30 inches of linear seating per chair. They can be stacked and stored between 7:00 p.m. and 8:00 a.m. Step space over and beyond the required 15-foot walkway width can count as seating. Corners of steps offer prime seating arrangements and will count as seating if not obstructed by railings.

5. *Trees.* Within the open space area(s), one tree must be planted for each 500 square feet or portion thereof up to 2,000 square feet. One additional tree is required for each additional 1,000 square feet of urban open space. Trees planted on unenclosed urban open spaces must have a minimum caliper of four inches at the time of planting. . . . Trees planted on enclosed urban open spaces must have a minimum caliper of three inches at the time of planting.

6. *Food.* The provision of food facilities is encouraged. Food kiosks can count as open space, provided they do not exceed 150 square feet in area. No more than one-half of the open space may be used for an open air cafe. Litter receptacles must be provided at a minimum of four cubic feet of receptacle capacity for each 800 square feet of open space.

7. *Amenities.* The following amenities are permitted within an urban open space area: ornamental fountains, stairways, waterfalls, sculptures, arbors, trellises, planted beds, drinking fountains, clock pedestals, public telephones, awnings, canopies, and similar structures.

San Francisco. The city's 1985 Downtown Plan compels developers of downtown commercial buildings to provide open space at a ratio of one square foot for every 50 square feet of an office project, or for every 100 square feet of a predominantly retail project. The space must be built on site or within 900 feet of the project, and no more than 20 percent of it may be indoors. The plan "envisions a downtown where almost everyone will be within 900 feet . . . of a publicly accessible space to sit, to eat a brown-bag lunch, to people-watch, to be out of the stream of activity but within sight of its flow." The open space requirement may be met by building "a plaza, an urban park, an urban garden, a view terrace, a sun terrace, a greenhouse, a small sitting area (a snippet), an atrium, an indoor park, or a public sitting area in a galleria, in an arcade, or in a pedestrian mall or walkway. . . . " These spaces are reviewed according to the "type, size, location, physical access, seating and table requirements, landscaping, availability of commercial services, sunlight and wind conditions, and hours of public access." (See Insert 4 for standards.) The Downtown Plan includes a detailed chart listing the guidelines for each of the open space alternatives.

Insert 4.
San Francisco's Open Space Standards
(code excerpt)

[A public open space must:]
(1) Be of adequate size;
(2) Be situated in such locations and provide such ingress and egress as will make the area easily accessible to the general public;
(3) Be well designed and where appropriate be landscaped;
(4) Be protected from uncomfortable wind;
(5) Incorporate various features, including ample seating and, if appropriate, access to food service, which will enhance public use of the area;
(6) Have adequate access to sunlight, if sunlight access is appropriate to the type of area;
(7) Be well lighted, if the area is of the type requiring artificial illumination;
(8) Be open to the public at times when it is reasonable to expect substantial public use;
(9) Be designed to enhance user safety and security;
(10) If the open space is on private property, provide toilet facilities open to the public; [and]
(11) Have at least 75 percent of the total open space approved be open to the public during all daylight hours.

Additional code requirements, particularly those covering microclimatic impacts, including sun access and ambient wind velocities, also directly affect the quality and character of the city's public spaces.

Maintenance is a prominent issue. The code states that "continued maintenance of the open space," at no public expense, is to last "for the actual lifetime of the building." With the approval of the city planning commission, a developer may contract with a public or private agency to build and maintain the space, provided "the commission finds that there is reasonable assurance that the open space to be developed by such agency will be developed and open for use by the time the building, the open space requirement of which is being met by the payment, is ready for occupancy."

Like New York's regulation, San Francisco's code calls for an information plaque:

> Prior to issuance of a permit of occupancy, a plaque shall be placed in a publicly conspicuous location outside the building at street level, or at the side of an outdoor open space, identifying the open space feature and its location, stating the right of the public to use the space and the hours of use, describing its principal required features (e.g., number of seats, availability of food service), and stating the name and address of the owner or owner's agent responsible for maintenance.

San Francisco's zoning also distinguishes between open spaces that function as amenities within office and retail development and public parks that serve recreational purposes. Based on the assumption that new projects increase the demand on downtown parks, commercial developers must also contribute "$2 per square foot of the net addition of gross floor area of office use to be constructed" to a special downtown park fund, which payment is part of the city's system of development fees for transit, art, housing, and child care. All monies deposited in the fund are earmarked "solely to acquire and develop public recreation and park facilities for use by the daytime population" in the downtown. Every third year, the park fee amount is to be reviewed by a joint session of the recreation and park commission and the city planning commission. In addition, the commissions are directed to "jointly review the fee to determine whether inflation in land and development costs justifies an increase in the fee, and if they so find, shall recommend an amendment of the provisions of this ordinance to the board of supervisors."

Portland. Portland's compact 200-by-200-foot street blocks create a high air-to-building ratio, with generous amounts of light and open space in the downtown. Counting the street space and parks together, more than 50 percent of the 500-acre downtown consists of open space. By comparison, the amounts of open space in downtown Seattle and New York run somewhat less than 35 percent.[23]

Although a plaza bonus was initially considered as part of Portland's recent incentive zoning system, the bonus was dropped for fear of inadequate controls. This fear was fed in part by the several now-empty plazas that had appeared in the downtown during the 1960s. It was also fed by the city's recognition of the marketing value of the downtown's distinctly dense urban character (unique in the state of Oregon). The city planners try to reinforce this quality through their policies.

The availability of public open space, however, is an issue within Portland's 1988 Central City Plan. Exactions and incentives for private development of open space have been set for those locations in which deficiencies might well occur with increased building. Areas undergoing street vacations for the development of superblock sites larger than 75,000 square feet will be particularly affected by the open space requirement. The zoning dictates that at least 50 percent of the area of vacated streets must be developed as open space, and that a plaza must be created equal to at least 5 percent of the total area of the superblock.

Under the Central City zoning, height may be transferred from land privately developed and dedicated as open space to certain development sites. Height transfers, however, are not permitted into historic districts, view corridors, or sites bordering on the waterfront or public open spaces. In addition to review by the parks bureau, new open spaces are also subject to design review by the city's design commission.

Portland has accomplished what many other cities have attempted but failed to do: it has removed a freeway that blocked access to the river from the downtown. In conformance with Portland's Downtown Plan, the city in 1977 closed off a mile-long, six-lane highway on the west bank of the Willamette River and designated a 50-acre waterfront park, of which 20 acres have been developed as intensive recreational open space. In the meantime, detailed studies, as called for in the Central City Plan, have been undertaken to determine the cost of relocating another existing freeway (I-5) on the east side of the river upland, and of putting in its place parks and waterfront development sites, as has been done on the west bank.

Bellevue. Not surprisingly, Bellevue has no open space requirement. Recent zoning efforts are aimed at intensifying and solidifying the downtown core, rather than obtaining additional light and air. Greater density, however, is awarded for including plazas, arcades, and enclosed plazas in commercial developments. The code defines a plaza as "continuous open space, which is readily accessible to the public at all times, predominantly open above, and designed specifically for use by people as opposed to serving as a setting for a building."

In response to the region's damp climate, the city offers the enclosed plaza bonus; these spaces "must be readily accessible from a pedestrian connection . . . [and] be signed to identify the enclosed plaza as available for public use." Bonuses are granted for arcades as well. An arcade, a continuously covered area, "functions as a weather-protected extension of the publicly accessible space which it abuts."

Several years ago, Bellevue bought a 17-acre tract of school surplus land for a public park on the edge of the downtown business district. In 1985, a national design competition was sponsored. The first, seven-acre phase, completed two years later, was funded by a consortium of citizens and property owners. The initial success of this phase led to the passage of a bond issue for the second phase, now underway. The city fathers hope that development of the park will enhance the potential for residential building in its environs.

Seattle. The city's incentive zoning scheme offers density bonuses for a variety of public space uses, including rooftop gardens, parcel parks, urban plazas, harborfront open spaces, and street parks. Like many other downtowns swept up in the tower-in-the-park euphoria of the last two decades, Seattle has more than its share of wind-ridden, underused urban plazas. Those urban plazas sanctioned by the 1985 zoning must comply with rigorous bonus criteria and design guidelines. For example, no plaza will earn bonus credits if built on a block where a plaza already exists. To ensure that plazas are built in appropriate locations, the city has mapped out those blocks where plaza bonuses are permitted, giving developers advance notice of eligible sites.

Seattle's code states that plazas should be located on pedestrian streets and connect with transit tunnel stations or major transfer points for surface transit operations. The city also encourages plazas on corner lots. At least 50 percent of a plaza's perimeter must be lined with retail uses, and there is an art requirement to boot. As *special* public benefit features, candidates for the urban plaza bonus are scrutinized more thoroughly than are applicants for *general* public benefit features, and proposed plazas are subject to discretionary review.

In the case of the Washington Mutual Tower, the city at first insisted that the plaza be located on Third Avenue, where pedestrian traffic was heavy. Because the area received no sunlight, however, the city was persuaded to make a special exception and permit the developer to place the plaza on the sunnier Second Avenue. Consequently, no other project within 300 feet of the plaza on Second Avenue will be allowed to earn density credits for a plaza.

With the recent passage of a citizen initiative that places additional limits on building heights and densities in the downtown, the city is reevaluating its bonus schedule and considering making many of the open space options requirements instead. (See Chapter 1, "Incentive Zoning," for further information on the 1989 CAP initiative.)

OPEN SPACE RETROFITS

Many early urban plazas and other public open spaces that were built with scant attention to functional criteria, spurred by incentive zoning codes that failed to require that the spaces be usable, have been "retrofitted." These spaces are being renovated, not because they are in a state of disrepair but because they simply do not work. Plaza rehabilitations are also being undertaken to convert passive spaces into income-producing uses.

One of the country's earliest mixed-use projects, New York's Rockefeller Center, has undergone periodic retrofits since it was built in 1929. The outdoor ice skating rink, for instance, was first planned as a sunken plaza at the main entrance to the retail concourse. Underused, the plaza was converted in the early 1930s into an ice skating rink in winter and an open air cafe in summer. More recently, the rink was redesigned as part of a multimillion-dollar effort to rejuvenate the retail complex.[24]

Basing their work on that of William H. Whyte, a team of "space doctors" from New York's nonprofit Project for Public Spaces (PPS) has specialized in retrofitting plazas and open spaces since the late 1970s. The firm was called in to diagnose the case of Exxon Park, a 1960s-vintage midblock plaza stretching between 49th and 50th Streets on the edge of Rockefeller Center. The problem was that Exxon Park had been taken over by drug dealers. Significantly, the food stand was hidden behind a waterfall and invisible from the street; moreover, because the space was seen primarily as a short-cut between streets, people did not linger there. To discourage the drug dealers, Rockefeller Center had tried to box them out by erecting heavy fences, but this action, according to PPS, further blocked visibility from the street and stymied potential pedestrian use.

As recounted by Tony Hiss, PPS analysts noted that the park's two main drug dealers had instinctively employed sound retailing principles and effectively staked out for themselves the two spots in the park that were most visible from the street. So PPS decided to put a food-vending cart in the busier of those two spots—out by the front gate. That cart now does a roaring business. PPS also scattered tables and chairs throughout the park, and put a second food cart in the middle of the park. This served three purposes: it slowed down people who wanted to use the park as a crosswalk; it made tables and chairs something you could see from the street; and it created more pools of privacy.[25]

People walking by the park on 50th Street, who now have a view of greenery, food carts, chairs, tables, and other people, as opposed to the previous rather grim glimpse of a mostly bleak space, have a reason to stop. Whyte describes this slowing-down process as "window shopping," much like people's behavior outside a department store. "In the case of a park or a plaza," he says, "it serves as the mechanism that allows the life of the street to flow into an adjacent open space."[26]

Physical design modification is but one of several variables influencing effective open space use, and Whyte further recommends the introduction of maintenance requirements, as well as plaza management and programming—regular staging of events such as performances and concerts to attract clusters or crowds of people.

RETROFITS AND MODIFICATIONS THROUGH ZONING

Just as custom-tailored design and maintenance criteria for new spaces are increasingly mandated by today's zoning regulations, so are retrofits of plazas and arcades encouraged by land use codes. Cities such as Charlotte, San Francisco, and Seattle promote retrofits of older, underused urban plazas and arcades. According to Charlotte's code, "Buildings and plazas constructed prior to the adoption of this section may be changed to include any of the amenities and features required or encouraged by these standards, such as the provision of food facilities, movable chairs, and alteration of ledges to make them sittable."

Seattle's zoning looks at the retrofitting of plazas and other public benefit features that have been bonused under the city's previous code. These amenities, embracing urban plazas, shopping plazas, shopping arcades, and voluntary building setbacks that earned extra commercial space under the earlier zoning, must remain in place for the life of the project. They may only be modified according to the specific code provisions, which bring the modifications under the discretionary review of the director of the city's department of construction and land use. For exam-

ple, plazas may be altered or even reduced in size, as long as the changes are consistent with the intent of the bonus rules as prescribed under the current zoning for urban plazas and parcel parks (see Insert 5). Seattle architect William Bain, Jr., notes that the earlier code virtually forced office developers to build open spaces to maximize their commercial space. Ten square feet of commercial space was awarded for each square foot of plaza, and six square feet for each square foot of arcade.

Insert 5.
Seattle: Modification of Plazas and Other Bonus Features (code excerpt)

Section 23.49.34

A. The modification of plazas, shopping plazas, arcades, shopping arcades, and voluntary building setbacks which resulted in any increase in gross floor area under Title 24 of the Seattle Municipal Code shall be encouraged in any downtown zone if the change makes the plaza, arcade, or setback more closely conform to the requirements of this chapter. The director shall review proposed modifications to determine whether they provide greater public benefits and are consistent with the intent of the Public Benefit Features Rule, as specified in this section. . . .

B. Except as provided in Subsections E2 and E3, no modification to a plaza or other feature listed in Subsection A may be made under this section if it will increase the total floor/area ratio (FAR) of the structure. Except as permitted in Subsections E2 and E3, no reduction in the area of the bonused feature may be made for any uses, except retail sales and services, human service uses, or daycare centers, unless the loss of area is offset by the conversion of existing floor area in the structure to uses exempt from FAR calculation in the zone.

C. Plazas and shopping plazas
Modifications to plazas and shopping plazas for which increased gross floor area was granted under Title 24 shall be permitted, based on the classification of the plaza on Map IE.
   1. Type I plazas
   Type I plazas shall continue to function as major downtown open spaces. Modification of these plazas and/or reductions in plaza size shall be permitted if the director finds that the modified or remaining plaza is consistent with the intent of the Public Benefit Features Rule for urban plazas and parcel parks.
   2. Type II plazas
   Type II plazas do not function as major downtown open spaces, but they shall continue to provide open space for the public. Modification of these plazas and/or reductions in plaza size shall be permitted if the director finds that the modified or remaining plaza is consistent with the intent of the Public Benefit Features Rule for urban plazas, parcel parks, hillside terraces, and rooftop gardens.

D. Shopping arcades
   1. Exterior shopping arcades
   When street-level uses are eligible for a floor area bonus in a zone in which an existing exterior shopping arcade is located, the existing shopping arcade, or a portion of the existing shopping arcade, may be converted to retail sales and service uses if the conversion will result in greater conformity with the street-facade development standards of the zone, and if the minimum sidewalk widths . . . are met. No

bonuses shall be given for any retail space created by conversion of a shopping arcade. . . .

2. Interior shopping arcades
Portions of existing interior shopping arcades may be modified and/or reduced in size, so long as any pathway which connects streets or other public open spaces is maintained at a width of at least 15 feet and it continues to allow comfortable and convenient pedestrian movement. The visual interest and the sense of space and light in the shopping arcade shall be also maintained and enhanced if possible. . . .

E. Arcades
The director shall use the following standards to determine whether an arcade may be filled in, and to determine the uses that may be permitted in a former arcade:

1. Arcades that provide essential pedestrian connections, such as a connection to a bonused public open space or access to public parks, shall not be filled in.

2. Arcades that do not provide essential pedestrian connections may be filled in. In downtown areas where bonuses may be granted for shopping atriums and shopping corridors, an arcade may be filled in only with uses which qualify for a retail shopping bonus. . . .

3. If an arcade is filled in with a use which does not qualify for a retail shopping bonus . . . , new public benefit features shall be required for any additional floor area.

4. Overhead weather protection shall be provided when an arcade on a street or public open space is filled in. No additional floor area shall be granted for the required overhead weather protection.

F. Voluntary building setbacks
Voluntary building setbacks may be filled in to provide retail sales and service uses, provided that the conversion maintains the minimum required sidewalk width . . . and will result in greater conformity with the standards for required street-level uses, if any, and street-facade development standards for the zone.

Several downtown developers have opted to retrofit plazas and other private open spaces according to the code modification provisions. The first of these plaza modifications was part of a $5 million renovation of a 50-story office tower built in the late 1960s. Twenty years ago, the sleek international-style Seafirst Bank Building added interest to the Seattle skyline with its trademark profile. However, when Seafirst Bank sold its headquarters building to JMB Realty of Chicago in 1983, the new owner wanted to enhance the bleak concrete expanse, as well as fill in some of the empty space with income-generating retail uses.

The NBBJ Group, architects of the original structure, welcomed the chance to soften and enliven the austere space, which had been dictated under the old code; they redesigned the space along the lines of the 1985 code modification provisions. Some 15,000 square feet of retail space, including several food services, was added to the plaza perimeters, and a solar-heated, glassed-in winter garden with a coffee bar was built along the north edge of the Fourth Avenue plaza. The NBBJ team also added plantings and pub-

"Before" and "after" views of plaza retrofit at the former Seafirst Bank Building, Seattle. Henry Moore's sculpture "Three-Piece Vertebrae" (right foreground) is a Seattle landmark.

lic seating, a sheltered pedestrian passage from a sidewalk to the building lobby, and a canopy over another sidewalk (see photographs). Together, these changes transformed the plaza into a major public space in the downtown and effectively energized the area.

Too bad that downdrafts from the building and nearby high rises cause such fierce gusts during certain times of the year that safety lines are sometimes strung across the plaza to give passers-through something to hang onto.[27]

STREETSCAPES

A rising trend in downtown zoning is to treat streets as part of the public open space network. These elements of the network are highly significant because streets occupy some 25 percent of the land mass in most downtowns, and in such cities as Portland, Oregon, and Washington, D.C., the percentage is much greater. Until recently, highway engineering dominated the management and design of streets and catered mainly to automobiles, traditionally regarded as the primary users of streets. Similarly, public agencies generally focused on supporting the needs of road travelers. Thus, a perhaps disproportionate amount of public space was devoted almost exclusively to serving motorized traffic. Traffic engineering was directed primarily toward the expansion of street capacities to accommodate more and more automobiles.[28]

Most contemporary planning approaches discount this largely outmoded paradigm. Instead, city officials and planners, traffic engineers, architects, and landscape architects are admonished to "conceptualize streets as [continuous] networks of public open space"[29] serving a full range of different uses and users. This new pluralistic approach has prompted some cities to adopt street classification systems for their downtowns. By setting up a hierarchy of streets with specialized functions (major arterials, collectors, transitways, and local access streets, with differing allocations of space between pedestrian and vehicle use for each street class), cities can better balance enhanced pedestrian environments with convenient vehicular access.[30]

Seattle has named eight distinct street categories in the downtown, which seem to have been determined largely by analyzing pedestrian traffic flow—access streets, different classes of pedestrian streets, street parks, and undeveloped streets. The downtown zoning ordinance contains a street classification map. Having surveyed and recorded pedestrian circulation patterns throughout the downtown, the city has composed differing street-level design requirements based on the pedestrian traffic volume.[31] For example, along those streets designated Class I pedestrian shopping streets, 60 percent of the street-level facade must be transparent, and blank walls are limited to 15-foot segments along the street frontage. On the Class II pedestrian streets, where pedestrian traffic is lighter, the transparency requirement and the blank wall limits are decreased. Likewise, the percentage of ground-floor space that must be kept for retail uses varies with a street's category.

Streets in downtown Portland, Oregon, are classed by their general functional characteristics. The three classes are traffic access streets, nonautomobile streets, or principal bicycle streets. Regardless of their principal functions, though, all streets must have suitable provisions for pedestrians and bicycles. One stated purpose of the street classification system is "to establish within downtown integrated and effective systems for the movement of automobile traffic, transit vehicles, pedestrians, and bicycles, and to establish a basis for reducing conflicts among these movement systems."

BACK TO THE GRID

Streetscapes are not only shaped by circulation patterns and principal functions. They are also determined by the scale and spacing of the street grid. Cyril Paumier writes: "The most basic element[s] of downtown's urban design framework [are] its street system and the extent to which that system creates a predictable and unifying pattern of similarly sized blocks and regularly spaced intersections. A consistent pattern of blocks creates a strong organizing structure for downtown development and has an important influence on the scale of buildings."[32]

For example, William Penn laid out the heart of Philadelphia as a "greene countrie towne," with streets aligned on a grid, an open space in the middle, and a parklike square in each of the four corners. Penn gave the city what Paul Goldberger calls "the strongest and clearest symbol of the public realm of any city in the country" and a "sense of clear, coherent order."[33]

Another example is 18th-century Paris, where building height was determined by street width—higher on wide streets and lower on narrow streets—a principle that Baron Haussmann continued in his reconstruction of the city. In the same way, New York City's first zoning regulations were based on the relationship between street width and building height.[34]

The city of Portland is known for its walkable downtown, where pedestrians need only travel 200 feet between crosswalks. The city's gridiron system, with its tight, ramrod-straight 200-foot-long blocks, makes for a readable urban landscape. Maintaining the integrity of the city's tight grid is the first of Portland's more than 22 downtown design guidelines. "Portland's small blocks and frequent streets provide greater open space, light, air, and more direct pedestrian travel than is typically available in city centers. When the ground floors of new development projects are allowed to occupy more than a single block, these characteristics of the downtown are lost." Architectural writer Gideon Bosker describes the "miniaturizing ethos" of Portland's streets and the expansive north/south avenues that "strategically orient downtown buildings towards the sun."[35] Developers are discouraged from creating superblocks in this downtown.

One reason that downtown Portland is extraordinarily legible as a grid is that most major projects take up full-block sites, a factor which, in conjunction with the city's height limits, largely determines the building envelopes. Within this block system, all sides of a building are equally visible. There are no "back" doors.

In direct contrast, many of the streets in Bellevue were never platted, so that the many resulting 600-foot superblocks have directly influenced development patterns. For example, one explanation for the rush of recent development in downtown Bellevue, besides the area's robust economic climate, is that blocks are so long that fewer lots are required for a single project; this makes it easier to assemble land for major development. Apparently, these superblocks were preserved by the city's previous slow real estate market, which exerted no pressure to divide the blocks into smaller parcels. In turn, Bellevue's superblocks helped cause the proliferation of the asphalt-surface parking lagoons that took over the CBD when the development climate was less attractive than it is now.

STREETSCAPE CONTINUITY

Much has been written about the need for a "unifying visual matrix," [36] allowing the viewer to rapidly scan an urban scene and understand the streetscape as a whole. "Visual continuity," notes Cyril Paumier, is particularly important "to individual merchants whose success depends at least in part on the ease with which potential patrons can locate and identify their businesses." [37] Street patterns, block sizes, locations of open spaces, and building/sidewalk relationships all contribute to the streetscape morphology. Architectural techniques such as uniform building heights, matching cornice lines, and legible building entrances also are being used increasingly to give the streetscape a sense of closure and continuity.

Whether inspired by the grand boulevards Baron Haussmann planned for Paris during the Beaux Arts period or by the neat, tight gridiron circulation system of l9th-century New York, cities are looking more and more to historical street prototypes.

Jonathan Barnett remarks that "the continuity that . . . [New York's] pre-l961 zoning imposed on the street was a virtue that was not appreciated until it was already lost." [38] In the traditional downtown, ground-floor retail shops were topped by offices to create a continuous rhythm along the public street. The occasional institutional uses (churches or government buildings) or businesses with institutional pretensions (banks or hotels) became conspicuous by

their disruption of the continuity of the shop windows and entrances. [39] These deliberate discontinuities nonetheless were part of the planned urban fabric.

Ronald Eichner and Henry Tobey observe that this pattern has been seriously ruptured in the last 30 years with the construction of multiuse structures, "which do not necessarily result in lively multiuse streetscapes. Often, large mixed-use structures that look good on zoning maps because they appear to bring a lively mix of activities to the city have a deadening effect on surrounding streetscapes." [40] This happens where retail uses are embedded within private development and mall shops are internalized. Too often, the street edges of such buildings feature blank walls with inadequate direct sidewalk connections to the interior shopping center. Urban streetscapes are threatened by these faceless, impregnable fortresses that tend to sap the vitality from downtown streets.

Another culprit is the convention center, looming as a great concrete hulk in many cities, spanning two or three blocks with scarcely a window. As William Whyte writes,

Convention center experts say that this sealed-box format is the way it has to be. Otherwise there would be "leakage," or "contamination"—that is, natives without badges mixing it up with the others. Thus the tight seal. . . . The separation works. I've charted pedestrian activity on civic spaces adjoining some of these centers and found surprisingly little relationship between what's going on inside and what isn't outside. Within, there might be 4,000 ophthalmologists, but on the sidewalk and benches of the adjoining spaces only a handful of people. [41]

BLANK WALL LIMITS AND TRANSPARENCY REQUIREMENTS

The potentially damaging effects of such bone-crushing behemoths as convention centers and large-scale mixed-use projects have been thoroughly documented. As part of an effort to strengthen streetscapes and preserve visual continuity, downtown planning departments throughout the country are revising their zoning codes to elicit uniform street walls, animated street edges, and orderly public spaces. (These issues pertain intimately to retail continuity, as explored in Chapter 7, "Retail Uses.") As part of this effort, many downtowns, including Charlotte, Cincinnati, Seattle, and Portland, have enacted facade transparency requirements and blank wall limits in conjunction with street-level retail requirements.

Portland's regulation entitled the Limitation on Blank Walls, in effect since 1979, applies not only to all new construction but also to any additions, major alterations, or major repairs calling for building permits. The rule was expanded in 1988 to include all commercially zoned and multifamily areas within the downtown and the Central City and also applies to parking garages. (See Appendix A, which deals with design guidelines for parking garages.) At least half of a building's frontage must have see-through windows at the ground level. In some situations, artwork and/or display windows may be substituted to meet the requirement. In addition, buildings without lobbies, retail uses, or office space may provide windows affording glimpses into other active uses, such as pressrooms, classrooms, kitchens, or manufacturing space. However, parking lots, truck loading areas, and vehicular access ways are not considered active uses (see Insert 6).

Insert 6.
Portland, Oregon: The Limitation on Blank Walls
(code excerpt)

Section 33.702.193

A. **Purpose**. Blank walls on the ground-floor level are limited to encourage continuity of retail and consumer service uses; to encourage retail and commercial activities at street level; to provide a pleasant, rich, and diverse experience for pedestrians by visually connecting activities occurring within a structure to adjacent sidewalk areas; to enhance crime prevention by increasing opportunities for surveillance of the street from interiors of buildings; to restrict fortresslike facades at the street level; and to avoid a monotonous environment.

B. **Standards**.
   1. In RX and CX Zones, at least 50 percent of the length and 25 percent of the exterior wall area on the floor abutting sidewalks, plazas, or other public open spaces or rights-of-way must be devoted to windows affording views into retail, office, or lobby space, pedestrian entrances, or retail display windows.
   2. This limitation on blank walls does not apply to sides of buildings having residential units located adjacent to the exterior ground-floor wall.
   3. Buildings having less than 50 percent of their ground-level floor area in retail, office, or lobby use, but containing other active uses found during the design review process to be of visual interest to the pedestrian may provide windows affording views of the active use as an alternative to Paragraph 1 above. (Examples of such uses are pressrooms, classrooms, kitchens, or manufacturing processes.) Parking areas, truck loading areas, and vehicular access ways are not active uses.
   4. Buildings having less than 50 percent of their sidewalk-level space in retail, office, . . . lobby, or . . . other visually interesting active uses may substitute artwork and/or display windows to meet the blank wall provisions of Paragraphs B.1 and B.2 above, if the proposed display window or artwork is found to meet the intent of this section as stated in Paragraph A above, during the design review process. (Artwork and displays relating to activities occurring within the building are encouraged.)

C. **Compliance**. All new construction and all major remodeling projects are subject to this requirement and must comply. Major re-

modeling projects are those where [*sic*] the building floor area is being increased by 50 percent or more, or where [*sic*] the cost of the remodeling is greater than the assessed value of the existing improvements on the site (assessed value is the value shown on the Multnomah County assessment and taxation records for the current year). Multiple remodeling projects undertaken since the initial effective date of this chapter that cumulatively meet the above description of a major project are treated as a major project and must also comply, when the total cost of all projects [is] equivalent to 50 percent of the assessed value.

In Charlotte, North Carolina, "[w]orks of art, fountains and pools, street furniture, landscaping and garden areas, architecturally articulated facades, and display areas" may be used to comply with the blank wall limits in the downtown (see Insert 7). The regulation also applies to the first floor of parking garages. Cincinnati's transparency requirement complements the city's street-level retail requirement on designated streets. (See Insert 8 for the wording of Cincinnati's transparency provision.)

Insert 7.
Charlotte's Street Wall Guidelines
(code excerpt)

2. *Street Walls.* The first floors of all buildings, including structured parking, must be designed to encourage and complement pedestrian-scale activity. It is intended that this be accomplished principally by the use of windows and doors arranged so that the uses are visible from and/or accessible to the street on at least 50 percent of the length of the first-floor street frontage. Works of art, fountains and pools, street furniture, landscaping and garden areas, architecturally articulated facades, and display areas may also be considered in meeting this requirement. Where windows are used, they must be transparent. Where expanses of solid wall are necessary, they may not exceed 20 feet in length. The first floor and street level must be designed with attention to adjacent public or private open spaces and existing streetscape improvements. The provision of multiple entrances from the public sidewalk or open spaces is encouraged. Structured parking facilities must be designed so that the only openings at the street level are those to accommodate vehicle entrances and pedestrian access to the structure. The remainder of the street-level frontage must be either occupied retail space or an architecturally articulated facade designed to screen the parking areas of the structure, to encourage pedestrian-scale activity, and to provide for urban open space. *(See Figure 3053.6.1.2 [shown below].)*

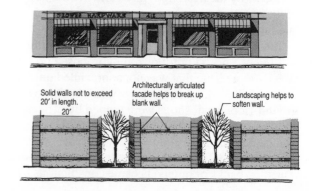

Solid walls not to exceed 20' in length.

Architecturally articulated facade helps to break up blank wall.

Landscaping helps to soften wall.

Just as street-level requirements are generally confined to the retail sector, so are blank facade limits more rigorous on high-volume pedestrian streets in commercial districts. In Seattle, for instance, the transparency (window) requirement is 60 percent of the street-level facade for Class I pedestrian streets but only 30 percent for Class II pedestrian streets and street parks. The percentage is also reduced on steep slopes, which pedestrians are less apt to use. Residential buildings are exempt from the facade transparency stipulations.

The Seattle code explicitly addresses situations "[w]hen the transparency requirements of this subsection are inconsistent with the glazing limits in the energy code." In these cases, the transparency requirement takes precedence.

REQUIRED BUILDING LINES

Renewed interest in defining public spaces through street walls and in reinforcing streetscape continuity is also reflected in the current crop of new downtown office towers, which push toward the outer limits of the lot line. Structures like the IBM and AT&T Buildings in New York create street walls with a vengeance. Jonathan Barnett notes that this recent trend defies those earlier zoning regulations (New York's 1916 Zoning Ordinance and progeny) with various setback requirements and bulk controls. These "tended to pull development inward, away from property boundaries, on the theory that the public interest most in need of protection is represented by the rights of adjoining property owners."[42]

Some cities, including Portland, Oregon, have implemented required building-line zoning provisions, whose purpose is

to maintain the urban quality of retail, office, or historic areas by preventing [that] loss of the sense of enclosure, the continuity of display windows, . . . and weather protection that would result from random decisions to provide plazas or building setbacks[.] [R]equired building lines are established along street lot lines in certain portions of the Downtown Development Zone. . . .

(See Insert 9.)

Many of the other zoning provisions discussed in earlier chapters of this book—view corridor mechanisms, height caps, and street-level retail requirements—as well as controls limiting curb cuts and loading dock areas, also serve to reinforce the visual continuity of the street wall.

STREETSCAPE DESIGN GUIDELINES

Streetscape design guidelines further strengthen the street edge. Special uniform paving treatments, for example, can be used to better define crosswalks and reinforce the pedestrian system. In much the same way, a vocabulary of well-designed street furniture, light standards and signage, finishing and material requirements, and landscaping and planting features can be used to help unify the streetscape. Cities typically undertake these streetscape improvements as part of capital improvement strategies to promote redevelopment within targeted downtown sectors or to create an identifiable image for a particular sector, such as a historic or waterfront district.

In some jurisdictions, the law requires private developers to comply with streetscape design guidelines. In Bellevue, for instance, the city's main street—the Major Pedestrian Corridor—will be constructed over time by developers whose projects abut the corridor alignment. When building on the corridor, developers must follow a comprehensive set of design guidelines. (Further discussion of Bellevue's pedestrian corridor may be found later in this chapter.) Similarly, projects built in Portland, Maine's Commercial Street Waterfront Core must provide specified streetscape amenities as part of the city's public access design guidelines, enacted in 1985.

A program of uniform streetscape improvements can also be used to integrate separate downtown functions such as the retail, transit, and pedestrian systems. In Portland, Oregon, both the 11-block transit mall coursing through the city's retail core and the light-rail transit line are carried out with similar paving materials, trees, lights, fountains, shelters, benches, and other street furniture. Each of the mall's sidewalks has been widened to 24 feet, and the sidewalk paving extends across each intersection, clearly separating pedestrian from motor-vehicle space.

GROUND-FLOOR DESIGN FOCUS

The imposition of transparency requirements, blank wall limits, and mandated build-to lines reflects the closer attention being paid to building/sidewalk relationships and to the design of the building base. The base is after all the part of the building that affects most directly the experience of the pedestrian on the sidewalk. Careful selection of building materials, massing, proportioning of facade openings, organization of the facades themselves, and spacing between structures can strengthen both visual continuity and streetscape variety.

Charlotte's 1987 amendments to its Uptown [that is, downtown] Mixed-Use District (UMUD) ordinance require that the bases of high-rise buildings (over five stories) be clearly differentiated from the upper stories, Under UMUD regulations, the bases must provide "design elements that will enhance the pedestrian environment. Such elements as cornices, beltcourses, corbelling, molding, stringcourses, ornamentation, changes in material or color, and other sculpturing of the base as are appropriate must be provided to add special interest to the base." The code also demands that special attention be paid to the design of those windows positioned in the base. "Band windows are discouraged." Instead, recessed "win-

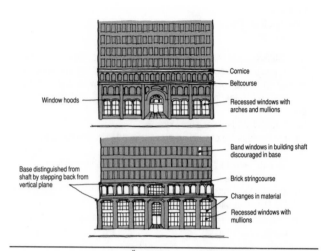

Source: Charlotte, North Carolina; "Delineation of the Building Base" (code illustration).

dows . . . distinguished from the shaft of the building through the use of arches, pediments, mullions, and other treatments are encouraged."

Charlotte's UMUD ordinance also addresses the design of building entrances and encourages entryways that are clearly delineated and inviting: "Doorways must be recessed into the face of the building to provide a sense of entry and to add variety to the streetscape. For structures less than 100,000 square feet, the entryway must be one square foot for each 1,000 square feet of floor area, with a 15-square-foot minimum. For buildings over 100,000 square feet, the entryway must be at least 100 square feet."

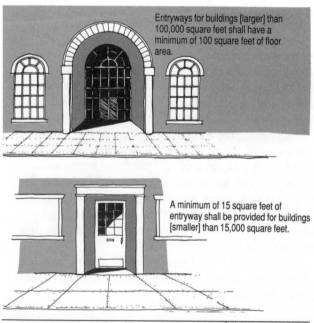

Source: Charlotte, North Carolina; "Delineation of the Building Entrance" (code illustration).

Street-level entryways influence retail activity as well as the degree of aesthetic variety. Particularly in the case of massive, seemingly impregnable mixed-use projects, retail activity may be deeply embedded within inward-gazing arcades. The addition of clearly marked entryways opening directly onto the sidewalk can help stimulate outside pedestrian activity and animate the street scene. As mentioned in the previous chapter, "Retail Uses," Charlotte mandates that 50 percent of its street-level footage be devoted to retail uses; this requirement may be reduced if individual entrances are provided to street-level retail tenants fronting on the sidewalk.

Likewise, the city of West Palm Beach awards density bonuses of 10,000 square feet for each additional building entrance. The following bonus criteria apply:

(1) Entrances shall provide access from a public sidewalk.
(2) Entrances shall have a minimum width of ten (10) feet.
(3) Doors shall be recessed a minimum of five (5) feet from the surface of the building at the entrance.
(4) The maximum bonus provided under this section shall not exceed five percent (5%) of the floor area allowed by the base floor/area ratio for the zoning district.

Structured parking facilities are notorious for disrupting the retail and visual continuity of downtown streets. Many cities, among them Pittsburgh, Bellevue, Orlando, Charlotte, and Portland, regulate the design of downtown parking facilities and have adopted design guidelines for construction of their bases. Parking garages in downtown Charlotte, for instance,

> must be designed so that the only openings at the street level are those to accommodate vehicle entrances and pedestrian access to the structure. The remainder of the street-level frontage must be either occupied retail space or an architecturally articulated facade designed to screen the parking areas of the structure, to encourage pedestrian-scale activity, and to provide for urban open space.

(Refer to Insert 7. Also, see the design guidelines for parking garages in the appendix.)

Finally, some cities, like Bellevue, have enacted explicit design guidelines governing building/sidewalk relationships. These street-edge guidelines assort streets according to the amount of projected pedestrian use and list the requisite conditions for each category, accounting for such elements as retail and commercial uses; transparent windows; street walls; multiple entrances; ground-level differentiation; canopies, awnings, or arcades; paving; seating; artwork; and landscaping. The 1983 guidelines regulate development on the downtown Major Pedestrian Corridor and on the three major public open spaces. (For details on Bellevue's pedestrian corridor, see the subsection below devoted to it.)

PEDESTRIANWAYS

PEDESTRIAN IMPROVEMENTS

If streets form the skeleton holding together the downtown, then pedestrian circulation is the lifeblood of the retail core. To generate that necessary degree of market synergy among downtown functions, people must be able to move easily between important activity centers.[43] Therefore, more attention is being paid to pedestrian circulation improvements in the downtown, especially in the vicinity of the retail spine.

Confined to urban renewal projects during the 1960s and 1970s, pedestrian networks are now being implemented in private construction through the use of several zoning techniques. Density bonuses, for example, are often awarded for pedestrian circulation improvements, which typically comprise sidewalk widenings, arcades, through-block connections, plazas, and urban parks. In Hartford, pedestrian circulation improvements are clearly defined (see Insert 10).

■ Repeat the rhythm of openings to maintain consistent streetscape.
■ Provide two smaller openings to parking deck instead of one large one.

Source: Charlotte, North Carolina; "Guidelines for Street Walls of Parking Garages" (code illustration).

(f) ... Improvements to which the public is assured access on a regular basis, or an area that is dedicated to and accepted by the city for public access purposes. Such improvements shall be directly accessible to the pedestrian circulation system. ... Such improvements shall include and be limited to sidewalk widenings, arcades, through-block arcades, plazas, and urban parks.

(1) Sidewalk widening: The widening of a paved walk at the side of a street. The widened area shall extend along the entire length of the lot or zoning lot and shall be open to the public at all times.

(2) Arcade: A continuous covered but not necessarily enclosed space which extends along the facade of a building and has at least two (2) entrances opening directly to a street, open space area, or sidewalk.

(3) Through-block arcade: A continuous covered space which runs through a building and connects a street, open space area, or sidewalk to a street, open space area, or sidewalk.

(4) Plaza: A continuous area which is open from the ground level to the sky for its entire width and length, which fronts on a street, sidewalk, or sidewalk widening, and which is directly accessible to the public at all times for use by the public for passive recreational purposes. The ground level of the plaza shall be constructed principally of hard-surfaced materials. An existing space between or next to a building or buildings shall not qualify.

(5) Urban park: A continuous area of land which is open from the ground level to the sky for its entire width and length, with the exception of recreational equipment or pedestrian amenities such as benches or lighting, which fronts on a street, sidewalk, or sidewalk widening and which is directly accessible to the public during daylight hours for scenic or leisure purposes. The ground level of this area shall be covered principally with plantings.

Through-block connections, taking the form of open air walkways, courtyards, covered arcades, or even lobby atrium spaces, are designed to complement existing downtown pedestrian networks. Located at grade but off the street, these pathways cut through development blocks and are most useful in cities with long blocks or in superblock projects. Through-block connectors function most effectively when they "reinforce the spine and primary connectors by running perpendicular to and providing links between them. ... They can also function as linkages between parking and the major retail streets." [44]

A through-block arcade may be defined as "a continuous covered space, which runs through a building and connects a street, open space area, or sidewalk to a street, open space area, or sidewalk" (Hartford's 1984 code). Some cities require pedestrian circulation improvements and offer through-block arcades as an option. New projects in Midtown Manhattan must pro-

Land Design/Research, Inc.

Through-block pedestrian connections make superblock projects more manageable while joining office buildings with public open spaces.

vide some of these amenities: sidewalk widenings, arcades, corner circulation space, building entrance recess areas, and through-block connections. The 1982 Midtown Zoning also mandates through-block circulation networks in certain midblocks west of Fifth Avenue.

In Bellevue, developers of superblock projects must build a pedestrian connection to "permit movement through the superblock from a perimeter walkway or sidewalk to publicly accessible spaces, adjoining structures, or parking areas." These connections must be developed as internal walkways or sidewalks, arcades, interior arcades, pedestrian skybridges, underground passageways, or tunnels.

Sometimes, pedestrian circulation amenities are meant to improve pedestrian comfort and designed to alleviate climatic or terrain conditions. Seattle's hill-climb assist bonus, for example, involves including escalators "to aid pedestrian movement in areas of concentrated employment and pedestrian activity on lots located along steeply sloping streets." Likewise, Bellevue and Seattle, which have protracted rainy seasons, offer bonuses for overhead weather protection features, enclosed plazas and shopping corridors, arcades, awnings, and marquees.

PEDESTRIAN MALLS

During the 1960s and 1970s, urban designers saw the separation of automobile traffic from pedestrian traffic as axiomatic, and cities across the country malled their downtowns. Cars were totally banned from several blocks, where trees, benches, and fountains were put in. The goal was to "halt the exodus of retailers and shoppers to suburban malls by making downtowns more like those malls, with a dash of park thrown in." [45] Fred Kent, who heads New York's Project for Public Spaces, views the malling phenomenon as an offshoot of the environmental movement of those two decades, during which the "mood of the times was definitely anti-urban, anti-city." [46]

While imitating suburban shopping malls, many downtown pedestrian malls lacked the virtues of shopping malls, namely, coordinated maintenance and hours, sufficient parking, and retail variety. In some instances, the lush vegetation planted in the transit malls obscured the shops and provided havens for derelicts and delinquents. The car-free zones generally sprawled over too many blocks, with too few pedestrians to form the necessary critical mass to support the retail. Moreover, by excluding the auto, pedestrian malls virtually excluded the customer. [47]

Although a few succeeded, a large number of pedestrian malls flopped, and many cities have undertaken costly mall retrofits. Although grass berms and landscaping may be visually pleasing, retail studies show that people like to shop where there are other people, where there is activity, noise, commotion, and energy. Eugene, Oregon, has reopened several blocks to cars, and other cities have turned the entirety of their malls back into streets. Within a year after Waco, Texas, ripped out the fountains and trees on its Austin Avenue pedestrian mall and reopened the street to car traffic, store vacancies reportedly dropped from 80 percent to 40 percent. [48]

The pedestrian mall debacle underscores some of the dangers of separating pedestrians from vehicular traffic, at least within the context of downtown shopping districts. Rather than segregating the two functions, most cities are now searching for new ways to balance them. One increasingly popular approach is the transit mall, exclusively used by pedestrians and buses, which not only provides convenient access to retail corridors by mass transit, but also limits automobile use and the attendant pollution and congestion.

At the same time, cities are seeking to use their streets more efficiently. Toward this end, Seattle's incentive zoning system includes density bonuses for street parks. Based on the concept of the *Woonerf,* popularized in Holland and West Germany, street parks integrate car and pedestrian use of the street space and provide a scheme of open spaces linking blocks within given sectors of the downtown. The purpose of the *Woonerf* is to reestablish the social character of the street, reclaiming it as human territory and not just the preserve of cars. [49] (See Insert 11 for Seattle's street park guidelines.)

Insert 11.
Seattle's Street Parks
(code excerpt)

1. Intent
   Street parks provide a continuous system of open spaces that link together blocks within an area of downtown. Street parks are designated on the pedestrian street classification map for the zone in which they are located. Improvements to street parks may qualify for a bonus when they are in accordance with the street park development procedure established by the Seattle Engineering Department.

2. Area and dimensions—Basic Standards
   a. Paving and landscaping improvements specified in the street park plan for the public right-of-way shall be made along the entire street park frontage of the lot extending to the center line of the street or other location specified by the street park plan.
   b. In lieu of development of the street park, voluntary agreements for fee payment to assist public development of the street park may be made.

3. Landscaping and furnishing—Design Guidelines

a. To ensure an integrated design treatment throughout the length of the street park, landscaping requirements shall be as specified in the street park plan.

b. Art shall be incorporated as set forth in the general conditions of this rule. The nature of the artwork and locations shall be determined as part of the street park development procedure.

4. Special conditions—Basic Standards

a. The area of the public right-of-way developed as a street park shall remain in the public domain.

b. All areas separated from the vehicular right-of-way by a curb, and all nonstandard features located between curbs, shall be maintained by the property owner for the life of the project.

c. On street parks without a curb, a determination shall be made regarding the area for which the property owner will assume maintenance responsibility or the amount of reimbursement required to cover the cost to the city for maintaining the area.

Finally, one other questionable strategy for enhancing the quality of the downtown pedestrian environment was building grade-separated pedestrian systems, popularly known as skywalks. Like pedestrian malls, skywalks were designed to alleviate the conflicts between human and car circulation in congested downtowns, as well as to link private development parcels. Instead of eliminating automobile traffic, however, skywalks simply removed pedestrians from the street level and spun a new network of elevated walkways connecting the upper levels of downtown buildings.

Most downtowns lack the pedestrian volume to support more than one street system. According to William Whyte's studies with time-lapse films, if the midday foot traffic at the 100 percent corner is "less than 1,000 people per hour, the city is beyond gimmickry. It has lost its engine." [50]

For this reason, skywalk networks too often have enjoyed economic success at the expense of street-level retail. More and more disenchanted with these unwanted side effects, many cities are now reevaluating their skywalk programs. (Chapter 9 of this book deals exclusively with skywalks.)

BELLEVUE'S PEDESTRIAN CORRIDOR

As part of its metamorphosis from a 1950s suburban Car City to an intensely urban place with a dense downtown core, Bellevue has developed a set of policies and zoning regulations aimed at improving the quality of the pedestrian environment. The backbone of Bellevue's downtown plan is the Sixth Street Pedestrian Corridor, or Major Pedestrian Corridor, which will function as the city's main street. More than 2,000 feet long, with three major public open spaces situated on its alignment, this east/west link will connect the retail hub and regional shopping center with high-rise office and mixed-use development to the east. The corridor is a required element of the city's 1981 incentive zoning code, which intensified building densities within the downtown and called for a variety of uses. The corridor will be built in increments by private developers whose projects abut it. In exchange, developers may exceed the maximum height limit and earn density bonuses. The bonuses may be banked for use in a later development phase or sold to another project within the core.

History. Bellevue's pedestrian corridor was inspired by several prototypes. One influence was the transit mall for the exclusive use of pedestrians and transit riders, as developed in Denver, Portland, Baltimore, and Minneapolis. Bellevue also looked to New York City's 1970s incentive zoning provisions for midblock plazas and galleries and through-block connections, which were designed to help pedestrians cut through the endless congested superblocks of Manhattan. [51]

The magnitude of private participation, however, distinguishes Bellevue's pedestrian corridor from similar projects. All major property owners on the corridor must participate in its design, construction, and maintenance and must deliberately shape and orient their buildings to fit the corridor network. [52]

At an early stage, the roughly 10 owners of property abutting the corridor decided to control their own destiny as far as possible and formed a pedestrian corridor committee. The committee balked at the city's initial idea of a public dedication with no compensation and successfully negotiated to win concessions in the form of increased height and density. The property owners agreed to provide public access for a period of 50 years, after which the agreement must be renewed.

A second contentious subject was timing. The city first wanted the corridor to be fully constructed within six months. Skittish over the recent failures of numerous pedestrian malls, the corridor committee argued that because the downtown lacked the necessary critical mass, it made more sense to develop incrementally. In contrast to most pedestrian malls, which are short-term public works projects, the corridor will be developed over some 10 to 15 years. Mark Hinshaw and Don Miles, who helped develop the corridor design guidelines, predict that the phased construction "will cause the finished product to seem less dated and more natural, with some portions having an older appearance or patina than others." [53]

Unlike most other street improvement projects, which "require the transformation of a defined urban streetscape, the corridor demands that an entirely new series of public and semipublic spaces be created together with their context." [54] Because the area designated for the corridor is primarily bordered by parking lots and undeveloped tracts, the planning constraints were entirely different from those for an existing street lined with retail and office buildings. In the latter case, existing businesses, garages, utilities, traffic patterns, and landmarks would have had to be accommodated. But starting from scratch, Bellevue planners could determine the preferred environment.

In 1981, the corridor committee, in cooperation with the Bellevue Downtown Merchants Association, hired the Seattle firm TRA Architects and the design consulting firm Don Miles Associates/PPS to develop corridor design guidelines. (Bellevue's current principal urban designer, Mark Hinshaw, worked for TRA at that time.) Before then, a survey had been made of over 1,200 employees and their spouses, probing the attitudes and preferences of potential users. Paid for exclusively with private funds, the present set of guidelines was achieved with the help of a committee consisting of the property owners, developers, and city staff and was adopted by the city council in 1983. (See Insert 12 for one of the design guidelines.)

Insert 12.
Bellevue: Sample Design Guideline for the Pedestrian Corridor (code excerpt)

12. *Pedestrian amenities*
   Intention
   To ensure that the corridor emphasizes pedestrian use.
   Accomplished by
   Providing generous amounts of seating in a variety of forms.
   Providing appropriate lighting, which shall be both functional and visually distinctive.
   Providing drinking fountains, litter receptacles, and restrooms.
   Providing directories and maps.
   Establishing a graphic system using a logo and international symbols.
   Encouraging artwork and decorative fountains.
   Providing handicapped access.
   Vegetation to complement pedestrian use (e.g., shade, wind protection, seasonal flowers, etc.).
   Considering safety, security, and fire protection.
   Principles addressed
   Artwork.
   Directional information
   Furnishings
   Places to sit

Design. Compared with the wide swaths made by many pedestrian malls, Bellevue's corridor will be compact: it may be no less than 45 feet and no more than 60 feet wide. The city intends that pedestrian movement take place along the corridor edges, where sidewalk cafes, shopping, and other active pedestrian uses will be concentrated (see Insert 13). Passive rec-

reation and special activities will occur in the middle of the corridor, which will be reserved for plantings, seating, kiosks, and other furniture. Between these two sectors, two pedestrian pathways will run. Secondary pedestrian-movement paths with commercial frontages will cut through development superblocks and feed into the Major Pedestrian Corridor. These secondary paths may lead to enclosed atriums and landscaped spaces.

Insert 13.
Bellevue: Illustrations for Corridor-Edge Amenities

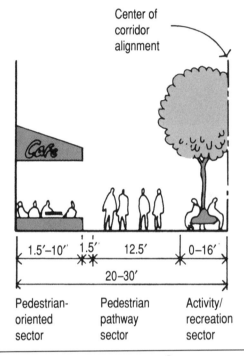

Source: City of Bellevue Design and Development Department.

The corridor design guidelines also contain massing provisions addressing sun-access and street-wall enclosure concerns (see Insert 14). Hinshaw and Miles note that "[s]treet furniture is designed to relate to the scale of a street rather than to that of a mall. For example, many mall projects typically have light fixtures in the height range of 12 to 14 feet. Light fixtures on the pedestrian corridor are 15 to 16 feet high, which is nearer the scale of traditional street lighting." [55]

Insert 14.
Bellevue: Guideline on Massing along the Corridor (code excerpt)

4. *Massing of abutting structures*
   Intention
   To create an intense urban place, giving consideration to open spaces and public areas, and giving special consideration to sun, shade, and air.

Accomplished by
Ensuring that the form and placement of buildings consider year-round conditions of sun and shade within the corridor.
Encouraging lower portions of buildings to be built to the corridor edge, but not necessarily in the same manner. Variations in use, design, and configuration should be encouraged.
Principles addressed
Spatial containment
Solar exposure

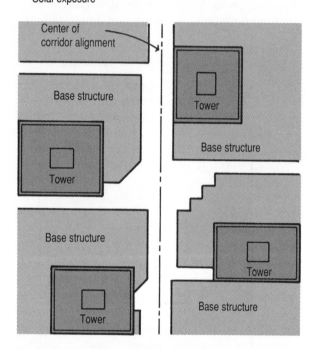

Hinshaw and Miles state that in evolving a desired image for the corridor, Bellevue looked to the best traditions of classic civic design and deliberately selected those architectural and street-furniture design elements that would survive the test of time.[56] For example, light fixtures incorporate a fruit motif commemorating the city's origin as the hub of a fruit-growing region. Benches, planting tubs, tree grates, and paving bricks were also chosen for their classic styles. Even drinking fountains, litter receptacles, and bollards were custom-designed.

Development on the Corridor. The corridor's western end has been built, including a major public open space fronting on Bellevue Square. In addition, the first major high rise to earn corridor density points has gone up. This is the 27-story office/retail complex developed by the Koll Company. Anchoring the eastern end of the corridor, the 1.5 million-square-foot Koll Center opened its first phase in 1987. More than 100,000 square feet of commercial/office space was acquired in exchange for building on the corridor and complying with the corridor guidelines. Much of that additional density has been banked for use in a later phase. As required by the zoning, the project provides retail "pedestrian-oriented uses" along the corridor,

located within greenhouse-styled pavilions and a weather-protected arcade. The zoning also called for the above-mentioned special street lights, benches, paving patterns, and tree grates, which the developer installed on the corridor alignment.

Besides the Koll Center, the corridor's eastern terminus is anchored by the bus transit center, strategically placed in the center of the office core. Built by the regional transit authority, the transit center had to comply with the corridor design guidelines and features the same classic light standards, street furniture, and pedestrian amenities as the adjacent Koll Center. The decorative metal work and, to top it off, the handsome domed clock tower underscore the transit terminal's civic function as a landmark in the downtown.

A civic center is also planned for the eastern end of the corridor. The first phase will contain a 500-seat performing arts center, a multipurpose exhibition/convention hall, and a dozen meeting rooms.

The first project to rise on the midsection of the corridor will be a 32-story office tower. Still in the planning stages, the Kohn Pedersen Fox–designed building will run along the corridor for 200 feet and earn density credits at a ratio of 16 to 1. It is expected

Mark L. Hinshaw

This lighting fixture, designed for Bellevue's pedestrian corridor, has a base cast with stylized fruit to commemorate the apple orchards and berry farms that predated downtown Bellevue.

Anchoring the corridor's eastern end is Bellevue's regional transit center.

that any unused density will be banked for use on a future project within the office sector. One of the main design challenges has been knitting the 550,000-square-foot project into the corridor. Street-level retail uses will be deliberately designed to complement pedestrian circulation patterns, with special attention to signage and visibility.

Evaluation. Although any long-term evaluation of the corridor would be premature, developers now building on the alignment view the location as a project amenity. A promotional brochure for one of several Wright Runstad & Company high rises in Bellevue states that Rainier Bank Plaza is located within blocks of "the ambitious Pedestrian Corridor, proposed for development over the coming years." Several retailers have approached corridor developers, expressing interest in locating on the corridor. Once sufficient corridor construction has been completed, with continuous retail frontage, it is anticipated that a central retail management (CRM) association will be founded for the purpose of setting uniform hours and marketing, and establishing maintenance protocols. (See Chapter 7 for a discussion of CRMs.)

From the city's perspective, a major benefit of the Bellevue approach is that building the pedestrian corridor will require almost no municipal funds. Construction of the individual corridor pieces can be triggered only by the development of abutting private land parcels. "In a very general sense, the city of Bellevue, in approving the pedestrian corridor scheme, has 'sold' development rights for the price of a coordinated downtown public open space system."[57]

One difficulty, however, of linking the provision of public amenities to the random operation of the real estate market is that the improvements depend on individual developers' timetables. Differing rates of development may cause temporary discontinuities in the pedestrian system. Moreover, it is questionable whether retail corridors and pedestrian pathways developed incrementally, and thus in piecemeal fashion, can function effectively. Hence, pedestrian traffic on Bellevue's corridor will likely be minimal until more pieces of the corridor are finished and until it is seen as the city's main street.

Some observers predict that the option to transfer bonus floor area to sites off the corridor will result in too much development too far removed from the corridor. This phenomenon is not likely to occur until the supply of downtown office space is fully absorbed. If, however, the city should decide to decrease the available density credits or lower the overall densities, the incentive to build on the corridor will be diminished.[58]

Notes
1. Paul Goldberger, "Good Buildings That Make Respectful Neighbors," *New York Times* (July 10, 1988).
2. Calvin Trillin in the *New Yorker* (March 6, 1989), p. 100. From a review of William H. Whyte's book *City: Rediscovering the Center* (see note 13 below for full citation).
3. Philip Langdon, "A Good Place to Live," *Atlantic Monthly* (March 1988), p. 43.
4. Paul Goldberger, "Public Space Gets a New Cachet in New York," *New York Times* (May 23, 1988).
5. Ibid.
6. Quoted in Langdon, op. cit., p. 55.
7. Cited by Gideon Bosker and Lena Lencek in "Portland, an Urban Theme Park," *Architecture* (November 1987), p. 52.
8. Paul Goldberger, "Robert Moses: Patron Saint of Public Places," *New York Times* (December 18, 1988).
9. Jonathan Barnett, *An Introduction to Urban Design* (New York: Harper & Row, 1982), p. 74.
10. Jerold S. Kayden, *Incentive Zoning in New York City: A Cost-Benefit Analysis*, Land Policy Roundtable Policy Analysis Series no. 201 (Cambridge: Lincoln Institute of Land Policy, 1978).
11. John J. Costonis, "Law and Aesthetics: A Critique and a Reformulation of the Dilemmas," *Michigan Law Review*, vol. 80 (1982), p. 379.
12. Ibid., p. 370.
13. William H. Whyte, *City: Rediscovering the Center* (New York: Doubleday, 1989), p. 233.
14. Ibid.
15. See Jerold S. Kayden, op. cit., p. 70.
16. See Whyte's discussion of Kayden's study in *City*, p. 233.
17. Robert S. Cook, Jr., *Zoning for Downtown Urban Design: How Cities Control Development* (Lexington, Mass.: D. C. Heath and Company, 1980), p. 88. (The book is out of print.)
18. Whyte is quoted in Robert H. McNulty, Dorothy R. Jacobson, and R. Leo Penne, *The Economics of Amenity: Community Futures and Quality of Life* (Washington, D.C.: Partners for Livable Places, 1985), p. 41.
19. Ibid.
20. Jonathan Barnett, "Designing Downtown Pittsburgh," *Architectural Record* (January 1982), p. 91.
21. Ibid., p. 82.

22.   See ibid., p. 91.

23.   See Michael S. Harrison, "Promoting the Urban Experience in Portland, Oregon," in *Public Streets for Public Use*, ed. Anne Vernez Moudon (New York: Van Nostrand Reinhold Company, 1987), p. 182.

24.   For a discussion of the retrofit of Rockefeller Center, see Stephen Davies and Margaret Lundin, "Department of Corrections," *Planning* (Chicago: American Planning Association, May 1987), pp. 28–29.

25.   Tony Hiss, "Experiencing Places," Part II, *New Yorker* (June 1988), p. 85.

26.   Ibid.

27.   As recounted by Whyte in *City*, p. 135.

28.   See Donald Appleyard, "Foreword" to *Public Streets for Public Use*, ed. Moudon, p. 11.

29.   Anne Vernez Moudon, "Introduction," ibid., p. 16.

30.   See Cyril B. Paumier, with W. Scott Ditch, Constance C. Diamond, and Diana P. Rich, *Designing the Successful Downtown* (Washington, D.C: Urban Land Institute, 1988), pp. 65–66.

31.   "Getting In on the Ground Floor," *Zoning News* (August 1987), pp. 1–2.

32.   Paumier et al., op. cit., p. 64.

33.   Paul Goldberger, "Philadelphia's Master Plan Rests on Its Streets," *New York Times* (June 12, 1988).

34.   Whyte notes Haussmann's influence on New York's 1916 zoning in *City*, p. 230.

35.   Bosker and Lencek, "Portland, an Urban Theme Park," p. 51.

36.   Paumier et al., *Designing the Successful Downtown*, p. 60.

37.   Ibid., p. 60.

38.   Barnett, *An Introduction to Urban Design*, p. 74.

39.   See Ronald B. Eichner and Henry Tobey, "Beyond Zoning," in *Public Streets for Public Use*, p. 277.

40.   Ibid.

41.   Whyte, *City*, p. 224.

42.   Barnett, *An Introduction to Urban Design*, p. 66.

43.   See Paumier et al., *Designing the Successful Downtown*, p. 27.

44.   Ibid., p. 71.

45.   Laurie M. Grossman, "City Pedestrian Malls Fail to Fulfill Promise of Revitalizing Downtown," *Wall Street Journal* (June 17, 1987).

46.   William E. Schmidt, "Replacing the Downtown Mall with Traffic," *New York Times* (December 13, 1987).

47.   See Grossman, op. cit.

48.   Ibid.

49.   See Norman E. P. Pressman's discussion of the *Woonerf* in "The European Experience," in *Public Streets for Public Use*, pp. 42–43.

50.   Whyte, *City*, p. 311.

51.   See Don C. Miles and Mark L. Hinshaw, "Bellevue's New Approach to Pedestrian Planning and Design," in *Public Streets for Public Use*, pp. 221–231.

52.   See ibid., p. 223.

53.   Ibid.

54.   Ibid.

55.   Ibid., p. 226.

56.   Ibid., p. 226.

57.   Ibid., p. 230.

58.   Ibid., p. 230.

CHAPTER 9

SKYWALKS

It is sad to see how many cities . . . are adopting exactly the approaches that will make matters worse. Most . . . programs have in common as a stated purpose "relief from pedestrian congestion." There is no pedestrian congestion. What they need is pedestrian congestion. But what they are doing is taking what people are on the streets and putting them somewhere else. In a kind of holy war against the street, they are putting them up in overhead skyways, down in underground concourses, and into sealed atriums and galleries. They are putting them everywhere except at street level.

–William H. Whyte[1]

Many cities are now debating the pros and cons of a time-honored type of downtown pedestrian corridor, lately being revived: the skywalk. Downtown skywalk systems have been around for a long time. Toronto's system dates back to the 1890s, Houston's to 1947, and St. Paul's to 1956. Alternative pedestrian networks have been built in more than 30 North American cities, and cities are building them still. Many older systems—including those in Syracuse, Milwaukee, Minneapolis, St. Paul, Duluth, Toronto, and Montreal—were undertaken to give pedestrians an escape from frigid winter streets.

But recent construction has been motivated largely by economics rather than by weather. A number of cities with relatively mild climates, such as Charlotte, Cincinnati, Los Angeles, and Dallas, have built offstreet networks of pedestrian bridges and, in some cases, tunnels in their downtowns. A 1986 survey of U.S. skybridge systems, conducted by the city of St. Paul, reported that economic development was the main motive for building such systems in 11 of the 24 responding cities. Weather was the primary reason in only five.[2] (See Insert 1.)

As James Thompson, director of traffic and transportation for Des Moines, Iowa, says, "You don't spend $10 million to build a big umbrella. . . . You do it to save the city."[3] Skywalks have proliferated during the last decade; cities have funded them as ele-

ments of their overall strategies to thwart the exodus of downtown stores to suburban malls.

Some skywalks have indeed become major generators of retail activity. The skywalk systems in U.S. downtowns link a variety of uses, including office buildings, convention centers, hotels, apartment buildings, and railway stations. Most commonly, however, they link retail establishments. Planning professor Kent Robertson notes that as systems mature, they attract more and more retailers in search of heavy pedestrian traffic flows, and the skyways take on the character of multiblock urban shopping malls.[4]

A 1986 survey reported that three-fourths of St. Paul's downtown retail business takes place on the skywalk level, where rents exceed ground-floor retail rents by about $2 per square foot. Clearly, retailing is alive and well on the skywalk systems of many U.S. downtowns. As one Charlotte (North Carolina) developer says, "The Overstreet Mall is Main Street Charlotte."[5]

SECOND-STORY CITY SYNDROME?

So where's the rub? "The biggest problem posed by surrogate streets," says William H. Whyte, "is not that they fail to function but that they function too well. Dilution is the consequence. A downtown can support just so many stores and restaurants, and it is a lively downtown if there are enough of them on its streets. Add another level and something has to give."[6] While business is flourishing on the skywalks, street-level retail sales often are plummeting. One reason many skywalk systems have damaged retail areas is that they frequently connect to parking garages, obviating the need to use sidewalks. In addition, structured parking facilities, which too often feature undifferentiated blank walls at the ground level, are major

Insert 1.
Grade-Separated Pedestrian Networks in North American Cities[1]

	Number of Blocks	Number of Bridges	Number of Tunnels	Year Begun	Most Recent Connection[2]	Ownership
Calgary	42	41	0	1970	3/85	Public
Cedar Rapids	10	12	0	1978	10/85	Joint
Cincinnati	15	18	0	1970	11/84	Joint
Dallas	36	15	26	1965	1/86	Joint
Des Moines	21	27	0	1982	6/86	Joint
Duluth	13	17	0	1974	12/85	Public
Edmonton	24	9	16	1970	3/84	Joint
Fargo	7	7	1	—	11/85	Public
Fort Worth	31	16	10	1968	1/78	Private
Houston	60	21	51	1947	1/85	Private
Lexington	6	6	0	—	7/86	Private
Milwaukee	13	11	0	1961	3/86	Joint
Minneapolis	32	34	2	1962	5/86	Private
Montreal	32	1	3[3]	1962	1/83	Joint
Rochester (New York)	18	6	1	1972	5/85	Joint
Rome (New York)	8	2	0	1977	1/77	Public
St. John (New Brunswick)	3	2	0	1983	12/83	Joint
St. Paul	33	39	1	1956	4/86	Public
Sioux City	11	13	0	1975	5/86	Joint
Spokane	13	16	0	1961	2/85	Private
Syracuse	8	6	1	1966	1/81	Joint
Toronto	20	3	13	1890	5/86	Private
Waterloo (Iowa)	4	3	0	1983	8/85	Public
Wichita	6	4	0	1964	1/75	Private

[1] The city of St. Paul surveyed 28 cities in June 1986; 24 responded, and four known to have grade-separated pedestrian systems—Atlanta, Buffalo, Omaha, and Rochester (Minnesota)—did not.
[2] As of summer 1986.
[3] Twelve kilometers.

Source: St. Paul Department of Planning and Economic Development, *A Survey of Downtown Grade-Separated Pedestrian Circulation Systems in North America*, December 1986. (Reprinted in *Urban Land*, December 1988.)

disrupters of downtown retail and streetscape continuity (as discussed in the previous chapter).

Although construction of Charlotte's Overstreet Mall may have helped persuade two department stores to remain downtown, the system has had mixed reviews. David Milder reports on a study that showed that 40 percent of downtown's onstreet merchants felt overhead retailing had hurt their business. [7] Overstreet Mall's siphoning-away of much of the already fragile street-level shopping has vertically segregated downtown retailing in Charlotte: The most expensive shops lining the skywalk are supported by affluent office workers, whereas the marginal street-level shops are frequented by lower-income city residents. The "upstairs bourgeois boutiquesville," in the words of architecture professor Colin Rowe, "appeared to be simply an added agent of ethnic discrimination. The

blacks were on the streets and the whites were in the skyway." [8]

This situation has occurred elsewhere. In his study on skywalks in five midwestern U.S. cities, Kent Robertson writes that

[t]he most pressing problem . . . is the tendency for the skywalks to exert a negative effect on retail sales and property values on the ground floor. . . . This relative scarcity of street-level economic establishments exerts a deadening effect on downtown street life, thus creating the perception of a lifeless downtown environment. While this problem is most severe in St. Paul, indications of this "second-story city syndrome" are evident in [Cincinnati, Des Moines, Duluth, and Minneapolis], too. [9]

In St. Paul's 1986 study, half of the 24 responding cities reported that skybridges did some damage to

The reevaluation of its skywalk system led the city of Charlotte to discourage the building of connections between the street and the overhead network.

street-level retailing, ranging from a "slight dampening effect" in Toronto to a "significant reduction in traffic" in Duluth.

The second-story city syndrome is partly a matter of physical design, of the failure to provide links between the skywalk system and city streets and transit stops. Because skywalks commonly connect to the peripheral parking facilities used by automobile commuters, direct entrances from the street level are scarce, and connections to public transit are rarely a high priority. Often, passersby cannot easily see skywalk entrances, particularly those embedded inside buildings. People may feel uncomfortable venturing too far into private space if they have to walk deep into a building's interior to locate a skywalk entry. Of the skywalk systems Robertson studied, Cincinnati's "appeared to be the least elitist, which is not only a function of demographics but also of the system's design, which provides direct connection to the sidewalk." [10]

Many skyways connect luxury hotels and high-end department stores with class-A office towers housing white-collar workers. Such buildings tend to intimidate low-end shoppers, who may feel they do not belong. Conversely, middle-class shoppers and strollers feel safer on the skywalk than on the sidewalk. "Presumably," writes Robertson, "there is a direct relationship between perceived security and the overwhelmingly homogeneous profile of the typical skywalk user ([a] female, high-income, white-collar worker)." [11]

This same segregation by class and race also occurs in downtowns with below-grade pedestrian networks. In Houston, for example, blue-collar workers, mostly blacks and Hispanics, use the outdoor sidewalks during the heat of the day, while white-collar workers traverse downtown in the comfort of air-conditioned tunnels. In San Antonio, searing summer temperatures drive tourists and conventiongoers to the River Walk, where temperatures tend to be 10 degrees cooler than on the street-level sidewalks, where less-well-off city residents congregate.

Once viewed as a quick fix for mobility and economic development problems, alternative pedestrian networks have brought about their own specialized problems and are undergoing rigorous reevaluation by many cities. Although business is booming on many skywalks, some critics claim the boom is really a matter of redistributed commercial activity. They question the value of an economic development initiative that spells the demise of street-level retail businesses.

LIMITING SKYWALK CONNECTIONS

"When you take a street away from ground level," comments Whyte, "you take away what makes it work—such as the intricate mixture of people, the shops, the hustle and bustle. What you are left with is a corridor." [12] Increased disenchantment with skywalks is reflected in the growing number of regulations governing their expansion and design. Within a city's building code, skywalks are typically treated as encroachments on the public right-of-way; this treatment requires that the engineering department issue special permits or grant discretionary review. An alternative tack, recently taken by some cities, is to bolster skywalk policy through the implementation of explicit zoning provisions.

PORTLAND, OREGON

Portland's downtown ordinance, for example, specifies use and design guidelines for overhead connecting bridges. Portland's "Structures over the Right-of-Way" guideline—one of 22 downtown design guidelines that encourage street life, promote pedestrian activity, protect views of the Willamette River and nearby hills, and respect the integrity of the city's unusually short (200-foot) blocks—instructs: "When placing structures over the public right-of-way, preserve significant views, pedestrian pathways, and public access to light and air, and provide active pedestrian spaces below."

In 1982, Portland adopted a citywide policy on "Encroachments on the Public Right-of-Way." Administered primarily by the city's engineering department, the ordinance distinguishes among Type I skystructures, "(intended only for the movement of people or goods) whose width is 14 feet or less"; Type II skystructures, "with a width ranging from 14 feet to 60 feet, or having a width less than 14 feet but containing a function other than the movement of people and goods, or having a height greater than 12 feet"; and Type III skystructures, "with a width of 60 feet or more, or a height greater than 12 feet." Different standards for the construction of above-grade, at-grade, and below-grade structures in the public rights-of-way are also enumerated for four discrete districts: the downtown retail core, the downtown, the pedestrian district, and the citywide district.

Within the retail core, for instance, overhead connections are only permitted under limited circumstances, mainly when they link second- or third-story retail space to other retail space or to short-term public parking. Also, a skystructure must be "essential to the project's function or economic feasibility," be "used only for pedestrian movement," and be open to the public. These connections must be glazed or have otherwise transparent walls.

In addition, the city of Portland dictates that expenditures for ground-level pedestrian improvements must at least equal those for new skybridge connections. The policy states that

[t]o protect the sidewalk as the primary pedestrian system, skystructures and underground walkways shall not be built in lieu of at-grade improvements. Improvements to the immediate street-level pedestrian environment and circulation system shall be made prior to, or in conjunction with, the above-grade or below-grade improvements.

Such improvements might include display windows, street-level shop entrances, improved building materials and finishes, or even upgraded paving materials. "The main reason for this unique requirement," states Portland city planner Michael S. Harrison, is to "maintain the sidewalk as the primary circulation space for pedestrians," so that new buildings connecting to the skywalk are less prone to be internally oriented. Within the retail district, all above-grade encroachments, underground malls, and walkways are reviewed by the design commission and the planning commission.

Controversy over skywalk connections for a proposed Cadillac Fairview mixed-use project (once slated to occupy the present site of the Pioneer Place project, now being developed by the Rouse Company) was a major element in the 1980 breakdown of negotiations on the proposal. Cadillac Fairview, concerned about merchandising the upper-level retail space and achieving a critical mass within the city's short blocks, had proposed blockwide skybridges with double-loaded retail uses. The city nixed plans for a skybridge, which would have blocked views of the Willamette River. In recent years, several permit requests for two- and three-story retail skybridges connecting multistory buildings to one another or to parking structures have also been hotly contested.

VIEW OBSTRUCTION

These experiences point up the fact that view protection is also a skywalk issue. Responding to the claim that skywalks clutter the skyline, more and more cities are regulating them with view corridor protection mechanisms. Des Moines, for example, reacting to the building of an overhead walkway that blocked a panoramic view including the state capitol, adopted rules to prevent skywalks from crossing certain streets; these measures will maintain views of such city landmarks as the Polk County Courthouse.

Portland's skywalk ordinance contains a view corridor map with differing standards depending on whether a proposed overhead connection obstructs a designated "visual focal point" that lies on a primary, secondary, or tertiary view corridor. This street-by-street inventory clearly bans skywalk connections in some areas (see Insert 2 for map).

Seattle also prohibits the construction of skywalks along "designated view corridors," and conditional use permits for existing connections must be renewed periodically. In the mid-1980s, the city refused to renew a permit for an overhead walkway that blocked a sweeping view of the downtown and ordered the property owner to dismantle the walkway. The order was challenged in court, and the city council recently approved the permit renewal.

CHARLOTTE

In 1987, Charlotte adopted downtown zoning amendments, in part to boost the ailing retail core, which had been eviscerated by Overstreet Mall as well as by many new ground-floor bank lobbies. These amendments require new development projects exceeding 100,000 square feet to devote half their net first-floor areas to retail uses. A reevaluation of the city skywalk system led Charlotte to discourage any new connections between the street and the second-story network.

This policy against expansion of the overhead network was vehemently opposed by Charlotte's development community. As W. Kent Walker, president of Charter Walker Properties, Inc., puts it, the Overstreet Mall has come to be the "raison d'être" for new development, which is often designed around it. The expectation of a connection to the skywalk is factored into downtown land prices. Walker, together with a bank-led partnership, is developing a $300-million mixed-use project on the city's main street, the Tryon Street

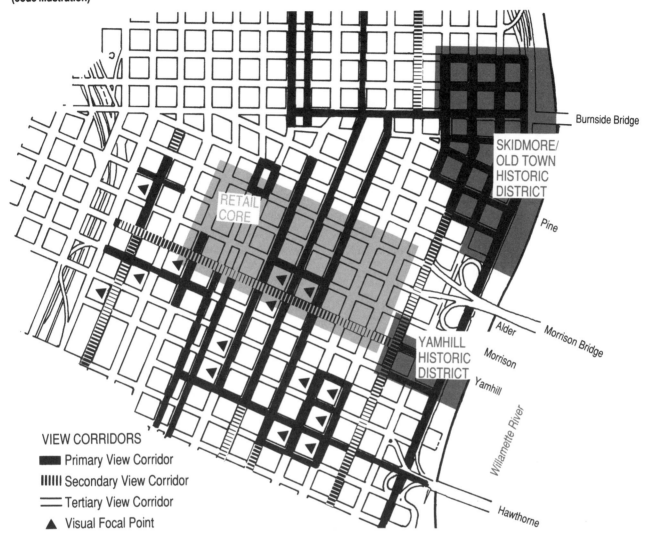

Burnside Bridge

SKIDMORE/
OLD TOWN
HISTORIC
DISTRICT

RETAIL
CORE

Pine

Alder

Morrison Bridge

YAMHILL
HISTORIC
DISTRICT

Morrison

Yamhill

Willamette River

VIEW CORRIDORS

■ Primary View Corridor

||||| Secondary View Corridor

— Tertiary View Corridor

▲ Visual Focal Point

Hawthorne

Mall. For this project, he had to remove portions of several skywalk connections. He feels obliged to replace them lest he be challenged by building owners who had expected eventual connections to the skywalk system.

Charlotte's anti-expansion policy has been modified. From now on, the city council must first approve any request to build an addition to the skywalk system. Then the proposed connection has to be reviewed by the planning department. Published review criteria set minimum width and interior height standards and address such issues as emergency vehicle access.

OTHER EXPERIENCES

As a rule, once a system is put up, enormous pressure arises to expand it. William H. Whyte notes,

however, that "[a] large capital investment is riding the offstreet system, and so is civic judgment. To be vindicated, the offstreet system must prosper, and to do this it must dominate. In most towns, there is simply not the market to support two full levels of business." [13]

Developers' expectations that new projects will automatically connect to the overhead system tend to be self-fulfilling. Nevertheless, these expectations are grounded in a certain reality. In St. Paul, for example, 1984 vacancy rates for buildings not connected to the skywalk system were four-and-one-half times higher than for buildings on the system. [14] In Fargo, North Dakota, where skywalks line 15 downtown blocks, rents in buildings connected to the skywalks have increased by up to 400 percent since 1983, while rents elsewhere in the city have risen by only 5 percent. [15]

DESIGN ISSUES

CINCINNATI

Whereas the idea of limiting and reevaluating sky-walks is catching on in many downtowns, Cincinnati's 1987 Downtown Development District regulations encourage expanding the skywalk network and offer incentives for building new connections. Bonus floor area, however, is granted only if a connection meets the criteria contained within the zoning ordinance. For instance, the connection must be designated on the skywalk overlay map; requirements for retail continuity and skywalk transparency must be met; and public access must be made available at all times, except between the hours of 2:00 a.m. and 6:00 a.m.

To qualify for bonus floor area, a new skywalk connection must meet the following code requirements:

(a) Be in a location as indicated on the DD District skywalk map.
(b) Connect without any step to the existing elevation of every portion of the skywalk that abuts the subject property.
(c) Be directly accessible by the public from an interior escalator, steps, or ramp to the ground-level atrium, arcade, lobby, sidewalk, or plaza.
(d) Be open to the public daily during all hours other than 2:00 a.m. to 6:00 a.m.
(e) Have a clear width of not less than 15 feet and a clear height of not less than 10 feet. Escalators shall not be deemed an impediment in the measurement of clear width or height.
(f) Be heated, air-conditioned, and illuminated to a level of not less than five footcandles at all times that it is open to the public.
(g) The owner shall agree to maintain and provide heating, air conditioning, and illumination for all portions of the skywalk that are within the public right-of-way to the center line of such right-of-way.
(h) The facades of the skywalk within the building shall meet the standards for retail continuity and transparency . . .
(i) The bonus floor area shall equal the skywalk floor area, multiplied by [a specified] factor . . .

As-of-right zoning is the overarching principle animating Cincinnati's Downtown Development District regulations. The skywalk rules are part and parcel of this approach: As long as the overhead connections are permitted on the skywalk overlay map, their construction is by-right and requires no special review procedure.

One reason for Cincinnati's satisfaction with skywalks is that here, second-story retailing seems to have flourished without hurting ground-floor shopping. Pedestrian traffic on both shopping levels has swelled in the 1980s, and city officials regard the skywalk system as a safety valve to accommodate increased congestion. The city's high density of development projects within a compact downtown core, in addition to the zoning requirement "that at least 60 percent of certain building frontages shall be exclusively devoted to retail uses," intensifies pedestrian activity. Also, in contrast to Charlotte, Cincinnati has seasonal extremes that may more readily justify climate-controlled elevated tubes as preferred alternative connectors.

ATLANTA

Downtown Atlanta, with some 30 skybridges linking parking decks to office buildings, hotels, and department stores, is also tussling with the skywalk question. The most controversial bridges are probably those at Peachtree Center, which was designed and developed by John C. Portman, Jr. Three years ago, Portman's request to build a 600-foot plexiglass-enclosed bridge connecting the center's mall with a parking garage was opposed by the city's urban design commission on the grounds that it would "advertise that you can't walk the streets of downtown Atlanta."[16]

The city's new long-range downtown plan, the Central Area Study II, states that "[p]roliferation of pedestrian bridges has affected street-level retail, [disrupted] visual continuity of the street, and, in some cases, diminished sidewalk activity." The plan recommends that pedestrian bridges be prohibited in future "where retail and other street or special district activities are important functions," and that new regulations should "designate zones where pedestrian bridges are not permitted, to protect historic districts and vistas from intrusion."

TRANSPARENCY

Explicit skywalk design criteria are set forth in the downtown zoning ordinances of Portland, Cincinnati, and Charlotte and form part of the overall development review process in Pittsburgh and Seattle. Glazing or transparency guidelines are consistent design requirements in all these cities. A see-through design preserves valued view corridors and vistas, like the spectacular views of Elliott Bay and Mt. Rainier from Seattle or of Mt. Hood from Portland, some of which are now hidden by opaque slabs of concrete the cities wish had never been built.

These transparency requirements may reflect a basic attitude about skywalks in U.S. cities—that they are mere connectors, so-called tubes of transition, and as such should be unobtrusive or invisible. On the other hand, the commonplace glass tube is often criticized as being monotonous, disorienting, and lacking in a sense of place. As architect Colin Rowe points out, invisibility was not the intention of the historical antecedents of the skywalk. Distinctive urban bridges built in the past—Florence's Ponte Vecchio, Venice's Bridge of Sighs, and Old London Bridge—were meant to function as elaborate articulated galleries or grandiose entryways and, most importantly, as places unto themselves.[17]

PUBLIC OR PRIVATE?

Skywalk design may also be influenced by ownership and funding structures. Compare St.Paul's all-public system with the privately owned Minneapolis skyway system, where all bridges are privately funded unless they connect directly to a city facility such as a parking garage. Many of the problems encountered by the Minneapolis system—nonuniform hours of operation, lack of security, uncoordinated signage, and design discordance—stem in part from multiple ownership. The individuality of each bridge's design robs the overall system of visual continuity.

In contrast, St. Paul's overhead connections share nearly identical design features. Some say the bridges' standardized pattern sets up a public or civic style and complements an orderly city dominated by governmental and institutional activity. Others feel the uniform design is monotonous.[18]

IN CLOSING

The downtown skywalk is a conundrum. Doubtless, many of these alternative pedestrian networks have injected new life into moribund retail cores. The skywalk systems in Cincinnati, Charlotte, and other cities are awash in commercial prosperity. Although the economic success of these systems is undisputed, urban experts nonetheless are concerning themselves increasingly with some of the unwanted side effects. Some cities have tried to mitigate these effects through skywalk regulation and design guidelines.

However, neither fine-grained regulations limiting the building of skywalks on view corridors nor sophisticated transparency rules and design guidelines can overcome what remains the basic issue, in the view of some commentators: that elevated pedestrian systems undermine the very *Ding an sich* of the downtown. Seeking to recapture those qualities that made downtowns lively before the onset of suburbanization, the urban design cognoscenti are focusing their attention on the ground, on open spaces, streetscapes, and sidewalks. According to architect Jaquelin Robertson, "There is [only] one level in the city. It is grade: where people walk, where trees grow, and where one has the best chance of solving almost all design problems. With few exceptions, one assumes a tremendous burden in traditional design terms when taking on a second-level scheme."[19] Or, as Whyte questions, "If you remove all the people from the sidewalks of downtown, do you really have a downtown anymore?"[20]

Notes

1. William H. Whyte, *City: Rediscovering the Center* (New York: Doubleday, 1989), pp. 6–7.
2. City of St. Paul Department of Planning and Economic Development, *A Survey of Downtown Grade-Separated Pedestrian Circulation Systems in North America* (St.Paul: author, December 1986).
3. Quoted in Lisa Belkin, "Skywalks and Tunnels Bring New Life to the Great Indoors," *New York Times* (August 10, 1988).
4. Kent Robertson, "Pedestrian Skywalk Systems: Downtown's Great Hope or Pathways to Ruin," *Transportation Quarterly*, vol. 42, no. 3 (July 1988), p. 470.
5. David N. Milder, "Crime and Downtown Revitalization," *Urban Land* (September 1987), pp. 16–19.
6. Whyte, *City*, p. 199.
7. Milder, op. cit., p. 19.
8. Colin Rowe, "I Stood in Venice on the Bridge of Sighs," in *Design Quarterly 129: Skyways* (Cambridge, Massachusetts: The MIT Press, 1985), p. 8. This publication was based on a conference on skyways, tunnels, and streets held at the Walker Art Center and the University of Minnesota.
9. Robertson, "Pedestrian Skywalk Systems," p. 474.
10. Ibid., p. 482.
11. Ibid., p. 408.
12. Whyte, *City*, p. 202.
13. Ibid., p. 203.
14. Robertson, op. cit., p. 478.
15. Belkin, "Skywalks and Tunnels Bring New Life to the Great Indoors."
16. Tom Walker, "Skybridges High, Dry, Debatable," *Atlanta Journal* (September 6, 1988).
17. Rowe, "I Stood in Venice on the Bridge of Sighs," p. 8.
18. Robertson, "Pedestrian Skywalk Systems," p. 481.
19. Jaquelin Robertson, "Private Space in the Public Realm," in *Design Quarterly 129: Skyways*, p. 4. (For full citation of *Design Quarterly 129*, please see note 8 above.)
20. Quoted in Belkin, op. cit.

CHAPTER 10

PARKING AND TRANSPORTATION

PARKING REQUIREMENTS

Many cities impose no minimum parking requirements in the downtown, partly because office developers generally choose to build parking facilities to appease lenders and attract tenants. The trend, however, in many innovative downtown zoning regulations, is to set requirements for both minimum and maximum parking amounts. In Hartford, for example, the city had not required parking until it passed the Downtown Development District zoning in 1984. Under the new zoning, the imposition of minimum parking standards (one space per 1,000 square feet of net office space) effectively downzoned the downtown area by more than 20 percent because the spaces had not previously been counted into the floor area calculation. To the dismay of the development community, moreover, the 1984 requirements made no distinction between above- and below-grade parking when calculating the total FAR for a project.

Hartford regulations now exempt below-grade parking from the FAR calculation, as do some other municipal codes, as an incentive for developers to incur the substantial added expense. Whereas an above-grade, multilevel parking garage costs approximately $5,000 per space to build, excluding land, below-grade parking costs run about $20,000 per space. Cincinnati's zoning grants an additional 350 square feet of commercial space for every underground parking space, and above-grade parking is exempt from the FAR count.

Parking requirements may be more lenient for those building types or uses encouraged in the downtown, such as historic buildings or daycare and human services uses. For many years, parking requirements tolled the death knell for historic structures, which

typically were built with no accessory parking. Happily, the approach in more recent years has been to exempt historic districts from these requirements. (See Insert 1 for a list of uses exempt from parking requirements in downtown Seattle.)

Insert 1.
Seattle's Parking Exemptions
(code extract)

Exceptions to the parking requirement shall be permitted as follows:
a. No parking shall be required for new uses to be located in existing structures, or when existing structures are remodeled.
b. No parking shall be required for residential uses.
c. No parking, either long-term or short-term, shall be required for the first 30,000 square feet of retail sales and service use on lots in areas with high transit access, as identified on Map IA. No parking, either long-term or short-term, shall be required for the first 7,500 square feet of retail sales and service use on lots in other areas.
d. No parking shall be required for the first 2,500 square feet of any nonresidential use which is not a retail sales and service use.
e. No parking shall be required when an existing structure is expanded by up to 2,500 square feet or less, provided that this exemption may be used only once by any individual structure.
f. No parking shall be required for any gross floor area in human service or daycare use.
g. In Pioneer Square Mixed zones, the Pioneer Square Preservation Board may waive or reduce required parking according to the provisions of Section 23.66.170, Parking and Access.
h. In International District Mixed and International District Residential zones, the International District Special Review District Board may waive or reduce required parking . . .
    In these zones, the parking requirements for restaurants, motion picture theaters, and other entertainment uses and places of public assembly shall be established pursuant to the requirements of Section 23.66.342, rather than the provisions of this section.

Likewise, in those cities that encourage downtown residential development, the minimum parking requirements for residential uses, which usually gener-

160

ate less traffic, are frequently lower than those for commercial uses. In some downtowns, parking for residential buildings is required but exempted altogether from the floor area count.

SHORT-TERM PARKING

Another trend in many downtowns is to distinguish between long-term and short-term parking. Short-term, or transient, parking is typically limited in time to fewer than four hours. Many cities are trying to enhance the quality of their downtown pedestrian environments by encouraging transit use and limiting the available parking for commuters. Still, the general consensus holds that in order to strengthen retail cores and compete with the suburban malls, short-term parking must be readily available to shoppers and visitors, as well as to the clients of the many downtown service providers—lawyers, accountants, and others.

In Hartford and Seattle, short-term parking is one of the bonus options available within the incentive zoning system (see Inserts 2 and 3). Portland's downtown zoning also has a 20 percent short-term parking requirement for office development, and this parking "shall be marketed, priced, or operated in a manner which encourages its use for short-term parking and discourages its use for long-term parking." Whereas Hartford developers need only develop a plan to ensure that such spaces will be used exclusively for transient parking, Seattle developers must comply with more detailed bonus standards, including that of instituting a rate structure favoring short-term use. Seattle also has a requirement for short-term parking, and the bonus is only available once this requirement has been met. Short-term parking requirements and rate structuring mechanisms are also crucial components in transportation management programs (see later section of this chapter on TMPs).

Insert 2.
Short-Term Parking Bonus in Hartford
(guideline accompanying code)

Transient Parking
– *Definition:* Parking spaces provided for short-term public use in a parking garage.
– *Criteria:* The applicant shall submit to the council a plan ensuring that such spaces will be used for transient, not monthly or employee, parking. A bonus for transient parking will not be recommended unless it has been found that the plan is satisfactory and conforms to the Downtown Development Plan and is detailed in the developer's transportation management plan.

Ratio 1:4

Insert 3.
Short-Term Parking Bonus in Seattle
(code extract)

1. Intent
   Short-term parking is intended to aid the vitality of the retail core by providing needed parking for shoppers and visitors.
2. Area and dimensions—Basic Standards
   a. A minimum of 25 spaces in excess of the amount established by the short-term parking requirement for uses on the lot shall be provided.
   b. Two hundred spaces in excess of the amount established by the short-term parking requirement for uses on the lot shall be the maximum number bonused.
   c. The location, size, and dimensions of parking spaces and access shall meet the requirements of the land use code.
   d. The area bonused shall include all areas used for short-term parking which is in excess of the amount of required short-term spaces, plus associated vehicular circulation, but the total bonused area shall not exceed 375 square feet per parking space.
3. Street orientation—Basic Standards
   Parking may be provided above or below grade, and shall be subject to the standards for the screening and location of parking for the zone in which the parking is located.
4. Access and hours of operation—Basic Standards
   a. Signs shall be located at all entrances to the parking which indicate the location of public short-term parking and parking rates. These signs shall be visible and readable by drivers from the street.
   b. Parking shall be available to the public during normal hours of retail operations. The minimum hours shall be from 9:30 a.m. to 7:00 p.m. seven days a week.
5. Special conditions—Basic Standards
   a. A rate structure that favors short-term parking shall be required for the bonused spaces.
   b. Parking shall not be rented other than on an hourly basis. No monthly or daily discount shall be permitted.
   c. The property owner shall enforce regulations necessary to ensure that parking is available for short-term use and submit an annual report to the director indicating the fee structure, hours of operation, and utilization.

Hartford developers and tenants regard transient parking features as standard building amenities, and the bonus has been used or proposed in most of the downtown office projects that have come on line since the city's incentive zoning regulations were adopted in 1984. The bonus is only allowed, however, on those streets with adequate reserve capacity, as designated in the Downtown Development Plan, and the city has rejected several applications.

SHARED PARKING

Some downtown zoning regulations also include provisions for shared parking. In Bellevue, Washington, the code permits up to a 20 percent reduction in the minimum parking requirement for providing "cooperative use of parking," with different peak hours of operation. A typical example would accommodate the patrons of a restaurant within an office building.

BICYCLE PARKING REQUIREMENTS

Any project in downtown Seattle containing 20 parking spaces must provide one bicycle storage space per 20 automobile spaces. In Portland, where the percentage of commuters bicycling to work is estimated at between 2 and 4 percent, or roughly 5,000 people a day, the city has a similar requirement; it also classifies certain streets in the downtown as principal bicycle streets (see Insert 4).

REGULATION OF SURFACE LOTS AND PARKING GARAGES

Many downtown land use codes also regulate surface lots and parking garages. Aside from the visual blight, the asphalt lagoons that consume vast areas of many cities also make for serious environmental difficulties related to excess runoff and microclimatic changes.

Some downtowns prohibit the removal of buildings and subsequent conversion of sites into unsightly surface parking lots. Surface lots in Seattle and Portland, Oregon, are only issued conditional permits, which must be renewed every few years. In Portland, concessions are made, however, for lots of 20 or fewer spaces serving a residential use, or for interim lots that form part of large-scale phased developments in which the phasing pattern temporarily means inadequate parking for the project (see Insert 5). Surface

lots for principal use in Orlando also are allowed only as conditional uses in the downtown, and accessory surface lots may extend along no more than 25 percent of the building site's street frontage on each block face.

DEMOLITION PERMITS

A related issue is the granting of demolition permits so that sites may be converted into surface lots. Cincinnati's code, which bans surface lots in the downtown, authorizes city agencies to grant demolition permits only if new construction permits are issued at the same time. Furthermore, any lot left vacant 180 days after demolition must be landscaped according to plans approved by the planning director. (See Insert 6 for code language.) The city, however, has waived this requirement on several occasions.

Richard Roddewig notes that this technique of linking issuance of a demolition permit to approval of plans for a new building is a principle commonly used in historic districts. "More and more," writes Roddewig,

> communities are becoming concerned that demolition permits issued without consideration of the prospects for, and likelihood of, immediate new construction on the site simply create surface parking lots and make it easier for land speculation in active downtowns. By prohibiting issuance of a demolition permit until application for a building permit for a new structure on the site is also in hand, Cincinnati hopes to encourage retention of existing buildings until the economic demand for a replacement structure is assured.[1]

Insert 6.
Cincinnati on Demolition Permits
(code extract)

Sec. 2406.1. Demolition. Except in cases of public emergency, no permit for the demolition of any building in the DD District shall be issued unless an application for a building permit for work to replace the building to be demolished has been filed with the director of buildings and inspections. Provided, however, the applicant may instead post a bond with the director of buildings and inspections to secure compliance with Section 2406.3. The bond shall be in the amount equal to $10 per square foot of the area of the lot on which the building to be demolished is located.

Sec. 2406.2. Maintenance of Vacant Lots. Every owner of any vacant lot within the DD District shall keep the lot clean, free from garbage, litter, standing water, debris, motor vehicles, whether or not abandoned, and all things causing the property to be detrimental to the public health, safety, welfare, or to the aesthetics of the DD District or properties in the vicinity.

Sec. 2406.3. Landscaping. Any lot within the DD District kept vacant for more than 180 days following the demolition of any buildings thereon shall be landscaped and thereafter maintained in good order. Landscaping shall be in accordance with a plan approved by the director of city planning following the procedures and standards set forth in Sections 2403.4 through 2403.10. The landscaping shall be appropriate to an urban park or garden. The lot shall be fenced as appropriate for public safety and aesthetics. All plant material shown on the approved plan shall be watered, fertilized, pruned, kept free from weeds and litter, and replaced if diseased, injured, or dead, consistent with good horticultural practices. Such lots shall not be used for storage.

On the other hand, developers often treat surface parking lots as part of the assemblage process and count on these lots as a means of generating revenue until projects are completed. For this reason, such limits on surface parking lots are economically disadvantageous to developers.

LANDSCAPING REQUIREMENTS

The larger the lot, the more serious the environmental problems. Therefore, many cities that still allow surface lots in their downtowns impose landscaping and screening requirements to break up the large expanses of asphalt. This move also helps to reduce the heat gain on these surfaces and to improve their appearances.

Tom Smith writes that in addition to enhancing the appearance of parking lots, careful landscaping

> can also be used to separate pedestrian and vehicular traffic and to delineate different functional areas within a lot, such as long-term employee parking and short-term visitor parking areas. Using landscaping to define parking areas typically helps to control traffic and lower traffic speeds, thereby ensuring greater safety and efficiency in the operation of the lot. The use of deciduous and flowering trees in a parking lot's interior can provide shade for the cars and the lot's surface. Dense perimeter landscaping can also muffle the noise of automobiles and reduce the glare of automobile headlights and parking lot lighting.[2]

(See Insert 7 for screening requirements for grade-level parking lots in downtown Charlotte, North Carolina.)

Insert 7.
Charlotte's Requirements for Screening Parking
(code extract)

3. *Screening*. . . . Grade-level parking lots must be screened from the street and pedestrian areas either by shrubs and/or evergreen trees planted at the most appropriate spacing for the species used or by solid walls or fences not exceeding four feet in height. Trees used to fulfill this requirement must be located on private property in planters, a planting strip, berm, tree lawn, any of which must be at least eight feet wide and at least two feet deep; the areas between the trees to be landscaped or grassed. The trees must be of a small maturing evergreen variety and be at least 10 feet tall at the time of planting. Plant material used to fulfill this requirement must be provided with an automatic irrigation system which does not rely on drainage from the street, sidewalk, or buildings. All plant material must conform to the "American Standard for Nursery Stock" published by the American Association of Nurserymen. The developer must provide written certification that the plant material meets this standard. Trees employed to meet the screening requirement may not be counted toward the street tree planting or urban open space tree requirements. Any lot which becomes vacant through the removal of a structure for any reason must be screened from all abutting public street rights-of-way in accordance with the provisions of this section. The type of trees used must be consistent with any approved streetscape plan for the area or the city's public street tree planting and landscaping program. . . .

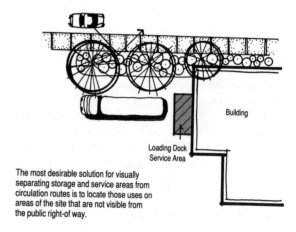

The most desirable solution for visually separating storage and service areas from circulation routes is to locate those uses on areas of the site that are not visible from the public right-of-way.

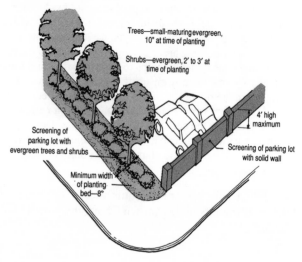

Trees—small-maturing evergreen, 10' at time of planting

Shrubs—evergreen, 2' to 3' at time of planting

Screening of parking lot with evergreen trees and shrubs

4' high maximum

Screening of parking lot with solid wall

Minimum width of planting bed—8'

RATIOS, REDUCTIONS, AND CAPS

BELLEVUE, WASHINGTON

Whereas cities like Hartford are instituting downtown parking requirements for the first time, a trend in many downtown zoning regulations is to cut back on parking requirements. Until 1981, for example, Bellevue's downtown regulations required office development to provide at minimum five spaces per 1,000 square feet of office space. No maximum was set. In 1981, the city adopted much lower parking requirements, with both minimum and maximum allowances designed to be reduced gradually. The code now dictates a minimum of two spaces and a maximum of 2.7 spaces per 1,000 net square feet of office. Whereas this ratio is considerably higher than Seattle's parking limits, it is far more restrictive than the typical suburban requirement, which is generally three to four spaces per 1,000 square feet.[3]

Bellevue's dramatic reduction of its parking ratios was part of its overall efforts to create a downtown with an intense and varied urban core. Shifting employees into more efficient modes of transportation, such as buses and carpools, was central to this campaign. The city's efforts included an incentive zoning system that promoted the construction of major dense, mixed-use projects within a concentrated area; creation of a pedestrian corridor linking the financial and retail sectors; and substantial capital investments for transportation improvements.

To slash the parking quotas, Bellevue recognized the need to develop alternative transportation modes and committed itself to expanding transit service. City officials entered into an agreement with Metro, the regional transit authority, to increase transit service concurrent with expansion of the downtown employment population. A $5 million "timed-transfer" transit center in the core provides half-hourly connections to other major communities in the region.

ORLANDO

Between 1970 and 1980, Orlando, Florida's population grew from 99,000 to 132,000. Projections of continuing growth, coupled with concern about downtown traffic congestion and parking availability, prompted the city in the early 1980s to secure federal assistance for transportation improvements. The city council also enacted a downtown parking overlay district to lower offstreet parking requirements for office (and office-plus-retail) development and adopted an incentive for further reductions in parking construction.

Under the ordinance adopting this incentive, developers could avoid construction of required parking by as much as 20 percent in exchange for contributing to a transportation management trust fund. Contributions would be based on 80 percent of the construction cost of each space avoided, with the presumed cost of a space set periodically by the city council. For example, the construction cost of a space in 1986 was set at $5,600, resulting in a proposed contribution per space avoided of $4,480. In actual practice, from 1982 to 1986, the city did not receive a single payment for the trust fund because lenders were leery of proposals calling for less-than-"adequate" parking for office and mixed-use buildings.

SEATTLE

In Seattle, the parking ratios vary according to transit access (see Insert 8). In order to exceed the maximum of one long-term parking space per 1,000 square feet of nonresidential use, one must apply for a spe-

Parking Ratios in Seattle
(code extract)

Chart 49.16A Parking Requirements
(expressed in parking spaces per 1,000 square feet of gross floor area of the use)

| Use | Long-Term Parking Requirement | | | | | | Short-Term Parking Requirement in All Areas |
| | Areas with High Transit Access | | | Areas with Moderate Transit Access | | | |
	Unrestricted Long-Term	Carpool	Total	Unrestricted Long-Term	Carpool	Total	
Office	0.54	0.13	0.67	0.75	0.19	0.94	0.1
Retail sales and service, except lodging	0.32	0.08	0.40	0.56	0.14	0.70	0.5
Other nonresidential	0.16	0.04	0.20	0.16	0.04	0.20	None
Lodging	1 space per 4 rooms (all areas)						None

cial exception. Such considerations as proximity to transit lines, the characteristics of the workforce, employee hours, and the likelihood of the extra parking's encouraging the use of single-occupancy vehicles are to be taken into account.

Seattle's zoning also allows developers to meet the minimum long-term parking requirement alternatively by paying into a general downtown parking fund. The determination is to be based on proximity of the site to public parking, the level of transit service to the lot, and proposals by the applicant to encourage building tenants to use alternatives to single-occupancy vehicles. Because the minimum requirement is relatively low and lenders are not eager to finance projects that have little or no on-site parking, no money has been paid into the fund.

The city's most recent major transportation improvement is a $400 million Metro tunnel containing five stations that will run for one and one-third miles through the office and retail sectors and connect with Interstate 5. The beauty of the dual propulsion system is that the diesel buses will convert to electricity within the tunnel, which will link with existing feeder and collector programs. Capable of whisking 18,000 passengers an hour through downtown, the tunnel will provide an exclusive right-of-way for buses (the same buses that go through neighborhoods or on the freeways). The tunnel, which will be completed by 1990, is meant to relieve the growing congestion caused by the swelling population and real estate development boom. Transit ridership to the downtown is now projected at some 21 percent.

RIDESHARING AND REDUCTION

Some regulations dictate that a percentage of parking spaces must be allotted to vehicles participating in carpools and other ridesharing programs. In Seattle, for instance, some 20 percent of long-term parking must be saved for carpools (see Insert 9). Also, long-term parking ratios for nonresidential uses in Seattle may be reduced by the employers' providing vanpools, or by carpooling in excess of the requirement (see Insert 10). In Portland, 15 percent "of the parking allocated for office use shall be for carpool use, provided it can be marketed." Ridesharing requirements are also typically integrated into transportation management plans (see next section of this chapter).

Insert 9.
Carpool Requirements in Seattle
(code extract)

2. Carpool spaces provided to meet the requirements of Subsection B1 shall either be:

a. Physically set aside and designated for exclusive carpool use between 6:00 a.m. and 9:30 a.m., and [not] leased to tenants for long-term parking, except as parking for carpools and vanpools. Required carpool spaces not used by carpool vehicles by 9:30 a.m. shall be used as public short-term parking with appropriate signage provided; or

b. Subsidized, provided that the subsidy shall be equal to at least 30 percent of the monthly market rate charged the general public for a parking space. Subsidized spaces shall be provided at the rate that carpools are formed.

Insert 10.
Parking Reduction Provisions in Seattle
(code extract)

3. The following substitution rates shall be used to reduce the long-term parking requirement for all nonresidential uses, except lodging:

   a. One vanpool may be substituted for six parking spaces. The unrestricted long-term parking requirement may be reduced no more than 10 percent for vanpool substitutions. If the proponent elects to use the vanpool option, the necessary number of vans meeting the standards of the commuter pool division of Metro shall be acquired, or a surety instrument acceptable to the director shall be posted; and vanpools shall be organized for employees in the structure. Before a certificate of occupancy may be issued, details of the vanpool program shall be spelled out in a memorandum of agreement executed between the proponent, his or her transportation coordinator, the director, and the Seattle Rideshare Office.

   b. Each carpool space in excess of those required by Subsection B1, which is physically reserved or subsidized according to the provisions of Subsection B2, may be substituted for one and nine-tenths parking spaces. No more than 50 percent of the total number of long-term parking spaces provided shall be set aside or discounted for carpools.

   c. A 15 percent reduction in the unrestricted long-term parking requirement may be achieved by providing free transit passes to all employees in the structure for at least five years.

Studies by ULI show that urban and suburban communities in at least seven states have enacted so-called parking reduction regulations, offering as "carrots" reductions in the amount of offstreet parking required by zoning.[4] Carrots are given in exchange for developer-financed ridesharing and transit services. Some regulations, such as those passed in Orlando and Seattle, offer developers the option of contributing to a trust fund to finance publicly managed commuter assistance programs. Although the potential reductions are hefty—from 20 to 60 percent of minimum parking requirements—they have rarely been used. Developers are usually reluctant to trade the guarantee of a set parking supply for the uncertain success of demand management.

PORTLAND'S PARKING LID

Portland's Downtown Parking and Circulation Policy, adopted in 1975 as the transportation component of the Downtown Plan, was a direct response to the requirements of the 1972 Clean Air Act. The stated public goals of the transportation policy are to encourage transit use, traffic flow management, economic development, and air quality compliance. During the more than 10 years since the policy was put in place, the air quality of the downtown has improved notably. Much of the improvement can be traced to such measures as the imposition of federal auto emissions standards, the city's biannual auto inspection program, and the limit on downtown parking spaces. The number of carbon monoxide violations has plummeted, from over 50 in 1975, to 19 in 1979, and to only one in 1987.

Another significant feature of Portland's parking and circulation policy is the primary importance given to pedestrians and to walking as a preferred mode of transportation. Because of the small-scale blocks (200 feet long), many of the pedestrian amenities that on larger blocks might be built into projects, such as benches and plazas, in Portland occupy the wide sidewalks, which have displaced some travel lanes.

Here, the pedestrian takes precedence over the automobile. This policy is reflected in the city's unique parking ratio structure. All offstreet parking within the downtown is by conditional use only and is reviewed by the hearings officer. Although Portland has parking ratios, they are only maximum standards, and in theory the city permits new commercial buildings to be constructed without any parking. The maximum range for office development is 0.7 to 1.0 space per 1,000 square feet, and, as in Seattle, the range varies with nearness to transit. Projects with large retail components and higher short-term parking needs are permitted more on-site spaces than straight office projects. Under the downtown's strict parking quotas, however, the few available parking spaces mostly go to tenant executives. Several commercial projects have been built with no parking. In the instance of one 20-story office project with no on-site parking, an arrangement was made to lease some of the spaces in a garage across the street. Minimum parking requirements do pertain, however, for residential development (see Insert 11).

Insert 11.
Portland: Maximum Parking Space Ratios
(code extract)

A. New parking which is proposed as a part of a new development or redevelopment may be approved, provided that the number of parking spaces does not exceed the number indicated by the following schedules of maximum parking space ratios.

B. The listed ratios are *maximums*. New nonresidential buildings may be constructed without parking spaces, or with fewer spaces than the maximum ratios would produce. . . .

C. Minimum residential parking requirements are: not less than one space per condominium unit, three-quarters of a space per rental unit, and one space per eight elderly housing units. . . .

Schedule (1) Maximum Parking Space Ratios for Office Developments by Parking Sector

Parking Sector (based on proximity to transit)	Spaces per 1,000 Square Feet of Gross Floor Area
A,D,H,K,L	1.0
B,J	0.9
C,G	0.8
E,F	0.7

Schedule (2) Maximum Parking Space Ratios for Types of Development Other than Offices

Development Type	Spaces per 1,000 Square Feet or per Habitable Unit
Residential	1.20 per Dwelling Unit
Hotel	1.00 per Rentable Unit
Retail	1.00 per 1,000 Square Feet
Medical	1.50 per 1,000 Square Feet
Educational	1.00 per 1,000 Square Feet
Manufacturing/Wholesale	0.70 per 1,000 Square Feet
Cultural/Entertainment*	0.25 per 1,000 Square Feet

*The listed ratio is for employee parking.

Parking for daytime use by patrons shall be determined on a case-by-case basis and be based on an analysis of demand and availability of parking in the area.
Parking for evening use by patrons will only be approved if existing daytime-use parking in the area is unavailable or insufficient for the need. Daytime use of spaces approved for evening-patron use will be reviewed and considered during the conditional use process.

THE LID INTRODUCED

By far the most controversial component of the city's parking program is the maximum parking inventory, sometimes referred to as "the lid." In 1975, an inventory was estimated of all existing and approved parking spaces in the downtown, and new development was forbidden to exceed the absolute limit of 40,855. Parking ratios and distribution policies were developed accordingly. Despite the creation of 10,000 new jobs since 1975, the addition of new spaces has been negligible. Since 1975, several redevelopment sites have been added to the downtown area, and in 1987 the lid was increased to 43,914.

When a project removes existing parking, the exchange is not one-for-one. The preexisting spaces go into the pool and are not automatically reallocated to the project but must come in under the ratios. In much

the same way, if a structure is built where no parking already exists, the parking reserve must be large enough to allow spaces for the new construction. Office development, which requests the most spaces, depletes the lid more rapidly than any other development type.

Some development replenishes the lid. For instance, the onstreet parking that was removed for the ll-block transit mall was added to the inventory. In addition, some residential towers have been built on surface parking lots, and the extra spaces went back into the reserve because residential and hotel parking are exempt from the lid. Development in historic districts and other parts of the city with low FAR limits may also contribute to the total parking reserve.

Although the lid has not yet acted as a constraint on new development, current estimates show the city is within 500 spaces of the allowed inventory. If the inventory limit were reached, the city would have to decide which spaces to remove.

The lid, as stated earlier, was originally adopted as a means of reducing the excessive level of carbon monoxide, in compliance with the Clean Air Act, and the 43,914 limit (1987) of permitted spaces is absolute. At some theoretical point, however, innovative transportation methods, such as synchronized signals, transportation management plans, promotion of mass transit use, and ridesharing programs, may be so successful in banishing air pollutants as to warrant adding more spaces to the inventory and raising the lid. Parking manager Elsa Coleman observes that although this scenario is possible, the present issues addressed by the lid really are more directly related to congestion, traffic flow, and transit support than to air quality.

Coleman warns that in cities lacking public transportation alternatives, a parking lid is not a realistic option. At the same time that Portland's Downtown Plan was being formulated, with its many features meant to deter automobile use, the city committed itself to public transit. By the time the Downtown Parking and Circulation Policy was enacted in 1975, the city had secured a $15 million federal grant to construct the two-thirds-mile bus transit mall on two major arteries coursing through the main retail and commercial districts. The ll-block bus mall furnishes exclusive bus lanes with limited auto access.

In 1986, the first phase of the city's light-rail system opened. The $214 million Metropolitan Area Express, known as MAX, stretches for 15 miles between Portland and the suburban city of Gresham. Within the downtown's "fareless square," passage on conventional transit and light rail is free at any time of the day. Ridership on MAX has surpassed all expectations. The Tri-Met transit agency predicted daily ridership at no more than 10,000 to 12,000, when in fact paid ridership has averaged about 20,000. Major peak-hour and weekend crowds require extra trains.

Because new jobholders are being accommodated on the city's expanding transit and light-rail systems, downtown jobs have increased by one-third without a significant surge in traffic. Within the last 10 years, the transit system has doubled its share of all work trips to downtown, and an estimated 48 percent of commuters rely on public transportation.[5]

THE LID'S EFFECT ON DEVELOPMENT

Although Portland's zoning permits office buildings to be constructed without long-term parking, most new projects provide on-site parking unless surface parking already exists nearby. Despite the apparent roaring success of the city's public transportation program, lenders remain skeptical and view the more liberal suburban parking ratios as a continuing threat. Indeed, when the downtown's aggressive parking ratios were first implemented, a host of projects shot up on the periphery of downtown, where the parking ratios were three per 1,000 square feet of office space, as opposed to 0.75 to one per 1,000 in the core.

From the very start, Portland's transportation program was more than an end in itself, intended as it was to spur economic development as well as augment air quality and aid traffic movement. Portland architect Greg Baldwin talks about the "shaping power" of transportation and notes that within a year after plans for the light-rail system were unveiled, every piece of property along the designated route changed hands at least once. Sections of the city along the rail route that had previously languished, like the Skidmore historic district, were suffused with new activity. The city's highest property values generally developed on those ridges of property next to the transit mall and the light-rail line.

TRANSPORTATION IMPROVEMENTS

Some downtown zoning codes offer increased density in return for making improvements to transit facilities. For instance, one of the bonus selections in Cincinnati's incentive zoning is a bus passenger shelter (see Insert 12). Pittsburgh also awards a floor area bonus for downtown transit-related facilities "designed and developed as an integral part of the total development project and not as mere connections."

The transit facilities must use city-dedicated bus lanes, where applicable, and must "be engineered to accommodate at least 4,000 persons during the peak hours of travel on a weekday." Likewise, transit tunnel access is one of the special public benefit features in Seattle's incentive zoning system to encourage new development to connect to the city's bus transit tunnel.

Insert 12.
Bus Shelter Bonus in Cincinnati
(code extract)

Sec. 2403.2.4. . . . In order to qualify for bonus floor area, a bus passenger shelter shall satisfy all of the following criteria:
(a) Be a sidewalk-grade-level, sheltered area of at least 200 but no more than 500 square feet.
(b) Adjoin a public sidewalk along a bus route operated by a public transit authority at a stop location specifically approved by the director of public works for the location of a bus passenger shelter.
(c) Provide at least 10 spaces of public seating sheltered from the rain.
(d) Provide a line of sight from within the shelter along the bus route to allow persons waiting for buses to observe their approach.
(e) All areas of the shelter shall be illuminated at all times to a level of a least five footcandles.
(f) Be maintained in good order and kept open for public use at all times for the life of the building or for as long as the location remains a stop along a bus route operated by a public transit authority.
(g) The bonus floor area shall equal the sheltered area of the bus passenger shelter, multiplied by [100].

New York City's subway station improvement bonus was the subject of a landmark 1987 court case. Boston Properties was to have earned an extra 20 percent of density for its Columbus Center project in exchange for upgrading an adjacent subway station. But a trial court found that this agreement contravened the explicit provisions for granting the discretionary bonus in New York's 1982 Midtown Zoning (see Insert 13 for the bonus criteria) and declared the contract null and void. (The reader will find further exploration of this case in Chapter 1, "Incentive Zoning.")

Insert 13.
New York: Bonus Criteria for Subway Station Improvements
(code extract)[1]

Floor area bonus
The amount of the *floor area* bonus shall be in the discretion of the city planning commission and may range from no bonus *floor area* to the maximum amount allowable by special permit, as set forth in Section 81-211 (Maximum floor/area ratios for nonresidential or mixed buildings). In determining the precise amount of *floor area* bonus, the commission shall make findings on the following:
(a) the degree to which the station's general accessibility, rider orientation, and safety will be improved by the provision of new connections, additions to circulation space, or easing of circulation bottlenecks;

(b) improvements in the station's environment by provision for daylight access, better orientation of riders, or improvements to noise control, air quality, lighting, or other architectural treatments;

(c) provision of escalators where justified by traffic or depth of mezzanine or platform below *street* level;

(d) convenience and spaciousness of *street*-level entrance and compatible relationship to the *development's* or the *enlargement's* ground-floor *uses*.

---

[1] All italics in New York inserts are original.

In San Francisco, improvements to the transit system are made through the use of another zoning technique. The city's transit impact development fee, a revenue-producing mechanism for San Francisco's Municipal Railway System (Muni), was developed to offset the anticipated rise in costs generated by the construction of new office projects downtown. Implemented in 1981, the transit fee was later integrated into the 1985 Downtown Plan as part of the city's comprehensive system of development fees, which also go toward housing, public art, daycare centers, and open space.

The transit improvement fee in San Francisco is assessed at the rate of $5 per square foot of office space. Each building's fee covers the estimated transit improvement costs over a 45-year life cycle, which may be paid in installments over several years or in a lump sum following construction. Since 1981, the city has collected $48.4 million (including interest) for transit improvements. Of that amount, the city has spent $5.3 million, most of which went toward expanding peak-hour services and defending the fee successfully in several court challenges. Within the next five to 10 years, the city expects to collect $20 to $25 million from projects now underway or approved. These revenues, like the city's housing contributions, are limited by the current cap of 475,000 square feet annually on downtown office construction.

The California Supreme Court upheld San Francisco's fee in 1987 and, in a later decision, found that it could also be imposed retroactively on 13 major downtown projects under construction before the ordinance went into effect. The case was appealed to the U.S. Supreme Court, but the Court refused to review it and the fee remains intact.

TRANSPORTATION MANAGEMENT PROGRAMS

Whereas parking ratios and reduction programs affect available parking supply, transportation demand management (TDM) or traffic systems management programs attempt to control demand. Traffic manage-

ment calls for employers to reduce employee automobile trips; it encourages greater use of mass transit, carpools, and other alternative modes. In effect, traffic management reduces traffic demands from new development, in contrast to methods that increase traffic capacities.

TDM systems were first used in the suburbs to alleviate rush hour traffic through either ridesharing or flexible work hours. More elaborate demand management techniques, however, are increasingly required as conditions of approval for new development in downtowns. As such, they are being written into the zoning regulations. Transportation management plans (TMPs) and transportation demand management programs (TDMs) target consumer demand according to mode of transportation, time of day used, mileage covered, and trips per day. These programs, whether mandated or optional, promote or require various trip reduction measures, including rideshare-matching services and vanpool leasing/coordination, on-site employee transportation coordinators, transit subsidies, and staggered work hours.

HARTFORD

Hartford, for example, mandates that applications for site plan approval of downtown projects include both preliminary and final transportation management plans. These essentially consist of traffic studies indicating "access to and from the site; pedestrian and vehicular circulation and parking; [and] the impact of the proposed access, circulation, and parking on the city's pedestrian and vehicular circulation system." (See Insert 14 for more of Hartford's wording.)

Insert 14.
Hartford's TMP Rule
(code extract)

[Section] 35-6.21. *Transportation management plan.* All applications for site plan approval and/or a special permit for developments in the B-1 Downtown Development District and the B-2 Downtown Development Perimeter District shall include a preliminary and final transportation management plan. The purpose of the transportation management plan is to clearly indicate access to and from the site; pedestrian and vehicular circulation and parking; the impact of the proposed access, circulation, and parking on the city's pedestrian and vehicular circulation system; and conformity to the Downtown Development Plan and the Hartford Plan of Development.

. . .

(2) *Final transportation management plan.* A final transportation management plan shall include, at a minimum, a written statement with appropriate supporting documentation, describing the following information:

(a) The number of on-site parking spaces required by the provisions of Section 35-6.17.

(b) The number and types of parking spaces to be provided on site, such as employee parking, transient parking for on-site uses, transient parking for off-site uses, parking for high-occupancy vehicles, parking for compact cars, and handi-capped parking.

(c) The number, location, and type of any parking spaces to be provided off site and the method of transporting persons between the off-site facility and the project site.

(d) Alternative modes of transportation, such as mass transit, carpools, vanpools, and bus pools available and to be provided.

(e) Expected usage of the alternative modes of transportation.

(f) Location of all vehicular and pedestrian entrances and exits.

(g) The impact of the proposed development on the city's vehicular and circulation system, including the numerical impact on a.m. and p.m. peak-hour volumes and [on] peak-hour link and intersection capacities for all streets and intersections within three (3) blocks of the project site.

(h) How the proposed access and pedestrian and vehicular circulation and parking conform to and implement the recommendations of the transportation and circulation elements of the Downtown Development Plan.

Hartford's code also allows developers to cut back on the number of required nontransient offstreet parking spaces by up to 30 percent in exchange for implementing a TMP "demonstrating a comprehensive approach to reducing the parking demand at the site" (see Insert 15). So far, no developer has undertaken such plans to reduce parking requirements. The explanation given is that lenders would refuse to finance projects without the maximum permitted complement of spaces. Another deterrent is that, in the case of speculative development, it is difficult to formulate a plan before a tenant mix is known.

Insert 15.
Hartford on Reductions in Required Offstreet Spaces
(code extract)

(3) *Reduction in required number of on-site parking spaces.* The court of common council is authorized to allow the reduction of the on-site, offstreet parking spaces required in the B-1 Downtown Development District in accordance with the provisions of this section in instances where the reduction is in accord with an approved transportation management plan and will reduce traffic and congestion on city streets; where alternative modes of transportation are provided to get to and from the site; and where the reduction of the on-site parking is in conformance with the Downtown Development Plan and will provide for a more appropriate form of development.

(a) Up to ten (10) percent reduction in the number of required nontransient offstreet parking spaces is permitted when the applicant and/or employers who are tenants of the applicant's project agree to the following:

1. [Designate] an employee transportation coordinator responsible for promoting ridesharing and public transit use among employees.

2. Participate in areawide ridematching system or provide a ridematching program at the site.

3. Designate a minimum of twenty (20) percent of the nontransient offstreet parking spaces to be offered at a dis-

count parking rate for vehicles containing three (3) or more persons. If there is to be no charge for parking, then reserve a minimum of twenty (20) percent of the nontransient offstreet parking spaces for vehicles with three (3) or more persons. The reserved preferential spaces shall be located in close proximity to the building entrances, relative to the other spaces, and shall be clearly signed or marked "Reserved—Minimum Three Persons per Vehicle."

(b) Up to a thirty percent (30%) reduction in the number of required nontransient offstreet parking spaces is permitted when the applicant submits a transportation management plan demonstrating a comprehensive approach to reducing the parking demand at the site. The reduction granted shall be commensurate with the parking demand reduction projected by the transportation management plan. The plan will be reviewed by the city manager to determine the adequacy in reducing parking demand through increased ridesharing and applicant and/or employer commitment to the program. Reductions shall be computed based on levels of auto occupancy and transit ridership determined by the city manager to be applicable to the area in which the site is located. In addition . . . , a minimum of three (3) of the following techniques shall be provided . . . .

1. Provision of vanpools or subscription bus service for employees.

2. Subsidy of employee use of high-occupancy vehicles such as carpools, vanpools, and bus pools.

3. Instituting a parking charge and not permitting such charge to be employer-subsidized.

4. Provision of parking cost subsidies for high-occupancy vehicles, if a parking charge exists.

5. Provision of, or participation in, shuttle services from off-site parking facilities owned or leased by the applicant or employers who are tenants of the applicant's project.

6. Provision of subsidized transit passes.

7. Any other technique or combination of techniques acceptable to the city manager and capable of reducing nontransient parking demand at the work site.

. . .

(4) *Transportation management, continuing character of obligation.* Where a final transportation management plan is approved by the council, the applicant shall covenant to ensure continued compliance. . . . The covenant shall be for a term of twenty (20) years. . . . Such covenant shall be recorded on the land records and shall run with the land.

State environmental impact acts allow some cities to impose conditions on new projects to mitigate those adverse traffic-related effects described in environmental impact statements. This approach is followed in some East Coast states, such as New York and Virginia, but is most prevalent on the West Coast. For instance, Seattle and Bellevue use the power delegated to them under the Washington State Environmental Policy Act (SEPA) to require that major new projects submit TMPs, a requirement that has also found its way into the downtown zoning codes of both cities.

SEATTLE

Since 1979, Seattle has encouraged developers to offer HOV (high-occupancy vehicle) incentives to building tenants. In 1985, the city's zoning codified the requirement that all major developments and institutions must begin transportation management programs. Since that time, new provisions have required that projects 10,000 square feet or larger must hire a building transportation coordinator (BTC); promote ridesharing semiannually; establish a commuter information center; set aside at least 20 percent of long-term parking for the exclusive use of carpools, or provide such parking on demand at a significant discount; and supply one bicycle rack for every 20 parking spaces. Parking reduction credits are awarded for vanpools at the ratio of 1 to 6 and to carpools at the ratio of 1 to 9, up to a maximum of 50 percent from code parking requirements. Free transit passes for all building workers may be distributed in exchange for a 15 percent reduction in unrestricted long-term parking requirements.

All elements of Seattle's transportation management program must be in place before a certificate of occupancy can be approved. Building traffic coordinators must submit quarterly reports of program performance and commuting habits to the Seattle Commuter Services Office. In 1985, average daily ridesharing participation involved 5,810 commuters, with an annual subsidy of $528,000.

SAN FRANCISCO

San Francisco's Downtown Plan calls for transportation management programs and "transportation brokerage services" within the city's commercial sectors to "minimize the transportation impacts of added office employment in the downtown . . . by facilitating the effective use of transit, encouraging ridesharing, and employing other practical means to reduce commuter travel by single-occupant vehicles." On-site transportation brokerage services are required for new buildings, additions, or conversions in which the added floor area for office use comes to at least 100,000 square feet:

> Prior to the issuance of a temporary permit of occupancy . . . the project sponsor shall execute an agreement with the department of city planning for the provision of on-site transportation brokerage services and preparation of a transportation management program to be approved by the director of planning. . . .

(See Insert 16 for TMP/brokerage services criteria.)

Insert 16.
San Francisco's Rule on TMPs and Brokerage Services (code extract)

Sec. 163. Transportation Management Programs and Transportation Brokerage Services in C-3 Districts.

(a) *Purpose.* This section is intended to assure that adequate measures are undertaken and maintained to minimize the transportation impacts of added office employment in the downtown, in a manner consistent with the objectives and policies of the Master Plan, by facilitating the effective use of transit, encouraging ridesharing, and employing other practical means to reduce commute travel by single-occupant vehicles.

(b) *Requirement.* For any new building or additions to or conversion of an existing building in C-3 Districts where the gross square feet of new, converted, or added floor area for office use equals at least 100,000 square feet, the project sponsor shall be required to provide on-site transportation brokerage services for the actual lifetime of the project, as provided in this subsection. Prior to the issuance of a temporary permit of occupancy . . . , the project sponsor shall execute an agreement with the department of city planning for the provision of on-site transportation brokerage services and preparation of a transportation management program to be approved by the director of planning and implemented by the provider of transportation brokerage services. The transportation management program and transportation brokerage services shall be designed:

1. To promote and coordinate effective and efficient use of transit by tenants and their employees, including the provision of transit information and sale of transit passes on site.

2. To promote and coordinate ridesharing activities for all tenants and their employees within the structure or use.

3. To reduce parking demand and assure the proper and most efficient use of on-site or off-site parking, where applicable, such that all provided parking conforms with the requirements of Article 1.5 of this code and project approval requirements.

4. To promote and encourage project occupants to adopt a coordinated flextime or staggered-work-hours program designed to more evenly distribute the arrival and departure times of employees within normal peak commute periods.

5. To participate with other project sponsors in a network of transportation brokerage services for the downtown area.

6. To carry out other activities determined by the department of city planning to be appropriate to meeting the purpose of this requirement.

BELLEVUE

Since the early 1980s, Bellevue has espoused alternatives to single-occupant vehicle (SOV) use through its parking restrictions, transit program, and requirement that developers of downtown office projects hire transportation coordinators and promote HOV (high-occupancy vehicle) use as part of their organized transportation management plans. In an effort to accelerate the downtown's transition from a low-density, auto-dependent center into a denser, more pedestrian-oriented core, the city first supplied these programs as policy on an informal, ad hoc basis and later formalized them into zoning requirements.

History of Bellevue's Transportation Management Program. In 1981, the city set up mode-splitting goals at 35 percent, that is to say, 35 percent of employees in new projects were either to take transit, to participate in vanpool or ridesharing programs, or to use other HOV alternatives. Unhappily, the split that was actually achieved was closer to 10 to 15 percent. There were no monitoring or enforcement mechanisms, and people parked illegally on private lots and in residential neighborhoods.

Now, rather than simply work toward a perhaps arbitrary percentage goal, the second generation of downtown development in Bellevue must meet exacting performance standards, and penalties have been set for projects generating more parking than can be handled on site. Developers must set aside money guaranteeing performance; the sum will be refunded two years after the date of occupancy, if achievement of the transportation management goals can be demonstrated. If not, the city is authorized to spend the money to subsidize vanpools or take other measures to mitigate traffic impacts.[6]

Bellevue's requirement for a TMP is administered through the development review process. A transportation demand management (TDM) requirement was recently added to the code, and specific TDM performance criteria, now being developed, will also be comprised within the zoning.

In addition, the Washington State Legislature in 1988 passed the Local Transportation Act. The Act authorizes local government to charge developers impact fees within certain transportation benefit districts to finance off-site transportation improvements. Before this enabling legislation, the assessment of "involuntary" development fees had been statutorily prohibited by state law. The city of Bellevue is now considering the imposition of impact fees over and above transportation improvement assessments for the downtown.

Recently, apocalyptic traffic jams and increased impatience with the city's traffic mitigation tactics galvanized 8,200 Bellevue residents into signing an initiative. They demanded that the city council take immediate action to improve traffic conditions. The city responded by passing a temporary ordinance in September 1988 requiring developers either to pay up-front fees covering the full costs of improving streets and intersections in congested areas, or to forgo building. The temporary ordinance was replaced by a permanent one that establishes a baseline level of adequate service for all major intersections.

To implement the permanent ordinance, the city developed a sophisticated computer model of traffic conditions for major intersections and for roadways leading to major freeway intersections. Plugging the projected traffic volumes from a proposed development into the computer model, the system shows the traffic impacts of a project over scores of intersections. If the model determines that the project will degrade traffic conditions below a given standard, the project sponsor must invest in the necessary traffic improvement measures before commencing construction.

Some Problems with Bellevue's TMP. One criticism has been the lack of cost-effectiveness. The developer and owner of an MXD called Bellevue Place, Kemper Freeman, Jr., says that some of the original traffic mitigation techniques recommended by the city were sorely lacking in cost/benefit analysis and that the $16 million worth of mitigation costs first proposed for his project by the city exceeded his total land costs. Instead of paying the mitigation costs as they stood, Freeman chose to contract with the transportation management association (TMA), which proposed alternative mitigation measures and shrank his mitigation costs to some $2.7 million.

When the TMP requirement in Bellevue was administered on an ad hoc basis, developers pointed out they did not know in advance what the traffic mitigation conditions would be and complained the conditions were imposed arbitrarily. This was especially so for those developers whose projects were among the first to come in under the new requirement; these developers felt they were at a competitive disadvantage against other downtown projects that had more liberal parking allotments. Codification of the TMP requirement and specific performance criteria should overcome this equity objection.

GENERAL TMP ISSUES: BELLEVUE AND ELSEWHERE

An additional difficulty is the impracticality of devising TMPs for service-sector employees. Ridesharing, vanpools, flexible hours, and incentives to use transit are most effective on large single-employer sites, with back-space office workers (most often computer and technical support staff), or with other types of employees who can be organized easily into work shifts. Bellevue is growing rapidly into a major service center, and although new Bellevue projects will house some back-office users, much of the space will be occupied by service-sector tenants—accountants, brokerage offices, branch law firms, and the like—that may prove resistant to locking themselves into fixed work hours. Also, in the case of a speculative development, it may be difficult to devise a TMP before the tenant mix is determined.

Another reality to be reckoned with is that parking is viewed in many cities as an employment "perk" and therefore as a project amenity enhancing a building's value. Developers persistently raise the objection that aggressive long-term parking rationing puts them at a disadvantage compared with the suburbs and makes it harder to get financing. For example, in Hartford, implementation of the TMP is voluntary and can earn a developer as much as a 30 percent reduction in the on-site long-term parking requirement. Yet the provision has yet to be used. In Seattle, developers can reduce substantially their parking obligations by imposing various traffic mitigation measures, but everyone is coming in at the maximum. Similarly, downtown Portland has no minimum parking limits, and most projects provide on-site facilities all the same.

Moreover, structured parking earns quantifiable value under traditional appraisal methods, so that most developers and their lenders hesitate to cut voluntarily their on-site parking allotments. Zoning requirements thus tend to set the accepted market standards.

A related question that needs answering when devising parking ratios and HOV alternatives is, to what extent can the market be forced? When Bellevue originally reduced its parking ratios in 1981, the intent was to drop them further by 0.3 every two years. By trial and error, however, the city learned that the market of the early and mid-1980s simply would not support any more reductions. The present allocation of 2.7 spaces maximum per 1,000 square feet of commercial space inevitably will drop in the future, but there is no longer a fixed schedule. City officials hope that by clamping down on the supply, they can raise the cost enough so that commuters will in time turn to transit.

Matthew Terry, director of design and development in Bellevue, notes that the city's most aggressive mode-split objective, at 44 percent, is modest compared with downtown Seattle's situation. In Seattle, roughly 30 percent of the shoppers and 40 percent of the office workers already use transit. Bellevue is still auto-driven and struggling to effect an attitudinal change that Terry says will take at least a decade.

With regard to enforcement, most jurisdictions know it is not easy to ensure that the spaces meant for short-term parking will not be taken by commuters, or that spaces set aside for carpools or vanpools will not be poorly marketed and remain empty. One approach is to set up a rate structure favoring short-term parking, a required measure in Seattle, where greater density is granted for providing short-term spaces.

To complicate matters, parking coordinators, who also frequently function as building managers, have many other responsibilities. For this reason, some developers and employers form TMAs, which distribute ridesharing and matching information, market the traffic reduction incentives, and enforce the TMP provisions.[7]

Finally, yet another difficulty is that, although the TMP requirements are imposed on the developer, the actual implementation responsibility (subsidized transit passes, incentives for ridesharing, and so on) generally is borne by another party (employer or building tenant). For this reason, Bellevue requires as part of its approval process that developers pay a certain deposit to ensure that the TMP objectives will be met. When the objectives have clearly been reached, the money is refunded. This seems an effective method of guaranteeing a developer's sustained commitment to the success of a project's TMP.

In some jurisdictions, developers risk losing performance bonds, letters of credit, or funds in escrow if local governments decide to take over poorly run TDM programs. The simplest enforcement mechanisms are covenants. In Hartford, a covenant lasts for 20 years and "shall be recorded on the land records and shall run with the land."

Notes

1. Richard J. Roddewig, in unpublished report presented at session of the land use, planning, and zoning committee at the 1988 midyear meeting of the American Bar Association.
2. Tom Smith, "The Greening of Parking Lots," *Zoning News* (April 1988), p. 1.
3. The most recent edition of the Institute of Transportation Engineers' *Parking Generation* reports that for general office buildings smaller than 50,000 square feet, the range is slightly lower than 3 to 4, but buildings in the 50,000- to 100,000-square-foot range show higher parking ratios because they contain a higher density of employees. (Cited in Robert T. Dunphy, "Traffic and Parking: A New Generation of Information," *Urban Land* (May 1988), p. 8.)
4. Reported in upcoming ULI book on transportation management for employers and developers.
5. See Steve Dotterer, "Portland's Arterial Streets Classification Policy," in *Public Streets for Public Use*, ed. Anne Vernez Moudon (New York: Van Nostrand Reinhold Company, 1987), p. 174.
6. For a closer look at Bellevue's TMP, see Kemper Freeman, Jr., William R. Eager, and Christina J. Deffebach, "A Market-Based Approach to Transportation Management," *Urban Land* (July 1987), pp. 22–26. The article is an informative case study examining how one developer responded to the city's TMP requirement.
7. See ibid. for description of Bellevue's transportation management association.

CHAPTER 11

HOUSING

Cities nationwide are striving to create a lively 24-hour downtown with the bustling sidewalks, fast-paced nightlife, and overall élan that distinguish such world-class cities as Paris, London, Rome, New York, and San Francisco. However, these characteristics, which depend on the availability of specific downtown services and activities, require a certain critical mass, provided in part by local residential neighborhoods. Apart from their role as consumers, downtown inhabitants perform an "eyes-on-the-street" function, discouraging vandalism and other crimes. Their support of municipal services as tax-payers, of course, is also crucial.

Downtown housing is a paradox. In those downtowns awash in economic prosperity, the commercial development boom of the 1980s has apparently propelled land values beyond the prices private-sector housing developers can pay. On the other hand, in less prosperous cities, investors are skittish about committing to residential development, which is seen as high in risk. Although the potential gluts of commercial building in some cities may eventually spark interest in downtown housing, the choice of most residential developers inevitably will be market-rate units rather than affordable ones. But the population in many downtowns consists mainly of low-income renters, individuals who cannot afford to move to the suburbs, much less to make the steep monthly payments for the luxurious new condominiums being built downtown.

Because of these inherent economic disincentives, many cities have had to regulate downtown housing through subsidies and exactions and fashion a raft of zoning tools to speed this kind of development. However, before a city implements mechanisms either to cajole or coerce developers to construct downtown housing, it first may be necessary to amend existing zoning regulations to allow residential development within designated sectors. Because Euclidean-style zoning has traditionally segregated residential from other uses, many downtowns have had to set up special hybrid districts permitting housing to be built within commercial or even industrial sectors of the downtown. Such zones are generally labeled commercial/residential districts, mixed/commercial, or mixed-use districts. Under Portland, Oregon's 1988 Central City Plan, for example, all commercial sectors and one industrial sector are mixed-use zones that allow housing construction within either mixed-use or single-use projects.

SURVEY OF AVAILABLE MECHANISMS

INCENTIVE TOOLS

Cities with full-blown incentive zoning systems, such as Bellevue, Washington, Cincinnati, Portland, Hartford, and Seattle, simply include housing among their bonus options. In those cities that use special purpose mixed-use districts, additional density may be gained by developing housing within the district. A related incentive is lowered parking requirements for residential uses, whether standing alone or as components of mixed projects. Bellevue, Washington, permits significant parking reductions for residential units incorporated into commercial development, to help offset costs in mixed-use projects. Burlington, Vermont, grants as much as a 50 percent reduction in the on-site parking requirement for any type of residential building in the downtown. Instituted on a case-by-case basis, this reduction has encouraged the adaptive use of several structures, which have been converted to residential. In contrast, Seattle makes no parking requirement at all for residential uses in the downtown.

Another kind of incentive entails accelerating the permit review process for residential projects, as Seattle does. Also, some inclusionary housing programs (promoting the inclusion of affordable or low-income units within market-rate residential projects) are incentive-based; within certain districts in New York City, for instance, developers of market-rate housing projects may gain up to a 20 percent density bonus for including low-income units. Alternatively, inclusionary zoning regulations may allow in-lieu cash payments.

Some cities exempt residential building from height and density restrictions. In some commercial areas of San Francisco, projects that include moderate-income housing can exceed FAR limits, as long as they comply with the governing height and bulk limits. In Portland, Oregon, mixed-use projects can go over the height limits by as much as 75 feet if the bonus height area is devoted to housing; the residential portions of such mixed-use projects are exempt altogether from the FAR calculation. Bellevue, Washington, makes larger height and FAR concessions for residential construction: In pursuit of its overarching goal of creating a neighborhood in the downtown, the city also nurtures the development of those local services that support residential neighborhoods—supermarkets, libraries, art galleries, hardware stores, and drugstores, as well as charitable and social service organizations—and exempts these uses from the FAR count.

These incentives are often targeted at special housing markets. Burlington, Vermont, for example, awards density credits for elderly housing and greater height for low-income projects. Likewise, the residential incentives in Seattle are now limited to the production of moderate- and low-income housing.

MANDATORY TOOLS

Although many of the above incentives make downtown residential development more attractive, commercial development in most cities invariably commands higher revenues. Thus, some cities have found it necessary to mandate some housing mechanisms. For instance, Hartford's voluntary residential density bonus has proven almost completely ineffective. In 1987, therefore, the city passed the mandatory Housing Overlay District (HOD) zoning, requiring new projects within certain areas to devote a percentage of their floor area to housing.

A basic technique for ensuring the development of residential uses within desired areas is to downzone. By downzoning areas peripheral to the downtown, thus limiting office development to the densest office core, cities can effectively write down land costs in the periphery and enhance the opportunity for residential buildings there. Bellevue has reinforced its policy

of steering office development to the downtown by severely curtailing the allowable density and height of office structures within certain districts outside the business core. Whereas FARs within the 144-block core may reach 10.1 in some downtown locations, peripheral areas have been downgraded to an FAR of 0.5, which limits a commercial building to be built on a 100,000-square-foot lot to some 50,000 square feet. Seattle's incentive zoning ordinance takes a similar tack by limiting some of the downtown mixed/residential areas to an FAR of 5, thereby driving down land costs in those areas and targeting them for housing.

In like fashion, Portland's Central City Plan, which sets aggressive housing goals of developing 5,000 new housing units within the next 20 years, has downzoned some 10 acres of land to residential. Before implementing the plan, the city also rezoned 60 acres within the CBD to require housing as the principal land use activity.

Among other mandatory mechanisms are involuntary inclusionary housing provisions. Seattle's downtown code requires that "at least 10 percent of the units in new structures containing more than 20 dwelling units shall be maintained as affordable housing . . ."

One of the more recently touted zoning tools to ensure that at least some housing gets built in the downtown is the so-called "office/housing linkage" requirement. In Boston and San Francisco, developers of major office projects must agree to construct a certain amount of housing or pay a comparable fee into a housing trust fund to obtain a building permit. (As will be discussed later, linkage programs also can be implemented on a voluntary basis as part of a city's incentive zoning system.)

Finally, some cities with visible homeless populations have enacted housing preservation ordinances (HPOs) and antidemolition ordinances, which generally protect single-room-occupancy (SRO) and other types of low-income housing. Most of these ordinances are authorized under a city's general police powers, rather than its zoning authority, and therefore exceed the parameters of this discussion.

MIXED-USE DISTRICTS AND HOUSING OVERLAYS

Special purpose districts and overlay zones are being used increasingly in fully built-out cities as vehicles for change. These tools normally preserve existing desirable uses or establish an area of special character, particularly in those neighborhoods of unusual social, cultural, ethnic, environmental, or historical significance that are threatened by redevelopment pressures. In exchange for helping to realize these public objectives, developers generally receive some form of zoning relief, typically greater building densities.

Special purpose districts, in common with floating zones, overlay zones, planned unit development provisions, and other flexible zoning techniques, are intended to inspire more inventive developer responses to special physical conditions, changed economic circumstances, or shifts in technology or consumer preferences that more traditional zoning approaches have tended to stifle.

Tailor-made zoning has been specifically crafted for cultural, arts, and theater districts and for "combat zones," as well as for waterfront, garment, retail, and preservation districts. As mentioned in an earlier chapter, Portland, Maine's waterfront harbor zone severely curtails all development on the Casco Bay that is unrelated to marine use; and capital cities such as Austin, Tallahassee, and Washington, D.C., have "capitol interest" or "capitol dominance" zones preserving views of their capitol buildings and monuments.

At last count, New York City had created 34 special purpose districts, many of which are aimed at preserving the character of distinct, moderately dense residential neighborhoods. "Special districts are not new; only their pervasiveness is a recent phenomenon."[1] The cause of this phenomenon Richard Babcock calls the "penicillin effect"—if it works here, do it again there.[2]

In theory, overlay zones do not supplant the underlying zoning but impose an additional layer of uses or design review requirements within a targeted geographic area to achieve given goals. Zoning provisions unrelated to the overlay mission essentially remain intact. Special purpose districts, on the other hand, are complete mini–zoning ordinances. They may specify everything: uses, parking requirements, density and height limits, setbacks, massing, and incentives. Separate design review criteria are frequently developed for each special district.

In practice, however, overlay zones and special districts are indistinguishable and are used more or less interchangeably. Some cities also may use the techniques of planned unit developments and special design zones to regulate those city sectors that share a single purpose.

SHORT CASE STUDY: WASHINGTON, D.C.'S SPECIAL PURPOSE MIXED-USE DISTRICT

The District of Columbia's Commercial/Residential (CR) Mixed-Use District was enacted in the mid-

1970s expressly for the West End—a 12-block transitional area west of the rapidly expanding office corridor and east of the residential and retail concentrations of Georgetown. The area, which was zoned commercial/light-industrial, excluded residential uses and had an FAR of 4. As development pressures mounted, it was feared that the rash of medium-sized office buildings would kill any opportunities for housing.

The replacement CR zone "encourage[s] diverse compatible land uses, which may include a mixture of residential, office, retail, recreational, light-industrial, and . . . miscellaneous uses." It provides increased density with the inclusion of residential or hotel uses in a project: within this district, hotels qualify as a "transient residential" use. Under the special zoning, the total FAR for all buildings and structures within a lot may not exceed 6, and no more than 3 out of the 6 may be devoted to uses other than residential. To maximize the allowable density, therefore, a project must contain a residential component. The allotment of residential and nonresidential uses may also be distributed among projects within the same block, provided the aggregate does not exceed the total FAR limits within the district.

Since the zone was adopted in 1974, more than 2.5 million square feet of space for offices, hotels, condominiums, and retail uses has been built in the West End. By treating hotels as a residential use, however, the CR zone has encouraged market forces to alleviate the city's mid-1970s hotel shortage at the expense of housing. Although the planning office expected some hotels to be built in the area, they did not anticipate the extent of hotel construction. Within the CR zone, new office and retail space now exceeds over 2 million square feet, and more than 1,300 new hotel rooms or suites and 240 condominium and cooperative apartments have been added. A majority of the new structures involve mixed uses: office with residential, office with retail, or other combinations.

Although the original intent was to cultivate an economic mix of housing (moderate to high-end), most new units built in the West End since the CR zone was put in place are rentals or condominiums targeted at empty nesters or at one- or two-person households at the high end of the income scale.[3]

The prognosis for future residential building within the zone appears relatively favorable. Several mixed-use projects built in the CR zone during the early 1980s were stymied by the recession, forcing developers to slash prices on housing units, thus tainting the image of residential development in the area. This negative perception, which at first discouraged lenders from investing in residential uses and diverted funds to hotels instead, has largely dissipated. Moreover, the city's hotel market is temporarily saturated. In several recent projects, the residential component has fared considerably better than expected, with some projects preleasing almost 100 percent of the housing units.

In summary, the CR zoning fathered the potential for residential development in the West End, although the zoning clearly was not the motivating force that shaped the development climate there. Without the regulatory stick, however, developers inevitably would have chosen to build office towers, which command far higher rents. One developer, for example, initially covenanted to build a residential structure in the second phase of a planned unit development (PUD) in exchange for density concessions on an adjacent office building. The developer later claimed that a strictly residential project within the CR zone was not economically feasible and successfully negotiated to reduce substantially his residential obligation within the PUD's second project, which will combine office and housing.

HOUSING OVERLAYS

Just as special purpose residential districts may be either mandatory or voluntary, so may housing overlays be implemented as either incentives or exactions. Hartford, Portland, Oregon, Boston, and Washington, D.C., have designated specific areas in the downtown where commercial developers are induced or forced to devote a percentage of their project space to residential use.

HARTFORD

The city's 1984 voluntary residential density bonus proved ineffective in generating new housing stock in the downtown (see later section of this chapter on housing bonuses), and the seemingly insatiable appetite for new office space increased the pressure to convert those remaining sites set aside for residential to commercial uses. Therefore, in 1987, Hartford's city council passed the mandatory Housing Overlay District (HOD), which is applicable to designated areas within the CBD. The purpose "is to establish a residential development requirement for land areas determined to be desirable for housing development but designated for mixed-use/office development by the underlying zoning district designation. . . . " Within these mapped areas, at least 25 percent of the gross floor area originally proposed for office or parking structures must instead be devoted to residential use.

The residential requirement is triggered by buildings with FARs of 5 or more and with a minimum lot area of 10,000 square feet. Residential space built to meet the 25 percent HOD requirement is also exempt from the FAR calculation. Once the 25 percent requirement has been met within the HOD, the residential density bonus is available for those office projects located within the Downtown Development District.

As of this writing, the housing overlay mandate has influenced the programming of a mixed-use project next to Bushnell Park, on the fringe of the CBD. The first phase of the 29-story condominium tower will contain 202 apartments, to be followed by subsequent phases that will contain office, retail, and more residential units. The location, overlooking the park, is advantageous for residential development, and therefore the housing component is seen as a lesser gamble than it might otherwise be.

PORTLAND, OREGON

Portland's 1988 Central City Plan calls for residential development in those city sections most conducive to and attractive for housing, including sites along the Willamette River, close to major public open spaces, or near both light-rail transit and major retail centers. The residential exaction, affecting some 100 acres of commercially zoned land within the CBD, requires that at least 15 dwelling units be developed as part of a project for each acre of land on the site. The housing may be provided within a single-use or a mixed-use building. Occupancy of the nonresidential portions is not permitted until the residential components have been completed.

BOSTON

Boston's 1987 Interim Planning Overlay District (IPOD) for the downtown is a temporary zoning measure in effect for two years, until the Boston Redevelopment Authority formulates a permanent comprehensive ordinance. Comprising 11 planning districts, the IPOD includes various height subdistricts as well as housing priority areas. In March 1989, the zoning commission passed permanent regulations for the Midtown Cultural District, part of the IPOD, which covers a 27-block area between Back Bay and the financial core.

Within each of the housing priority areas, developers must provide different percentages of housing. The triggering mechanisms for determining the housing obligation also vary. For example, the requirement in the mostly residential Chinatown-Bay Village Housing Priority Area is 75 percent of the gross floor area of any proposed project, whereas in the housing priority area for the Chinatown CBD, the percentage is 50 percent. Within the more industrial leather district, the requirement is 25 percent for projects exceeding 10,000 square feet. The Midtown zoning established a fourth housing priority area for designated sites facing the Boston Common; for these sites, the residential requirement is 75 percent.

WASHINGTON, D.C.

In 1981, the District of Columbia created the Hotel/Residential (HR) Incentive District, an overlay zone aimed primarily at encouraging hotel building near the Washington Convention Center, which was then under construction. The zone's secondary aim was to further the long-term public policy goal of promoting downtown housing. The HR zone allows hotel or housing developers a density bonus of 2 FAR, subject to the city's height limit of 130 feet for commercial structures in the HR district. Zoning in the underlying districts permits a maximum FAR of 6 or 6.5 and maximum heights of 90 feet. Over a hotel footprint of 10,000 square feet, for example, the bonus would yield an additional 55 rooms or give a 20 percent boost to a 250-room hotel.

Hotel industry experts initially persuaded city officials that the incentive zone was necessary by claiming that steep land costs in the downtown prevented hotels from competing with office buildings, which could bring in higher revenues from a given site. Indeed, in 1980, about half of the city's hotels were still located in residential areas. No major new hotels were being built near the convention center, and the concern was that none would be added in the future.

Since the HR overlay was enacted, several hotels have been built or are underway in the incentive zone. As a spinoff, the zone has inevitably improved the climate for hotel building in its vicinity; a 917-room convention hotel has been erected near the convention center but in an existing district (which allows an FAR of 8.5).

Two of the new hotels in the overlay zone are components of mixed-use projects. In both instances, senior company officials note the bonus was not used to increase the hotel size. Market factors dictated the number of hotel rooms. Effectively, the bonus was used instead to increase the office space, which raised potential revenues for the overall project and thus reduced the risk of hotel building in an area perceived in the early planning stages as problematic.

One developer believes the bonus, along with lowered interest rates, enabled a decision to proceed earlier with the project than might otherwise have been feasible. Another developer says the bonus helped in obtaining acceptable financing sooner than normally.

By 1987, the city's hotel market was generally saturated, and Washington suffered from an oversupply of hotel rooms, particularly of higher-priced lodging. The resulting slowdown in overall construction is unrelated, therefore, to the density premium in the HR overlay. Perhaps disappointingly, so far, the incentive zone has triggered almost exclusively hotel rather than housing production. Given the city's strict height cap, a density premium of 2 FAR appears inadequate to counterbalance the high land cost per FAR square foot that office rents can now justify. Until residential demand results in higher sales or rents, and/or until land prices are driven or written down, the overlay zone is unlikely to stimulate major downtown housing production.

In one instance, the HR zone did lead to an office/housing linkage project. Under a planned unit development provision, a developer has pledged seed money for 150 units of low- and moderate-income housing, to be built several blocks north of the downtown HR zone in exchange for an increase in office density. In fact, the existence of the HR zone partly inspired the local linkage concept, which is now administered on an ad hoc basis.

HOUSING BONUSES

Downtown housing is almost always one of the bonus features available within incentive zoning systems. Cities like Cincinnati, Hartford, Orlando, Bellevue, Portland, Oregon, and Seattle award surplus density and, in some instances, surplus height for incorporating residential uses into commercial projects. In these instances, "residential" is generally defined as housing only. Bellevue's residential bonus, for example, specifically excludes hotels and motels.

HARTFORD

Boasting one of the country's lowest office vacancy rates in 1988, Hartford is an anomaly on the national scene. With announced proposals calling for some 9 million square feet of new commercial space, Hartford's market for class-A office space is booming. But, although 80,000 people work in Hartford's downtown, less than 1 percent of the citywide population of 136,000 lives in the downtown. And the 1980 census reports that 25 percent of the city's residents live below poverty level. The city's 1984 Downtown Plan stated that 6,437 new housing units would be needed there in the 1980s and that 5,970 substandard housing units would have to be rehabilitated by 1990.

This program comes to an estimated total cost of $688 million. The compact (200-acre) downtown has a serious housing shortage, and the city has adopted several zoning strategies to address this problem.

The 1984 Downtown Plan comprises two distinct bonuses promoting housing construction in the downtown and distinguishes clearly between residential uses and "visitor- and convention-related housing," namely, hotels. Eight additional square feet are awarded for each square foot of housing, up to a maximum of 4 FAR. In contrast, the hotel bonus yields only one additional square foot of office space per square foot of hotel space and caps at an FAR of 1.

As of 1988, only one project had been approved to use Hartford's bonus for residential construction. A $200 million 59-story office/condominium/retail complex will contain some 80 housing units. The project will earn additional rentable space through the provision of other preferred uses, including pedestrian-oriented retail, transient parking, and preservation of a historic structure. The bonus will permit it to soar to 878 feet, nearly 100 feet higher than Boston's John Hancock Tower.

Under Hartford's downtown code, developers may also choose to earn extra density by contributing to a linkage trust fund. (Linkage programs receive closer attention in a later, so-named section of this chapter.) Payment is due from developers at the time of filing for building permits. It is anticipated that the 878-foot mixed-use project referred to above will pay about $400,000 into the trust fund.

The linkage funds need not be spent in the downtown and will likely be used for varied citywide neighborhood improvements, including constructing parks and refurbishing vacant lots, in addition to building affordable housing.

In 1987, the rate of payment into the trust fund was boosted from $5 to $15 for each square foot of bonus floor area. By 1988, no project had yet paid into the fund. The housing trust fund is distinct from the low-income housing fund, made up of contributions collected under Hartford's housing preservation ordinance (HPO).

There appears to be a market for luxury downtown housing. But many developers are waiting to see whether the 500 high-end residential units slated to come on line in the downtown and its peripheries in the next several years will be readily absorbed. No market-rate units have been built in this central area since the 1970s.

Only one project has been approved to use the visitor- and convention-related housing bonus. The latter will be used to generate a density gain for a 316,000-square feet, 30-story speculative mixed-use/office project with a connecting 27-story luxury hotel.

Because the downtown zoning ordinance offers a generous selection of bonus features, developers need not rely on housing bonuses to earn increased density. The housing bonus ratio, at 1 to 8, is greater than that offered for any other amenity but is still insufficient to outweigh the perceived economic risk. Since the Downtown Development District was implemented in 1984, the downtown will have gained 3.4 million square feet of commercial, 186,000 square feet of residential, and 130,775 square feet of hotel space. Although the bonus obligation may be met entirely through high-end housing, developers hesitate to build more units in an area that will soon be supporting some 500 luxury condominiums and rentals, until the resulting market has been tested.

Disappointed with the lack of production under the incentive approach and concerned that prime residential sites might be taken for office projects, the city passed a mandatory housing overlay in 1987 to preserve key residential sites within the CBD. Meanwhile, for more than four years, the city council has wrestled with various proposals for a mandatory office/housing linkage system; none has yet been adopted.

ORLANDO

Orlando's downtown code contains a separate bonus category for mixed-use development. Developers may choose from these categories of uses: multi-family dwellings, office, light retailing/personal services, eating and drinking establishments, hotels/motels, entertainment services, and public benefit uses. To qualify for a bonus, a project must contain at least three of the above uses. (See Insert 1 for code language.) Downtown developers have in fact chosen to use other amenity options rather than build multi-family dwellings.

Insert 1.
Orlando's Mixed-Use Bonus
(code extract)

Section 58.2223. . . .
Bonuses for mixed-use development shall be awarded only where the following standards are met:

Bonuses Available
For the first two use categories
  from the list below which are included
  in the development . . . . No Bonus
For each use category after the second . . . . 1.0 FAR
Maximum FAR available under this bonus . . . . 3.5 FAR

Eligible Use Categories —To be awarded the bonuses available for mixed-use development, the development must include uses from the following list of categories. The uses from each category must total at least the percentage shown at right of [the] net floor area of the entire development:

(a)	Multifamily Dwellings	10.0%
(b)	Offices	10.0%
(c)	Light Retailing/Personal Services	5.0%
(d)	Eating and Drinking Establishments	1.0%
(e)	Hotels/Motels	10.0%
(f)	Entertainment Services	1.0%
(g)	Public Benefit Uses	2.5%

Section 58.2224. *Housing in a Mixed-Use Development*

NOTE: This bonus is only available for a development also qualifying for the mixed-use development bonus.

Bonuses Available

For at least 40 percent of gross floor area
    devoted to multifamily dwellings . . . . 0.30 FAR
For each additional 10 percent of gross floor area . . . . . 0.15 FAR
Maximum FAR available under this bonus . . . . 0.75 FAR

Morever, the city awards an intensity bonus of 0.5 FAR for moderate-cost housing, with the requirement that at least 2 percent of the total construction costs be contributed to the city's low-income housing trust fund. Alternatively, developers may provide a proportionate number of low-rent units on site. Although no developer has opted to use the bonus in the downtown, it has been used in other parts of the city.

PORTLAND, OREGON

Portland resisted using the incentive zoning approach until 1988, which saw the passage of the Central City Plan. The earlier downtown ordinance, however, did contain a single density bonus for residential development. In place since 1979, the provision, which grants additional floor area for housing at an FAR rate of but 2 to 1, has been used only once.

The residential density bonus enacted under the Central City Plan, which covers the CBD and not just the downtown, uses a ratio of 3 to 1 and applies to all commercial and light-industrial areas (see Insert 2). To preserve a site's full potential for nonresidential development, the space allocated to housing is not calculated into the total FAR, so that in effect there is a double bonus. Also, to encourage use of the bonus in the near future, the ratio is more generous for those projects with residential components built within the first 10 years of the plan than it is for those built in the second decade.

Insert 2.
Portland: The Housing Bonus
(code extract)

[Section] 33.702.060. . . .
1. **Residential Bonus Provision.** Projects in the Central City Plan District in CX and CE Zones will receive bonus floor area of up to an additional floor/area ratio of 3:1 if they include residential use. Projects which include housing built under building permits issued prior to July 1, 1998, may commit up to two-thirds of bonus floor area to nonresidential uses. Projects built based on building permits issued after July 1, 1998, may commit up to one-half of their bonus floor area built to nonresidential uses. Residential portions of mixed-use projects receiving this bonus must be completed and receive a certificate of occupancy at the same time, or before, a certificate of occupancy is received for any nonresidential portion of the project. Future continuation and maintenance of the residential development provided to qualify for this bonus must be assured by the property owner executing a covenant with the city in conformance with the requirements of Section 33.702.090 of this chapter.

The city has targeted use of the bonus on more than 15 acres of the CBD. Projects within these targeted areas must exercise the housing bonus option before taking advantage of the other eight bonus selections. As well as density increases, the city also offers height bonuses, which in the case of housing may amount to as much as a 75-foot increment beyond prevailing height limits.

INCLUSIONARY HOUSING

Inclusionary housing programs—first used in the suburbs as a means of combatting exclusionary zoning practices—attempt to integrate residential neighborhoods socially and economically. Although labeled "inclusionary," most such programs, which may be required or incentive-based, permit the production obligation to be met on or off the site.

SEATTLE

Within the downtown, "at least 10 percent of the units in new structures containing 20 dwelling units shall be maintained as affordable housing." The affordability requirement, however, has not been enforced beyond initial sale or rental. Although the city is considering raising the percentage, the legal status of the inclusionary provision apparently is vague, and there is some concern that changes to the present innocuous requirement may provoke legal challenges.

NEW YORK

New York City's inclusionary housing program, passed in 1987, permits up to a 20 percent increase in allowable FAR for market-rate residential buildings in exchange for the purchase of air rights for lower-cost housing. Intended to promote economic integration and diversity in dense residential neighborhoods (with FARs of 10) on the Upper West and East Sides, the bonus may only be used within defined boundaries. The market-rate housing must be built within the confines of the community district containing the low-income housing. If put up in a nearby district, the market-rate units may be no farther than a half-mile away from the low-income units. Before the bonus may be acted on, a certificate of occupancy must first be issued for the low-income housing. Generally, the latter must be managed by a qualified not-for-profit organization (see Insert 3). Because the program permits a geographic radius of one-half mile, some commentators question whether the goal is to achieve integrated housing or just to stimulate housing production.[4]

Insert 3.
New York on Inclusionary Housing
(code extract)[1]

23-91
General Provisions

In the district indicated, an inclusionary housing program is established to preserve and to promote a mixture of low- to upper-income housing within neighborhoods experiencing a shift from mixed- to upper-income housing and thus to promote the general welfare.

. . .

23-92 (cont'd.)
Lower-Income Household

A "lower-income household" is a *family* having an income equal to or less than the income limits (the "80 percent of SMSA limits") for New York City residents established by the U.S. Department of Housing and Urban Development pursuant to Section 3 (b)(2) of the United States Housing Act of 1937, as amended, for lower-income families receiving housing assistance payments.

Lower-Income Housing

"Lower-income housing" [is] *standard units* occupied or to be occupied by *lower-income households*. *Lower-income housing* shall not include *standard units* assisted under city, state, or federal programs, except where such assistance is in the form of:

(a) real estate tax abatements and exemptions which are specifically limited to the *lower-income housing*, or

(b) operating assistance that the commissioner of the department of housing preservation and development determines will be used to enable households with incomes of not more than 62.5 percent of the "80 percent of SMSA limits" to afford such *lower-income housing*.

Lower-Income Housing Plan

The "lower-income housing plan" is the plan accepted by the commissioner of housing preservation and development which sets forth the developer's plans for creating and maintaining the specified *lower-income housing* pursuant to this program, including, but not limited to, choice of *administering agent*, tenant selection, rent levels in the *lower-income housing*, and income verification of tenants pursuant to Subsections (b), (c), and (d) of Section 23-94 of this resolution.

23-93
Floor Area Compensation

The *floor/area ratio* of a *development* may be increased from 10.0 to a maximum of 12.0 at the rate set forth below, if the developer of such *development* provides *lower-income housing* pursuant to Section 23-94 (Lower-Income Housing Requirements).

For each square foot of *floor area* provided for *lower-income housing* pursuant to the options listed in Column A and which meets the requirements set forth in Section 23-94 (Lower-Income Housing Requirements), the *floor area* of the *development* may be increased by the number of square feet set forth in Column B.

Options

Column A	Column B
On-Site New Construction	3.7
On-Site Substantial Rehabilitation	3.2
Off-Site New Construction (Private Site)	4.0
Off-Site New Construction (Public Site)*	2.5
Off-Site Substantial Rehabilitation (Private Site)	3.7
Off-Site Substantial Rehabilitation (Public Site)*	2.2
Preservation	2.0

*Public sites are those made available for this program by a public agency at nominal cost.

Each structure erected and recorded as a separate *building* at the department of buildings as of January 1, 1987, may be considered individually in determining if *lower-income housing* provided pursuant to this program shall be considered as substantial rehabilitation or preservation.

. . .

23-943 (cont'd.)

(b) Rent charged to *lower-income households* shall not be increased to reflect the costs of any renovation made in order to qualify such units under the inclusionary housing program, even though such increases may be permitted under other laws regulating maximum rent levels in these units.

(c) The commissioner of housing preservation and development may require any improvements to that *building* or to the housing necessary to ensure that, with normal maintenance, the *lower-income housing* will continue to provide a decent, safe, and sanitary living environment for the life of the increased *floor area* in the *compensated development*.

(d) The *lower-income housing* shall be maintained and leased to lower-income households for the life of the increased *floor area* in the *compensated development*.

(e) The developer of a *compensated development* must demonstrate to the satisfaction of the commissioner of housing preservation and development that, for three years prior to the submission of the *lower-income housing plan,* no harassment occurred that resulted in removal of previous tenants of units proposed to become *lower-income housing* preserved pursuant to this section.

---

[1] In New York inserts, all italics are original.

"Normally, an arcane land use regulation that tries to generate housing for the poor at no easily discernible public cost might be expected to languish as an unused option in zoning law," writes *New York Times* reporter Alan S. Oser.[5] Expectations, however, are not so low for New York's inclusionary incentive, which is predicted to produce an eventual 200 to 300 units of low-income housing per year.

In certain parts of the city, such as the Upper West Side, where bonuses for plazas and arcades have been eliminated, the inclusionary housing bonus is the only way to reap a 20 percent as-of-right increase. In places where alternatives are still available, the inclusionary bonus may still be attractive: It allows developers to maximize valuable ground-floor space for high-rent retail, for example, rather than give up the space for a plaza.

The density boost is greater for new construction than for preservation of existing stock, so it is unsurprising that all the low-income housing projects are newly built. Still in its infancy, the program has resulted in some 60 new units in three buildings, with an additional 101 units in two buildings under negotiation.

OFFICE/HOUSING LINKAGE PROGRAMS

Whereas inclusionary zoning attempts to socially integrate uses that are mainly residential, linkage policies essentially allocate the responsibility for supplying housing. "Linkage, or linked development, is a policy that taps a currently burgeoning type of land use, such as commercial development, in order to finance the construction of housing or to promote some other social need, such as job training or employment." [6]

Housing density bonuses may be implemented through the technique of office/housing linkages. Under this system, commercial developers have the options of contributing a fee for the production of housing, usually low- and moderate-income, or of erecting the units themselves. Additional density is typically earned in one of three ways—by constructing the housing units on or off site, by forming a partnership with a residential developer to build the housing, or by giving to a housing trust fund. Various permutations of office/housing linkages have been enacted throughout the country, in such cities as Boston, San Francisco, Palo Alto, Hartford, Seattle, Santa Monica, Jersey City, and more recently Menlo Park, California, and Cambridge, Massachusetts. (See Insert 4, next page, for table.)

The rationale for San Francisco's first Office/Housing Production Program (OHPP), adopted in 1980 and the prototype for many later systems, was that "growth in downtown office space draws new employees whose housing needs alter the housing market, thus creating problems for lower-income families. Hence the 'link' between new offices and more housing." [7]

Linkages may be voluntary or mandatory. In Hartford and Seattle, for instance, the voluntary linkage option is one of several available through the incentive zoning program in each city. Miami and Cambridge have enacted linkagelike systems that are incentive-based. In sharp contrast, in Boston and San Francisco, developers must provide affordable housing for the mere privilege of building major projects. The triggering mechanism for Boston's linkage program is application for some form of zoning relief. Arguably, then, the program is incentive-based and not an exaction. Nonetheless, almost every major development proposed for downtown Boston calls for some form of zoning relief, so that the linkage provision is virtually unavoidable. Whereas San Francisco's requirement is limited to office structures, Boston's linkage obligation applies to hotels, retail projects, and institutional buildings as well as office towers.

Although linkage programs generally revolve around the office/housing nexus, some also entail job training. Boston's program, for example, earmarks $1 out of the $6 linkage fee for job training. Since 1986, when the job training fee was created, nearly $300,-000 has been committed, and $1.1 million more is anticipated. Developers may elect to contribute to a jobs trust fund or to offer an on-site job training program that employs low- and moderate-income workers.

San Francisco and Boston have the two most active linkage programs in the country.

SAN FRANCISCO

San Francisco's 1980 pioneer program, which first looked to the California Environmental Quality Act (CEQA) for authorization, was technically an impact mitigation measure. Originally called the Office/Housing Production Program, or OHPP, this earlier system involved no explicit affordability requirement. In 1985, the city enacted the Office/Affordable Housing Production Program (OAHPP), which requires that 62 percent of the units be affordable.

Between 1985 and 1989, the housing fee, which affects projects of 50,000 square feet or more, has risen from $5.34 per square foot of office space to $5.78, to cover construction cost increases. Most contributions are in the form of payments to housing organizations that sponsor construction. Only about $4 million has been contributed directly to the city's housing trust fund, $3 million of which has been spent.

As of 1988, contributions had assisted the production of more than 5,690 housing units—4,026 newly constructed and 1,664 rehabilitated. These contributions are generally packaged with monies from federal and other housing programs. The 11 office

Insert 4.
Housing Linkage Programs[1,2]

City	Date Adopted	Area and Uses to which Applicable	Fee Requirement (or equivalent production commitment)	Results to 1988[3]
Palo Alto, California	1979	All buildings over 20,000 square feet	$2.69/square foot over 20,000 square feet (mandatory)	Payment of $2.4 million, which has assisted production of 200 units
San Francisco, California	1980	Downtown office buildings over 50,000 square feet	$5.69/square foot over 50,000 square feet (mandatory)	Commitments of $29.7 million, which has assisted production of 4,026 new units and 1,664 rehabilitated units
Boston, Massachusetts	1983	Office, retail, institutional buildings over 100,000 square feet anywhere in city	$5.00/square foot over 100,000 square feet, paid over seven years if in downtown, 12 years if in neighborhood (mandatory)	Commitments of $45 million, which has assisted production of over 2,000 units
Jersey City, New Jersey	1985	All commercial buildings	About one unit for each 2,595 square feet (based on formula) (mandatory)	Commitments of $9 million and direct development of 704 units
Santa Monica, California	1986	All office buildings over 15,000 square feet	$2.25/square foot up to 15,000 square feet, and $5.00/square foot over 15,000 square feet (mandatory)	Commitment of $400,000, plus production of about 150 units negotiated prior to present program
Menlo Park, California	1988	All commercial buildings over 10,000 square feet	$1.33/square foot over 10,000 square feet, or (for lower-intensity uses) $0.53/square foot (mandatory)	None
Cambridge, Massachusetts	1988	All buildings developed under special permits in three defined districts	$2.00/square foot over 30,000 square feet	None
Miami, Florida	1983	Office buildings in defined downtown districts	Optional zoning density bonus: $4.00 per bonus square foot	Contributions of $700,000, unexpended
Seattle, Washington	1984	Downtown office buildings	Optional zoning density bonus: $15.30 per bonus square foot in core, $10.00 in expansion district	Production of 274 units
Hartford, Connecticut	1984	Downtown commercial buildings	Optional zoning density bonus: $15.00 per bonus square foot	Commitment of $400,000 and direct development of 90 units

[1]Excluding inclusionary housing requirements for residential buildings.
[2]According to a ULI survey, August–September 1988.
[3]To August 1988.
Source: *Urban Land* (December 1988).

developments approved since passage of the 1985 ordinance have accrued a total housing obligation of 1,098.9 units.

Proposition M's imposition of a stricter office building cap in 1986 effectively limited housing linkage contributions to about $2.5 million per year. (See Chapter 4, "Design Review Overdose, San Francisco–Style.") Furthermore, the "beauty contest" necessi-

tated by the cap, combined with the soft office market, has slowed office building approvals in recent years. In the 1989 round of the beauty contest, office sponsors evidently decided that submitting a specific housing mitigation plan might help them in the selection process: each of the four competing developers opted to enter into an agreement with a housing sponsor rather than pay directly into the city fund.

BOSTON

Boston's linkage program shows no such signs of slowing down. As of January 1989, 37 office, retail, and institutional projects had generated commitments to make almost $47 million in housing linkage payments. Over $24 million of this amount has been paid to assist the construction or rehabilitation of 2,355 housing units in 27 affordable housing projects. Eighty-four percent of these units will be in the affordable price or rent range.

Boston's program demands that downtown developers pay a housing fee of $5 per square foot of space over 100,000 square feet, over a seven-year period. The fee may be paid over 12 years if the project is outside the downtown. As in San Francisco, most developers elect to make payments directly to housing sponsors; only $3 million has been paid into the city's housing trust fund. The trust has awarded $2.9 million in cash grants and loans to nine applicants to build 250 housing units, of which 222 (89 percent) will be in the affordable price range.

In one application of Boston's linkage program, the Beacon Companies and Equitable Real Estate, developers of the recently opened mixed-use project Rowes Wharf, are contributing over $1.9 million in housing linkage funds to the Tenants Development Corporation, Projects III and IV, which involve 94 housing units of which 62 (66 percent) are affordable.

LINKAGES ASSESSED

Although Boston targets a percentage of its housing and job training obligation at those neighborhoods adjoining an office project or at their residents, the execution of the housing obligation in most linkage systems is not confined to the downtown but permitted throughout the city. On the theory that downtown growth often burdens the housing and infrastructure capacities of less affluent portions of a city, linkage programs attempt in part to harness some of the economic prosperity pouring into the downtown and funnel it to needier sectors. Therefore, another link in the office/housing nexus is the connection between downtowns and residential neighborhoods.

As ULI's development policy director, Douglas Porter, observes,

> proponents of downtown linkage programs argue that the development of new commercial space creates housing shortages, especially for low- and moderate-income residents. The housing needs of employees occupying the new space, goes the rationale, contribute to housing cost increases and to the conversion of lower-cost housing, both of which decrease the supply of housing available for low- and moderate-income residents. To mitigate this negative impact, therefore, developers should contribute to programs that produce such housing. This is the jobs/housing link that is used to justify such programs. [8]

Linkage critics, however, find this argument specious. San Francisco economist Claude Gruen notes that "[a]dditions to the supply of office space do not create office employment any more than cribs make babies." [9] These critics claim that employment growth stimulates housing demand, and office buildings merely accommodate this growth. In other words, changes in housing markets are caused by city and regional employment growth, not by office construction. This is why many developers believe that "housing problems are a citywide, if not a regional, phenomenon for which all residents and taxpayers should take responsibility." [10]

Finally, one effective method for easing the potential financial burden of linkage requirements is to allow contributions to be phased over a period of time, rather than paid in a lump sum when the building permit is issued. Boston's linkage fees, for instance, are phased over a seven-year or 12-year period, depending on the locale of the project. And at $6 per square foot paid over seven years (the housing/job training linkage fee paid by downtown developers), the rents are raised by only 1 or 2 percent, a minimal increase in a thriving market. [11]

TDRs

Another zoning tool that helps support the construction and rehabilitation of downtown housing stock is the use of air rights transfers called TDRs. TDRs have also been designed to encourage several other goals, ranging from the protection of agricultural land, coastal mountain ranges, forests, and wetlands to the preservation of historic landmark structures and cultural institutions. The transfers are based on a system of compensating owners for the difference between the value of their property as a resource and its speculative value for development. [12]

The forerunner of TDRs is the so-called zoning lot, in which the transfer area is confined to a single city block. As the system works in New York City, individual parcels on the same block that are contiguous for at least 10 feet may be merged into a single zoning lot through a declaration of single-lot status filed by parties holding interests in the adjacent parcels. Structures below the FAR limit may use these as-of-right zoning-lot mergers to transfer unused FAR allowances to vacant parcels in the same block for new development.

In New York City, zoning-lot mergers have been used primarily to reap additional density for skyscrapers. But Seattle's downtown code limits "combined-lot development," whereby lots with lot lines within 400 feet of each other may be merged with projects involving infill development or containing retail or affordable housing. (See Insert 5.)

Insert 5.
Seattle: Combined-Lot Development as Incentive (code extract)[1]

The Seattle Municipal Land Use Code, 23.49.130 Combined-Lot Development, allows lots with lot lines within 400 feet of each other to be combined for the purpose of calculating the permitted gross floor area, *when projects include affordable housing*. Affordable housing is defined as follows:

1. In a condominium or cooperative project, initial sales price must be established such that buyers pay no more than 30 percent of 150 percent of the SMSA median household income for all housing costs (including maintenance fees and utilities).
2. In rental projects, rents (including utilities costs) must remain at or below 30 percent of 150 percent of area median income for one year after the first tenant occupies the unit.
3. To qualify for this provision, the combined-lot development must include a minimum of 1 FAR of affordable housing. Buildings containing affordable housing must have a minimum of 50 percent of the building floor area in affordable housing use.

[1] Italics imposed for clarity.

In the late 1960s, New York amended its zoning code to permit air rights transfers from locally designated landmark buildings to lots adjacent to one another within the same block, lots across the street from each other, or lots diagonally across an intersection from each other. These more flexible types of density transfers have come to be known as TDRs.

TDR programs work by shifting a part of the "bundle of rights" for a particular parcel to another piece of property. This transfer of future development potential from one property location (the "sending site") to another (the "receiving site") is generally calculated in terms of floor area. Once the transfer is made, legal restrictions prohibit the sending site from developing the unused air rights at a later date.

The unused air rights potential is typically calculated by subtracting the density of the existing structure (the one on the sending site) from the maximum base FAR permitted within that sector. For example, a historic structure with an FAR of 3, located in a 10 FAR zone, would have potential unused density rights to the tune of 7 FAR.

New York City's air rights inclusionary system for low-income housing (discussed earlier in this chapter) diverges from this rule of calculation. Here, the density increase is not indexed to the potential FAR of the sending lot. Instead, the air rights purchased for low-income housing may earn only a 20 percent density increase, so that, in this sense, they function more like density bonuses.

Most cities steer the density transfers to designated spots targeted for growth by limiting the allowable transfer sites to specific sectors. Much of the remainder of this chapter will describe the use of TDRs in several downtowns to boost residential development, particularly that of low- and moderate-income housing.

PITTSBURGH

Pittsburgh's zoning provides TDRs in two situations. When housing will be constructed on the receiving site, development rights may be transferred from any site in the Golden Triangle (the downtown). Otherwise, development rights may be transferred only from adjacent sites that now contain either historic structures or not-for-profit performing arts facilities. To date, development rights have been purchased and transferred from two theaters, but the TDRs for housing have not yet been used.

PORTLAND

Portland, Oregon's 1988 Central City Plan offers TDRs to encourage the preservation and maintenance of single-room-occupancy (SRO) housing. An SRO typically consists of a series of rooms that have access to shared kitchens and bathrooms. Existing or new SRO housing facilities may sell or otherwise transfer surplus development rights under the following conditions:

- The facility must be in good condition or be brought up to code standards;
- The SRO housing must be the primary use on the site;
- At least 60 percent of the SRO must be devoted to residential uses;
- The structure or structures must be maintained into the future; and
- If the housing is later removed, it must be replaced on the same site or elsewhere within the Central City before any new development may be occupied. (See Insert 6.)

Insert 6.
TDRs involving SROs in Portland (code extract)

33.702.030 Use Restrictions. Within the Central City Plan District there are additional restrictions which modify the uses allowed in the base zones. These restrictions are:

...

C. **Limitation on SRO Housing and Shelter Beds**. Within the North of Burnside District, the number of SRO housing units and shelter beds [is] limited. The boundaries of the North of Burnside District are shown on Supplemental Zoning Map A, located at the back of this chapter.

1. The maximum number of permanent shelter beds that may exist in this district is 252.
2. The maximum combined number of SRO housing units plus permanent shelter beds that may exist in this district is 1,282.
3. If all existing or potential permanent shelter beds are replaced by SRO housing units, the maximum number of SRO housing units that may exist in the district is 1,282. One SRO unit may be added for each shelter bed eliminated.

...

33.702.070 SRO Housing Transfer [of] Development Rights Provisions.

A. **Purpose**. Transfer of floor area potential from sites occupied by single-room-occupancy housing, SROs, is allowed in order to reduce the market pressure for removal of this needed and hard-to-replace housing.

B. **Qualifying Projects**. Those developments which qualify are vacant, existing, and new single-room-occupancy housing (SROs) located in a CX or CE Zone.

C. **Procedure**. Qualifying developments may transfer their surplus floor area potential to other sites in the Central City through a Type II procedure assigned to the hearings officer.

D. **Approval Criteria**. To be approved, the proposal must meet all the following:

1. The SRO housing structure is in good repair at the time of the transfer application, or is brought into a state of good repair as part of the development proposal to which floor area is being transferred. In the case of new construction, SRO housing will be built as part of the development proposal to which floor area is being transferred;
2. At least 60 percent of the SRO housing structure is used for housing;
3. Use of the SRO structure, from which floor area is transferred, will be predominantly for provision of SRO housing;
4. In the event that the SRO housing structure is removed, the number of SRO housing units lost will be replaced either on the site or at another location in the Central City. When replacement SRO units are provided, they must receive an occupancy permit at the same time or in advance of issuance of any occupancy permit for a new building on the former SRO housing site; [and]
5. The property owner executes covenants with the city which are attached to and recorded with the deed of both the site transferring and the site receiving the transfer of floor area, reflecting the respective increase and decrease of potential floor area and assuring future continuation and maintenance of the SRO housing [as required] . . .

E. **Limit on Transfers of FAR**. The maximum floor area increase achievable through the use of development rights transfers is established by Section 33.702.050, Subsection C.

SEATTLE

The city's TDR program is encompassed in the overall incentive zoning system. The program is tiered so that, in order to develop a project with an FAR between 15 and 20, a developer has no choice but to buy TDRs or density bonuses for the construction and/or rehabilitation of moderate- and low-income housing. (Development in the office core typically goes in at FARs of 17 and 18.) The amount of the potential development rights available for transfer is the difference between the existing floor/area ratio and the base FAR for that zone.

Housing TDRs are reserved exclusively for the preservation of low- and moderate-income housing. At least 50 percent of the floor area of a renovated project must serve low-income renters, those households earning less than 50 percent of the area median income. In addition, the seller must ensure that the building on the sending site will be rehabilitated to code standards and maintained for 20 years. Moreover, if 100 percent of the units on the sending site were low-incomes as of January 1, 1983, the rehabilitated structure must continue serving low-income households for a minimum of 20 years, an undertaking that calls for heavy subsidies.

Most of the downtown sectors contain eligible sending sites, although the receiving sites are limited to the office core and the mixed/commercial sector next to the Denny Regrade. Housing rehabilitation under the TDR obligation must be completed within one year from the time the air rights are purchased. In turn, the office developer has up to three years from the time construction begins to transfer the TDR credits to the commercial receiving site.

Seattle's code also provides TDRs to preserve Seattle landmarks and to spur compatible infill development within historic districts, as well as in the office sectors. While no transfers have yet been made from landmark structures since the program was enacted in 1985, several transfers have been made from low-income housing facilities.

Most of the 274 housing units newly built or rehabilitated in the downtown as a result of the city's zoning incentives for housing were achieved through TDR contributions. Of the approximately 173 moderate- and low-income units preserved through TDRs, roughly 155 are attributable to the Washington Mutual Tower, the only building that has been completed under the 1985 ordinance. Developer Wright Runstad & Company donated roughly $548,000 in TDRs, or $9.60 per gross commercial square foot. Low-rent housing produced through TDRs, like that produced through office/housing linkage programs, is heavily leveraged with supplemental private financing and public subsidy programs.

Some Seattle observers claim that the flood of vested projects in 1984 was largely responsible for the flat market for TDRs, which in 1987 and 1988 were selling at approximately $8 a square foot (although by 1989, the TDR market had more than doubled). Concerned that low-income housing stock would be lost in the interim while the market was dry, the city founded a TDR bank, seeded with $2.5 million. The bank will purchase development rights from residential buildings and hold them until the market is ripe for future sales to commercial developers.

EVALUATION OF TDR SYSTEMS

The modest success of Seattle's TDR approach is partly attributable to the system's simplicity. Developers need only make direct cash payments to a nonprofit housing group. Thus, they avoid the entanglements of obtaining certificates of approval from the Seattle Landmark Preservation Board or of complying with the federal preservation guidelines, as required for TDRs from historic buildings. Granted, a TDR seller must enter into an agreement to rehabilitate and maintain the structure involved. But making the one-time cash contribution is far less complicated than working with a nonprofit to produce the housing through the alternative density bonus option.

In addition, Seattle's 1985 plan integrates housing TDRs into the multitiered bonus system. In this way, the city virtually ensures that low-income housing will be constructed (through bonuses) or rehabilitated (through TDRs) in exchange for density gains. Under this zoning, developers wanting to build at floor/area ratios of 15 or greater have had no choice but to buy TDRs or produce low-rent housing for bonuses. However, a newly passed initiative has altered this mechanism. It slashes building heights and FAR limits in the downtown, precluding development at 15 FAR or above. This initiative, the citizen-sponsored Citizens Alternative Plan (CAP), discussed in a later section of this chapter, was implemented on June 1, 1989.

Although CAP forbids building at 15 FAR in the downtown, it also greatly lowers the base for housing. Within the densest office sector, Seattle developers must now provide housing if they want to exceed an FAR of 7; beyond an FAR of 10 and up to 14, downtown developers must purchase TDRs for low-income housing. The 1985 zoning had permitted as much as half of the TDR allocation to go toward moderate-income housing. But CAP dictates that the TDRs can now be used only for low-income housing, thus requiring heavier subsidies.

Contrasting with Seattle are those downtowns where the by-right FAR limits are excessively generous or where the code presents many bonus selec-

tions. These cities are preempting their own TDR markets in the receiving zones. Developers, then, may lack the inducement to buy TDRs. Of the approximately 50 jurisdictions with TDR schemes, actual transfers have transpired in no more than a dozen.[13]

New York City's TDR landmarks program is a case in point. Though the program is among the most active in the country, during the 19 years of its existence less than 15 transfers have been made for the more than 700 landmark buildings across the city.[14] The reason is simple: there are easier ways to gain density. The first choice of New York developers is to use the as-of-right zoning-lot merger, which is exempt from review procedures. The second choice is to apply for a higher density classification. Only after these options have been exhausted does a developer seek to buy TDRs and submit to the strenuous review.[15]

At the opposite end of the spectrum, San Francisco expunged density bonuses from its 1985 Downtown Plan and largely replaced them with TDRs. Increased density may only be acquired through the purchase of TDRs for historic buildings or open space, or through the inclusion of housing in downtown commercial buildings. The plan mandates the preservation of 251 "significant" buildings and offers incentives to promote the retention of 183 "contributory" buildings, which have a lesser historic value but still enhance the overall architectural and cultural character of the city.

When designing an incentive system, planning departments must conduct extensive feasibility studies to accurately assess the commercial value of each bonus selection and determine the density ratio assignable to each bonus. Just as a bonus system must correspond to economic reality, so must a TDR program be grounded in the marketplace and reflect economic realities. It may also be necessary to include a monetary increment to overcome initial skepticism or confusion, as well as to offset extra costs associated with participation in the program.

Pricing levels must be continually monitored, and if a TDR bank is used, it must be adequately funded. TDR banks, which help stabilize TDR prices, should be funded at a level high enough to buy and sell at least 25 percent of the development rights transacted.[16]

Another issue revolves around determining the location and size of a city's potential receiving zone or zones. Developers routinely claim that the receiving sites are too limited and that the value of the TDRs would be amply enhanced if transfers were permitted on more sites. On the other hand, the planners, who design the TDR programs, are loath to unleash additional density without adequate controls and seek to channel it into those parts of the city that can best accommodate the growth.

Should timing be a major factor in TDR regulations? Opinions differ. In Seattle, rehabilitation of low-rent residential structures must be completed within one year of the purchase of air rights; construction of new housing by an office developer must not take more than three years or the developer cannot apply TDR credits to a commercial receiving site. TDRs in San Francisco, though, have no timing requirement. Air rights need not be transferred from sending to receiving parcel at the time of purchase but may instead "float" unattached until the development rights are exercised.

From an economic-development viewpoint, the most important piece of property within a TDR system is not the resource to be protected but the receiving site. This is the property that benefits from the density increase. The success of the system ultimately depends on the potential development opportunities on the receiving sites. For example, if the receiving zones are already built up, so that it is nearly impossible to assemble large enough parcels to absorb any greater density, or alternatively if the zones are unattractive economically or inappropriate for large-scale projects, the system will not work. Richard Roddewig characterizes TDR programs in such situations as "constitutional 'eyewash,' the minimum scheme[s] necessary to provide the appearance of compensation to property owners and protected areas with no serious design to ensure that the program [will] work." [17]

CASE STUDY: SEATTLE'S HOUSING INCENTIVE PROGRAM

In the early 1980s, Mayor Charles Royer proposed a mandatory linkage approach to downtown housing growth. The Seattle business community adamantly opposed the idea, and the housing obligation was instead treated as a voluntary option within the 1985 incentive zoning system.

From the start, an inherent tension within the city's housing policy has surrounded the question of whether to favor middle-income or low-rent residential opportunities. The final goal is to reach a population of 40,000 downtown residents, with 25,000 already achieved by the year 2000. When the downtown zoning was being formulated, most downtown housing units were either high-end condominiums or low-end rentals, and the city fathers did not want to worsen this bimodal split. The Royer administration, therefore, was firmly committed to promoting the development of mixed-income downtown residential neighborhoods, with a special emphasis on middle-income housing.

On the other hand, the city's powerful housing lobby aimed to direct all efforts toward retaining low-income housing stock. According to one set of calculations, some 17,000 housing units were lost between 1960 and 1986. Many of these were low-rent accommodations, so that by 1985, only 7,311 low-income units remained in the downtown. (Some of this loss, of course, can be ascribed to rent increases rather than to demolition.)

The city's 1985 incentive housing program attempts to address both concerns and encourages construction of both middle-income and affordable housing through the use of housing density bonuses. It also fosters the preservation of the remaining low-income units via the transfer of development rights.

Unlike most other incentive programs, which treat housing as but one of many bonus alternatives, Seattle's hierarchical system is weighted so that, to exceed an FAR of 7 within the most concentrated commercial core, developers must either build or contribute money toward downtown housing. (Interested readers may refer to Chapter 1, "Incentive Zoning," for further details on Seattle's zoning system.)

Developers are offered density bonuses in return for cash contributions to the state's housing finance commission or for actual construction of new housing units, rehabilitation of vacant units, or purchase of development rights from occupied low-income units (see Insert 7). Although a cash-contribution option exists, the weighted bonus system comes down in favor of production and rehabilitation, and these alternatives cost developers roughly 30 percent less than making cash payments. As a result, no money has been paid to the state.

Insert 7.
Seattle's TDR Housing Program

Example:

A hotel is proposed in the DOC 2 [office core] which will require 36,000 square feet of housing bonus above the intermediate FAR. The owner of an apartment building who rents to low-income tenants (incomes less than 50 percent of area median) needs to rehabilitate his building.

The building is located in the DOC 2 Zone. The owner agrees to maintain the housing as low-income housing for 20 years, in accordance with the transfer of development rights [TDR] housing program guidelines. The building has a developed floor area of 23,000 square feet. The amount of development rights available for transfer is the difference between the developed floor area and the base FAR of 8 in the DOC 2. There are 34,000 square feet of development rights which could be transferred. The commercial-building owner and the housing owner negotiate a sale price which will finance needed rehabilitation and a maintenance reserve.

The hotel developer uses the cash option of the housing bonus program to satisfy the remaining obligation of 2,000 square feet.

Calculation: Commercial x Bonus Value = Cash Contribution
2,000 sq. ft. x $10.00/sq. ft. = $20,000

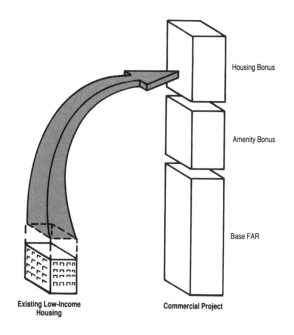

Source: City of Seattle Department of Community Development.

PERFORMANCE OPTION

The primary purpose of the 1985 housing bonus program is to encourage the addition of moderate-income housing units to the downtown. "Moderate-income" households are those with incomes less than or equal to 150 percent of the region's median income; in 1987, the median income for a single-person household in Seattle was $25,100.

The ratios for the bonus credits are partly determined by the income levels of the renters. The lower the income, the higher the subsidy. New construction and substantial renovation serving more modest households earn bonus credits at a faster rate than those serving higher income levels. The approved rents must be locked in for a period of 20 years, although certain buyout options are available after 10 years (see Insert 8).

As a matter of policy, the city gives special nurturance to the production of moderately priced units in the downtown mixed/residential sector called the Denny Regrade, where base FARs have been reduced to 5. In this area, the bonus value is $20 per square foot of housing, and the rental rate is locked in for only one year.

After groundbreaking on a commercial project, a developer has two years to meet the performance obligation. If no housing is produced within two years, the city is authorized to assign the developer's letters of credit (put up as security) to the state housing finance commission, which can use the money to fulfill the housing obligation.

Insert 8.
Seattle's Housing Bonus Program:
The Performance Option

Example:
An office developer wants to reach the maximum allowable FAR in the DOC 1 Zone. The amenity bonus has been used to achieve the intermediate FAR. . . . The square [footage] within the building requiring a housing bonus is 142,000.

A housing developer proposes a co-venture involving a low-income new-construction housing project. The project would serve tenants with incomes below 50 percent of the area median and include 32 600-square-foot, one-bedroom units. This project would qualify for a housing bonus ratio of 7.6.

Calculation:
New Housing x Bonus Ratio = Gross Commercial
19,200 net sq. ft. of Low-Income Housing x 7.6 = 145,920 gross sq. ft. Bonus Commercial Space

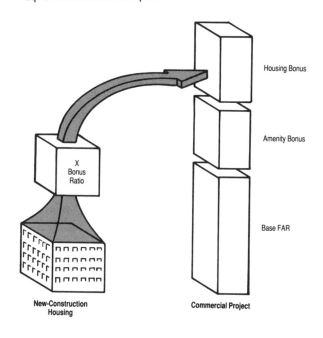

Source: City of Seattle Department of Community Development.

TDRs

Although the TDR option is part of the city's overall housing incentive program, TDRs essentially compete with housing bonuses. (Seattle's TDR program is examined more closely in the section of this chapter devoted to development rights transfers.)

HOUSING PRODUCTION

As of July 1988, some 274 housing units had been built or rehabilitated through Seattle's density bonus program. Most of these units were traceable to the 55-story Washington Mutual Tower. In pursuit of 13.3 extra stories of office space, developer Wright Runstad & Company contributed more than $2.5 million toward the construction of 101 new units in three buildings and the rehabilitation of 155 units. The developer paid a cash fee for the new construction and transferred development rights from three residential buildings to provide the rehabilitation funding. The contribution per commercial square foot came to about $9.60.

A portion of the new construction was financed with density contributions from two office buildings antedating the 1985 code. In one building, one and one-half floors of parking were converted into commercial space, and in the other, the same developer requested additional density to accommodate a 10,000-square-foot ground-floor corner space for a branch bank. This addition displaced some retail space that had earned bonus credits under the old code. Through the bonus modification provision in the 1985 code, the developer was permitted to modify bonused space in the two structures by contributing to the building and renovation of downtown housing units. (For further coverage of Seattle's modification procedure, see Chapter 1, "Incentive Zoning.")

One major criticism of the city's housing incentive program is its insuperable complexity and attendant uncertainty, which extend the application review time as they compound the legal fees. Wright Runstad's participation in the housing bonus program cost between $20,000 and $30,000 in legal fees. Senior Vice President Steve Trainer says that he would make a different choice today regarding the forming of a partnership with a nonprofit to produce new housing. Now, he would choose to fulfill his entire housing obligation through the buying of TDRs. This kind of purchase, as a one-time cash payment, represents the more direct and less cumbersome of the two procedures.

The alternatives available under Seattle's housing bonus program are not mutually exclusive. As illustrated by the Wright Runstad project, developers may meet their housing obligations through a combination of TDR payments and performance. In both instances, the city's department of community development is an advocate for both the commercial developer and the nonprofit builder and often serves as a liaison for both parties. Sometimes, the city issues an RFP for a particular project: Commercial developers may be re-luctant to work with housing nonprofits that have not first secured preliminary approvals of their proposals from the city.

One of the longstanding local housing nonprofits is the Seattle Housing Resources Group (SHRG), formed in 1980 under the leadership of the Downtown Seattle Association to develop, preserve, and rehabilitate low-income housing. The SHRG developed and now manages several of the housing projects built or renovated in part with contributions from the Wright Runstad tower.

EVALUATION AND PROPOSED CHANGES

Because Seattle's housing bonus program is an integral part of its incentive zoning—which mandates housing beyond a certain threshold—the city has had more success in stimulating housing production than many other cities that lack these mechanisms. This success has been furthered by the approximate 30 percent cost difference between housing production and payment into a state-managed fund, a difference that clearly favors performance over payment.

Despite the modest successes of the housing bonus program, however, the system is the subject of vociferous debate and reevaluation. One obvious reason for the lag in downtown housing development is that the rush of recent construction mostly involves commercial projects that secured use permits before the 1985 code: These projects were forced to obtain building permits within two years or risk losing their permit rights; moreover, they bore no housing obligations. Until this surplus office space is largely absorbed, developers are apt to feel cautious about bringing more commercial projects on line, at least in the immediate future. This caution further delays construction of buildings with housing bonus obligations.

A second reason the city is reevaluating its housing program is the rising concern about the loss of low-income housing stock since the state's highest court overturned the city's low-income housing preservation ordinance (HPO) in the 1987 *San Telmo Associates* v. *City of Seattle* decision.[18] Under the HPO, low-income housing owners wishing to demolish their property and replace it with a nonresidential use had to give tenants notice, help them find new housing, and rebuild a percentage of the destroyed units. Alternatively, property owners could pay an impact fee that benefited the city's low-income housing fund.

The court ruled that the municipally imposed impact fee constituted an illegal tax: it placed the burden of maintaining low-income housing on the few property owners with housing on their sites. The decision suggested that the city address the problem through legitimate means, such as rezoning or levying a tax on all city landowners.

Indeed, the overruling of the HPO has focused attention on low-income housing in particular. There is substantial pressure to target more of the housing credits at low-income development. This change, however, would conflict with the original modus operandi of the housing bonus program—that of stimulating a residential mix, strong in the middle-income range, as part of the overall effort to achieve 24-hour activity in the downtown. At the time the 1985 code was enacted, most construction permits for new housing in the downtown were being issued for high-end condominiums. On the other end, a multimillion-dollar levy for low-income housing had also passed in 1985, and some state money was still available for low-cost units. Therefore, the housing incentive system was seen by some factions as needed to fill the gap by encouraging the development of middle-income residential uses.

The present dissent is being voiced clearly by some critics. At the time of this writing, four years after passage of the 1985 code, these critics are asserting that middle-income housing (lodgings for households earning 120 to 150 percent of the median salary, with rents ranging from $800 to $1,000) increasingly is being built in the downtown without the aid of bonuses. Opponents are asking whether the subsidies are still necessary.

Meanwhile, with the passage of CAP, the city has had to completely rethink its housing program. CAP, or the Citizens Alternative Plan, which gleaned some 62 percent of the votes on May 16, 1989, calls for stricter height and density curbs and limits new office space to 500,000 square feet a year for the next five years (with 85,000 square feet set aside for low-rise structures). After this time, the limit will be raised to 1 million square feet annually until 1999. (CAP is examined more extensively in Chapter 1.)

The citizens' plan not only limits FARs in the densest office sector to 14 and heights to 450 feet (approximately 38 stories) but also triggers Seattle's housing obligation sooner. To build beyond an FAR of 7, office developers must participate in the housing or historic preservation program; above an FAR of 10, they have to buy TDRs for low-income housing.

Under CAP, housing bonuses now may be used only for the erection of moderate- and low-income units, with at least 50 percent of the bonus credits reserved for low-income households. Before CAP passed, the city council lowered the income levels that define both moderate- and low-income households.

These adjustments to the housing program depart notably from its earlier goal of stimulating a diverse housing mix in the downtown. Clearly, the recent changes reflect the current perception that public resources should be channeled toward preserving low-rent rather than middle-income housing.

CAP does not actually tinker with the remaining menu of bonus selections. One inevitable effect of the development lid, however, will be to cut down on the number of office projects applying for housing bonus credits, as for any of the other public benefit features. The only major city to fashion a similar office rationing program to the one in Seattle is San Francisco. And this city now suffers from curtailed housing linkage payments, which are effectively capped at $2.5 million a year.

Therefore, the planning office is considering a major revamp of the bonus system and possible elimination of some bonus selections altogether. Also, some open space options, such as those for parcel parks, street parks, rooftop gardens, and hillclimb assists, as well as for daycare and human services, may be mandated instead.

SUMMARY: NEW ZONING FOR HOUSING

The inventory of zoning techniques to stimulate downtown housing—mixed-use districts, overlays, inclusionary zoning, bonuses, linkages, and TDRs—is an ample one. However, many of these tools, particularly the ones that are incentive-based, have proven fairly ineffective. In many cities where commercial space commands much higher rents than residential, optional density bonuses, for example, are insufficient inducements. This has been the experience in Hartford, Cincinnati, Orlando, Portland, and many other cities. One reason Seattle's housing program has been more productive is that under its former incentive system, the housing obligation automatically applied to all buildings exceeding a certain size. Quite simply, Seattle developers planning to build office projects in the range of 15 FAR and above had to participate in the housing program.

Similarly, required linkage systems tend to generate more housing than optional ones. Such mandated approaches, however, are probably appropriate only for cities with healthy real estate markets. Developers invariably note that involuntary linkage exactions in some cities may make the difference between a marketable product and an unprofitable one. They warn that the cancellation of even one project because of the extra costs imposed by linkage could in some circumstances negate the potential gains from such a program. The question is whether the risk is worth the reward.

In 1987, Chicago developer Ralph Guthrie estimated that, over 20 years, a new 750,000-square-foot building in downtown Chicago would bring in some $176 million in state and local revenues, after public service costs and not allowing for inflation. In comparison, the contributions from linkage programs proposed at the time for Chicago were projected at $130 million, far less than the revenues from just one building.[19]

On the other hand, mandatory development fees within hot development markets can offer a positive alternative to growth limits. Faced with mitigating the impacts of a project—the effects on affordable housing, public transit, or child care—developers prefer paying fees to building less or not at all.

The residential production generated by even the most successful systems, however, is a mere pittance tossed at the intractable housing needs of most cities. Clearly, zoning cannot do it all. Whatever zoning tools a city uses to stimulate residential development must be packaged with tax incentives and other subsidies. The selection of zoning tools and other incentive mechanisms depends in part on the precise housing types a city wants to promote—low-rent, middle-income, market-rate, or (preferably) a combination of these.

The less-than-satisfactory results of many zoning tools for spurring housing development are usually more directly related to the market than to the failure of any one mechanism. In many cities, such as Pittsburgh, Portland, and Seattle, downtown housing is competing with attractive, reasonably priced residential neighborhoods lying conveniently near the downtown. The most difficult markets are generally newer cities in which downtown residential neighborhoods have never existed. These cities lack the essential amenities and services—groceries, hardware stores, clothing stores—necessary to support residential uses. Older downtowns can at least build on existing retail and support services. Developers can also renovate and add to existing housing stock, so that they are not operating in a vacuum.

The success of downtown housing, therefore, is closely tied to that of other public initiatives affecting the quality of urban living. Its fate is linked to the availability of neighborhood services, restaurants and other retail uses, entertainment and cultural facilities, adequate transportation, daycare, attractive public spaces, and other vital signs of urban health.

Notes

1. Clifford L. Weaver and Richard F. Babcock, *City Zoning: The Once and Future Frontier* (Chicago: American Planning Association, 1979), p. 120.
2. Statement made at a panel session on special districts at the American Planning Association's 1988 annual meeting in San Antonio.
3. Background history of CR Mixed-Use District provided by Malcolm D. Rivkin's report, *Urban Planning Testimony for Square 24*, prepared for Boston Properties before the District of Columbia Zoning Commission (September 1987), pp. 7–9.
4. Rachelle Alterman says that New York's inclusionary program is aimed at creating housing rather than integrated neighborhoods and perhaps should be called " 'housing-to-housing' linkage." See "Evaluating Linkage and Beyond: Letting the Windfall Recapture Genie Out of the Exactions Bottle," *Washington University Journal of Urban and Contemporary Law*, vol. 34 (1988), p. 17.
5. Alan S. Oser, "New Bonuses Spur Low-Income Units," *New York Times* (March 20, 1988).
6. Alterman, "Evaluating Linkage and Beyond," p. 6.
7. Douglas R. Porter, "The Linkage Issue: Introduction and Summary of Discussion," in *Downtown Linkages*, ed. Douglas Porter (Washington, D.C.: Urban Land Institute, 1985), p. 3.
8. ———, "Pain before Gain: Developers' Views on Housing Linkage Programs," in *Private Supply of Public Services: Evaluation of Real Estate Exactions, Linkage, and Alternative Land Policies*, ed. Rachelle Alterman (New York: New York University Press, 1988), p. 157.
9. Quoted in Alterman, "Evaluating Linkage and Beyond," p. 33.
10. Porter, "Pain before Gain," p. 157.
11. See ibid., p. 155.
12. See Richard J. Roddewig and Cheryl A. Inghram's comprehensive treatment in *Transferable Development Rights Programs*, Planning Advisory Service Report no. 401 (Chicago: American Planning Association, 1987).
13. See ibid., p. 1.
14. As noted in ibid., p. 8.
15. Ibid., p. 8.
16. Ibid., p. 27.
17. Ibid., p. 19.
18. 108 Wash. 2d 20, 735 P. 2d 673 (1987).
19. See Porter, "Pain before Gain," p. 155.

APPENDICES
INDEX

DESIGN REVIEW FOR PARKING GARAGES

Traditionally, building codes have dictated parking structure design. They have focused mainly on such matters as noise and fire protection, and by and large, they have proven totally inadequate to address the special design concerns of the more complicated parking facilities being built in downtowns today. The trend in many cities is to regulate downtown parking structures through zoning and to subject them to design review.

Is it possible to reflect the culture, geology, climate, and social patterns of a particular place in the designs of its parking garages? This was one of the overarching questions raised in a 1987 symposium on the "New Regionalism" held at the University of Texas at Austin. Architect Robert A.M. Stern pointed out that it had been possible in the 19th century to develop appropriate and functional designs for train stations; so, today, must "we . . . stop worrying about parking garages being horrors and consider them, like anything else, as architectural possibilities." [1]

Besides aesthetics, the increased attention to the design of parking garages has arisen in part from economics. Steep downtown land costs no longer justify building mere car containers, let alone surface lots, on prime downtown property. Property owners want more of a return than they can pull in from parking alone. Moreover, garages are no longer separate entities but often form part of mixed-use projects, where one goes not only to park, but also to eat, use a health club, and shop.

For these reasons, some cities favor developers' incorporating retail uses on the first floor of downtown parking structures. Of course, some garage retail uses make more sense than others. Convenience groceries and other food stores, dry cleaners, and photo shops where customers can easily stop on their way to or from work are likelier to succeed than, say, specialty retail or boutiques. On the other hand, forcing any retail uses in garages on the periphery of the downtown core is probably unrealistic.

Land Design/Research, Inc.

Many downtown design plans are hindered by the presence of parking facilities.

One major economic incentive for providing commercial uses within parking facilities has been the availability of tax-exempt bonds for public/private projects. Changes imposed by the Tax Reform Act of 1986, however, make this incentive less compelling, at least in the case of public garages.

An eminently reasonable design concern is that the unrelenting blank walls of the typical parking garage contribute nothing to the downtown streetscape. Indeed, in the central core, they may seriously disrupt retail continuity. Thus, some cities are requiring active uses on the first floors of downtown garages. In Bellevue, Washington, for example, "[i]ncorporating retail shopping space at ground level into parking structures whenever practical and appropriate" is one of the review criteria to be considered by the director of design and development as part of the design review process for the downtown. The city has also composed a simple set of performance standards for the construction of parking structures (see Insert 1).

Insert 1.
Parking Performance Standards in Bellevue
(code extract)

4. . . .The director of design and development may approve a proposal for a parking structure through design review (Part 20.30F). The director of design and development may approve the parking structure only if—

a. Driveway openings are limited, and the number of access lanes in each opening [is] minimized.

b. The structure exhibits a horizontal, rather than sloping, building line.

c. The dimension of the parking structure abutting pedestrian areas is minimized, except where retail, service, or commercial activities are provided.

d. The parking structure complies with the requirements of Section 20.25A.115 [dealing with design guidelines for building/sidewalk relationships].

e. A wall or other screening of sufficient height to screen parked vehicles and which exhibits a visually pleasing character is provided at all above-ground levels of the structure.

f. Safe pedestrian connection between the parking structure and the principal use exists.

g. Loading areas are provided for vanpools/carpools, as required by Paragraph F.3 of this section.

h. Vehicle height clearances for structured parking must be at least 7.5 feet for the entry level, to accommodate vanpool parking.

In Pittsburgh, downtown parking structures must undergo the city's project development plan review and comply with the 14 review criteria, which address such points as access for the handicapped, view protection, and open space. The discretionary review process, understandably, is not nearly as comprehensive for parking garages as for major mixed-use projects. Nonetheless, both public and private parking structures must meet the city's open space zoning provision, which demands that open space amounting to 20 percent of the lot area be provided at ground level.

As part of the PPG Place project (described in the main text of this book), the city remodeled one of its adjacent parking garages to include ground-floor retail and also offered street-level shopping in its new garage near PPG Place. Another project, One Oxford

Center, was also required to build retail uses along two of the four sides of its new parking structure.

In Portland, Oregon, parking garages are subjected to the same development review as all other new construction and major renovations within the Central City. This procedure entails application of the 22 design guidelines. In addition, the obligatory build-to lines in designated areas of the downtown, the required percentage of retail or personal service uses at the street level, and the limits on blank walls are applicable to parking garages, as to other structures. In Portland, design review for public projects is just as comprehensive as for private ones, and indeed this thoroughness is reflected in the animated ground floors of some of the city's downtown public garages.

As part of the overall effort to pique pedestrian interest and preserve streetscape continuity in downtown Charlotte, North Carolina, the entrances to parking garages must follow a consistent and predictable pattern. The only openings allowed at street level are for auto or pedestrian circulation, and retail space is to be built along the rest of the parking deck's frontage, to spur pedestrian activity.

In Orlando, Florida, the criteria vary with the amount of pedestrian traffic on the street where the parking facility stands. For parking garages on pedestrian streets, "[a]t least 75 percent of [ground-floor] parking garage frontage, exclusive of the entrance driveways, shall consist of active uses other than parking, such as offices, retailing, services, entertainment, etc."

Parking garages on secondary pedestrian streets in Orlando must have a "landscaped, pedestrian-oriented setback of at least 20 feet." The setback requirement is waived, however, for any part of the parking garage frontage that offers active ground-floor uses. The code states that this requirement "is intended to create pleasing pedestrian-oriented spaces. Other design alternatives which achieve this intent may be approved by the appropriate reviewing authority." The code also stipulates that the façades of all parking facilities should "achieve architectural unity" with those of principal structures.

In Cincinnati, design review is mandated only for those projects with major parking facilities. Design review is not automatic for other types of development in the downtown but is only triggered in given situations or when a developer voluntarily submits to it. Cincinnati is also one of the few downtowns to award density bonuses for on-site below-grade parking; the bonus space accrues at the rate of 350 square feet per parking space provided.

Unlike Portland, Pittsburgh, or Bellevue, which have passed explicit development review criteria or design guidelines for the downtown as an entity, Cincinnati has no such written design guidelines *except* for parking garages. These guidelines emphasize the façades of parking facilities, which should achieve "a sense of scale, rhythm, and texture" (see Insert 2).

Insert 2.
Cincinnati: Design Review Guidelines for Parking Garages (code extract)

Garages subject to design review pursuant to Section 2405.10 of the Downtown Development, DD, District regulations of the zoning code shall conform to the following guidelines, which shall apply to façades facing any street greater than 50 feet in width or the skywalk:

a) Parked cars shall be screened from public view from every adjacent public way greater than 50 feet in width.

b) Garage entrances and exits shall be designed and located so as to minimize hazards to pedestrians.

c) Façades shall contain openings that, in their scale, size, and placement, are compatible with the same qualities of openings in surrounding buildings.

d) Façades shall contain articulations to achieve a sense of scale, rhythm, and texture.

e) The façade of the ground-level floor shall be differentiated from upper floors to establish the appearance of a base to the building. By way of example, this differentiation can be achieved through the use of several of the following techniques.
   i) A taller ground floor.
   ii) A change in color.
   iii) A change in material.
   iv) A change in detailing.
   v) Banding at the top of the ground floor.
   vi) Other architectural means.

f) The design of façades shall not reveal or imply sloping floor levels that may be behind the façade.

g) Façades shall be compatible with the design, materials, and overall character of surrounding buildings with regard to the scale, color, and texture of materials, form and massing, and design detailing.

Note

1. Michael McCullan, "Garage Mechanics," *Progressive Architecture* (November 1987), p. 106.

BELLEVUE'S FAR AMENITY SYSTEM
(code excerpts)

Section 20.25A.030.C
FAR Amenity Standards

1. Pedestrian-Oriented Frontage

Building frontage devoted to uses which stimulate pedestrian activity. Uses are typically sidewalk-oriented and physically or visually accessible by pedestrians from the sidewalk. Uses which compose pedestrian-oriented frontage include, but are not limited to, specialty retail stores, groceries, drugstores, shoe repair shops, cleaning establishments, floral shops, beauty shops, barber shops, department stores, hardware stores, apparel shops, travel agencies and other services, restaurants, and theaters. Banks and financial institutions are not pedestrian-oriented uses.

Design Criteria

1. Pedestrian-oriented frontage must abut a sidewalk, plaza, or arcade.
2. A pedestrian-oriented use must be physically accessible to the pedestrian at suitable intervals.
3. Pedestrian-oriented uses must be visually accessible to the pedestrian at the sidewalk, plaza, or arcade level. . . .

2. Plaza

A continuous open space which is readily accessible to the public at all times, predominantly open above, and designed specifically for use by people as opposed to serving as a setting for a building.

Design Criteria

1. Must abut and be within three feet in elevation of a pedestrian connection so as to be visually and physically accessible.
2. Must provide protection from adverse wind, wherever practical.
3. At least 10 percent of the plaza surface area must be landscaped.
4. Must provide at least one sitting space for each 100 square feet of plaza.
5. Must be enclosed on at least two sides by a structure or by landscaping which creates a wall effect.
6. Minimum size is 500 square feet in CBD-OB; 1,000 square feet in other land use districts.
7. Maximum size of bonusable plaza square footage is 1,500 square feet in CBD-OB; 5,000 square feet in other land use districts.
8. Minimum horizontal dimension is 20 feet.
9. Must provide opportunities for penetration of sunlight.
10. May not be used for parking, loading, or vehicular access.

3. Landscape Feature

A continuous open space located at or near grade whose principal feature is an unusual and pleasing landscape form. The purpose is to serve as a focal point and a visual landmark, rather than as a specific location for pedestrian activity.

Design Criteria

1. Must abut the intersection of two public rights-of-way or perimeter walkways or sidewalks in order to receive the full bonus available. One-half of the available bonus will be awarded if the landscape feature abuts a right-of-way or pedestrian connection but is not located at an intersection.
2. Maximum area is 1,000 square feet in CBD-O-1, CBD-O-2, CBD-MU , and CBD-OLB, and 500 square feet in CBD-OB. No bonus is awarded if the landscape feature exceeds the maximum size.
3. Must be visually accessible from abutting rights-of-way or walkways or sidewalks.

4. Enclosed Plaza

A publicly accessible, continuous open space located within a building and covered to provide overhead weather protection while admitting substantial amounts of natural daylight (atrium or galleria).

Design Criteria

1. Must be accessible to the public at least during normal business hours.
2. Must be readily accessible from a pedestrian connection.
3. Must be signed to identify the enclosed plaza as available for public use.
4. At least 5 percent of the area must be landscaped.
5. Must provide at least one sitting space for each 100 square feet of area.
6. Must be coordinated with pedestrian-oriented frontage to the maximum extent possible.
7. Minimum horizontal dimension is 20 feet.
8. Minimum area is 750 square feet.

5. Arcade

A continuously covered area which functions as a weather-protected extension of the publicly accessible space which it abuts.

Design Criteria

1. At least 50 percent of the linear frontage must be developed as pedestrian-oriented frontage which complies with the design criteria of this section. This pedestrian-oriented frontage may be counted separately to gain floor/area ratio exceeding the basic FAR through the amenity incentive system.
2. Pavement below must be constructed to provide for drainage.
3. When adjacent to a public walkway or sidewalk, design must provide opportunity for connection to adjacent development across property lines.
4. Must have a horizontal rather than a sloping orientation across the building façade.

5. Must present a coordinated design along its entire route.
6. Must be accessible to pedestrians at all times.
7. Minimum height is eight feet above finished grade.
8. Maximum height is 20 feet above finished grade. No bonus is awarded if the maximum height is exceeded.

6. Marquee

A permanent overhead canopy projecting from the elevation of a building, and designed to provide continuous overhead weather protection to the areas underneath.

Design Criteria
1. Must be developed over a walkway or sidewalk.
2. Pavement below must be constructed to provide for drainage.
3. Must have a horizontal rather than sloping orientation along the building elevation.
4. Design must be coordinated with building design.
5. Minimum height is eight feet above finished grade, except as otherwise required in the uniform building code (BCC 23.10).
6. Maximum height is 12 feet above finished grade. No bonus is given if the marquee exceeds the maximum height.
7. To insure daylight penetration, the ratio of the marquee's projection from the building to its height above finished grade may not exceed 3:4.

7. Awning

A rooflike structure of fabric stretched over a rigid frame projecting from the elevation of a building designed to provide continuous overhead weather protection.

Design Criteria
1. Must be developed over a walkway or sidewalk.
2. Pavement below must be constructed to provide for drainage.
3. Must have a horizontal rather than sloping orientation along the building elevation.
4. Design must be coordinated with building design.
5. Minimum height is eight feet above finished grade.
6. Maximum height is 12 feet above finished grade. No bonus is awarded if the awning exceeds the maximum height.
7. To insure daylight penetration, the ratio of the awning's projection from the building to its height above finished grade may not exceed 3:4.

8. Landscape Area

An outdoor landscaped area providing visually or physically accessible space for tenants of the development of which it is a part.

Design Criteria
1. This area must be in addition to any landscape development required by the land use code.
2. May not be used for parking or storage.
3. May be located at grade or on top of a structure.
4. At least 30 percent of the area must be planted with evergreen plant materials.

9. Active Recreation Area

An area which provides active recreational facilities for tenants of the development of which it is a part.

Design Criteria
1. May not be used for parking or storage.
2. May be located out of doors, on top of, or within a structure.
3. Recreational facilities include but are not limited to racquetball or handball courts or health clubs.

10. Residential Uses[1]

Design Criterion
1. Area devoted to service cores and community facilities may be used to obtain bonus floor area. No area devoted to parking or circulation may be used for this purpose.

11. Underground Parking

Design Criteria
1. The amenity bonus applies only to that structure or portion of a structure located below the average finished grade around a building.
2. Must be covered by a structure or developed open space.

12. Above-Grade Parking Located under Principal-Use Residential Structure[2]

Design Criteria
1. Parking must be enclosed.
2. Exterior surface must be the same material as used on the principal-use building.

13. Public Meeting Rooms

Design Criteria
1. May include fixed-seat auditorium or multipurpose meeting rooms.
2. Must be available for public use, but may operate under a reservation or nominal fee system.
3. Must provide seating for at least 50 persons.

14. Sculpture[3]

Any form of sculpture or other artwork located outside of the building.

Design Criterion
1. Must be displayed near the main pedestrian entrance to a building.

15. Water Feature[4]

A fountain, cascade, stream, water sculpture, or reflection pond. The purpose is to serve as a focal point for pedestrian activity.

Design Criteria
1. Must be located outside of the building and be publicly visible and accessible at the main pedestrian entrance to a building or along a pedestrian connection.
2. Water must be maintained in a clean and noncontaminated condition.
3. Water must be in motion during daylight hours.

16. Major Pedestrian Corridor[5]

The Major Pedestrian Corridor located on or in the immediate vicinity of N.E. 6th Street between 102nd Avenue and 110th Avenue, N.E.

Design Criterion
1. Must comply with the requirements of Section 20.25A. 100.E.1.

17. Child Care Services[6]

A use providing regular care and training for children, generally for less than 24 hours, outside of the immediate family or kindergarten-through-12th-grade education system. . . .

Design Criteria . . .
2. Floor area for this amenity *may* also be counted as pedestrian-oriented frontage. . . .

18. Retail Food[6]

A self-service retail enterprise which sells food, beverages, and household goods for consumption off the premises.

Design Criteria
1. Minimum gross floor area shall be 15,000 square feet.
2. Maximum bonusable area is 30,000 square feet.
3. Floor area for this amenity *may* also be counted as pedestrian-oriented frontage. . . .

19. Public Restrooms[6]

A room or rooms containing toilets and lavatories for the use of the general public, with only limited control for purposes of personal safety.

Design Criteria
1. Shall be located on the ground floor of the building.

2. Shall be open for use by the public during normal business hours, although access may be monitored by a person located at the restroom facility.
3. Shall be handicapped-accessible.
4. Shall be signed to identify its location.

20. Performing Arts Space[6]

Space containing fixed seating for public assembly for the purpose of entertainment or cultural events (live performances only).

Design Criterion

1. This bonus shall apply only to performing arts spaces that are less than 10,000 square feet.

21. Space for Nonprofit Social Services[6]

Space which is made available, rent-free, to charitable and social service organizations which provide emergency assistance, health services, referral services, or other specialized social services directly to the public.

Design Criteria

1. Such space shall principally provide outreach functions rather than administrative functions.
2. Maximum bonusable area is 5,000 square feet.
3. Bonus floor area for this amenity *may* also be counted as pedestrian-oriented frontage. . . .

22. Donation of Park Property

Property which is donated to the city, with no restriction, for park purposes.

Design Criteria

1. The need for such property in the location proposed must be consistent with city-adopted policies and plans.
2. The minimum size of a donated park parcel is 10,000 square feet.
3. Donated park parcels need not be contiguous with the site for which development is proposed.

. . .

[Bellevue's Amenity System: Further Requirements]

E. Transfer of Bonus Floor Area:

1. Where floor area may be transferred:
   Bonus floor area earned through the amenity incentive system for a specific parcel of land may be transferred to any other property within the Core Design District, or to any property in the same ownership which abuts or is across an abutting public right-of-way from property which includes the Major Pedestrian Corridor.

2. Amount of floor area transfer:
   No more than 25 percent of the gross floor area of a proposed project may be transferred floor area. This limitation does not include floor area generated by construction of the Major Pedestrian Corridor or major public open spaces.

3. Recording required:
   The property owner must record each transfer of floor area with the King County Division of Records and Elections and with the Bellevue City Clerk.

4. Notwithstanding any provision of this code, no transfer of floor area occurs when all property is included in one project limit.

---

[1] Excludes hotels and motels.
[2] Parking qualifying for this bonus must serve a residential use. It must be located under a structure which contains a residential use, and all bonus floor area must be devoted to residential use.
[3] Measured in units of $100 of appraised value.
[4] Measured in units of $100 of appraised value, or actual construction cost, whichever is greater.
[5] Bonus floor area may be achieved through the provision of this amenity only in conjunction with a permit to construct the Major Pedestrian Corridor. . . .
[6] Floor area may be excluded from calculation of maximum floor/area ratio.

INDEX

Artwork, public, 39–41, 83–84; visual arts space, 41; water features, 41–42; maintenance issues, 42.

Atlanta, Georgia: skywalk policy, 158.

Austin, Texas: view protection, 99, 102.

Bellevue, Washington: zoning history, 19, 124, 148–149; bonus for human services facilities, 43; administrative design review (ADR), 64–67; "pedestrian-oriented frontage" requirement, 125–127; Bellevue Square, 125–126; Bellevue Place, 126; urban plazas, 136–137; design guidelines for building/sidewalk relationships, 145; Major Pedestrian Corridor, 148–151; Koll Center, 150–151; Rainier Bank Plaza, 151; parking ratios and parking reduction incentives, 164; transportation management program (TMP), 171–173.

Berkeley, California: Elmwood Commercial District, 115; commercial overconcentration and quantitative zoning, 115.

Blank Wall Limits, 141–142. *See also* Transparency Requirements.

Bonus. *See* Incentive Zoning.

Boston, Massachusetts: zoning history, 8; bonus for community service facility, 45; daycare, 47–48; shadow controls, 89; limits on street-level winds, 96–97; housing overlay district, 177–178; linkage, 184.

Build-To Lines, requirements for, 109–110, 143. *See also* Streetscapes and Continuity.

Burlington, Vermont: view protection, 99; incentive for elderly housing, 174.

Caps on Commercial Development: Seattle's Citizens Alternative Plan (CAP), 24–25, 121–122, 191; San Francisco's Proposition M, 71–75.

Centralized Retail Management (CRM), 108.

Charlotte, North Carolina: shadow controls, 89; retail uses, 119–121; open space, 134–135; blank wall limits, 142; design guidelines for parking structures, 145; skywalk policy, 154, 156–157; screening requirements for surface parking lots, 163–164.

Cincinnati, Ohio: zoning history, 8–9; public art, 39; daycare, 45–48; design review, 57; transparency requirement, 143; skywalk policy, 158; demolition permits, 162–163; bus shelter bonus, 168.

Continuity: retail continuity, 109–111; streetscape continuity, 141. *See also* Streetscapes, blank wall limits.

Coral Gables, Florida: Mediterranean Overlay District, 56–57.

Daycare, 45–52; as requirement, 46–48; as incentive, 48–49; regulatory hurdles, 50; in-lieu fee option, 50–51; liability issues, 51; costs and subsidies 52.

Denver, Colorado: view protection, 99, 102.

Design Review, 53–68, 70–76, 82–86; legal considerations, 58–59; evaluation, 58, 67–69, 84–86; street-edge standards, 65, 143–145; costs, 67–68; design guidelines for Bellevue's Main Pedestrian Corridor, 149–150; design guidelines for parking garages, 195–197. Case studies: Pittsburgh, 59–61; Portland, Ore., 61–64; Bellevue, 64–67; San Francisco, 70–76, 82–84.

Employment and Job Training, 42–43.

Environmental Issues, 87–105; background of environmental review and environmental impact statements, 87–88, 103–104; light access and "Waldram diagram," 88–90; shadow controls, 90–94; San Francisco's Proposition K, 90–94; shadow testing, 91–92; costs, 93, 103; street-level winds, 96–98; wind testing technology, 97; mitigation measures, 98; view protection, 98–102; environmental simulation techniques, 100–101, 104–105; legal considerations, 102; evaluation and testing costs, 102–104.

Floor/Area Ratio (FAR): definition, 9, 11 (footnote 1). *See also generally* Chapter 1, Incentive Zoning, 12–38.

Hartford, Connecticut: zoning history, 9, 14, 117–118; bonus ratios, 17; visual arts space, 41; employment and job training, 42–43; daycare, 48; 180 Allyn Street, 48; design review, 55–56; zoning for retail uses, 116–119; State House Square, 118–119; parking requirements, 160; short-term parking incentive, 161; transportation management program, 169–170; Housing Overlay District (HOD), 175, 177; housing bonuses, 178–179.

Historic Preservation: relation to incentive systems, 10; relation to retail districts, 107–108, 121; relation to parking requirements, 160; TDRs for historic preservation, 184–185, 187.

Housing, 174–192; survey of zoning mechanisms, 174–175; mixed-use districts, 175–177; housing overlays, 177–178; housing bonuses, 178–180; inclusionary housing, 180–182; linkage (office/housing), 182–184; TDRs, 184–188; evaluation, 191–192. Case study: Seattle, 188–191.
Housing Overlay Districts, 177–178.
Human Services Facilities, 43–45.

Incentive Zoning (*see generally* Chapter 1, 12–38): selecting bonus features, 14–15; calculating bonus values, 17–19; evaluating bonus systems, 25–26; enforcement and maintenance, 26–29; modifications of bonused space, 32–33; legal issues (Columbus Center case), 34–38. Case studies: New York City, 12–14; Portland, Ore., 20; Seattle, 20–25.

Linkage (office/housing linkage), 182–184; evaluation, 184, 191–192. Case studies: San Francisco, 182–184; Boston, 184.

Mixed-Use Districts, 175–177. *See also* Housing *and* Special Districts and Overlay Zones.

National Environmental Policy Act (1969), 87, 104.
New York, New York: zoning history, 6, 12–14, 33–34, 78; ULURP (Uniform Land Use Review Procedure), 13, 53; urban plazas, 27, 30, 130–132; Columbus Center controversy, 34–38; special districts, 55, 176, 110, 116; Battery Park City, 57–58, 129; "Waldram diagram" and light access, 90; retail uses, 107, 114, 115–116; Fifth Avenue Special District, 110, 116; bonus for subway station improvements, 168–169; inclusionary housing bonus, 180–182; TDRs, 184–185, 187.

Open Space, public (including urban plazas), 130–139; maintenance issues, 29–30; retrofits and modifications, 134, 137–139. Case studies: New York City, 130–132; Pittsburgh, 132–134; San Francisco, 135–136; Portland, Ore., 136; Bellevue, 136–137; Seattle, 137.
Orlando, Florida: public art requirement, 39; retail and streetfront continuity, 110–111; parking reduction incentive, 164; housing bonuses, 179–180.
Overlay Districts. *See* Special Districts.

Palm Beach, Florida: Worth Avenue Special District (for retail uses), 114–115.
Parking, 160–168; design guidelines for parking garages, 145, 195–197; short-term parking, 161; shared parking, 161–162; bicycle parking, 162; surface lots and garages, 162; demolition permits, 162–163; landscaping requirements, 163; parking reduction incentives, 164–166; parking lids, case study: Portland, 166–168.
Pedestrian Malls, 147. *See also* Pedestrianways.
Pedestrianways, 145–151; pedestrian improvements, 145–147; pedestrian malls, 147–148; pedestrian corridors, case study: Bellevue, 148–151.
Pittsburgh, Pennsylvania: design review, 59–61; PPG Place, 60; view protection, 100; open space, 132–134; TDRs, 185.

Plazas. *See* Open Space.
Portland, Maine: Commercial Street Waterfront Core (waterfront design guidelines), 144, 176.
Portland, Oregon: zoning history, 10, 20; bonuses for public art and fountains, 40–42; daycare, 45; design review, 61–64; RiverPlace, 62–63, 81; retail approach, 108–109; Justice Center, 109; open space, 136; limitation on blank walls, 141–142; building-line requirement, 143; skywalk policy, 155, 157; bicycle parking, 162; regulation of surface parking lots, 162; parking and circulation policy, 166–168; parking lid, 167–168; Metropolitan Area Express (MAX), 167–168; housing overlay district, 177; housing bonuses, 180; TDRs for preservation of single-resident-occupancy buildings (SROs), 185–186.

Quantitative Zoning, 115. *See also* Retail Uses, commercial overconcentration.

Retail Uses, 106–127; relation to historic preservation, 107–108, 121; retail continuity, 109–111; enforcement, 113–114; quality control issues, 114; commercial overconcentration and quantitative zoning, 114–115. Case studies: New York City, 115–116; Hartford, 116–119; Charlotte, 119–121; Seattle, 121–124; Bellevue, 124–127.

San Francisco, California: zoning history, 70–72, 82–84; public art, 40–41, 83–84; employment brokerage services, 43; daycare, 46-47; design review, 70–76, 82–84; "beauty contest," 72–73; commercial growth cap (Proposition M), 71–75; sculptured rooftops, 80; TDRs, 83; shadow ban (Proposition K), 91, 94, 103; 343 Sansome Street, 93–94; limits on street-level winds, 96; view protection, 100–101; commercial overconcentration, 115; open space, 135–136; transportation management program requirement, 171; linkage, 182–184.
Sculptured Rooftops, 79–82.
Seattle, Washington: zoning history, 18, 20–25, 31–33; Washington Mutual Tower, 22–23, 49, 51–52, 81–82; Citizens Alternative Plan (CAP), 24–25, 121–122, 191; public art, 39; human services facilities, 43–45; daycare, 45–46, 48–52; Pacific First Centre, 48–49; design review of bonus selections, 56; retail discussion, 121–124; Century Square Tower, 124; open space, 137; bonus space retrofits and modifications, 138–139; former Seafirst Bank Building, 42, 139; short-term parking, 161; parking reduction incentives, 165–166; transportation management program, 171; inclusionary housing, 180; TDR housing program, 186–188. Case study of housing program, 188–191; evaluation of program, 190–191.
Shadow Controls, 89–94; San Francisco's Proposition K, 90–94; shadow testing, 91–92; costs, 93, 103.
Skywalks, 153–159; equity issues, 153–155; limiting skywalk connections, 155–157; view obstruction, 156; design issues, 158–159.
Special Districts and Overlay Zones, 54–55, 175–180; Mediterranean Overlay District, Coral Gables, 56–57; overlays for view protection, 98–99; Fifth Avenue Special District, New York City, 110–116; shopping overlay

(SHOP) district, Washington, D.C., 112–113; Worth Avenue Special District, Palm Beach, 114–115; mixed-use districts, 175–177; Hartford's Housing Overlay District (HOD), 175, 177. Case study: Washington, D.C., 176–178.

Street Parks, 147–148.

Streetscapes, 139–151; continuity, 141; blank wall limits and transparency requirements, 141–143; build-to-line requirements, 143; streetscape design guidelines, 143–144; ground-floor design focus, 144–145; pedestrianways, 145–151; street parks, 147–148.

Through-Block Connections and Arcades, 146–147. *See also* Streetscapes, pedestrianways.

Transfer of Development Rights (TDRs) *(see generally* 83, 184–188): for historic preservation, 83, 187; in connection with view protection, 102; for housing preservation, 184–188; evaluation, 187–188. Case study: housing TDRs in Seattle, 186–187.

Transparency Requirements, 142–143. *See also* Blank Wall Limits.

Transportation Improvements, 168–169; for bus shelters and subway stations, 168–169; San Francisco's transit improvement fee, 169.

Transportation Management/Demand Programs (TMPs), 169–173; evaluation, 172–173. Case study: Bellevue, 171–172.

View Protection, 98–104; legal considerations, 99; relation to skywalk connection policy, 156.

Washington, D.C.: shopping overlay (SHOP) district, 112–113; Commercial/Residential Mixed-Use District, 176–177; Hotel/Residential Incentive District, 178.

West Palm Beach, Florida: bonuses for street-level building entryways, 145.

Wind Testing, 94–97; technology for measuring street-level winds, 97; mitigation measures, 97–98; costs, 103.

Woonerf. See Street Parks.